Inside Politics

BY THE SAME AUTHOR

Mulroney: The Making of the Prime Minister
From Bourassa to Bourassa: Wilderness to Restoration
Free Trade: Risks and Rewards (ed)
Leo: A Life (with Leo Kolber)
Politics, People & Potpourri

L. Ian MacDonald

Inside Politics

Published for *Policy* Magazine
by
McGill-Queen's University Press
Montreal & Kingston · London · Chicago

© McGill-Queen's University Press 2018

ISBN 978-0-7735-5362-0 (cloth)
ISBN 978-0-7735-5370-5 (ePDF)
ISBN 978-0-7735-5371-2 (ePUB)

Legal deposit second quarter 2018
Bibliothèque nationale du Québec

Printed in Canada on acid-free paper

We acknowledge the support of the Canada Council for the Arts, which last year invested $153 million to bring the arts to Canadians throughout the country. Nous remercions le Conseil des arts du Canada de son soutien. L'an dernier, le Conseil a investi 153 millions de dollars pour mettre de l'art dans la vie des Canadiennes et des Canadiens de tout le pays.

Library and Archives Canada Cataloguing in Publication

MacDonald, L. Ian, author
  Inside politics/L. Ian MacDonald.

A collection of columns and articles.
Sequel to Politics, people & potpourri.
Issued in print and electronic formats.
ISBN 978-0-7735-5362-0 (cloth) – ISBN 978-0-7735-5370-5 (PDF) –
ISBN 978-0-7735-5371-2 (ePUB)

1. Canada – Politics and government – 2006–2015.
2. Canada – Politics and government – 2015–.
3. Politicians – Canada. I. Title.

FC655.M33 2018   971.07'4   C2017-907280-3
                                  C2017-907281-1

This book was typeset by Marquis Interscript in 11/14 Sabon.

For my girls, Grace and Zara
With special thanks to their Moms

CONTENTS

Author's Note ix

1 Election 2011 3
2 Election 2015 13
3 Stephen Harper 18
4 Tom Mulcair 35
5 Justin Trudeau 47
6 The Senate Expense Scandal 79
7 The FISC and the Economy 91
8 Energy and Pipelines 109
9 The Mission against ISIS 122
10 The 2012 Quebec Election 139
11 Language and Identity Politics 149
12 The 2014 Quebec Election 158
13 America 174
14 Here and There 210
15 People 293
16 Tributes 326
17 Cottage Country 350

AUTHOR'S NOTE

This is my second collection of columns and articles, a sequel to *Politics, People & Potpourri*, also published by McGill-Queen's University Press (MQUP) in the fall of 2009.

Inside Politics seemed like an obvious choice for a title of a book along similar lines. In the years since, much has happened in the politics of Canada and Quebec, as well as to the leaders who have defined and shaped the first two decades of the 21st century in our country.

In Canada, the Harper decade of Conservative rule gave way to a majority government led by Justin Trudeau and his "sunny ways" – a reference not to his own father but to the signature of another great prime minister, Sir Wilfrid Laurier, more than a century ago.

The change of tone, from Stephen Harper's socially introverted personality and all-consuming message control, also marked generational change in Ottawa. Harper was born in April 1959, at the end of the Boomer Generation following the Second World War. Trudeau was born on Christmas Day in 1971, as part of Generation X. Harper was born in New Brunswick, grew up in middle-class Toronto, and gravitated to Calgary. Trudeau was born to parents who lived at 24 Sussex, was a survivor of their broken marriage, and became, as he told CBS's *60 Minutes* in 2016, "a snowboard instructor ... a bouncer in a nightclub ... a whitewater river guide" and a teacher, before becoming a freshman MP from Montreal in the parliamentary class of 2008.

Harper was a born strategist who worked at becoming a retail politician. Trudeau was a born campaigner who worked at becoming a strategist. Whenever I spoke to Harper during his time in office, I never had a sense that he was longing to be out on the campaign trail. Whenever I spoke to Trudeau, I always thought it was the only place he wanted to be. When I once asked him how it was going out there on his constant tour, while he was leading the third party in the House, he replied: "I'm doing what I was born to do, and if you write that, I'll kill you."

There is no more majestic moment in a democracy than a peaceful change of government from one party to another. This is what Canadians witnessed during the two-week transition from a Conservative to a Liberal government in 2015, a change so seamless that Harper and Trudeau appeared together at the National War Memorial just three days after the election on the first anniversary of the terror attacks that claimed the lives of two Canadian soldiers. With their joint wreath-laying, Harper and Trudeau transformed a solemn memorial moment into a splendid and unifying occasion, signifying continuity as well as change.

In a career of writing about politics and politicians, I've been fortunate to have my work informed by a period of service in government, first at the centre in Ottawa and then at our embassy in Washington. From 1985–88, I was privileged to serve as principal speechwriter to Prime Minister Brian Mulroney. The speeches I worked on with him included his address to the United Nations General Assembly on apartheid in 1985, his speech to the House on the abolition of capital punishment as well as on the Meech Lake Accord in 1987, and his address to a joint session of the U.S. Congress in 1988. And in the 1988 election, transformed into a referendum on the Canada-U.S. Free Trade Agreement, Mulroney carried the entire Progressive Conservative campaign on his shoulders. He was the greatest campaigner of his time.

I've often been asked what it was like to write for him. I've always said it was like being the jockey for Secretariat in the Belmont Stakes – you just let him run and win by 31 lengths.

There is nothing like working in a Prime Minister's Office or the Privy Council Office to give one a sense of how government works. These two central agencies in the Langevin Block are the seat of power in Canada. Holding the pen for a Speech from the Throne was an education on the size, scope and scale of government. Every department in government lobbies the PMO for a paragraph, or at least a mention, in a throne speech. Serving in the PMO alongside public servants working on budgets, trade and constitutional deals, while reconciling seemingly irreconcilable interests, was more than an education. It was a paradigm shift in my understanding of politics and public policy, and where they coincided.

During my time as minister of public affairs at the Canadian Embassy in Washington from 1992–94, I learned, day in and day out, the absolute truth behind one of the great clichés of diplomacy: relationships matter. Canadians operating at our embassy in Washington carry an advantage both on Capitol Hill and at the White House that only a few countries can claim: the benefit of the doubt. Our conversations with the U.S. government begin from a default posture of good will. That mutual respect has been tested at times in our recent bilateral history, and it should never be taken for granted.

In the present decade, it is Harper and Trudeau who have marked the political touchstones of the 2010s in Canada. Their two successful election campaigns, Harper's in 2011 and Trudeau's in 2015, are the opening chapters of this book.

The 2011 campaign was significant because it gave Harper a majority government and relegated to third place a Liberal Party led by Michael Ignatieff, a globally recognized authority on human rights whose failure to adapt to the retail game of politics made Harper seem downright extroverted.

The 2015 election was significant because it delivered a judgment not just on what Canadians felt about the Conservative Party after 10 years in office, but a positive verdict on how Trudeau rebuilt the Liberal brand from the ground up, from tripling its membership, to re-establishing its fundraising, to recruiting a strong cohort of new candidates. He made the Liberals competitive again, won the ballot over the NDP on the question of change, and then moved to majority territory when Canadians decided to throw the bums out, or actually, to throw the *bum* out.

Two long-form magazine articles in 2011 and 2015 give both Harper and Trudeau full credit for their very different majority victories, one on a theme of continuity and the other on change. The first is from *Policy Options,* the magazine of the Institute for Research on Public Policy, of which I was then editor in the days when it still had a print edition. The second is from the 2015 election edition of *Policy,* Canada's bi-monthly magazine of politics and public policy, of which I am editor and publisher. Our print edition is not a retail product, but a niche publication delivered to a guaranteed audience of MPs, Senators, deputy ministers, the National Press Gallery, as well as Maple Leaf Lounges across Canada and VIA business class lounges in the Montreal-Ottawa-Toronto triangle. It's an audience of political decision makers, opinion and business leaders and we are very proud of what we've built at *Policy* since its launch in 2013. I want to thank associate editor Lisa Van Dusen, graphic designer Monica Thomas, web editor Nicolas Landry and social media editor Grace MacDonald, not to mention our superb writers, for their contributions to building the *Policy* brand.

These two elections, as noted, form the political bookends of the present decade in Canada. And in between, there are the events, personalities and issues that have shaped the political narrative and policy debate, from fiscal frameworks to clean energy and pipelines, from the Senate expense scandal and democratic reform, to national security at home and the re-profiled mission against ISIS abroad.

These debates, which dominated arguments under the Harper administration, continue as a political conversation under the Trudeau government, only from a different policy perspective.

And then there was Quebec, with its two elections in 2012 and 2014. Quebec campaigns are different than those in other provinces in one important sense – they are the only provincial elections in which the future of the country itself is at stake. The 2012 election resulted in a minority Parti Québécois government that was unable to pursue its objective of sovereignty. Instead, it played a dangerous game of identity politics with its Charter of Quebec Values, to say nothing of the usual language debates over French on signs, the most ludicrous one being *pastagate*, over menus in Italian restaurants.

Pierre Karl Péladeau would prove to be a game-changer in the 2014 election, but not in the way the PQ hoped. In a single 10-second sound bite announcing his arrival as a PQ candidate, he pumped his fist and declared his goal "to make Quebec a country." Standing beside him as he said it, smiling and leading the applause, was the PQ's leader, Pauline Marois. In that moment, the campaign was transformed into a referendum on a referendum, something most Quebecers didn't want to live through again. Leading at the start of the campaign with over 40 per cent in the polls, the PQ plummeted to the mid-20s by election day, which saw the arrival of a Liberal majority government led by Philippe Couillard, who had proven in the campaign that not only could he take a punch, he could also land one.

In the present decade there have been two very different views of Canada's role in the world under the Harper and Trudeau governments. As articulated by Harper's Foreign Affairs Minister John Baird, Ottawa's world view was one of "No More Honest Broker," a policy under which Canada took sides on human rights in the Commonwealth, and lined up behind Israel at all times and in all circumstances. Trudeau, in his first whirlwind world tour as prime minister, had a very different message: "Canada is back." From a policy of choosing sides under Harper in the first half of the decade, Canada was clearly moving to a policy of re-engagement as an honest broker in the second half.

Re-engagement with the United States was definitely the theme of Trudeau's first visit to Washington and the White House in March 2016. Where Harper never had anything more than brief working visits to the White House, Trudeau received a state dinner from President Barack Obama, the first in nearly two decades for a Canadian prime minister. The working and social aspects of the visit marked an important renewal in Canada-U.S. relations, and a warmth not seen since the days of Mulroney's relationship with Ronald Reagan and the first George Bush.

It would prove to be a very different state of affairs in managing Canada-U.S. relations following the surprise election of Donald Trump as president in November 2016. Trudeau and his staff pivoted adroitly and managed a successful first meeting with Trump at the White House in February 2017. Throughout the transition and the early months of the Trump presidency, Trudeau and his team solicited Mulroney's advice on getting along with Trump and his senior advisers, the former PM's friends and winter neighbours in Palm Beach.

The years covered in this book include some significant political anniversaries worth recalling. The 50th anniversary of John Diefenbaker's Bill of Rights in 2010; the 25th anniversary of the Meech Lake Accord as well as the 25th anniversary of the negotiation of the Canada-U.S. Free Trade Agreement in 2012. Also noted, the 100th anniversary of the Château Laurier in 2012. Oh, if the walls could talk.

In a columnist's job, you meet a lot of personalities along the way. I've met my share of fascinating people, some of them profiled in these pages. There is also a chapter of tributes to some remarkable people, including my former father-in-law, Tom Van Dusen, a close adviser to two prime ministers, Diefenbaker and Mulroney. Jim Flaherty was my oldest friend. And I was privileged to call Jean Béliveau a friend.

The collection closes with some summer updates from cottage country, and our place in the Gatineau Hills of Quebec, only 45 minutes from the Peace Tower, but far from the madding crowd of Ottawa. It being the cottage, there's always something going wrong, but at day's end, when the sun sets off the end of our dock, it doesn't get any better than that. By the way, our cottage at sunset is the image on the back cover of the book, with my daughter Zara standing on the beach.

There are the usual people to be acknowledged and thanked for their help in putting this collection together, beginning with Philip Cercone, executive director of McGill-Queen's University Press. This is my fifth book with MQUP, and it's both a pleasure and privilege to work with Philip and his great team, including Ryan Van Huijstee. In an era when print publishing has been challenged by digital and tablet books, MQUP has met the test and is thriving, not only in terms of its academic reputation, but its retail sales, both in Canada and the United States as well as Europe.

Special thanks to Gwenda Wright of the Earnscliffe Strategy Group in Ottawa, for assembling the archive in hard copy, then putting together the edited electronic version of the manuscript. Thanks also to Chantal Limoges at Navigator Ltd., in Montreal, for her support in pulling together photo copies of the manuscript.

Next I must thank the editors of my column over this period, beginning with David Johnston and previously Wayne Lowrie at the *Montreal Gazette*. Special thanks to *Gazette* editor-in-chief Lucinda Chodan, who personally located hundreds of columns after they had been dropped from the newspaper's website. At the *Ottawa Citizen*, which published a bi-weekly column from 2012–14, I want to thank David Watson, who was always a pleasure to work with.

At *iPolitics*, deepest thanks to James Baxter, the founding editor and chief executive of Canada's must-read political website. James had the courage and vision to start *iPolitics* in 2010, and it's been a continuous pleasure writing for it since 2014. Particular thanks to Doug Beazley, deputy editor for opinion, who handles my column, and sees to it that I never miss a deadline. Thanks, as well, to Ian Shelton, former deputy editor for news and technical whiz who sent me two years of columns in a single email. "It's a big file," he cautioned, "about 360,000 words." With another 750,000 words from the *Gazette* and *Citizen*, the archive ran to some 1.2 million words, or more than 1,000 articles.

Winnowing the file down to a manageable size for a collection was one of the challenges in pulling this book together. But it was also part of the fun. If journalism is the first draft of history, it's equally important to see how the work stands the test of time. If the writing isn't prescient and perspicacious, it doesn't meet that test.

The reader is the best judge of that.

L. Ian MacDonald
Montreal and Lac-St.-Pierre-de-Wakefield
August 2017

Inside Politics

FROM 905 TO 416:
THE GTA MAJORITY

At 6.00 a.m. on the second Monday of the spring campaign, Jim Flaherty was at the Pickering GO station, meeting commuters on their way to work in Toronto. From 905 to 416, the two area codes making up the Greater Toronto Area which would on May 2 deliver the long-sought Conservative majority.

At the finance minister's side was Chris Alexander, the former Canadian ambassador to Afghanistan, and star Conservative candidate against Liberal incumbent Mark Holland in the riding of Ajax-Pickering, whom he would go on to defeat by six points.

At the two entrances of the station, Alexander's volunteers handed out his campaign pamphlet to voters and asked if they wanted to say hello to Flaherty and the candidate. Herding cats. Sleepy cats.

"Come and meet our finance minister," Alexander said over and over again.

"Nice to meet you," Flaherty said. "How are you doing today?"

"Keep up the good work," several voters told him. "You're doing a great job."

Two GO bus drivers actually got off their buses to come over and shake Flaherty's hand. You don't see that every day.

"How does it feel here?" Flaherty was asked.

"Good, very good, maybe too good," he said. "It feels like 1995 at Queen's Park." The year of Mike Harris and the Conservative sweep that ousted the NDP

I

ELECTION 2011

government of Bob Rae, the only man ever to have days named after him for the wrong reasons.

In the final days of the 2011 campaign, with the spectacular rise of the NDP in Quebec, bad memories of a disastrous NDP government would help Stephen Harper close the deal for a national majority in Ontario.

The Conservatives would elect 22 new MPs from Ontario. 73 in all, up from 51 in the last House. But it was the GTA that produced the majority. Where the Conservatives held 11 seats in 905 at dissolution, they would win 21 out of 22 on election day. And where they had no seats in 416, and hadn't won a seat in the city since 1988, they won nine out of 23 seats in Toronto itself.

In all, the Conservatives gained 19 seats in the GTA, taking them across the majority threshold. Overall, the Conservatives won 166 seats, 11 more than required for a majority, up from 143 in the last House. The Liberals, who had 32 GTA seats before the election, were left with only seven. Their leader, Michael Ignatieff, lost his own 416 seat of Etobicoke Centre.

And the Conservatives, astonishingly, are now the GTA party.

When the election was over, Flaherty convened a GTA caucus meeting at the ministers' regional office in downtown Toronto. "We couldn't fit everyone around the table in the boardroom, there were members who had to stand," he said later. "We used to meet in a phone booth."

For the Conservatives, the road to a majority always ran through 905. To their own surprise, it also ran through 416, where their best case in the war room before the election was that they might win four or perhaps five seats. Nine seats in 416 was way beyond their expectations.

The Conservatives' sweep of 905 began in the banquet halls of its multicultural communities. The first messenger was Immigration Minister Jason Kenney, who had spent several years flying into ethnic dinners in Toronto. And the message was that Conservatives shared their entrepreneurial spirit and family values, while the Liberals had, for far too long, taken their votes for granted.

The second messenger was Flaherty, the popular finance minister who himself represented the 905 riding of Whitby-Oshawa and was minister responsible for the GTA. He campaigned tirelessly up and down the 401 and 407, with a few side trips into the city on the Don Valley Parkway.

And the third messenger was Harper himself, pouring it on in the final days of the campaign, charging through Ontario, warning of the dangers of an opposition coalition, one now led by the NDP, with Ignatieff reduced to the role of passenger in the back seat. In the last five days of the campaign, when he pivoted from the Liberals to the NDP, Harper finally proved he had the stamina and the smarts to be a closer. On May 1, as part of a cross-Canada sprint on the final day of the campaign, he delivered a strong stump speech in London, where the Conservatives would unexpectedly win all three seats in the southwestern Ontario city.

"The choice in this election is increasingly stark," he said. "You can have an NDP government or a Conservative government."

He continued: "In this election, Mr. Ignatieff has taken the Liberal Party away from its roots, and in an NDP direction ... so let's be clear, a vote for the NDP is a vote for an NDP government. And a vote for the Liberals is now a vote for an NDP government. And let me speak very clearly to traditional Liberal voters. I know that many of you do not want NDP economic policies, that you do not want NDP tax hikes, and that is why to make sure the next Parliament does not raise taxes, Canada needs a strong, stable, Conservative majority government."

While some Ontario Liberals switched to the NDP to prevent Harper from getting a majority, many more Blue Grits voted for the Conservatives to make sure he got one. In the final five days of the campaign, the Liberals plummeted six points in Ontario in the Nanos daily tracking poll, while the Tories got a ballot box bounce on election day, as voters streamed to the polls to block an NDP-led coalition. Martha Hall Findlay, a popular and personable Liberal MP, defeated in her 416 riding of Willowdale, later called it a "double whammy," saying she got "squeezed from both sides."

Call it the reverse echo effect, which attested to the influence of the polls. Reading the polls and coverage of the Orange Wave in Quebec, Ontarians thought it was a very good thing for Canada that Smilin' Jack Layton and the NDP were taking down the Bloc. But they wanted no part of an NDP-led coalition to defeat a Conservative minority government. So, thanks to Layton's historic gains in Quebec, the voters handed Harper his majority in Ontario.

You could feel it on the doorsteps in a new subdivision in Flaherty's riding on Easter Saturday. First-time homeowners, many of them too young to remember Rae Days, spontaneously told Flaherty that "you have to get a majority to stop the NDP." They'd heard about the accidental and disastrous NDP government from their parents, and the best thing about that from the Conservative perspective was that Rae himself was still around – as a Liberal.

On election night, the numbers turned up perfectly for the Conservatives in Ontario. They won 44 per cent of the Ontario vote, while the Liberals and NDP were virtually tied at 25 per cent. Harper couldn't have scripted better splits than that, resulting in 73 Conservatives, 22 New Democrats and only 11 Liberals across the province.

Thus was born the Harper Coalition, Ontario and the West. As Conservative Senate Leader Marjory LeBreton later noted: "West of the Ottawa River, we won 48 per cent of the vote."

For the Liberals, as they surveyed the wreckage of their campaign, the numbers were eloquent. It was easily their worst showing in history, both in share of the popular vote and seats in the House. Their worst previous share of the pop-vote was 26 per cent under Stéphane Dion in 2008. Ignatieff won less than 19 per cent in 2011.

And their worst previous score in terms of seats was 40 under John Turner in the Mulroney landslide of 1984, in what was then a 282-seat House. Ignatieff's Liberals won only 34 seats in a 308-seat House, numerically and proportionately a much worse score than even the Turner debacle. The Liberals find themselves, for the first time in history, the third-place party in the Commons.

To go along with their 11 seats in Ontario, the Liberals won only four in the West, seven in Quebec and 12 in the Atlantic, and none in the three northern territories. And this from a party that in 2000, only a decade ago, won more than 100 seats out of 106 in Ontario because of the splits on the right between the Canadian Alliance and the Progressive Conservatives.

This was the party that, just three decades ago, won 74 out of 75 seats and 68 per cent of the votes in Quebec, in the exceptional circumstances of the prelude to the first referendum, where Quebecers wanted Pierre Trudeau as their federalist champion.

In 2011, the Liberals were reduced to seven seats and only 14 per cent of the vote in Quebec, all of those seats in non-francophone ridings on the island of Montreal.

Given the Liberals' standing as the most successful brand in Canadian politics in the 20th century, it was as if McDonald's had suddenly fallen to third place in fast-food in the 21st century. Except that it didn't happen overnight. It happened over three decades of neglect of the most storied political franchise in Canadian history.

Two events in the fall of 1980 would have long-term disastrous consequences for the Liberals. The first was the National Energy Program, which left the Liberals out of the game in the West from that day to this. And the second was the failed First Ministers' Conference on the Constitution, which ultimately led to patriation with the entrenched Charter of Rights in 1981 and 1982, over the objections of Quebec, principal home to one of Canada's two official language communities. Or as Trudeau himself described Quebec at the time: "Le foyer principal du Canada français."

The patriation of the Constitution was followed by the death of the Meech Lake Accord in 1990, a seminal moment in which the principal negative actors were Trudeau and Jean Chrétien. The demise of Meech gave birth to the Bloc Québécois, which Lucien Bouchard led to 54 seats and 49 per cent of the vote in the 1993 federal election. This was followed by the blowback of the 1995 Quebec referendum, which in turn begat the federal waving of the Canadian flag that resulted in the sponsorship scandal and the Gomery Commission. This sustained the Bloc's narrative of grievance in the 2004 and 2006 elections.

The Conservatives' self-inflicted wounds in 2008, over cultural cuts and kiddie crime, enabled the Bloc to get through that campaign with 49 seats, even though its popular vote fell to 38 per cent from 49 per cent in 2004 and 42 per cent in 2006.

The declining trend line of the BQ should have been a signal that the Bloc brand of poutine stands was in trouble in 2011. A party born in grievance had no narrative of grievance. Gilles Duceppe got away with it for a while, but he proved in 2011 to be not only tired and old, but totally tone deaf to the voices of his own people.

And in a single sound bite in a speech to a Parti Québécois policy convention in Montreal on April 17, Duceppe created the surge that took Jack Layton and the NDP all the way from the low 20s in the Nanos daily tracking poll to the mid-40s on election day, the point where the rising tide lifts all the boats, electing 59 members of the NDP in Quebec, to only seven for the Liberals, five for the Conservatives and four for the BQ.

"We have only one task to accomplish," Duceppe said at the PQ convention. "Elect the maximum number of sovereignists in Ottawa and then we go to the next phase – electing a PQ government. A strong Bloc in Ottawa. The PQ in power in Quebec. And then everything again becomes possible."

Et tout redevient encore possible. This was a direct echo of the Yes slogan in the 1995 referendum campaign, *Oui, et tout devient possible.* Duceppe would lose his East End Montreal seat of Laurier-Ste.-Marie by more than 5,000 votes and more than 10 points to the NDP's Hélène Laverdière, a retired official from the Foreign Affairs department. Layton himself campaigned in the riding on Easter Saturday, pulling nearly 2,000 people to a rally without bussing anyone in.

Duceppe was playing the separatist card at a separatist meeting, and while it might have played well in the room, there was a much larger audience that was appalled by the prospect of another referendum that would divide Quebecers and perhaps break up the country. To make matters worse,

Duceppe brought out Jacques Parizeau to campaign with him a week later. Duceppe might as well have campaigned with the ghost of Leonid Brezhnev in the streets of Moscow. Parizeau personified all the bad memories of the 1995 referendum.

Quebecers might show up for another referendum, but that didn't mean they wanted one. So what did they do? They went, spontaneously, to Jack Layton, *le bon Jack,* a good guy. Layton had been growing in the Nanos tracking poll, from the mid-teens at the outset of the campaign, through a four-point bump after his appearance as a *gars sympa* on *Tout le monde en parle*, the Radio-Canada talk show that draws up to 1.8 million Quebecers on Sunday night, an audience bigger than Habs hockey, even in the playoffs.

Quebecers saw and heard that Layton had won the English-language debate on April 12 with Michael Ignatieff, delivering a haymaker on the Liberal leader's poor attendance in the House. It played into the French-language debate the following night, where Layton more than held his own with Duceppe. Replying to Duceppe's argument that neither one of them could become prime minister, Layton responded, with a smile, that this was rather arrogant on the part of the BQ leader.

Though this was Layton's fourth national campaign, he succeeded in re-inventing himself in Quebec. While his French was imperfect, his accent was colloquial. Layton reminded Quebecers, especially by showing up in a Canadiens sweater during the playoffs, that Montreal was his team, as well as his home town, despite having spent decades in Toronto. In a matter of weeks, he became a favourite son in Quebec, the most powerful card in the deck of Canadian politics in that province.

Quebecers caucused over their choice *autour de la table de la famille* on Easter weekend, a week before the vote. They decided that Jack was indeed their guy. And that they were going to vote for him. In the last week, the trend to the NDP in Quebec became as hard as the boards at the Bell Centre.

From 23 percent in the Nanos tracking poll on the day of Duceppe's disastrous speech, the NDP grew to 43 percent in Quebec on election day. Meanwhile, the Bloc plummeted from 39 percent on April 17 to 23 percent on May 2, a loss of more than a point a day. In previous elections, the Liberals and then the Conservatives in 2006 had benefited from polarization as the default choice of federalist voters as the Block the Bloc party. But none of the federalist parties played that card in 2011. The voters decided to Block the Bloc entirely on their own.

As a result, the Bloc was reduced to a rump of only four seats, losing its standing as a recognized party in the House. Not only did the Bloc lose staff and research funding, it lost its place in question period. Where it used to have three or four questions a day, its small deputation, sitting as private members, will be fortunate to get one question every couple of weeks. And it will lose the federal subsidy of $2 per vote on which it has subsisted for years. Having received 1.7 million votes as recently as 2004, it won only 889,000 in 2011, nearly one million fewer votes in Quebec.

Where did the Liberal campaign go so disastrously wrong, sliding from a peak of 32 percent at the end of March in the Nanos daily poll to a historic nadir of 18.9 percent on election day? The answer is everywhere and in every way.

For openers, the Liberals forced an election Canadians didn't want, over an issue, contempt of Parliament, about which voters were generally indifferent. They had a message that couldn't be sold, and a messenger, Ignatieff, who couldn't sell it.

"You know how many questions I got at the door about contempt of Parliament?" asked Conservative cabinet minister John Baird, who was re-elected in Ottawa West-Nepean. "Four. Exactly four questions. I got six questions on the long form census, because it's Ottawa. And I got 30 complaints about changes to a local bus route."

The Liberal frame of contempt was also counterintuitive in the sense that Harper had managed his way through two minority Houses in five years, and that Flaherty had successfully steered five consecutive budgets through minority Parliaments, including one in the midst of the steepest synchronized global recession in 60 years.

Harper had a simple ballot question, majority or minority, words that had been banned from the Conservative vocabulary in his previous three elections. And Ignatieff was dogged from the beginning by hypothetical questions about whether he would bring down a Conservative government and form an opposition coalition. Roll the video of the Three Stooges Coalition from 2008. This played right into Harper's narrative and framed his ballot question.

There was also an element of institutional entitlement in Ignatieff proposing another frame, that of "a red door or a blue door," when as it turned out, there was also an orange door.

For the first half of the campaign, hardly anything moved. "Mother's Day when I wake up to see that Nik Nanos has the Conservatives 10 points ahead," said former Prime Minister Brian Mulroney, who from the beginning of the campaign to the end privately predicted a Tory majority, though he warned that "anything can happen in the debates, as I know from my own experience."

What happened is that Ignatieff took one on the chin from Layton over his poor attendance record. "If you want to be prime minister, you'd better learn how to be a Member of Parliament first," Layton said. "You know, most Canadians, if they don't show up for work, they don't get a promotion. You missed 70 percent of the votes."

Instead of replying that he was out meeting voters, doing his real job as Opposition Leader, Ignatieff stuttered and stumbled a lame reply that no one could remember. Ignatieff, the most experienced television performer and debater on the stage, was never in it after that. As a telling point – the Liberals had raised $3 million in the campaign up to the debates, but only $10,000 came in on the day after the English debate.

And then in his feature-length interview with CBC News anchor Peter Mansbridge the following week, Ignatieff allowed himself to be drawn into a discussion on the conditions under which he would form a coalition, the very question his advisers had implored him to avoid.

Mansbridge politely persisted, and Ignatieff finally went there. "All right, let's run it out so we're all clear," Ignatieff said. "If Mr. Harper wins the most seats and forms a government, but does not secure the confidence of the House, and I'm assuming that Parliament comes back, then it goes to the governor general, that's what happens, that's how the rules work. And if the governor general wants to call on other parties or myself, for example, to try to form a government, then we try to form a government. That's exactly how the rules work, and what I'm trying to say to Canadians, I understand the rules, I respect the rules, and I will follow them to the letter and I'm not going to form a coalition government and I'm prepared to talk to Mr. Layton or Mr. Duceppe or even Mr. Harper and say, Look, we have an issue and this is how I want to solve it. Here's the plan that I want to put before Parliament. You know, this is the budget that we would bring in and then we take it from there."

Game over. If the Conservatives couldn't win a majority after a gift like that, which again played perfectly into Harper's narrative, then they wouldn't deserve one. There was an enduring and annoying professorial quality about Ignatieff. Here he was turning a dangerous hypothetical question into a lecture on constitutional convention, when his answer should have been "Ask the governor general, I'm campaigning to lead a Liberal majority government."

When the Liberal slippage reached the point where they were overtaken by the NDP in the polls due to the orange surge in Quebec, the bottom fell out of their campaign in Ontario. And in the closing stretch, the Liberals, who had always been the party of strategic voting, saw their voters in Ontario flock to the NDP and the Conservatives.

And there were two elections, the one in the bubble and the one on the ground. Trapped in the bubble, hunched over their Blackberries sending tweets to each other, most members of the National Press Gallery missed the story on the ground. With rare exceptions such as *National Post* columnist John Ivison, who actually broke out of the bubble and went out on his own to talk to real live voters, most journalists travelling with the leaders were content to stay in the cocoon. There was the daily spat on Harper's tour of how many questions he would take every day, when no one in the real world cared. Then there was the spectacle of the CBC's Terry Milewski asking Harper if he was "a coward or a chicken" for declining a one-on-one debate with Ignatieff. It is impossible to imagine any member of the White House press corps being so disrespectful to the president of the United States. But then, journalism is the only profession in which inappropriate behaviour is not only tolerated, but encouraged.

On the ground it was very different from the bubble. Voters were angry about the election, and even knew how much it cost – $300 million that, as Flaherty would tell people at his many stops in 905, could be put to better use for taxpayers.

On the second Sunday of the campaign, Flaherty set out down the 401 from his home in Whitby to visit five 905 ridings, with a side trip into 416 for an evening fundraiser.

All five 905 ridings were held by the Liberals, three of them won by margins of five points or less. All of them were in play. Flaherty's role was to fire up campaign volunteers to get out the vote.

"We are on the cusp of a majority," Flaherty told a crowd of 500 at Parm Gill's committee room in Brampton-Springdale. "It matters for the brilliant future of Canada that we have a majority." Gill would beat Ruby Dhalla by 20 points.

At every stop, Flaherty openly campaigned on the "M" word that was not allowed to pass the lips of Conservative candidates in the previous three elections. And this led him to the prospect of an opposition coalition in the event the Conservatives were returned with a third consecutive minority government.

"They've done it before and they'll do it again," Flaherty said, recalling the Three Stooges Coalition. "What they tried to do was take over the government. The finance critic of the NDP sat in my office and said, 'You may be finance minister now but you won't be in a week. We're taking over.'

"We've come out of the recession in better shape than any other country in the world, with nearly half a million new jobs," Flaherty continued. "We have a wonderful reputation in the world. Tim Geithner, the US treasury secretary, calls us 'virtuous Canada.' In the UK, they've had draconian cuts, with 400,000 civil servants laid off." The partisan crowds liked the narrative of Canada coming safely through the economic storm. It had the added virtue of being true, and told by the guy who was at the wheel. "As a member of Parliament from the GTA, I get lonely in Ottawa," Flaherty said. "We need more members from the GTA. It matters for the brilliant future of Canada that we have a majority."

There was the "M" word again.

Down in Mississauga South, Stella Ambler was running against long-time Liberal incumbent Paul Szabo. He won in the 2008 election by less than five points. Ambler would beat him by 10 points.

"I've had Jim as a boss," said Ambler, who used to run his Toronto ministerial office. "But I'd love to have him as a colleague."

"This is a riding we should win," Flaherty said on the drive back into Toronto for a Rosedale fundraiser for Mark Adler. In York Centre, the Jewish vote was on the move to Harper because of his staunch support for Israel. "The Jewish vote is 24 per cent of the riding," said Adler, grandson of a holocaust survivor. "And 70 per cent of it is coming to us." On election day he would beat hockey legend Ken Dryden by 15 points.

Flaherty visited six ridings that day, and the Conservatives would win every one of them. And in Liberal Fortress Toronto, the Conservatives would win the multicultural and Jewish vote, core constituencies of the Liberal Party, not by a little, but by a lot.

On the morning of the election, Flaherty looked at the last set of poll numbers and liked what he saw – the splits in Ontario that didn't even capture the Conservatives' ballot box bounce.

"We're there," he said. "We're good. It's a majority."

June 2011

2
ELECTION 2015

FROM ORANGE CRUSH TO ORANGE CRASH: THE FRONT-RUNNER CAMPAIGN THAT WASN'T

On the Sunday after the election call, and three days after the first leaders' debate, NDP senior campaign adviser Brad Lavigne met a friend for brunch at the Métropolitain Brasserie, a favoured hangout of Ottawa's political class.

Sitting in a corner booth by the bar, he stirred his coffee and considered the NDP's front-running status in the polls, which then had the party in the low 30s. The NDP's internal numbers showed the same thing.

"We've never been here before," he said.

Which kind of turned out to be the problem.

Not only had the NDP never been there before, they hadn't expected to be in first place at the outset of the campaign. Nor, as it turned out, did they have a narrative for a 78-day marathon rather than a normal 37-day campaign.

From a nadir of 20 per cent in the polls last fall, the NDP had hoped to grow to the high 20s by the beginning of summer.

Their fortunes began to take a turn for the better over the winter after Tom Mulcair shook up the Office of the Leader of the Opposition, bringing in Alain Gaul, who had been with him in the environment minister's office in Quebec City, to be chief of staff in the OLO. In no time, what had been a dysfunctional OLO became one where decisions were made and things got done.

Mulcair then reached out to two key members of Jack Layton's political entourage to run the NDP campaign. Layton's former chief of staff, Anne McGrath, was brought back as campaign director. And Lavigne, who had been Layton's principal secretary at OLO and previously campaign director in the 2011 Orange Wave election, left his consulting gig at H&K Strategies to become senior adviser in the campaign. Mulcair's announcement of his return, at a Wednesday morning caucus in January, prompted a spontaneous ovation.

By the time of the Broadbent Institute's annual Progress Summit at the end of March, the NDP was on the move. Over drinks at the bar of Ottawa's Delta Centre Hotel, Lavigne and McGrath were very forthcoming about the priorities for the coming campaign.

"The first objective," Lavigne said, "is to hold on to what we've got."

In other words, to finish no worse than second in the election, and to hold on to both the OLO and Stornoway. In an expected minority House, this would leave Mulcair and the NDP in the driver's seat in any talks with the Liberals about a working arrangement to defeat a Conservative plurality.

By the beginning of May, the NDP had already grown to the high 20s, with the Liberals having plunged from first to third place since the previous October. The Liberals' sharp decline in the polls could be measured from the moment of Justin Trudeau's memorable gaffe that Stephen Harper wanted to "whip out our CF-18s" and show everyone how big they are.

It was a smart-ass remark about a serious issue – the mission against ISIS in Iraq, later expanded to Syria. The Liberals waffled on both, saying they supported the troops but opposed the mission. In the first parliamentary debate – on the six-month deployment of CF-18s and the presence of 60 elite Joint Task Force "trainers" of Kurdish insurgents in northern Iraq – Trudeau failed to speak in the House. By the time of the second House debate, on expanding the Kuwait-based air mission to Syria and extending it by a year, the Liberals were jammed between Conservative support and NDP opposition.

Then, in the wake of the shooting of two soldiers on Canadian soil last October 20 and 22, the Liberals voted in favour of the Conservative security legislation, Bill C-51, to the great annoyance of progressive voters, who migrated to the NDP. It was one of Mulcair's finest moments as NDP leader.

And then came the Notley effect. After the surprise election of Rachel Notley and the NDP in Alberta on May 6, the federal NDP had a five-point bump in the polls. The conversation went like this: if the NDP can win in Alberta, they can win anywhere, even Ottawa.

But this proved to be an illusion. Within weeks of the writ on August 2, the Notley effect dissipated and then disappeared, leaving the NDP back in the high 20s, where they had started.

From the beginning, the NDP ran a front-runner campaign, when they were never really in front. The NDP's strategy of caution was apparent from Day One. Mulcair made his opening statement at the Museum of History in Gatineau, with Parliament Hill as a gorgeous backdrop. Then he walked away from the podium without taking any questions, and he looked uncomfortable in doing so. The decision to take no questions was simply an attempt to control the message by staying on it. While Mulcair took no questions, even Stephen Harper was taking five of them in front of Rideau Hall. Later, in Vancouver, Trudeau took as many questions as reporters wanted to ask. Mulcair then took the next day off.

And in the first leaders' debate hosted by *Maclean's*, Angry Tom was replaced by Happy Tom, a weird-looking guy with a smile pasted on his face, even as he was pointing an accusatory finger at his opponents. He looked inauthentic. Even as Trudeau was finding his feet in the first debate as well as four subsequent ones, Mulcair never found his voice.

And then Mulcair pledged to present balanced budgets, while Trudeau outflanked him on the left by promising three years of deficits, including $10 billion in each of the first three years of a Liberal government, before returning to balance in 2019.

This was Mulcair's decision to present himself as a fiscal moderate. Or as Lavigne put it privately at the time: "We're the NDP, we have to balance the budget."

He was referring to bad memories of NDP deficits in Ontario under Bob Rae, in British Columbia under Mike Harcourt, and even the $6 billion structural deficit Notley inherited from the ousted Progressive Conservatives in Alberta.

Then came the niqab debate.

After the Federal Court of Appeal ruled that a Muslim woman could wear a niqab during a citizenship ceremony, the Conservatives immediately said they would appeal, and overnight the identity issue hijacked the campaign in Quebec.

For Mulcair, the niqab was a disaster in Quebec, while Trudeau turned it to his advantage in the rest of Canada.

In Montreal on September 23, Mulcair delivered a carefully calibrated speech in which he noted that a veiled woman must reveal herself in private to citizenship officials, and is thus entitled to wear the niqab at a citizenship ceremony.

The NDP numbers then tanked in Quebec outside Montreal. The niqab issue figured prominently in the two French-language leadership debates on September 24 on Radio-Canada and October 2 on TVA.

The NDP had gone into the campaign in first place, polling in the low 30s, with the Liberals mired in third place in the mid-20s. The story of how they traded places is one for the history books.

First of all, the 78-day campaign played to Trudeau's acknowledged strength – his retail game. He was very good in crowds, endlessly posing for selfies that ended up on Facebook and Twitter. The buzz wasn't just in the room, it was also on social media. It wasn't just his stamina that carried through the marathon campaign; by the end of it, he came to personify generational change.

For the Liberals, Trudeau's deficit position was the differentiator from the NDP on change. In the process, he outflanked the NDP on the left, while Mulcair was positioning a socialist party to the right on the fiscal framework. This was right out of the Kathleen Wynne playbook from the 2014 Ontario election, and it was no accident – the Liberal campaign was run by the same people.

Trudeau also inoculated himself on the deficit question simply by saying he would run one. Progressive voters – who had left the Liberals for the NDP over issues such as Trudeau's support of the Conservative security legislation, Bill C-51 – returned to the Liberal fold. The size didn't matter. A deficit is a deficit. Period.

For his part, Stephen Harper overplayed his hand on the niqab, especially in English-speaking Canada, where voters recoiled at his musing about banning the niqab in the public service. The Conservative overkill included an announcement by two ministers, Chris Alexander and Kellie Leitch, of a snitch line to report "barbaric cultural practices." It was the precise moment when Red Tories gave up on this Conservative Party and crossed to the Liberals.

Coming in the 10th and penultimate week of the campaign, it seemed like a kind of tipping point against the Conservatives. By then, a campaign meant to be about the economy, had been transformed into one about values. The economy was the Conservatives' signature issue, and the announcement of the Trans-Pacific Partnership free trade agreement on October 5 should have played to their strength. But while it was Harper's best and most prime ministerial moment of the campaign, on what the first George Bush famously called "the vision thing," it proved to be a one-day story rather than a game changer.

Then came the four-day advance poll over Thanksgiving. Some 3.6 million Canadians voted over the long weekend, many of them as couples and families, having talked turkey around the family dinner table. The advance poll turned out to be nearly 20 per cent of the vote. The final turnout of 17.5 million was 68.4 per cent of eligible voters, up from 61 per cent in 2011 and 58 per cent in 2008. It was the highest turnout since 1993.

And it was Quebec, unexpectedly, that joined Ontario to hand Trudeau his surprise majority. No one saw that coming.

In two years, he has taken the Liberals from third place to government, a remarkable achievement.

Polling in the mid-20s in Quebec as late as the final weekend, the Liberals won 35 per cent of the vote and 40 seats on election day, where most seat projections gave them no more than 20 seats. The NDP meanwhile, was reduced to 25 per cent in Quebec and only 16 seats. The Conservatives won only 17 per cent, but it was an efficient vote, delivering 12 seats in the 418 Quebec City region, while the Bloc Québécois won 19 per cent and 10 seats.

Call it the mirror effect. Quebecers looked across the Ottawa River, saw what was happening in Ontario, and joined them in electing a Liberal majority.

With 184 seats in the new 338-seat House, Trudeau didn't just win government, he made history.

November 2015

3

STEPHEN HARPER

CETA: A BIG DEAL

The Comprehensive Economic and Trade Agreement between Canada and the European Union is the biggest trade deal since the Canada-U.S. Free Trade Agreement.

But it won't be anything like that in terms of its emotional impact and gut wrenching political debate.

For one thing, Canadians aren't afraid of being absorbed by the Europeans, as they were by the Americans. Remember? We were going to lose our health care, our culture, our very identity. The border between Canada and the United States would be erased. We would become the 51st state.

For another, it is because of the benefits derived from free trade that Canadians have a different mindset today. As the father of free trade, Brian Mulroney, said last year on the 25th anniversary of negotiating the FTA: "We're a much more confident, outward looking people."

Had he not taken the issue to the people, and carried the day in the 1988 free trade election, our economy would be much poorer today. Nor would there have been a North American Free Trade Agreement, negotiated with the U.S. and Mexico in 1992.

Where Canada had only $100 billion of exports to the U.S. when the FTA was implemented in 1989, exports peaked at $400 billion in 2000. During the 1990s exports created four new Canadian jobs out of five. Exports to the U.S. have been impacted negatively by a higher dollar, and took another hit during the recession of 2008–09, but have since recovered to around $330 billion, or about 75 per cent of all Canadian exports. A 2012 BMO Financial Group economic impact study found that foreign direct investment from the U.S. into Canada had increased from $76 to $325 billion, and that the Canadian economy grew by $1.1 trillion and 4.6 million jobs over the period.

The Canada-EU deal will be nothing like that, though a 2008 federal forecast predicts it will add $12 billion to the economy, and create up to 80,000 jobs.

But it is an even bigger deal than the Canada-U.S. FTA in the sense of how sweeping it is, taking 98 per cent of tariffs off the table when implemented. There were whole industries left out of the FTA, such as softwood lumber and beer, because they were too politically problematic.

"This is a big deal," Stephen Harper said in Brussels Friday at an appearance with EU President Jose Manuel Barosso. "Indeed, it is the biggest deal our country has ever made. This is an historic win for Canada."

It's also an historic win for him. It's the first time he's delivered on a big idea. With the Europeans now turning to talks with the Americans, CETA could well become the template for a North American-EU agreement, as the Canada-U.S. FTA became the model for the NAFTA. Then there's the talks among 12 countries in the Trans-Pacific Partnership, not to mention the prospect of a bilateral FTA with China and other rising Asian economies.

As in any trade negotiation, agriculture and supply management were major barriers to a deal that has been four long years in the making. Alberta cattlemen will get access to Europe for their beef, as will Quebec pork farmers.

Then there's dairy, and the 12,500 farmers who work under supply management. They've won wider access to the European market for dairy products – milk, yogurt and cheese, in return for Canada allowing in more European cheese. This may not play well among farmers and cheese makers, who know how to make their voices heard.

But the government also offered some comfort in suggesting assistance to affected sectors during a transition period. The Canadian wine industry was supposed to go out of business when wine was included in the Canada-U.S. FTA, but instead it has become extremely competitive.

On intellectual property, Canada's research-based pharma companies won a major point in a two-year extension of patent protection, allowing them to fend off the inroads of generic drug makers.

And here's an interesting one – government procurement will be opened up at the federal, provincial and municipal levels.

The provinces have been at the table from the beginning with the feds. In fact, the idea for a Canada-EU agreement began with Jean Charest in 2007, when he pitched it to the Europeans at the Davos conference, and then proposed it to the Council of the Federation. With the provinces onside, Harper was able to get the Europeans to the table. Charest may have left the Quebec premier's office, but his vision was important, and he deserves a lot of credit.

So does Harper, in that he stayed with it. "He took it on and drove it," Charest told colleague John Ivison from Beijing, where he was on a trade mission for his law firm. Keeping the provinces on board, and getting a major trade agreement with 28 countries, is no mean feat.

It's the sort of thing that historians will write about when measuring Harper's legacy.

And as Mulroney himself says: "This is a very significant achievement."

October 2013

∞

SHOOTING HIMSELF IN THE FOOT

The lead-up to the Conservative policy convention in Calgary was supposed to be a walk in the park for Stephen Harper.

You know, the speech from the throne, and the Canada-Europe free trade agreement. A big agenda for the second half of a majority mandate, and a major achievement – the biggest trade deal in the quarter-century since the Canada-U.S. Free Trade Agreement, certain to be a template for a larger North American-European agreement. Did we mention the economy? Unemployment below seven per cent for the first time since the Great Recession of 2008–09? Or one million new jobs created since then? Or the strongest fiscal framework and lowest debt-to-GDP ratio in the G7? Or Ottawa being on track to balance the books in 2015?

That's a narrative of success. The Senate expense scandal? Well, the RCMP was on the case, and so was the auditor general. Let them do their work, report their findings and recommendations.

After the convention.

In other words, leave well enough alone. Or as my mother used to say, in Irish terms, "Feed a cold, starve a fever."

But then, in the rollout of the speech from the throne and the CETA deal, the Conservatives decided to introduce motions in the Senate suspending three of their own former members of the Red Chamber, appointed by Harper himself, for "gross negligence."

Right, the Senate expense scandal. And this, again, before anything had been heard from the RCMP, much less the AG.

No one in Ottawa believes this was the idea of Claude Carignan, the new leader of the government in the Senate.

Everyone knows this came from the Prime Minister's Office. What were they thinking? Obviously, they thought they'd get this off the table before the convention.

But here's what happened instead.

The motions suspending the three Conservative senators without pay and benefits amounted to turning the Senate into a kangaroo court, while suspending the presumption of innocence, the core value of British common law.

Oh, and then they gave microphones to Mike Duffy and Pam Wallin, who know how to use them. They've only been in Canadians' living rooms for the last 40 years.

They'll be teaching this, years from now, in COMMS 101, on how not to run a political communications issue.

These wounds are entirely self-inflicted.

Harper, who shouldn't be anywhere near this story, instead finds himself at the centre of the storm over a personal cheque for $90,000 his former chief of staff, Nigel Wright, cut for Duffy to repay ineligible expenses.

When the story broke last May, Harper at first expressed confidence in Wright, then accepted his resignation "with regret." Then in an interview with a Halifax radio station on Monday, Harper said Wright had been "dismissed." In the House the next day, he said Wright had been "removed," adding, "On our side, there is one person responsible for this deception and that person is Mr. Wright."

So, now Wright gets thrown under the bus, too. It's getting pretty crowded under that bus.

At first, Harper maintained that Wright was acting alone, but last week allowed that "a few" people inside PMO and the government may have known about the cheque.

Then it turns out there was a second cheque for $13,000 cut by the Conservative Party's lawyer through his firm, to cover Duffy's legal expenses, and billed back to the party. If party lawyer Arthur Hamilton knew about this, who else did? Which is the problem with this story – the tick-tock. What did the PM know, and when did he know it? And the vote in the Senate, which was to have taken place before the Calgary convention, won't occur until sometime next week. So the Senate story played right into a convention that the suspension resolutions were meant to pre-empt. Instead, the Senate story has dominated the news cycle for two weeks, during which it wouldn't have been a story at all if only the PMO had left it alone. Who knows how long it would have taken the RCMP and auditor general to report, and what they would have recommended? The Conservatives have taken a significant hit on two core attributes of their brand: integrity and competence.

Meanwhile, back at the convention, the prime minister's Friday night keynote had become an important moment. Would he talk about Senate reform? He was certain to tout his achievements. Among the policy resolutions was a hardy perennial: one member-one vote vs. all ridings are created equal. This debate has been going on since the Canadian Alliance and Progressive Conservative parties merged a decade ago. For the PCs, the equality of ridings, all having the same number of delegates to leadership conventions, is a fundamental principle. But the old Alliance crowd keep bringing it up at every convention.

On Friday, the PC argument prevailed again on the convention floor as two resolutions on changing the method for selecting a leader were voted down. Harper would have been relieved by that. The last thing he needs now is a house divided.

November 2013

SURROUNDED BY ULTRA-LOYALISTS

Just before the holidays in 2013, Stephen Harper announced the return of his former communications director, Dimitri Soudas, to be executive director of the Conservative party.

With the appointment of former campaign director Jenni Byrne as deputy chief of staff in the Prime Minister's Office last year, and Ray Novak's promotion to chief of staff, Harper is now surrounded by ultra-loyalists in both the party and PMO. They are there for the prime minister. Period. Good to go for the PM, in a manner of speaking.

The Soudas appointment, at a time when Harper was reported to be reflecting on his future, was a statement, pointedly to his own party, that he isn't going anywhere and has every intention of running again in 2015.

While the political class takes that statement at face value, it has failed to stop speculation, even within the party, and especially the caucus, that Harper may step down before the fixed-date election scheduled for October 2015.

There are a number of reasons for that, and one of them is a thing called time. Another is that Harper can't have another year like 2013 going into an election in 2015.

In other words, 2014 is make or break for Harper's leadership of the country, and of his party. To borrow from the weather networks, he needs relief from a "Polar Vortex," a daunting political cold front.

Harper is coming up on eight years in government on February 6, and by the scheduled time of the next election, he will have been in office for nine years and nine months. Let's call it 10 years – a decade. That's three terms in office.

The most compelling campaign narrative is "time for a change." Except for "throw the bums out." Harper is on the threshold of both.

Winning four terms in a row would be historically an odds-against proposition. Since confederation, only Sir John A. Macdonald and Sir Wilfrid Laurier have won four consecutive elections. And each won four straight majorities. Even Mackenzie King, though he formed six governments and was Canada's longest-serving prime minister with 22 years in office, never won four in a row. Pierre Trudeau won four out of five elections from 1968 to 1980, including the smallest minority ever in 1972, but never won four consecutive elections. Jean Chrétien is the last leader, before Harper, to have won three straight elections, all majorities, but was deposed by his party before having the chance to contest a fourth.

So history is aligned against a fourth consecutive Harper victory in 2015, and all of that history was written before the arrival of the Internet and social media such as Twitter and Facebook. What would Sir John A., and Sir Wilfrid have done with 140 characters and Likes thumbs up?

Before Harper can even begin to think of winning a fourth straight election in 2015, he needs a couple of channel changers, even game changers, in 2014. First, he needs the Senate expense story to go away, and that means the RCMP not preferring charges in the Wright-Duffy affair. Harper and the PMO have no control over that, but they can try to move on to better story lines, notably the economy.

The first thing the PM's message managers should do is get him out of question period, where he's been getting killed by NDP Leader Tom Mulcair. There's no need for the PM to be in question period three days a week, when two days would suffice – Wednesday as caucus day and either Tuesday or Thursday on the margins of that. There's no need for PMO to feed the opposition and media beast, a race to the bottom.

And then, Harper does much better when he's outside the Ottawa bubble. Even though his Davos-style conversation with the Vancouver Board of Trade on Monday was disrupted by environmental protestors walking right onto the stage, he was very cool. While the RCMP should be concerned about such a serious breach of security, he did well to shrug it off, saying, "it wouldn't be BC, without it."

He also did well last month at the Montreal memorial service for Paul Desmarais, capturing in both languages his importance as a visionary leader of Canadian business, and a Canadian patriot.

And Harper's higher instincts were superb in his personal invitations to former prime ministers, opposition and First Nations leaders to join him on his flight to and from South Africa for the memorial services for Nelson Mandela. The fight against apartheid is a proud bi-partisan Canadian story and Harper understood that. As Brian Mulroney put it later: "He couldn't have been more gracious to everyone."

So, let's see more of that. The high road. Our country needs it. So does Harper.

January 2014

NO MORE HONEST BROKER

Stephen Harper's speech to the Israeli parliament was everything Benjamin Netanyahu could have hoped for, and then some, when he welcomed his guest as a voice of "moral leadership" in the world.

"In standing up for the truth, your voice, Stephen, has become an indispensable one," Netanyahu told Harper on his arrival in Israel, the day before his address to the Knesset, a first by a Canadian prime minister.

You don't hear that every day – first name diplomacy in public. You don't hear the kind of speech Harper made every day, either.

There were no diplomatic nuances in Harper's address. He made it very clear that Canada supports Israel, at all times, and in all circumstances. "Through fire and water, Canada will stand with you," Harper said, prompting a standing ovation.

He was also heckled by two Arabic-Israeli members of the Knesset, who then walked out, when he spoke of the new anti-Semitism of boycotting Israel. But that was to be expected. Harper could have laughed it off, and should have, by saying he felt right at home, just as in question period.

Harper had already made the requisite call on the Palestinian Authority's leader, Mahmoud Abbas, and made the expected announcement on aid to the Palestinians. And in his speech, he endorsed a two-state solution, one in which each recognized the other.

In which case, as he put it, Israel would be the first to propose a Palestinian state at the United Nations, with Canada right behind it. There was an echo of history in that – Israel was born at the UN in 1948, with Canada's support for the partition of Palestine.

But Harper's foreign policy is a departure from the honest broker traditions personified by Lester B. Pearson, who was then undersecretary of state for External Affairs.

If anything, Harper's foreign policy can be called "no more honest broker," and his position on Israel is the centre piece of what could be called a principled or "values-based" foreign policy.

And there's a big debate about this in the Canadian foreign policy community. For the honest broker school of traditionalists, Harper has turned his back on Canada's constructive role as a mediator in all the clubs to which it belongs, from the UN and the Commonwealth to la Francophonie. Harper calls this, as he did in his Knesset speech, "going along to get along," and says there will be no more of that.

This is how his foreign minister, John Baird, put it in a speech to the UN General Assembly last fall. The honest broker crowd can disagree with Baird, and that would include many in his own department of Foreign Affairs, but it must be said that he's very articulate on behalf of the "principled" foreign policy.

You name the issue, and nowadays Canada has its own position on it. From Syria to Iran, from human rights in Sri Lanka to gay rights in Russia. You can look it up under quotes from Baird.

On Syria, he notes the Assad regime is negotiating the handover of chemical weapons whose possession it previously denied. On Iran and its nuclear ambitions, Baird has said, "we can't have a Kumbaya policy on Iran," which puts Canada offside with the U.S. led P5+1 negotiations to ease economic sanctions in return for the Iranians dialing back their nuclear program. "Regrettably," Baird has said, "we don't have a lot of confidence or a lot of trust in the regime in Iran." On Ukraine, Baird went into the street with protestors in Kiev's Independence Square in December and said Canada stood with them against their own government and big brother in Moscow. He's a strong proponent of gay rights in Russia, and not just in the run-up to the Sochi Winter Games. And he's equally a strong opponent of forced marriages of girls and young women.

As Baird put it in a recent interview. There are those who believe "that Canada is somehow a referee in the world ... No, we have interests, we promote Canadian values, and that's tremendously important."

And when Canada finds itself misaligned with the U.S., Britain and France? Baird points out that Brian Mulroney broke with Ronald Reagan and

Margaret Thatcher, "his two closest friends" on the world stage, on the issue of apartheid in South Africa and freedom for Nelson Mandela.

Like every successful foreign minister, Baird understands that he has one client – the prime minister. But Harper also knows that Baird has his back.

The size of the Canadian delegation to Israel, including 21 rabbis, may suggest political motives by Harper, seeking votes in the Jewish community. But when he first enunciated his positions on Israel, back in 2006, he didn't have those votes.

So when he speaks of Canada and Israel as "the greatest of friends and the most natural of allies," he means it.

January 2014

A GOOD EXIT

There is no more majestic moment in the life of a democracy than a change of government – the peaceful handover of power from one party to another.

That transition was symbolized by the memorial service at the National War Memorial on the first anniversary of last year's attacks which took the lives of two soldiers on Canadian soil, one at the monument itself.

A solemn occasion was transformed into a splendid one when Stephen Harper and Justin Trudeau laid a single wreath together at the place where Cpl. Nathan Cirillo fell.

The outgoing prime minister, and the incoming one, stood united at a moment that reminded us of the blessings of our country. They then sat together with their wives for the remainder of the ceremony, while the governor general spoke eloquently about the Canadian way of life.

The image of the joint wreath-laying symbolized not only an orderly transition, but generational change. Harper's hair has gone grey in office, as Trudeau's will over time.

It was very much to Harper's credit that he invited Trudeau to appear with him, and to Trudeau's credit for having said yes. One of the tests of a prime minister is whether he or she has a sense of national occasion, and both men have it.

Harper doesn't receive enough credit for his sense of occasion, in fact. He demonstrated it when he invited former prime ministers to accompany him on the plane to Nelson Mandela's funeral, and when he offered state funerals for Jack Layton and Jim Flaherty. At Flaherty's funeral, Harper delivered a touching and funny eulogy that captured the essence of the late finance minister.

When a prime minister leaves office, it isn't the time to demean him or diminish his record. That's inappropriate and in very bad taste. Rather, it's a moment to thank him for his service to the nation. It's a time for grace notes, not piling-on.

To begin with, it should never be overlooked that Harper united the right and gave Canada the democratic alternation it needed in 2006 after 13 years of dynastic Liberal rule. He governed skillfully through two minority Houses before finally securing a majority in 2011.

His signature issue was always the economy and, with Flaherty, he steered Canada through the shoals of the Great Recession of 2008–09. In the recovery period, the Canadian economy created 1.3 million jobs.

The crash in the oil patch and other energy commodities also happened on his watch, but he can hardly be faulted for that. He made an important speech in London in 2008 in which he declared that Canada would become the world's next energy superpower – but he was unable to follow through by enabling the private sector to complete the pipelines needed to carry oil and gas to tidewater. Unforeseen issues of social licence arose. In his own mind, this must stand as one the great disappointments of his nearly 10 years in office.

The Harper decade also should be remembered for his historic apology to First Nations in the House for the tragic legacy of residential schools, an issue addressed by the Truth and Reconciliation Commission he appointed.

In terms of federal-provincial relations, Harper – like Jean Chrétien before him – was not fond of meeting premiers as a group. But he was a classical federalist, always respecting the division of powers in the 1867 Constitution Act. He managed to turn down the temperature between Ottawa and the provinces – especially with Quebec, which he had Parliament recognize in 2006 as "a nation" within a united Canada.

In foreign affairs, Harper pursued what his former foreign minister John Baird called a "principled foreign policy" that departed from Canada's former role as an "honest broker" in the world. This was controversial, to the say the least, and will be debated for years to come. For the first time since the founding of the UN, Canada failed to secure a seat on the Security Council.

At the end of the day, it must be said that Harper missed an opportunity to leave office gracefully. A fourth term was always an unlikely prospect; no prime minister since Sir Wilfrid Laurier has won four consecutive elections.

Now, Harper has to think about what to do with the rest of his life. Former prime ministers sometimes enjoy success in the private sector, as Brian Mulroney has with his corporate law practice. Harper isn't built that way; being a rainmaker is the last thing that would interest him. But he would be in demand on the speakers' circuit and could write a very good memoir of his time in office.

As for the critiques of his government, and his admittedly controlling style – they can be left for another day. And as for the future of the Conservative party – the party must, before it chooses a new leader, engage in a serious conversation about how it lost its way in the campaign by overplaying the identity card, turning off many of its moderate supporters.

In the days and months to come, there will be plenty of time for reflection and recriminations on the Conservative campaign.

Meantime, as Stephen and Laureen Harper prepare to vacate Sussex by November 4, they deserve the thanks of Canadians for their service to our country.

October 2015

UNDOING A LEGACY

One of the most remarkable features about the Trudeau Liberals' first five months in office is the speed and efficiency with which they are undoing the legacy of Stephen Harper.

It began their second full day in office, when the new government announced it would restore the mandatory long-form census. It was a substantive and symbolic reversal of the previous government's policy. Since then, they've kept their thumbs firmly on the delete key – which carried them right into last week's budget, where they unleashed the wrecking ball.

Niqabs at citizenship ceremonies? No problem. Harper famously ran against that and lost, and deservedly so.

Bill C-24? The Liberals announced last month they're going to repeal the law that strips dual citizens of their Canadian citizenship for convictions of terrorism, treason or espionage. "A Canadian is a Canadian is a Canadian," Justin Trudeau declared during the campaign.

Bill C-51, the Anti-Terrorism Act? The Liberals supported it in the House, promising to amend it once they took office to align its security and privacy provisions with the Charter of Rights, and to curb the powers of the Canadian Security and Intelligence Service and the Communications Security Establishment. The Liberals haven't got around to tabling amendments yet, but they will.

The mission against ISIS? It's been re-profiled from the deployment approved by Parliament under the Harper government, with Justin Trudeau recalling the six CF-18s from their base in Kuwait and tripling the number of special forces advisers on the ground in the region from 69 to 207.

Omnibus budget bills in the House? The Liberals vow you've seen the last of them.

The Fair Elections Act? Done like dinner. The Liberals were the chief beneficiaries of voter pushback on that one – a massive turnout among First Nations voters and students angry at the voucher provisions in the legislation. A bill intended to suppress voter turnout actually increased it.

But if you want to see where the campaign to undo everything Harper did in office is really making strides, look to the budget.

The first of many legacy casualties is the Balanced Budget Act, adopted by the Harper government in 2015. The Liberals obviously must repeal it if they're going to run a $29.4 billion deficit in the next fiscal year, and nearly $100 billion in deficits over the four-year course of their mandate. Not content to leave it at that, the budget turns a screw on the Conservatives, stating: "The balanced budget legislation enacted by the previous government is inconsistent with the government's plan to return to balanced budgets responsibly, and in a manner that supports economic growth." (Not that the Liberals have a plan to return to balance, but that's another story.)

Child care? The Universal Child Care Benefit was a signature policy of the Harper era, with taxable cheques of $100 per month mailed to families for each child under the age of six. Harper ran on this as one of the "Five Priorities" that got him elected in 2006. In the recent budget, the UCCB, the Canada Child Tax Benefit and the National Child Benefit Supplement have all been rolled into the new Canada Child Benefit – means-tested but tax-free.

There's more. The Conservatives loved boutique family tax benefits. Well, income-splitting for couples with children under 18 is gone. So are the Children's Fitness and Arts Tax Credits.

Old Age Security? The budget cancels the Conservatives' raising the age of eligibility from 65 to 67, beginning in 2023. This, the budget says, "will put thousands of dollars back in the pockets of Canadians as they become seniors."

The tax cut for small business? Forget about it. The Conservatives were going to cut the small business tax cut from 10.5 per cent to 9 per cent, effective in 2019. The Liberals have just cancelled that – or, as the budget states, "further reductions in the small business income tax rate (will) be deferred." That will cost small business $900 million to 2019. Ouch.

First Nations? What had once seemed a promising relationship between Harper and Assembly of First Nations Chief Sean Atleo fell apart when his leadership collapsed over dissident chiefs' opposition to the First Nations

Control of Education Act – and nearly $2 billion of education funding fell off the table. Indigenous peoples' opposition to Harper intensified over his refusal to appoint a commission of inquiry into missing and murdered Indigenous women. The Liberal budget provides $40 million for a two-year inquiry into MMIW and girls, and another $96 million "to support the capacity of Aboriginal Representative Organizations to engage with the government."

That would be the AFN chiefs, as well Métis and Inuit leaders. (Sounds like a plan. A travel plan.) Overall, the budget allocates $8.4 billion over four years for Indigenous education, water and housing. That's a huge win for Perry Bellegarde, Atleo's successor as head of the AFN.

Arts and culture? Where the Conservatives deeply cut CBC funding, the Liberals are providing an additional $675 million to the public broadcaster over five years. "Reversing past cuts will allow CBC-Radio-Canada to invest," the budget states. While they're at it, the Liberals are topping up the Canada Council for the Arts by a further $550 million. In all, the Libs are increasing arts funding by $1.9 billion over five years.

Here's another one – an undo of an undo. The Liberals are reinstating the Court Challenges Program dismantled by Harper in his first budget in 2006. Funding for official languages court challenges was later restored, but Harper had made his point. Now the Liberals are making theirs with $12 million over five years for "bringing cases to the courts that clarify and assert their Charter rights."

So what does it say about Harper's leadership of the country that his legacy can be so easily dismantled, at least in the short term?

It tells us he was a transactional leader, not a transformative one. In the last half century, there have been only three transformative prime ministers: Lester B. Pearson (the flag, the Auto Pact, medicare and the Canada-Quebec Pension Plans), Pierre Trudeau (official languages, multiculturalism and the Charter of Rights) and Brian Mulroney (free trade with the U.S. and Mexico, the Acid Rain Accord and Canada's leadership role in the post-Cold War world).

No successor to their governments would have tried to undo those legacies. Jean Chrétien ran against NAFTA but had the good sense to endorse it on taking office in 1993. While not a transformative leader, he was a successful prime minister. Harper, in time, may also be seen as a successful three-term leader. Just not one who transformed the country.

March 2016

A TRANSACTIONAL PM

There are three kinds of political governance – transformational, transactional and transitional. Stephen Harper was a transactional prime minister.

In the modern era, since the end of the Second World War, Canada has seen only three transformative leaders – Lester Pearson, Pierre Trudeau and Brian Mulroney.

Pearson gave Canada the maple leaf flag, the Canada-Quebec Pension Plan, universal health care and the Canada-U.S. Auto Pact. All of this in two minority Liberal governments from 1963–68, supported by Tommy Douglas and the NDP. Pearson's social programs crossed the line into provincial jurisdiction, but he was the father of "cooperative federalism," who found a way to harmonize provincial prerogatives with the national interest.

The first Prime Minister Trudeau changed the face of Canada with the Official Languages Act, multiculturalism, and the Canadian Charter of Rights and Freedoms. He built a tolerant society, or as he put it in the 1968 Liberal leadership campaign, "a just society." The Charter is truly a transformative achievement.

A country whose constitutional tradition was steeped in the division of powers between Ottawa and the provinces was transformed into one in which individual rights were entrenched in the Constitution Act of 1982. Not to be overlooked is Trudeau's leadership role in the 1980 Quebec referendum, in which he personified the Canadian option, and gave three speeches for the ages.

Mulroney was a transformational leader on the economy and the environment, as well as in asserting a Canadian leadership role on issues such as apartheid. The Canada-U.S. Free Trade Agreement and later the North American FTA created nearly five million new jobs, according to figures from the Ministry of International Trade. Since the Canada-U.S. FTA was implemented in 1989, Canada's GDP has grown from $600 billion to $2 trillion today.

On the environment, Mulroney's transformative legacy includes: the 1987 Montreal Protocol on ozone depletion; the 1991 Acid Rain Accord with the U.S.; Canada's leadership role in including bio-diversity with sustainable development and climate change at the 1992 Rio Earth Summit; the cleanup of the Great Lakes and St.-Lawrence River; the creation of eight new national parks; and the Green Plan in bringing issues to cabinet. On the world stage, Mulroney led the movement to end apartheid and free Nelson Mandela, over the opposition of Ronald Reagan and Margaret Thatcher, his two closest allies. Canada supported the re-unification of Germany in 1990 and was the first country to recognize the independence of Ukraine in 1991.

Mulroney used to say that political capital was meant to be spent rather than hoarded, and there's no doubt that by the time he left office, Canadians were glad to see the back of him. But as with Pearson and Trudeau, he left a nation transformed in ways that weren't fully understood at the time.

Other prime ministers since Mackenzie King – Louis St.-Laurent, John Diefenbaker, Jean Chrétien and Paul Martin – were successful but transactional leaders. And three – Joe Clark, John Turner and Kim Campbell – were transitional figures.

As for his own place in the pantheon of leadership, it's obviously early days yet for Justin Trudeau. But it's interesting that he told his caucus not to think three years ahead to the next election, but 30 years ahead to what kind of country they will leave. On federal-provincial relations, First Nations, Canada-U.S. relations and the environment, he clearly intends to bid for a transformational ranking.

Where does Harper fit in? He was definitely a transactional prime minister, with a decidedly mixed record on important files such as the economy, energy, federal-provincial relations, First Nations and Canada-U.S. relations.

But he wouldn't have been in power for nearly a decade if he hadn't first united the right, in the merger of the Canadian Alliance and Progressive Conservative parties. What Harper got from that was the storied Conservative brand, which enabled the former western Reform movement to grow its geographic reach into Ontario, Quebec and the Atlantic. In winning a plurality of seats in the 2006 election, Harper's Conservatives provided alternation in government after 12 years of dynastic Liberal rule. He governed adroitly through two minority Parliaments before finally securing a majority in 2011.

And then he stayed too long, and ran a terrible campaign in the 2015 election, which the Conservatives thoroughly deserved to lose. But Harper did win three elections in a row, the second Conservative leader – other than Dief – since Sir John A. Macdonald to have done so.

There's no doubt that the economy was his signature issue. With Jim Flaherty at Finance, Harper's government steered the economy safely through the dangerous waters of the Great Recession in 2008–2009. In the recovery since then until Harper left office, the Canadian economy created 1.2 million new jobs. Ottawa also ran up $160 billion of new debt, though the Conservatives did return to balance, running a small surplus of $1.9 billion during their last full fiscal year in office.

In 2009, Flaherty also created the Tax Free Savings Account, which more than half of Canadian taxpayers signed up for, according to a BMO survey. The Conservatives also lowered the business tax rate from 21 to 15 per cent, the lowest business tax in the G7 and one of the reasons Bloomberg named Canada as the second-best place in the world to do business.

The Universal Child Care Benefit of $100 a month was one of Harper's five priorities in the 2006 election, and there's no doubt it helped the Conservatives win in the cities and suburbs. So did the $1,000 child's fitness and arts class tax credit – boutique tax breaks were a Conservative specialty.

Harper did successfully negotiate the Comprehensive Economic and Trade Agreement between Canada and Europe, and the present government is moving to implementation, not without challenges across the EU. Canada also signed the Trans-Pacific Partnership with 11 Pacific Rim nations, including the U.S. and Mexico, though it's far from certain to be ratified in the U.S., and is not supported by either presidential candidate. But there's no doubt CETA and TPP are big picture deals.

But one has only to look at the Liberals' first budget to see how easily Harper's legacy has been undone. The Liberals have rolled back the doubling of TFSA contributions to $10,000 a year. The UCCB and the National Child Benefit Supplement have been replaced by the Canada Child Benefit, means-tested but tax free. The fitness and arts tax credit is being eliminated next year. There's no more income-splitting for couples with children under 18.

In non-fiscal matters, the new government restored the long-form census, will be amending the Anti-Terrorism Act, Bill C-51, and has re-profiled the mission against ISIS, recalling six CF-18s from the Middle East while deploying more Canadian trainers of Kurdish forces in northern Iraq.

On energy, Harper proclaimed in a London speech in 2008 that Canada would be the world's next energy superpower, but then was unable to deliver the necessary pipelines to tidewater on the Pacific, Atlantic and U.S. Gulf coasts. Canada has been unable to diversify its oil markets beyond the U.S., resulting in a continuing Canadian discount to the world price.

In New York, Harper once said the Keystone XL pipeline was "a no-brainer," which was not how Barack Obama and the White House saw it. The deterioration of Canada-U.S. relations on Harper's watch is part of his legacy on a file in which the standard of excellence was set by Mulroney.

On First Nations, Harper deserves full marks for his 2008 apology in the House – his finest moment in Parliament, and for establishing the Truth and Reconciliation Commission. It's not Harper's fault that some Assembly of First Nations chiefs sabotaged their leader, Shawn Atleo, taking down the

First Nations Control of Education Act, while demanding the $1.9 billion in federal funding that went with it.

On federal-provincial relations, Harper didn't like meeting the provincial and territorial leaders, doing so only once in his decade in office, during the 2009 global downturn. On the other hand, he was a classical federalist, who respected the division of powers. And for Quebec, he introduced a 2006 resolution recognizing Quebecers as a nation within a united Canada.

Resigning his seat last week, Harper made the announcement in a 90-second video posted to Facebook and Twitter. He stood alone in a conference room that looked like the opposition leader's boardroom in the Centre Block. It's not clear when the message was taped. He made his own claims on posterity, and thanked Canadians "for having given me the honour of serving the best country in the world."

The Harper-haters, in both mainstream and social media, were still having a hard time letting go of him, and letting him go.

It was left to Justin Trudeau, following his caucus meeting last Friday, to set the appropriate grace notes, thanking Harper for his service to the country.

"As a prime minister who's also a father," Trudeau said, "I can understand the sacrifices that have to be made in terms of having a young family while upholding this responsibility for Canadians." And he went out of his way to thank Laureen, Ben and Rachel Harper.

August 2016

4

TOM MULCAIR

No one, but no one, is talking about another Quebec referendum any time soon. But we have to be ready for one, right? Just in case Pauline Marois calls an election and is returned with a majority government, plunging Quebec into unprecedented uncertainty.

Yeah, right.

So what is going on in Ottawa with the New Democratic Party proposing a private member's bill (PMB) to amend the Clarity Act, which calls for a clear answer to a clear question on a referendum?

As the House resumed on Monday, the NDP was baited by the Bloc Québécois, which proposed its own PMB to repeal the Clarity Act altogether.

What the NDP is proposing is essentially its 2005 Sherbrooke Declaration, which held that 50 per cent plus one would be enough to carry the day in a referendum, as was the case in the 1980 and 1995 referendums held by the Quebec government.

In the view of NDP Leader Tom Mulcair: "The side that wins, wins."

Not exactly, according to the 2000 Clarity Act, passed by the Chrétien government and upheld by the Supreme Court. It was the near-death experience of the 1995 referendum, in which the No side prevailed by only one point, 50.58 to 49.42 per cent on a soft sovereignty-partnership question, which prompted the feds to define clear rules of the game for negotiating the breakup of the country.

But this isn't about that. It's about Mulcair trying to play both sides of the street.

It's not clear how much the NDP's Sherbrooke Declaration opened doors of soft nationalist Bloc voters to the party six years later in the 2011 election. That was about Jack Layton, the man with the cane, *le bon Jack*.

But this is certainly about shoring up the NDP's new base in Quebec, which returned 59 Quebec MPs in that election, propelling the party from fourth to second place in Parliament.

Nor is it clear if either PMB will ever come to a vote in the House, as they have to take a priority number and are way down the list. In any event, neither would ever pass, as the Conservatives and Liberals both support the Clarity Act, as informed by the Supremes.

Yet while Mulcair was playing to the 50 + 1 gallery, the NDP was also proposing stronger language for a referendum question, such as: "Should Quebec separate from Canada and become a sovereign country?"

Mulcair knows perfectly well that no Quebec government will ever write a referendum question using the word "separate" or "separation."

Mulcair knows this from his own time on the front lines of the debate in the National Assembly, and before that as a young lawyer for Alliance Quebec, which was a federalist front.

No one can say he hasn't done his part in the long struggle to keep Canada whole.

Nor has he been speaking out of both sides of his mouth on the question of 50 + 1. He has been saying exactly the same thing in Toronto as in Ottawa or Montreal.

Yet he is playing a double game.

And on Monday he got called out on it by Liberal leadership candidate Justin Trudeau, who represents the east-end Montreal riding of Papineau, where he defeated a popular Bloc incumbent in 2008 and was easily re-elected in 2011. Trudeau knows a soft nationalist when he sees one.

"You cannot be half-pregnant on the question of Canadian unity," Trudeau said on the leadership campaign trail in Calgary. "It's a very careful political calculation by him to appeal to his strong nationalist base in Quebec." Exactly right.

As Trudeau also pointed out, Mulcair's 50 + 1 gambit does not bode well for any kind of non-aggression pact, united front or merger between the NDP and the Liberals, to block the Conservatives and Stephen Harper in the next election.

While the Liberals are a party of the pragmatic centre, some things are fundamental to their brand. The Charter of Rights is one. Official languages and multiculturalism is another. And so is the Clarity Act, part of the party's living legacy.

Nearly a year into his leadership, Mulcair has been generally impressive in the role. He's skated the loony left wing of the party into the boards. He kept his young Quebec MPs out of the Quebec election. He's imposed total discipline on his caucus.

Mulcair is also moving the NDP closer to the centre on major policy issues. And he's very good on his feet in the House.

Maybe he just wants to get the 50 + 1 thing behind him, so he can say the NDP's position is clearly on the record, and on the floor of the House itself.

Another referendum? Not in his time in Parliament.

January 2013

YEAR ONE AS LEADER

On the first anniversary of Tom Mulcair's election as leader of the New Democratic Party, the question is whether he has exceeded expectations.

It's a bit like companies putting out year-end numbers. Did he beat the street? What's his visibility going forward? And what new products is he offering to increase his market share?

In these terms, Mulcair's record as CEO of Team Orange is positive to mixed.

Yes, he has exceeded expectations, especially considering that he was replacing Jack Layton, who did for the NDP what Steve Jobs did for Apple. It's a pretty tough act to follow.

After Layton's death in August 2011, and the weak interim leadership of Nycole Turmel in the House, the NDP decided it needed an experienced parliamentarian.

With 13 years in the Quebec legislature, and five more in the House of Commons, Mulcair fit the job description down to the ground.

First, he moved quickly to impose impressive discipline on the NDP caucus. And you thought Stephen Harper was a control freak. Mulcair prevented his Quebec MPs from taking sides in Quebec's student unrest last spring, when some of them had just written final exams themselves.

In last summer's Quebec election, not one NDP member from Quebec publicly endorsed either the Parti Québécois or Québec solidaire. When it's considered that several of Mulcair's young Quebec members had previously written cheques to QS, that's quite an achievement. This was a real test for

Mulcair; he needed to impose top-down discipline from the Opposition Leader's Office, and he did.

In question period, Mulcair is an effective leadoff hitter, but his developing problem is that he's also trying to bat cleanup. On some days, he takes the entire opening round of questions. He needs to give his front benchers more airtime. He also needs to work on his sense of humour. He still gives the impression of being a pit bull.

In terms of policy offerings, Mulcair's leadership is a work in progress. He tried to appeal to Ontario voters by saying Canada was suffering from Dutch disease when there is no evidence, other than our petro dollar, to support this argument.

And his visit to Washington this month was a disaster. The international stage is different than the floor of the House – not an appropriate place to trash-talk the government of Canada. Bad mouthing the Keystone XL project, which, incidentally, involves thousands of union jobs on both sides of the border, was a bad idea.

But Mulcair's worst play was to suggest that 50-percent-plus-one was enough in a Quebec referendum, when the Clarity Act requires a clear answer to a clear question. He opened a Pandora's box, for no reason. It's costing him votes in Ontario and English-speaking ridings in Quebec, and has cost him an MP who crossed to the Bloc Québécois because Mulcair implied Ottawa would have a role in shaping the question. "The side that wins, wins," Mulcair said. But he lost in bringing it up.

What Mulcair is missing is a story, a narrative, so that voters can get to know him better. It comes down to this: Who is this guy, and where does he want to take the country?

Canadians don't know that he's the second oldest of 10 children, of a francophone mother named Jeanne Hurtubise and an Irish father named Harry Mulcair. As the second oldest of 10 kids, this means he looked out for his siblings. More than the big brother, at some points he would have been a stand-in for his parents. This is a story all parents, especially mothers, would find compelling.

Mulcair's personal journey, from McGill law to the National Assembly, is one of an ambitious achiever. But he clearly hasn't forgotten where he came from. On the day of his election as NDP leader, he wore his McGill tie to the convention, just as Mike Babcock wore his behind the Team Canada and Detroit Red Wings benches for Olympic gold and Stanley Cup games. "It's my lucky tie," Mulcair said recently.

Mulcair took heat last year, including from Harper, for carrying a French as well as Canadian passport. The answer is that his wife, Catherine Pinhas, was born in France to Jewish immigrants from Turkey. And that her parents, Sephardic Jews, were Holocaust survivors. Next question.

And even on the 50 + 1 dust-up, Mulcair has a strong personal narrative. He has no lessons to take from anyone in opposing separatism, having fought for a Canadian Quebec in the trenches of two referendums. In the second one in 1995, in his riding of Chomedey, the other side tried to prevent thousands of No votes from being counted.

But it's up to him to lay down those markers, to tell those stories. In order for the voters to trust him, they first need to know him.

March 2013

MULCAIR'S NARRATIVE

There are touchstones in Tom Mulcair's life, events that come full circle.

When he first ran for the Quebec legislature in the suburban Laval seat of Chomedey in 1994, he was returning to the neighbourhood where he grew up.

"On my first day of door-knocking," he wrote in his new autobiography, *Strength of Conviction,* "I went back and walked my old *Gazette* delivery route."

When he launched the French and English versions of the book in Montreal, he chose a bar called Les Bobards on St.-Laurent Blvd., in the Plateau Mont-Royal, where he had held his victory party in 2007 when he won the federal byelection in Outremont. Once again, full circle.

The joint was jumping, crowded with the personal and professional contacts of a lifetime – friends from his youth in suburban Montreal, colleagues from McGill Law School, staffers from the National Assembly who are with him still as Opposition leader in Ottawa.

Geoff Chambers, for example, has known Mulcair since they worked together at Alliance Quebec, the minority English-language activist group, back in 1983.

Chambers was sitting at the bar with his uncle, Charles Taylor – McGill professor, co-author of Quebec's landmark 2008 report on reasonable accommodation of ethnic minorities, and lifetime NDP activist. Chuck Taylor famously ran and lost to a guy named Pierre Trudeau in Mount Royal back in 1965. His role at Les Bobards was to introduce Mulcair.

"One thing that stands out about Tom," said Chambers, "is his loyalty to his friends."

It probably begins with family. Mulcair was the second oldest of 10 kids in a rambunctious and roaring Irish-Catholic family, the big brother to eight siblings. "In a large family," he wrote, "as anyone who was raised in one can attest, you learn to take your responsibilities early. The older children help to bring up the younger ones."

His parents' struggles to make ends meet can only be imagined. Mulcair's father had attended Loyola, a Jesuit high school for boys, and his son easily passed the entrance exam. But here there was no full circle – his father informed him the family couldn't afford the tuition, then less than $1,000 per year.

When he was 10 and 12 years old, Mulcair had paper routes with the *Montreal Star* and *The Gazette*. As a 14-year old high school student at Laval Catholic, Mulcair worked a summer job for $1.25 an hour at a clothing factory in Montreal's *schmatte* district.

This also came full circle at his book launch, in a way; the *schmatte* guys have lunch at Schwartz's and dinner at Moishe's, just a few blocks south of Les Bobards on St-Laurent. Over smoked meat at lunch and steaks at dinner they can be overheard complaining about their costs – including the help.

As a student at McGill, Mulcair paid his way through law school by working summers in the construction industry, tarring roofs. Just the way to get through a hot Montreal summer.

After completing his first year of law, in the summer of 1974, he met a French girl from Paris at a friend's wedding. Mulcair and Catherine Pinhas have been together ever since. Their backgrounds could not have been more different – he came from a struggling Irish-Catholic family, she from an affluent Jewish family from the well-to-do Paris neighbourhood of Neuilly. Her people, originally from Turkey, were Sephardic Jews and Holocaust survivors. They have two sons, both graduates of McGill, one a cop and the other a college professor.

Two things stand about the first half of Mulcair's book. One is that it's completely authentic, an account not only of his formative years but of a vanished place and time – English-Catholic Montreal in the middle of the 20th century.

The other is that Mulcair obviously wrote it himself, because the voice is entirely his. He wrote on his BlackBerry, on planes, trains and automobiles. (Quite an endorsement of the BlackBerry keyboard. I've written columns on mine, but a book? That might be a first.)

Mulcair also tells a compelling story about his years in Quebec City and his eventual recruitment by Jack Layton and the NDP. It didn't end well between Mulcair and Jean Charest in Quebec. As Environment and Parks minister in 2006, Mulcair opposed the development of Mont-Orford Park in Charest's backyard in the Eastern Townships. Charest called him in and the two men had a conversation that went something like this: *You're demoted. No, I quit.* In the end, no development ever went ahead.

Months later, Mulcair and Catherine had dinner with Layton and Olivia Chow at Mon Village, in Hudson, where Layton grew up. The restaurant is a well-known stop on the road between Montreal and Ottawa and – full circle again – it was there that Mulcair met Layton's former principal secretary, Brad Lavigne, and persuaded him to return as his senior campaign adviser.

It's only when Mulcair moves on to talk about his party leadership that his book turns into a campaign pamphlet, with the usual pre-election posturing and positioning. For example, in a chapter on the 1995 Quebec referendum, there's a conspicuous insert on the NDP's 2005 Sherbrooke Declaration and Mulcair's support of a 50 + 1 Yes vote being enough to break up the country.

"One of the worst mistakes we can make is to deceive voters the voters that in voting Yes they are voting for something else," he writes. "Some say it would be unthinkable to let the country break up on a vote of 50 per cent + 1 ... I say it would be unconscionable to let our relationships as Canadians degenerate that far."

So, he wasn't improvising or thinking out loud over St.-Jean-Baptiste, when he said he was "proud" of the Sherbrooke Declaration. It's in his book. And while this position might help Mulcair on the margins with the soft nationalist vote in Quebec, it will hurt the NDP in the rest of Canada, where there is very little support for the idea of repealing the 2000 Clarity Act requiring a clear majority to a clear question.

He also wrote about how, when he left the Charest government, "the Conservatives came calling." He mentioned "a senior Conservative who was an old friend from Quebec City." This would have been Lawrence Cannon, then the senior Quebec political minister in the Harper government. They met at the Garrison Club in Quebec City, and Cannon was interested in Mulcair joining the Conservatives as a candidate.

Mulcair wrote that he was more interested at the time in becoming chair of the National Round Table on the Environment and the Economy (NRTEE). "I had put forward my name and had been short-listed to head the agency."

Had the Conservatives appointed him to head the NRTEE – had they not shut it down two years ago, Mulcair never would have become NDP leader. He never would have become leader of the Official Opposition. And Stephen Harper would not now be trailing him in most polls. Full circle.

August 2015

KEEPING THE IN-LAWS HAPPY

A political party is a family – and in the NDP, Tom Mulcair is a son-in-law. As he has discovered since the election, it's one thing to marry into the family, quite another to keep the in-laws happy.

Many of them don't like the way Mulcair, a political transplant from the Quebec Liberals, has been running the family business. They weren't happy with the revamped product line offered in the election. And they're going to say so at the mandatory leadership review at the party's biennial convention in Edmonton this weekend.

Mulcair is rather like a CEO facing a shareholder revolt at the annual meeting; he just needs to get through it. All he needs, according to the rules, is 50 per cent plus one. In the real world, he needs to be somewhere in the 60s, preferably at the higher end. Mulcair himself is on record now saying he thinks he need a 70 per cent result to give him the authority to stay on.

Edmonton isn't that easy to get to, and it isn't a cheap flight, either. But party officials are expecting a high turnout of 1,500 delegates. Mulcair needs about 1,000 supporters on the convention floor. At this point, no one really knows whether he's there yet. Says one top NDP strategist, "It feels like the mid-60s."

The Broadbent Institute's annual Progress Summit in Ottawa last weekend offered a close up of the party's mood. The cocktail chatter and corridor conversations were largely about the leadership review.

Overheard at the hotel bar: "If I'm going to dump someone, I want to know who is going to replace him." That's a very good point.

If Mulcair were to step aside, who would be in the running? Nathan Cullen from British Columbia would be one obvious possibility. Megan Leslie would be another, even though she lost her Nova Scotia seat in the Liberal sweep of Atlantic Canada. She has star quality, she would represent generational change and she's perfectly bilingual. Niki Ashton from Manitoba ran against Mulcair in the 2012 leadership race, has kept her own counsel on the leadership review, and probably would be a contender this time as well.

At the Broadbent gathering of the NDP clan, quite a bit of anger was still evident, especially among defeated candidates. And not just about Mulcair dragging the party from the left to the centre of the political spectrum, but equally about the cautious conduct of the campaign itself.

One defeated candidate from the Toronto region wondered aloud: "Until the election was called, Mulcair was taking all kinds of questions and doing very well. Then on the first day, he took none, and walked away from the podium. Meanwhile, in Vancouver, Justin Trudeau stood there and took as many questions as reporters wanted to ask."

And then Mulcair took the next day off. Then, rather than barnstorming the country, Mulcair launched a tour that was more of a stately procession.

In politics, as in hockey, the worst thing you can do is sit on a lead.

"It was a classic front-runner's campaign," said one former MP who supported Mulcair for the leadership four years ago. One former stalwart of the Ed Broadbent era put it another way:

"It was a risk-averse campaign. It wasn't that Mulcair was outflanked on the left. It was the aversion to *risk*."

Trudeau's campaign wasn't risk-averse. He took a huge gamble in promising stimulative deficits – which proved to be the game-changer in the election, differentiating the Liberals from the NDP and winning the ballot question of change. Meanwhile, Mulcair was aligned with the Conservatives in promising balanced budgets. This did not pass unnoticed with the NDP's base on the left.

Nor did it go unnoticed, less than two weeks before the election, when Avi Lewis, Naomi Klein and kindred spirits on the left issued their Leap Manifesto on the environment, clean energy and Indigenous peoples, with the obligatory denunciation of free trade.

This came at a bad moment for Mulcair. Just when he needed to reverse the slide in his campaign, the Toronto-based movement leftists appeared to be deserting the cause.

And while Mulcair had been a dominant parliamentary figure who regularly demolished the Conservatives in question period, it was never clear that the voters would hand the country over to the guy holding the knife to the government's throat. But at least Angry Tom – the guy in the House – was authentic. Happy Tom, the guy who turned up for the leaders' debates, was not.

The one spot in the campaign where Mulcair passed the authenticity test was the release of his book, *Strength of Conviction*. The first half of the book was a revelation – a page-turner about growing up in a big family in Montreal, meeting and falling in love with his wife Catherine, working his way through university and law school with summer jobs that included roofing.

It was a moving story, and it offered him a chance to present a campaign narrative more in tune with who he is, where he came from and his hopes and dreams for our country.

It would be good to hear from that guy this weekend. It certainly couldn't do him any harm.

April 2016

LEADERSHIP LOST

The NDP suffered the worst possible outcome at its Edmonton convention, ditching its leader and allowing its policy agenda to be hijacked by the loony left.

Either wound is potentially fatal. Each was entirely self-inflicted. It may take a generation for the party to recover from both.

It's hard to say who had the worse Sunday afternoon, Tom Mulcair in losing the NDP leadership, or Jordan Spieth in blowing a five-shot lead in the closing nine holes of the Masters. Both will be talked about for decades in political and golf circles. Both collapses were unprecedented.

Since leadership reviews were invented in Canada, half a century ago, Mulcair is the first incumbent to be rejected outright by his party. Joe Clark called a Progressive Conservative leadership convention in 1983, saying his 66.9 per cent support was "not good enough." Which is how Brian Mulroney became party leader that year and prime minister in 1984.

Jean Chrétien avoided a Liberal leadership review he would have lost to the Paul Martin forces. Ahead of a summer caucus in 2002, he announced he would retire within 18 months. A caucus revolt and subsequent leadership review were averted, and Chrétien served another year as prime minister, completing a decade in office in November 2003. It was the only time a sitting prime minister with a comfortable majority was ousted by his own MPs, proving Mulroney's adage that "you can't lead without the caucus."

In Mulcair's case, he went to Edmonton with the approval bar having been set at 70 per cent by outgoing party president Rebecca Blaikie. But few NDP strategists expected Mulcair to do that well, the general sense being that he would be in the grey zone, somewhere in the mid-60s, a weak but survivable endorsement. By Saturday, even Mulcair's organizers sensed they were slipping below 60 per cent, but no one thought he would be defeated. The 52–48 vote against him shocked everyone on both sides in the hall into silence. It was an OMG moment.

A funny thing happened on the way to Edmonton, more people showed up than were expected. Hundreds more. And as one former campaign strategist put it, "they weren't going there to vote for the status quo."

Mulcair himself made what may have been a tipping-point error in an interview with CBC anchor Peter Mansbridge on the eve of the convention, when he said he would be prepared to leave oil in the ground if that's what the party wanted, as the radical wing is demanding in their Leap Manifesto.

It was a weak leadership moment and a big mistake, in that it infuriated the home town team, Premier Rachel Notley and her year-old NDP government, struggling with a $10 billion deficit due to the collapse of oil prices. Then there's the Canadian discount the Americans receive on Canadian oil as our only customer. As she pointed out in her convention keynote Saturday, Canada can't even get the world price, low as it currently stands, unless it can build pipelines east and west to tidewater so we can diversify to global markets. Pipelines, she pointed out, "are built by Canadian workers, with Canadian steel." Oh, and 70,000 Albertans have lost their jobs in the energy sector.

And with that, the convention became polarized over policy as well as leadership, with the far left Leap Manifesto as the focal point of fury on both sides.

Given the continuing recriminations from a failed campaign, and the clear divisions between the radical and moderate left, it's not clear that Mulcair could have won delegates over with his speech just before the vote.

Speeches don't win conventions anyway, and Muclair certainly didn't win anyone over with his. He needed a rousing barn burner, but instead delivered a teleprompter text full of NDP boilerplate rhetoric. There was one touching moment when he departed from his text and spoke about his dad being a diabetic and an amputee, struggling to find the money to pay for his meds. Mulcair choked up and had tears welling in his eyes. It was an emotionally powerful plea for pharmacare as well as universal health care, a case Mulcair had made on the campaign trail.

For the rest, he recited a hit parade of NDP heartland issues and was rewarded with half a dozen standing ovations. Then a majority of the same people went and voted against him.

Mulcair's concession speech, as painful as it must have been, may have been his finest moment as NDP leader. "Don't let this very divided vote divide us," he said. It was a moment of incredible grace under pressure, a very classy exit speech.

Mulcair will remain as leader in the House, as he should. While the NDP has been relegated to third party status, he remains a dominant figure. Welcomed back with a standing ovation from all sides as he rose in question period Tuesday afternoon, he was in top form, holding the government's feet to the fire. He raked the Liberals over the coals on Justice Minister Jody Wilson-Raybould attending a Liberal party fund raiser organized by a Bay Street law firm, as well as offshore tax havens in Panama and elsewhere and a revolving door culture of former Revenue Canada managers joining big accounting firms like KPMG. It was vintage Mulcair.

He can remain until his successor is chosen, and that could be as long as two years. Or he may decide, perhaps at the end of the spring sitting, that he's had enough.

It will be for others to clear the policy train wreck that divides the party between trust fund socialists from Toronto versus the real world of the Alberta NDP, to say nothing of the downside in Quebec of dumping a Quebecer as leader. Only the Liberals will benefit from that.

As for the NDP, while it didn't adopt the Leap Manifesto in Edmonton, the party agreed to discuss it at the riding level. Are they really going to have this divisive conversation in 338 riding associations?

April 2016

5

JUSTIN TRUDEAU

TO RUN OR NOT TO RUN

Justin Trudeau has a decision to make – to run or not to run for the federal Liberal leadership.

This is not a Hamlet-like dilemma, but a significant decision in terms of his family, lifestyle and career. At 40, he's at a good place in his life, with two young children at home in Montreal, and learning his job as a parliamentarian and opposition backbencher.

A run for the Liberal leadership would change all that. And in the event he won, how competitive would he be, in the House and on the hustings, with Stephen Harper and Tom Mulcair? This is not a charity boxing match, but the real deal.

Trudeau is very personable, well liked on all sides of the House. He's also been very careful about earning his way, rather than trading on the family name. This has been the case since he won a competitive race for the Liberal nomination in Papineau riding, the east-end Montreal seat then held by the Bloc Québécois. As far as that goes, it was his father who had the free ticket to ride, with the safe seat of Mount Royal handed to him on a platter back in 1965.

Not that the Liberal leadership is there for the asking, but Trudeau would enter as the frontrunner, on name recognition alone. This would also give him an inherent advantage in fundraising, no small matter, since leadership campaigns are subject to the severe restrictions of the Accountability Act.

Gone are the days when friends and corporations could write big cheques. Paul Martin raised and spent $10 million for the 2003 leadership campaign. Bob Rae and Michael Ignatieff spent no more than $2 million in 2006. And some of the other contenders are still paying off their debts from that leadership race. So in a campaign where donations are limited to $1,100 per person, being Trudeau doesn't hurt.

Where he'd be tested is on his ideas of the country, and his road-map for leading the Liberals from the wilderness back to the promised land of power.

Which raises the question of whether this is a prize worth seeking, much less winning.

The Liberals are in a place, third place, where they've never been before. In 2011, they won less than 20 per cent of the popular vote. For more than a century, since the time of Sir Wilfrid Laurier, the party's power base has been Ontario and Quebec. In the Chrétien era, when the right was split between the Reform Party/Canadian Alliance and the Progressive Conservatives, the Liberals twice won 100 seats in Ontario. And in the pre-referendum election of 1980, Trudeau's father won 74 out of 75 seats in Quebec. Today, the Liberals have only 11 seats in Ontario, and eight in Quebec, including a floor crosser from the NDP. In the West, where there are 92 seats, the Liberals hold only four.

The re-building job is enormous, and about to become even more daunting. The present House of Commons of 308 members will be expanding to 338 seats for the fixed-date election scheduled for October 19, 2015.

Twenty-seven of those 30 seats will be west of the Ottawa River, 15 of them in Ontario and six each in Alberta and British Columbia. Most of the new Ontario ridings will be in the suburban 905 area code around Toronto, where the Conservatives currently hold 21 out of 22 seats. Even in Toronto itself, where they had been shut out since 1993, the Conservatives now hold nine out of 23 seats in 416.

Similarly, most of the new seats in Alberta will be in the suburbs of Calgary and Edmonton, and the Conservatives already hold all but one of the current 28 seats in the province. The same holds for BC, where the lower mainland around Vancouver will get more seats and where the main competition for the Conservatives is the NDP, not the Liberals.

In the 338-seat House, the Conservatives will be heavily favoured to win all but a handful of those 27 new seats west of Quebec. The math of a majority is about to become easier for Harper. And make no mistake, unless he's hit by a bus he'll be running again. As for Mulcair, he has the advantage of being opposition leader, and while he can be a bit of pit bull, he's a proven commodity in the House. His job is to position the NDP as the alternative to the Conservatives, a left-right choice, with the Liberals possibly being squeezed out in the middle.

If Trudeau were to run and win the Liberal leadership, he would normally be looking at two elections before the Grits returned to office.

So he's not just looking at spending the next seven months of his life on the road, but perhaps the next seven years. He'd have to want it pretty badly.

But good for him if he answers the call.

September 2012

TRUDEAU HAS YET TO BE TESTED

When all the media buzz subsides over Justin Trudeau's bid for the Liberal leadership, there are two questions that will frame his campaign.

First, what's his idea of Canada and its role in the world?

And second, what's his plan for rebuilding the party?

He can answer these questions however he likes, in a series of major policy speeches, in a bunch of newspaper commentaries or both, collected as a book.

Nearly 30 years ago, when Brian Mulroney was running for the Conservative leadership, the rap against him was that he had no ideas. So he had his policy adviser, Charley McMillan, pull together some speeches as a book called *Where I Stand*.

"You want policy? There's my policy," he often said in 1983, and got on with the real business of winning a competitive convention.

For Trudeau, on his sense of Canada and its place in the world, the question isn't his father's idea of Canada, but his own.

This begins with the Constitution and the division of powers, the central bargain of Confederation.

What's his sense of Ottawa's role on such issues as health care and post-secondary education, not to mention such shared jurisdictions as the environment and immigration? Then, what would be his response to the demands of the present separatist government of Quebec?

As for Canada's place in the world, how would he build the Canadian brand? The Harper government and Foreign Affairs Minister John Baird have rebranded from the honest broker image, one where Canada joins all clubs and takes no sides, to a values-based policy that includes staunch support of the Israelis in the Middle East. Then there's Canada-U.S. relations, and the rise of Asia. What's Trudeau's sense of those important files?

And then there's the economy and fiscal frameworks.

These aren't trick questions, and no one is trying to trip Trudeau up. They're fundamental, and he simply has to know what he's talking about.

This is why they have places called the Canadian Club, the Empire Club and the Board of Trade.

Leadership candidates go there and put their ideas out in the public space.

This is also why leadership campaigns are a team sport, and Trudeau has put together a very good team. Gerry Butts, for example, used to be principal secretary to Dalton McGuinty at Queen's Park, and now heads the World Wildlife Federation in Canada. He's one of the smartest people in the room.

Two things stand out about Trudeau's leadership team. They represent generational change, and they don't have scores to settle from the Liberal Party's War of the Roses between the Jean Chrétien and Paul Martin clans. There is no prospect of the Liberals returning to government as long as they are feuding with one another. The people around Trudeau don't carry any of that baggage.

And then there's the question of rebuilding the party, the party of Laurier, St.-Laurent and, so far as that goes, Trudeau. In the last election, the Liberals won 11 seats in Ontario and seven in Quebec, out of 181 ridings in the two provinces that maintained the party's fortunes for more than a century. To say nothing of the Liberals winning only four out of 92 seats in the West.

Not to mention that, in the next election, there will be 30 new seats in the House, 27 of them west of Quebec, and most of them in the suburbs, such as the area code 905 region around Toronto, already dominated by the Conservatives.

Never mind flash polls that show Trudeau would defeat Stephen Harper and Tom Mulcair. Those are just about name recognition. No party has ever jumped from third to first place in one election.

The first thing Trudeau should be saying about the rebuilding job is that it's going to take time. It means fundraising, finding good candidates, building a ground game and putting forward policies that will enable the Liberals to capture the centre of the electorate rather than being squeezed out by the Tories on the right and the New Democrats on the left.

A competitive race includes debates with several serious candidates, even if they are just running for the next time.

If nothing else, Trudeau needs to be tested. Among other things, Canadians need to know whether he can take a punch, and not in a charity match, but in the political arena.

For those who dismiss him as a lightweight, he can only exceed expectations.

October 2012

TRUDEAU BRINGS MORE THAN NAME TO LEADERSHIP RACE

There could be as many as nine candidates for the federal Liberal leadership, but it's not shaping up as a competitive race. The field consists of Justin Trudeau and the others.

However, one serious candidate will join the race Wednesday when Martha Hall Findlay announces her leadership bid in Calgary, where she's a fellow at the University of Calgary School of Public Policy. While Alberta isn't exactly the Liberal heartland, she's making an interesting point by announcing her campaign kickoff there. She also has a serious network of friends and supporters.

She has just paid off her debts from the 2006 Liberal leadership race, where she was the first candidate to endorse Stéphane Dion after the first ballot. Elected to Parliament from a Toronto riding in 2008 and defeated in 2011, she will if nothing else give Justin a run in the ideas department.

Montreal MP Marc Garneau, Canada's first astronaut and former head of the space agency, is also itching to join the race. So that would make three candidates with name recognition.

But all prospective candidates, other than Trudeau, have two major challenges – money and organization.

For openers, it will cost each candidate $75,000 just to enter the race, in three instalments of $25,000. That isn't a lot of money, but such is Trudeau's early lead that other would-be candidates are having trouble raising the deposit.

The party has capped spending at $950,000, which reflects election-finance rules that now include leadership campaigns. Stung by the sponsorship scandal, Jean Chrétien left a 2003 campaign finance reform that excluded corporate donations and limited individual donations to $5,000.

Since the law didn't take effect until 2004, it didn't prevent Paul Martin from raising and spending $10 million for the 2003 Liberal leadership. Then Stephen Harper came along with the 2006 Accountability Act, which then limited personal donations to $1,000, indexed to inflation, and now at $1,200.

The thought of running a serious six-month leadership campaign for only $950,000 is counterintuitive. Normally, that would hardly cover a candidate's travel and accommodation, to say nothing of hospitality. Yet, in contrast to Trudeau, most prospective candidates would be looking to run on fumes.

As Sir Wilfrid Laurier once famously said: "It is not enough to have principles, we must also have organization."

Nowhere is organization more important than leadership campaigns.

Once again, advantage Trudeau. His campaign carries none of the baggage of the Chrétien-Martin leadership wars, nor the incompetence of the Dion-Ignatieff years, which left the storied Liberal brand on the verge of irrelevance.

For example, Trudeau has attracted two outstanding campaign advisers in Gerald Butts and Dan Gagnier. Butts was principal secretary to Dalton McGuinty at Queen's Park, and Gagnier was principal secretary to David Peterson in Ontario and later chief of staff to Jean Charest in Quebec. It was Gagnier who guided Charest back to majority territory in 2008 after he was reduced to a minority in 2007.

Gagnier joining Trudeau's team last week is one more indication that Trudeau should be taken seriously, not just in terms of the leadership campaign, but in rebuilding the Liberal party beyond that.

The Liberals don't want or need nine podiums on the stage of their leadership debates, and the entry fee alone should result in a winnowing of the field.

But neither do the Liberals want a coronation. They had that with Michael Ignatieff, and it didn't end very well. The entry of Hall Findlay and Garneau means that Trudeau will be tested on his ideas of party and country.

In spite of the advantages of the family name, he has a history of earning his way, from winning a contested Liberal nomination in his riding of Papineau to paying his dues in Parliament. He would be the first to say that he'd benefit from a competitive race.

November 2012

A LEADER NAMED TRUDEAU

Forty-five years ago this week, on April 6, 1968, the Liberal Party of Canada chose Pierre Trudeau as its new leader. He proposed a "Just Society," and the convention marked the beginning of the modern era in Canadian politics.

But it was by no means a done deal going in. It took four ballots, at a very competitive convention, for Trudeau to obtain a majority of delegates.

The field was incredibly deep – it included Robert Winters, John Turner, Mitchell Sharp and the first Paul Martin. And Joe Greene, who was living proof that great speeches win standing ovations but not conventions.

It was a delegated convention, decided on the floor, and the excitement was breathtaking. Had Turner taken his delegates to Winters, rather than releasing them when he was eliminated on the third ballot, the convention and history might have turned out very differently.

In any event, Trudeau went on to lead the party and the country for 15 years and four terms in office, interrupted only by the nine-month interregnum of the Joe Clark Conservative minority government in 1979. The Liberals were then regarded as Canada's natural governing party – from the time Lester Pearson took office in 1963 to Paul Martin relinquishing power in 2006, the Liberals were in government for 32 out of 43 years.

It is a very different Liberal Party that will gather for its leadership showcase in Toronto on Saturday, 45 years to the day from the first Trudeau's accession to the leadership. And it will be a very different occasion, as the event will mark the opening of one week of voting in a preferential ballot, the result of which will be announced the following weekend in Ottawa.

All the excitement will be made-for-television. The outcome is a foregone conclusion, though. Now, as then, the winner will be named Trudeau.

Justin Trudeau is very different from his father, and deserves to be considered on his own merits and his own terms.

But the son's leadership race is like the father's in one important sense: He is running both as the outsider and the choice of the party establishment.

And make no mistake, even relegated to third place in the House, this is an establishment party, based in the Montreal-Ottawa-Toronto triangle. The Liberal establishment has financed Trudeau's campaign, and put their considerable talent behind it.

But it's obviously a party in very different circumstances that the younger Trudeau will be inheriting, one that will have to climb over two others, the New Democrats and the Conservatives, to regain the promised land of government.

The Liberals have only 35 members in the House, and their caucus is not exactly deep with talent. Their best performer is the outgoing interim leader, Bob Rae, whom Trudeau would be well advised to keep on as House leader while he hits the hustings.

As the third party, the Liberals don't get a lot of time in question period anyway, and Trudeau hasn't found his feet there yet.

In any event, his job isn't in the House, it's in the country, rebuilding the party, from one province and one riding to the next.

And nowhere more so than in Ontario and Quebec, the two provinces that were, for a century, the mainstays of the Liberal dynasty. In the Chrétien years, when the right was divided, the Liberals routinely won 100 seats in Ontario.

But if Trudeau is not looking at a walk in the park, he didn't expect one going into politics. In 2008, he won a competitive nomination in Papineau and defeated a popular Bloc Québécois incumbent. And he held on to his seat in 2011, when he might well have been swept away by the rising NDP tide.

He may have inherited the family name, but he has never traded on it. And he has talents of his own. As this campaign has demonstrated, he is personable and authentic, and those are important attributes in this game.

Trudeau has the gift for retail politics and has used social media to his advantage. His challenge will be to transform his Twitter supporters into door-knockers.

One thing Trudeau has going for him is the inherent value of the Liberal brand. His father once ran a campaign on the slogan "The Land is Strong." The brand is strong, too.

April 2013

ONE CAMPAIGN ENDS, ANOTHER BEGINS

The press gallery above the House of Commons is normally close to empty during question period, which most reporters watch from their offices, when they watch it at all.

On Monday, it was standing room only, with overflow in an auxiliary gallery behind it. The joint was jammed for Justin Trudeau's first day in the House as leader of the Liberal Party.

Which turned out to be much ado about nothing. As leader of the third party in the House, Trudeau had to wait his turn to ask Stephen Harper why he was doing nothing for the middle class, a cohort of voters Trudeau discovered during his leadership campaign. The prime minister's answer was as forgettable as Trudeau's question.

Meanwhile, opposition leader Tom Mulcair, just back from the New Democratic Party convention in Montreal, was in high dudgeon on the issue of temporary foreign workers displacing Canadians in the labour market. Overall, Mulcair had a good weekend at the convention. The NDP is officially no longer a socialist party, though its members still call themselves brothers and sisters. The convention, held in a city that Mulcair has long made his home, was also intended to fill in some gaps in his personal narrative, as a father and family man. Yet back in the House on Monday, it was as if he was determined to show Trudeau up in terms of righteous indignation.

But Trudeau doesn't do sound and fury, and if he stays on plan, won't be in the House very much anyway. Question period doesn't play to his strengths as a retail politician. And as the leader of the third party, there isn't much there for him. As one of his advisers put it: "The plan is to liberate him from question period." When the House is sitting, look for him to be there on Wednesdays, caucus day, and perhaps Tuesday or Thursday as well.

For the rest, his job isn't in the House. His job is in the country, rebuilding the party, recruiting candidates and filling the campaign war chest. He has already been quite successful as a rainmaker, having apparently raised $2.3 million for his leadership campaign, well over the party's limit of $950,000. What's more, he can legally donate the surplus back to the party.

His campaign also created a ground game. "There were 12,000 volunteers on the ground," says an adviser. "They made 200,000 phone calls, real phone calls, not robocalls."

Winning by the margin he did, with more than 80 per cent of the turnout of 104,000 voters on a preferential ballot, Trudeau will be leading a united party, one that badly needs to put decades of infighting behind it.

As if to make the point, Jean Chrétien was warming up the crowd at Trudeau's coronation ceremony on Sunday, ripping the Conservatives and NDP, and doing some management of his own legacy.

At one point, he referred to his government's sound fiscal management, of balancing the budget in 1997 and paying down debt thereafter. Even at that moment, he could not bring himself to mention the name of his finance minister, Paul Martin, who was sitting right in front of him.

Unwittingly, Chrétien opened the door to the biggest applause line in Trudeau's prepared acceptance speech.

"It doesn't matter to me if you were a Chrétien Liberal, a Turner Liberal, a Martin Liberal or any other kind of Liberal," Trudeau declared. "The era of hyphenated Liberals ends right here, tonight."

The Liberal War of the Roses dates to John Turner's resignation from Pierre Trudeau's cabinet in 1975, before his return from Bay Street in 1984. Turner's leadership was constantly undermined by the Chrétien clan. And Chrétien, a sitting prime minister, lost his caucus and was deposed by Martin in a very Canadian coup.

Trudeau's team is largely unscarred by all that. Some of them don't even remember it. But the party, beginning with its former leaders and their clans, still have to put their past behind them. On Sunday, Chrétien and Martin's paths never crossed as they worked different sides of the room, and sat for separate interviews with TV anchors. It was enough for the Trudeau campaign just to get the two of them in the same room.

"This is the last stop of this campaign, and the first stop of the next one," Trudeau said.

And he took aim at the Conservatives as a party that plays divisive tactical politics.

"We are fed up with leaders who pit Canadians against Canadians," he said, "West against East, rich against poor, Quebec against the rest of the country, urban against rural."

It is early days until the next election in October 2015, but between now and then, this guy will be out there, working the crowd, honing his message of "hope and hard work." Based on the leadership campaign, the Conservatives and NDP would both do well not to take him lightly.

April 2013

A QUESTION OF JUDGMENT

Even though Justin Trudeau voluntarily disclosed his outside income from speaking fees four months ago, there was a sense then that the story would come back to bite him.

Which it has.

The problem with his disclosure, then and now, isn't so much the amount he was billing for appearances, but the people he was getting the money from – charities, not-for-profits, schools and universities.

Trudeau has revealed that, since becoming an MP in 2008, he has received $277,000 for outside speaking events, including $72,000 for four speeches last year. This was all before he declared his intention to seek the Liberal leadership.

For all of these appearances, he had a permission slip from the federal ethics commissioner.

But while he has been very above board, and set a high standard for transparency, this isn't about his ethics; it is about his judgment.

In fairness, Trudeau didn't go looking for these gigs. The clients came to him through his agent, Speakers' Spotlight.

The one that haunts him now is the $20,000 he accepted from the Grace Foundation, which supports a nursing home in Saint John, NB. The organizers lost $21,000 on the event, more than they paid him. (An ironic footnote to the story is that Justin's paternal grandmother was named Grace Elliott Trudeau.)

The foundation chairperson wrote to Trudeau asking for the money back, saying that "a refund would meet our needs and would provide a positive public impression." When the story blew up on Friday, Trudeau's office politely blew off the refund request. The public impression was anything but positive. He looked like he was stiffing an old folks' home for 20 grand.

By Sunday morning, he was having second thoughts. In obvious damage-control mode, Trudeau made a Father's Day appearance with Kevin Newman on CTV's Question Period in which he said he wanted to "do the right thing," and offered to sit down with all his former speaking-engagement clients to see if they were happy and, presumably, refund the fee if they weren't. In other words: If you ask, I'll give back the money.

Saskatchewan Premier Brad Wall, for one, thought Trudeau should refund the $20,000 he was paid to speak to a Literacy for Life conference in Saskatoon last year. According to Wall, elected officials shouldn't be paid to make speeches. Period.

Trudeau also received $20,000 last year for a speech to the Canadian Mental Health Association. Not only is this a not-for-profit, but his own mother, Margaret Trudeau, is one of Canada's most famous advocates for improved mental health outcomes. Hello!

Finally, Trudeau charged Ontario's Queen's University $12,000 for a speech last year at a time when he was the Liberal party's higher education critic. (He has also done paid appearances before school boards and other learning stakeholders while serving as his party's youth critic.)

There are two issues here, and neither is very complicated.

The first is a potential conflict of interest. An MP should not be accepting money, even if earned and unsolicited, from a stakeholder in whose space he's a shadow critic.

And the second is accepting money from a university in circumstances other than an endowed lecture. Speaking at universities, whether to small class groups or convocations, is generally regarded as part of giving back. It's an honour.

Trudeau also shouldn't have accepted $20,000 from Rogers Media for a speech shortly after he was first elected, in 2008. The telecommunications industry is regulated by the feds.

The question of outside income and speakers' fees paid to parliamentarians could be referred to the Commons Ethics Committee, but that would result only in a media circus. Or it could be considered in camera by the House Board of Internal Economy, where the rule of common sense would prevail.

Many backbench MPs continue their practices as lawyers, doctors, accountants or members of other professions. Some retain their business interests. There's no conflict in that.

But MPs shouldn't accept paid speaking appearances from charities, non-profits and organizations in the public education or health sectors, or in any regulated segment of the economy.

Trudeau recently proposed a very constructive and commendable solution on parliamentary expenses, in response to the Senate expense scandal: that all parliamentarians post their expenses online on a quarterly basis.

He may inadvertently be performing a similar service on the issue of outside speakers' fees paid to parliamentarians.

June 2013

A SENATE GAMBIT

Two leadership attributes are evident in Justin Trudeau's gambit on reforming the Senate.

First, he's not afraid of thinking big. And second, his inner circle is a close knit group that can keep a secret.

Trudeau and his entourage were working on his Senate move over the entire holiday break, and not a hint of it leaked before his surprise announcement last week that 32 senators were no longer members of the Liberal caucus. They were just as stunned as the entire political class, including the media.

In the short term, Trudeau has achieved a pre-emptive takeout of the auditor-general's upcoming interim report on Senate expenses. Trudeau has inoculated himself and the Liberal brand against any damaging revelations in the AG's report. The AG and his staff have been asking senators about everything from cab slips to cell phone bills. What began as a comprehensive audit has become a forensic one. Both the Conservatives and Liberals can expect to take a hit.

But Trudeau won't have to throw anyone out of his caucus, he's already done that by expelling all Liberal senators from caucus. It can be said that he's suspended the presumption of innocence, as Stephen Harper did in kicking out three Conservative senators last fall, before the RCMP reported its finding on their expenses.

The Trudeau team clearly understands the first rule of damage control – get the bad news out, take the hit and move on, as they did last year by proactively disclosing Trudeau's speaking fees, including at universities and schools, while he was a sitting MP, and the party's youth and higher education critic. Again last month, they disclosed he had mistakenly charged his office for minor travel expenses related to several paid appearances, and wrote a cheque to cover it. Trudeau called it "an honest mistake." End of story.

But that's just tactics. In larger strategic terms, Trudeau has seized the moment on an issue where he was previously squeezed between the Conservatives and the NDP.

From his Reform-Alliance days, Senate reform has been one of Stephen Harper's signature issues. He has long advocated for an elected Senate, and has referred the matter to the Supreme Court, which will find that he needs a constitutional amendment to do so, whether under the general amending formula of Parliament and seven provinces representing 50 per cent of the population, or under the unanimity provisions of the Charter of Rights.

As for the NDP, it has for more than half a century held for the abolition of the Senate, though it couldn't do that without a constitutional amendment, either. But Tom Mulcair's position is simply that as prime minister, he wouldn't appoint any senators.

Which, in a way, is also Trudeau's position.. He wouldn't appoint any senators, but would have them appointed by a group of eminent persons, along the lines of nominations to the Order of Canada.

The problem for Trudeau or Mulcair, should either become prime minister after the October 2015 election, is that neither could get a bill passed by a Conservative controlled Senate. And the governor general signs legislation only when it's passed by both Houses of Parliament.

There are 105 seats in the Senate, and the Conservatives currently hold 57 of them, with 32 Liberals (they are still sitting as Liberals), seven independents and nine vacancies. Seven more Senate seats will open up between now and the fixed date election, six of them this year, as these senators reach the mandatory retirement age of 75. At some point, Harper will have to decide whether to fill them or not.

The second problem with Trudeau's proposal is legitimacy. This is not like the Order of Canada, where the chief justice of the Supreme Court is the chair of the advisory council.

The Senate is supposedly the House of the Provinces (so styled by Trudeau's father in one of his many constitutional proposals). There's actually a solution available to this problem, and it's the Meech Lake formula under which senators were either elected as in Alberta, or named from lists provided by provincial legislatures, as in Quebec. Some outstanding Quebec senators were appointed during the Mulroney years, notably Roch Bolduc, the former head of the Quebec public service, and Claude Castonguay, the father of Quebec health care.

Trudeau's proposal runs into another problem – his party's own constitution. He can look it up under "Chapter 13 – Caucus," which states: "In this Constitution, the 'Caucus' means those members of the party who are members of the House of Commons or the Senate of Canada." As for conventions like the one to be held in Montreal the week after next, "each member of the caucus" is an automatic delegate. And proposed amendments "must be submitted in writing to the national president at least 27 days before the convention."

There's no doubt Trudeau has struck a chord with his proposal, as in the Senate is broken and needs fixing. But the devil is definitely in the details.

January 2014

ONE FOR THE LEADER

Well, that was easy.

The Liberal Party's constitution stipulates that their senators are automatically members of caucus. And when Justin Trudeau expelled 32 Liberal members from caucus, he missed by six days the 27-day notice period for proposing amendments to the party constitution.

No problem. In the final policy session of the Liberal convention in Montreal Sunday morning, the plenary adopted a sense of the convention resolution that allows the national executive to "interpret the constitution in a manner consistent" with the new Liberal caucus.

It passed 525 to 32 – by an amazing coincidence the same number of senators kicked out of caucus. And with that Trudeau, who had been taking it in from a front row seat, was outta there. By the time the co-chairs got around to proposing a big thanks to him, he had left the building. It's not every day a leader gets a standing ovation *in absentia*.

The Liberals didn't even bother to offer him up for a closing news conference or scrum, to the predictable annoyance of the media. As if voters would be also be irritated, particularly on a morning Canada had just won Olympic gold in men's hockey.

It was clear after Trudeau's keynote Saturday that his close entourage had no intention of doing a "media avail" at the closing of the convention. "When you've hit a walk-on home run, walk on," quipped Trudeau's top adviser Gerald Butts.

One reason to walk on was to avoid what happened to Andrew Leslie, the former commander of Canada's land forces, whose $72,000 in real estate fees and moving costs were in the news cycle last week. In an otherwise impressive political debut at a Friday keynote, Leslie divulged he had been talking to the Conservatives as well as the Liberals before joining the red team. This turned his subsequent newser into a drive-by shooting, with reporters demanding to know who was courting whom. In the middle of all this, the Conservatives sent out a series of chatty career move e-mail exchanges between the retiring general and the PMO. Welcome to the NHL, Andy.

It was the only mishap at a convention that was otherwise a significant success. While predictably thin on content, it was extremely well organized, and the delegates were in a very good mood. The Liberals did not look like a third place party – nor will they be after the next election. And this for a party left for dead after the 2011 election – and which, until Trudeau's accession to the leadership last year, it might as well have been.

A party that has been chronically in debt raised $11 million last year – more than $2 million in December alone, two-thirds of that in online donations. A party that could barely count 50,000 members now has more than five times that number. A party that couldn't find quality candidates is now seeing contested nomination battles everywhere (it helps if you went to Brebeuf or McGill with Justin). A party that was in the ditch is now on the march, cruising comfortably in first place in the polls.

All of which put the delegates in a very positive mindset. Journalists were also permitted to roam the floor freely and sit-in on most break-out sessions, in stark contrast to last October's control-freaky Conservative convention in Calgary, where Stephen Harper also skipped town without meeting the media.

In Montreal, there were two brands in the Liberal window, the party's and the leader's. The Liberal brand equity is in a party of government which, from the beginning of the 20th century, was in office for nearly 75 of the last 114 years. Trudeau's begins with name recognition. Most people 50 and over, as one Liberal strategist put it, "have known the guy since the day he was born, or think they do."

So the Liberal logo was literally hanging from the ceiling, and Trudeau's trademark slogan of "Hope and Hard Work" was the convention's theme. The hall looked very sharp.

And the delegates, who filled it to standing-room only for Trudeau's keynote, were in a mood to be on their feet. Trudeau didn't disappoint them.

On the issue of Senate reform in the wake of the expenses scandal, he pointed out that Harper, "as a candidate, promised that he would never appoint a senator. Not a single one. Then, after he got elected, he appointed 57 of them."

There was only one problem with Trudeau's delivery of his text: there wasn't enough French in it, only seven out of 39 minutes, as the French-language media did not fail to note. And this in Montreal. It's the kind of time allocation between the two languages usually heard in Toronto.

Most of Trudeau's speech was about Liberal positioning on "the middle class," which received no fewer than seven mentions.

Nathalie received several mentions, as well. Nathalie was everywoman, made up by Trudeau and his writers. She lives on the South Shore of Montreal, takes the Champlain Bridge to work in either an office or in retail in the city. She worries about the debt her family is carrying, worried she'll never have enough to retire, is "anxious about her future, probably even more so for her kids' future."

It worked in the hall, but on paper it was pretty thin. Afterwards, the hunt was on for Nathalie.

In the media centre, someone suggested that if Trudeau and wife Sophie's new baby is a girl, they'll have to name her Nathalie Justine.

February 2014

TRUDEAU'S RED TORY BASE

Justin Trudeau was playing to the base in his weekend keynote at the Liberal convention – the Progressive Conservative base, Red Tory voters who might consider becoming Blue Grits.

"People in Ottawa talk about the Conservative base as if it is some angry mob to be feared," Trudeau declared. "They are wrong. As you all know, the 5.8 million Canadians who voted Conservative aren't your enemies, they're your neighbours."

He went on: "I say this to grassroots Conservatives out there, in communities across this country. We might not agree about a great many things, but I know we can agree on this: Negativity cannot be this country's lifeblood. It may be the way of the Conservative party of Canada's current leadership, but it is not the way of those Canadians who voted Conservative."

After decrying negativity, Trudeau went on to do a negative riff on Stephen Harper. No one ever confused logic with rhetorical licence.

In a single page of his text, Trudeau mentioned the Conservatives and their voters no less than seven times, as many references as there were to the middle class in the entire speech.

But the outreach to Red Tories was the heart of the speech. These were once Brian Mulroney's voters, and Joe Clark's and Jean Charest's, and Peter

MacKay's before the Progressive Conservative party merged with the Canadian Alliance in 2003. Stephen Harper got what he wanted most in that deal, a storied national brand.

But there were a lot of voters who came with it, and for the most part they have stayed with Harper through the last four elections. Red Tories, like Blue Grits, are generally progressive on social issues, and conservative on economic ones.

For the most part, they live in cities and suburbs. Trudeau was right. They're your neighbours. They live on the West Island of Montreal, in the west end of Ottawa, in the area 905 belt around Toronto, in the Mount Royal subdivision of Calgary, and in the lower mainland of British Columbia.

In the 2011 election, Harper won a majority of 166 seats in the 308 seat House, with 39.6 per cent of the vote, with the New Democrats winning 103 seats and official opposition with 30.7 per cent of the vote, while the Liberals were relegated to third place for the first time in their history with 34 seats and only 18.9 per cent of the votes.

The new House will have 338 seats, with 15 of the 30 new seats in Ontario, six new seats in Alberta and BC, and three new seats in the greater Montreal area. Most of the 27 new seats outside Quebec are in cities and suburbs, where those Red Tories live.

They may already be trending to Trudeau and the Liberals. Recent polls put the Liberals in the mid-to-high 30s in voting intention, with the Conservatives hovering around 30 per cent, and the NDP trailing in the mid-20s.

For the rest, Trudeau skipped town before the media could ask him about the cost of commitments adopted by the Liberal policy plenary on Sunday morning. In his keynote, for example, he referred to "infrastructure that supports growth." In the policy session adopted a motion for an infrastructure program at 1 percent of GDP. That's $18 billion, three times next year's projected surplus after seven years of deficits.

But Trudeau's main problem this week isn't explaining the cost of his promises, but explaining himself, after making light of the situation in Ukraine during an appearance on Radio-Canada's *Tout le monde en parle*.

"It's very worrying, because Russia lost in hockey, they'll be in a bad mood," Trudeau said. "We fear Russia's involvement in Ukraine."

TLMEP is a place where politicians go to die. The wildly popular show is taped on Thursday and airs on Sunday. They have wine on the set. The host, Guy Lépage, and his sidekick Dany Turcotte, have the nicest way of setting guests up for a fall.

But Trudeau tripped himself up. He shouldn't have joked about Ukraine. There's nothing funny about it. And he shouldn't have waited until Tuesday before apologizing, as he did on Twitter. "I'm sorry to have spoken lightly of the very real threat Russia poses to Ukraine," he tweeted. He called the Ukrainian embassy, apologized to the ambassador and signed the book of condolences.

But by then, he had already taken a hit. There are 1.2 million Canadians of Ukrainian descent. Most of them vote.

March 2014

TRUDEAU 2.0

Given their precipitous decline in the polls, doing nothing was not an option for Justin Trudeau and the Liberals heading into the summer.

From first to third place in the EKOS-*iPolitics* poll, from 39 to 23 per cent in only nine months: that's pretty much the textbook definition of "plummeting." It's a political narrative that has the Liberals and NDP trading places – not just in the polls but as the perceived party of change.

With only four months to the election, and only days before the last sitting of this Parliament, Trudeau and the Liberals couldn't go into the summer looking like losers with nothing to offer.

So they pushed the re-set button in Ottawa, and essentially pre-launched their campaign and platform under the banner of Real Change. Not just change, as in 'time for a change'. But Real Change. Surrounded by Liberal candidates in a ballroom at the Château Laurier, Trudeau had plenty of good attack lines on Stephen Harper and the Conservative decade in government. But his real target was the other guy, Tom Mulcair, who has stolen Trudeau's thunder as the presumed agent and beneficiary of change.

"We're not going to do what some would cynically do," Trudeau said, referring to Mulcair promising to abolish the Senate when it can't be done without the unanimous support of the provinces; five premiers are already opposing it. Trudeau's right about that. His own proposal for the PM to appoint non-partisan senators recommended by a committee of eminent persons is perfectly within the constitutional bounds confirmed by the Supreme Court in the landmark Senate reference case.

But the Senate is hardly what candidates get an earful about at the door. Home delivery by Canada Post – that's different. For months, Mulcair has been saying the NDP would maintain and restore home delivery of the mail.

Trudeau made the same promise Tuesday, that the mail would continue "to be delivered to your home." Neither Trudeau nor Mulcair can say what this would cost, but it's a certain vote-getter.

Trudeau also wants the Canada Revenue Agency to treat taxpayers as clients and end its "political harassment" of charities with political agendas. This doesn't cost anything. It's an echo of the run-up to the 1984 election, when Brian Mulroney launched a sustained attack in the House on Revenue Canada, insisting that it treat taxpayers with "courtesy and respect at all times."

Most of what Trudeau proposed was low-cost to no-cost and some of it was pretty bold in terms of parliamentary reform. "This place is broken," he said, "and together we're going to fix it." Jack Layton said the same thing in 2011 and it became the template for the NDP campaign.

For example, Trudeau said the October election would be the last one based on the first-past-the-post system. Within 18 months, a Liberal government would propose a reformed electoral system with either preferential ballots or some kind of proportional representation.

Trudeau has also signed on to gender parity in all appointments, including the cabinet. "My Liberal cabinet," he declared, "will have an equal number of men and women." That rocked the house. In Quebec, one of Jean Charest's success stories was gender parity in all his cabinets, to the point where no one thought anything of it.

Trudeau also said he would strengthen the role of MPs, allowing more free votes. He would have whipped votes only on bills implementing the Liberal platform, on questions of confidence such as the throne speech and budget, and on 'values' issues arising from the Canadian Charter of Rights and Freedoms.

That's interesting. Just last year, Trudeau said his caucus members must support a woman's right to choose, an issue that's always been considered a question of conscience by Liberals and Conservatives alike. Not that there's ever going to be another vote on abortion in the House – no government of any political stripe would ever call one. But the right to choose is certainly not a charter value. (Indeed, Pierre Trudeau, father of the Charter of Rights, once wrote privately to Cardinal Emmett Carter of Toronto to say that he would invoke the notwithstanding clause to override any law permitting abortion on demand.)

Trudeau also would expand access to information to cover cabinet ministers' offices – including the Prime Minister's Office. Should he become prime minister, he might live to regret that. And with ATI in ministers' offices and the PMO, presumably including the PM's own department of the Privy Council Office, there's a risk that advisers and officials would no longer write about anything important in an email.

Trudeau would also restore the long-form census and encourage evidence-based policy, allowing government scientists to speak up rather than suppressing their opinions. Trudeau said he wants "policy based on facts, not made-up facts based on policy."

And Trudeau tried to put some distance between himself and his own support for C-51, the Anti-Terrorism Act, pointedly noting its potential harm to civil liberties and privacy, and insisting again that he would amend and improve it in government. There's no doubt that Trudeau and the Liberals have taken a hit among progressive voters on C-51 – to the benefit of the NDP, which clearly opposed C-51 as well as the extension of the limited military mission in Iraq and Syria.

Trudeau's event was the second major Liberal policy announcement in little more than a month. Their middle class tax cut and child care rollout ended up getting lost in the excitement over the NDP win in Alberta, and it was hard to distill into a sound bite. While it would cut the middle class tax rate from 22 to 20.5 per cent for people earning between $45,000 and $89,000 per year, it would also raise the top marginal rate from 29 to 33 per cent for those earning over $200,000, pushing their taxes north of 50 per cent in several provinces, including Ontario and Quebec. The Liberal child care package would be limited to families earning less than $150,000 a year – means-tested but tax-free.

The only thing that came of that tax announcement is that people who make over $200,000 have largely stopped writing cheques to the Liberals. Why would they give them money when Trudeau wants to take it away?

But on Tuesday, Trudeau got what he badly needed – a pretty clean launch to the re-booting of his campaign. At least the Liberals knew they were in trouble, and are trying to do something about it.

June 2015

PING PONG

Brian Mulroney used to call it the "ping-pong" effect: voters in Quebec and Ontario looking back and forth across the Ottawa River, watching to see what the people on the other side are doing.

And that's what happened in Monday's election, with Quebecers breaking to the Liberals in unexpected numbers to give Justin Trudeau a surprise majority government.

Quebecers love a winner. In the closing two weeks of the campaign, Trudeau looked like a winner. With the Liberals pulling away to a double-digit lead in Ontario in the final days, Quebecers jumped aboard the Trudeau bandwagon, giving him 40 seats – about twice as many as expected in any projections.

So Quebec proved to be the margin of Trudeau's majority of 184 seats in the new 338-seat House. He didn't just win the Island of Montreal – he swept the suburban area-450 suburbs of the north and south shore. He won in the lower Laurentians, the Eastern Townships and the Gatineau.

It was all in the numbers. Polling in the mid-20s as late as the final weekend in Quebec, the Liberals ended up winning 35 per cent of the Quebec vote. The NDP, with 25 per cent, won only 16 seats. The Conservatives won just 17 per cent of the vote but it was a highly efficient vote, concentrated in the Quebec City region – and it delivered 12 seats. The Bloc Québécois, with 19 per cent, won a surprising 10 seats, though Gilles Duceppe lost his Montreal riding of Laurier–Ste. Marie again to the NDP's Hélène Laverdière.

Who will speak for Quebec in the House? All four parties. But the Liberals will speak for Quebec in government, something which was not part of anyone's election scenario. And in a majority government at that.

How did this happen? How did the NDP slide from the mid-40s in Quebec to the mid-20s in voting intention in a matter of just three weeks? There has never been such a freefall. From a minimum projected 60 seats at the end of September, the NDP finished with just 16 on election day.

Two things happened to Tom Mulcair. First, the niqab thing erupted going into the French-language leaders' debates. Second, Mulcair lost on the ballot question of which party would be the agent of change.

On September 23, the eve of the Radio-Canada debate, Mulcair gave a speech at the Bonsecours Market in Old Montreal in which he issued a plea for tolerance and calm on the matter of Muslim women wearing the niqab at a citizenship ceremony.

Pointing out that any woman wearing the veil would have to reveal her face to citizenship officials in private, he said women should not be prevented from wearing the niqab at a swearing-in. He made the case like the lawyer he is – but the niqab put both the Conservatives and the Bloc back in the game in Quebec.

By then, Mulcair and the NDP were already losing to the Liberals on which party would be the agent of the change desired by two-thirds of Canadian voters.

The NDP went into the campaign in first place, polling in the low 30s, with the Liberals mired in third place in the mid-20s. The story of how they traded places is one for the history books.

First of all, the 78-day campaign played to Trudeau's acknowledged strength – his retail game. He was very good in crowds, endlessly posing for selfies that ended up on Facebook and Twitter. The buzz wasn't just in the room, it was also on social media. It wasn't just his stamina that carried through the marathon campaign; by the end of it, he had come to personify generational change.

And then, in a major turning point in the campaign, Trudeau said he would run deficits of up to $10 billion a year before balancing the books in 2019. Mulcair, meanwhile, said he would present a balanced budget from the beginning of an NDP government. "We have to balance the budget," said one of his advisers. "We're the NDP." In other words, the NDP was running to escape bad memories of the Bob Rae government in Ontario and Mike Harcourt's time as premier of British Columbia.

Trudeau's statement on deficits drew a line between the Liberals and the New Democrats. He outflanked the NDP on the left while Mulcair was positioning a socialist party to the right on the fiscal framework. The Liberal strategy was cribbed right out of the Kathleen Wynne playbook from the 2014 Ontario election, which was no accident: the campaign was run by the same people, notably public opinion specialist David Herle.

Trudeau also inoculated himself on the deficit question – by saying he would run one. Progressive voters who had left the Liberals for the NDP over issues such as Trudeau's support for the Conservatives' security bill, C-51, returned to the fold.

For his part, Stephen Harper overplayed his hand on the niqab, especially in English-speaking Canada, where voters recoiled at his musing about banning the niqab in the public service. The Conservative overkill extended to the strange idea of setting up a snitch line to report "barbaric practices."

This is Canada, for heaven's sake. We don't do that here.

In two years, Justin Trudeau has taken the Liberals from third place to government – a remarkable achievement.

A couple of years ago, I ran into Trudeau at a Jewish community tribute dinner in Montreal.

"How's it going out there?" I asked.

"I'm doing what I was born to do," he replied. "And if you write that, I'll kill you."

Doing what he was born to do has taken him all the way home to 24 Sussex. On his own terms. In his own time.

October 2015

A PM'S TOP TWO FILES

Brian Mulroney used to say that the top two files on his desk as prime minister were federal-provincial relations and Canada's relationship with the United States.

In the last two weeks, with the First Ministers' Meeting in Vancouver and his official visit to Washington, Justin Trudeau has demonstrated that he sees the same two bookends as top priorities of his government.

In this regard, he's temperamentally a lot more like Mulroney than his own father, who was constantly in conflict with the provinces and didn't really get along well with American presidents (with the exception of Jimmy Carter, who attended his funeral in 2000).

Mulroney got along famously with Ronald Reagan and the first George Bush, as well as Bill Clinton in the five months their tenures overlapped in 1993. Mulroney used to say that Canada-U.S. relations started at the top – that when a PM had the president's attention, the American system engaged.

What he got from Reagan was the 1987 Canada-U.S. Free Trade Agreement, complete with an exemption for Canada's cultural industries agreed to by a former Hollywood actor and president of the Screen Actors Guild. What he got from Bush was the 1991 Acid Rain Accord, which solved what was then the most pressing bilateral environmental issue between Canada and the U.S.

When Reagan died in 2004, Mulroney became the first foreigner ever to speak at the state funeral of an American president. On Friday, he became the first foreigner to eulogize a U.S. first lady when he spoke at the funeral of Nancy Reagan.

It was a timely reminder of the standard of excellence in Canada-U.S. relations, occurring the same week as Prime Minister Trudeau's visit to Washington and the White House.

Three things were quite clear during Trudeau's day at the White House and State Department on Thursday. First, he has made a strong personal connection with Barack Obama (they're calling it a bromance). Second, the White House spared nothing in the warmth of its welcome. Third, the president made sure the U.S. system engaged for Trudeau and the Canadian delegation in a way it hasn't since the Mulroney years.

It certainly never engaged that way during the Harper years. In nearly a decade in office, Stephen Harper never had more than a working visit at the White House, either with George W. Bush or with Obama. Harper mistakenly made approval of the Keystone XL pipeline project the template for the relationship, going so far as to call it "a no-brainer" on a visit to New York.

When Obama delayed and finally killed Keystone last year, relations between Ottawa and Washington went into the deep freeze. The White House stopped communicating with the PMO, which for its part froze out U.S. Ambassador Bruce Heyman. It was the worst period in Canada-U.S. relations since Jack Kennedy called John Diefenbaker "that SOB" and cut him out of the loop during the Cuban Missile Crisis of 1962. (Kennedy was delighted to welcome Liberal Prime Minister Lester B. Pearson to Hyannis Port after his election in 1963).

Similarly, several members of Obama's close political circle openly advised and consulted with Trudeau's campaign entourage, making no secret of their preferred outcome in the 2015 Canadian election.

So it was no surprise when Obama and his team received Trudeau and the Canadian delegation, literally and figuratively, with open arms.

Though it was an official visit by a head of government, the White House treated it as a state visit in all but name, from the welcome ceremony on the South Lawn to the Obamas and Trudeaus waving at the guests from the balcony of the South Portico. That was a first. Then the White House moved the state dinner from the State Dining Room which seats only 120 people to the East Room which allowed for more than 200. Even senior staff are usually invited only to the after-party at state dinners, but several members of Trudeau's PMO were included at the dinner.

And on content and tone, Trudeau and Obama both got it right in arrival remarks, the press conference in the Rose Garden and toasts at the dinner. Both benefited from strong staff work, notably in their "announceables" in the Rose Garden, but both also had perfect personal pitch throughout the day.

Asked by a White House reporter about the prospect of a Donald Trump or Ted Cruz presidency, Trudeau politely declined to go there.

"I have tremendous confidence in the American people," Trudeau replied, "and look forward to working with whomever they choose to send to this White House." Exactly right. It was Obama who referred to the Republican race as "a crack up," which of course made headlines on cable news channels.

Obama also has a good ear for Canadian accents and speech. In his welcoming remarks for the first official visit by a Canadian PM in 19 years, he playfully said, "It's about time, eh?" At the state dinner, he noted, "This is not dinner, it's supper." (My six-year-old daughter always insists on the same thing, using just those words.)

Trudeau has enjoyed two excellent weeks in Vancouver and Washington. And he deserves full marks.

He's shown that he has a sense of occasion. He's shown that he belongs at this level. And he has now taken ownership of the two biggest files on a PM's desk.

March 2016

CASTRO "CONTROVERSIAL"

Maybe it was the jet lag.

Justin Trudeau woke up Saturday morning in Madagascar, eight time zones ahead of Ottawa, and was informed that Fidel Castro had died Friday night in Cuba.

At noon local time, four o'clock in the morning back home, Trudeau's office issued a statement that the prime minister had obviously written himself.

It was profoundly personal but, politically, incredibly naïve and misinformed.

"It is with deep sorrow," the statement began, "that I learned today of the death of Cuba's longest serving president."

Hold it right there. Longest serving president? You'd think Castro had been elected for nearly half a century, rather than creating a communist dictatorship.

"Fidel Castro was a larger than life figure who served his people for almost half a century," the statement continued. "A legendary revolutionary and orator, Mr. Castro made significant improvements to the education and healthcare of his island nation.

"While a controversial figure, both Mr. Castro's supporters and detractors recognized his tremendous dedication and love for the Cuban people, who had a deep and lasting affection for 'el Commandante.'"

This would be the same tyrant who had thousands executed by firing squad, with thousands more suspected dissidents tortured in prison, while 1.5 million Cubans became boat people who fled to America.

On a personal level, Trudeau lamented the loss of a family friend who had served as a honourary pallbearer at his own father's funeral in Montreal in October 2000, in which the son became a public figure with his powerful "je t'aime Papa" eulogy.

"I know my father was very proud to call him a friend and I had an opportunity to meet Fidel when my father passed away," Trudeau's statement said. "It was also a real honour to meet his three sons and his brother, President Raul Castro, during my recent visit to Cuba."

Mourning a family friend was understandable and authentic. Putting Castro on a pedestal invited the kind of mockery and scorn that went viral within hours of Trudeau posting the statement from his website to his Twitter page. A Twitter hashtag #trudeaueulogies soon trended globally with tributes to other dictators along the lines of: "While controversial, Mussolini made the trains run on time." And so on.

Florida Senator Marco Rubio, himself a son of Cuban immigrants, wondered if it was fake news. "Is this a real statement or a parody?" he asked on his own Twitter account. "Because if this is a real statement from the PM of Canada, it is shameful and embarrassing."

Jeffrey Goldberg, editor of the liberal magazine The Atlantic, tweeted that it was "a sad statement for the leader of a democracy to make."

And even University of Ottawa's Roland Paris, who until summer served as Trudeau's foreign policy adviser in the PM's office, tweeted: "Since you're asking, it's not a statement I would have recommended."

Ouch!

Had he still been in PMO, Paris would normally have been on the trip to Madagascar for the summit of la Francophonie, and might have been in a position to prevent such an embarrassment to both Trudeau and Canada.

The international uproar caught up to Trudeau at his closing news conference in Madagascar Sunday afternoon. "He certainly was a polarizing figure," Trudeau acknowledged about Castro. "And there were certainly significant concerns around human rights."

There certainly were. It did not pass unnoticed that even as he gave a keynote to the Summit of la Francophonie on LGBTQ rights, he was lionizing Castro who had once rounded up gays and put them in "re-education camps."

Asked point blank by CBC whether Castro was a dictator, Trudeau admitted: "Yes." But he stood by his story, insisting that "on the passing of his death, I expressed a statement that highlighted the deep connection between the people of Canada and the people of Cuba."

Actually, he didn't, really, and that was a missed opportunity. In conclusion, he said: "I offer my deepest condolences to the family, friends and many, many supporters of Mr. Castro. We join the people of Cuba today in mourning the loss of their remarkable leader."

He could have spoken of the deep and abiding friendship between Canadians and Cubans, how 1.2 million Canadians vacation in Cuba every year, 40 per cent of its tourism industry.

Canadians have seen how Cubans, quite simply, endured Castro and managed to get on with their lives. It's evident even in their tail-fin fleet of 1959 Chryslers, Buicks, and Chevrolets, impeccably maintained cars that are now valuable antiques.

It was Opposition Leader Rona Ambrose who got it right in her statement Saturday night, when she said her "thoughts and prayers are with the people of Cuba who continue to endure (Castro's) long and oppressive regime, even after his death … my hope is that a better day is coming for the Cuban people, where they may live in freedom and where democracy, human rights and the rule of law are enshrined."

Trudeau flew home Sunday night, and the opposition will be waiting for him when he returns to the House. Among other things, the Conservatives will be pressing Trudeau for his assurance that he will not be attending Castro's funeral. That might be a tough one for him, since Castro paid him the courtesy of attending his father's service.

But this is a call Trudeau has to make as prime minister, not as his father's son.

November 2016

STRIKING A WORKING RELATIONSHIP WITH TRUMP

The media have been measuring the manner in which Justin Trudeau and Donald Trump hit it off by the length of their handshakes at the entrance to the White House and again in the Oval Office.

But leaving body language aside, the more significant language was in the joint communique (aigu) that was drafted ahead of the meeting and released during their working lunch.

The joint statement could have been written by Trudeau's officials, and signed off by the White House. And probably was.

On Canada-U.S. trade, for example, the communique extolled core messages that PMO advisers and cabinet ministers have been repeating over and over again to their counterparts on Team Trump.

"Canada is the most important market for 35 U.S. states," the communique reminded readers in the second paragraph, "and more than $2 billion in two-way trade flows across our shared border every day. Millions of American and Canadian middle-class jobs, including in the manufacturing sector, depend on our partnership." Trudeau repeated this virtually verbatim in his opening statement at their joint news conference.

In the next paragraph, the joint statement noted the imperative to "advance free and fair trade." The words "free and fair trade" are right out of Trump's mouth regarding the renovation of the NAFTA.

On energy and the environment, the communique noted that Canada and the U.S. have built "the world's largest energy trading relationship." And how. The Americans have been continuously reminded that Canada supplies 100 per cent of their imported electricity, 85 per cent of their imported natural gas, and 43 per cent of their imported oil, 3.2 million barrels per day in 2015.

The statement referred to the process for approving "the Keystone XL pipeline," which Trump could approve by issuing a presidential permit within 60 days of TransCanada having re-filed its application at the end of January. There's only the matter of Trump insisting it be built with American steel on the U.S. part of the route from Montana to Nebraska, where it would connect with an existing pipeline to the Gulf Coast. Both Trump and Trudeau support Keystone, and approval on the Canadian side remains in place from 2010. Interestingly, the joint statement also refers to "energy innovation, particularly in the clean energy sphere." Clean renewables are the growth segment in energy. For example, solar power now provides more jobs in the U.S. than either the coal mining or oil and gas extraction industries.

Notably absent is any reference to climate change or Trump's avowed intention to withdraw the U.S. from the 195-nation Paris Agreement to reduce GHG emissions to 30 per cent below 2005 levels by 2030. Instead the statement refers to "building on our many areas of environmental cooperation, particularly along our border and at the Great Lakes and we will continue to work together to enhance the quality of our air and water."

On defence and security, where Trump had called NATO obsolete, the joint statement refers to Canada and the U.S. as "indispensable allies in the defence of North America through NATO and other multilateral efforts." It also says the U.S. "values Canada's military contributions" including the fight against ISIS "and in Latvia." This means Canada will proceed with the deployment of 450 troops in leading a NATO mission there. In neighbouring Ukraine, the government announced Tuesday that 200 soldiers from Edmonton will relieve Canadian trainers posted there. No mention of Canada sending 600 soldiers on a peacekeeping mission to Mali, a very dangerous place where 100 foreign soldiers have been killed. Canada has already walked back that commitment, and a good thing, too.

Candidate Trump criticized NATO countries that failed to meet the alliance's target of defence spending as 2 per cent of GDP. The joint statement politely made no reference to Canada coming in at just under 1 per cent, or 23rd place out of 28 NATO members.

The most interesting initiative of the day was the creation of the United States-Canada Council for the Advancement of Women Entrepreneurs and Business Leaders, with five business women from each country on the board.

It was Trudeau's chief-of-staff Katie Telford who proposed the idea to Trump's close adviser Jared Kushner, who is married to Ivanka Trump, an advocate of enabling women in business. Which is how she came to be at the table in the cabinet room of the West Wing, sitting next to Trudeau and across from her father.

Trudeau's bona fides on women's issues are well established, notably with gender parity around the cabinet table. Trump's can only be described as a work in progress, though he said the right things at the start of the 35-minute round table.

The Canadian women around the table can also bring a value-added networking dimension with the White House on trade. For example, Linda Hasenfratz is CEO of Linamar, one of the leading auto parts makers in North America, whose products go back and forth across the borders many times in the automotive supply chain. She can be in touch with former investment banking executive Lina Powell, now Trump's adviser for economic initiatives. Other prominent Canadian women at the table included GE Canada CEO Elyse Allan and TransAlta Corp. CEO Dawn Farrell.

Trudeau struck an appropriate balance at the meetings with Trump, representing Canada's economic interests while declining the opportunity to lecture Trump on his immigration and refugee bans. "The last thing Canadians expect," Trudeau said at the joint newser, "is for me to come down and lecture another country in how they choose to govern themselves."

Quite right. And if there were no major deliverables at the summit, it was an important get acquainted session in which the prime minister did not put a foot wrong.

Besides, it can take years to develop major policy initiatives. In his prepared statement, Trudeau pointedly mentioned the 1991 Acid Rain Accord. Well, that was seven years in the making from when Brian Mulroney first raised the issue with Ronald Reagan in 1984, made it a centre point of his joint address to Congress in 1988, and finally signed off on it with the first George Bush in 1991.

Trudeau and his advisers deserve full marks for getting the relationship with the Trump administration off to a strong start.

February 2017

NAFTA BECAUSE WE HAFTA

There are two ways of renewing NAFTA, the first as a trilateral negotiation among the three North American nations, and the second as bilateral talks between the U.S. and Canada on the one hand, and Mexico on the other.

The latter is how the Trump administration wants to proceed, "tweaking" the NAFTA with Canada, while conducting a major renegotiation with

Mexico. Or as Kenneth Frankel, president of the Canadian Council of the Americas, put it at the opening of a Toronto symposium, "a hub and spoke effect, with the U.S. as the hub."

We've been in this movie before, back in 1990, when the first George Bush began the NAFTA process as a bilateral with Mexico, leaving Canada outside the talks. The American reasoning, as articulated by the U.S. Trade Representative Carla Hills, was that they already had the Canada-U.S. Free Trade Agreement negotiated in 1987, and now they wanted a bilateral deal with Mexico. Then as now, this was called hub and spoke.

"Knowing what President Bush had in mind for NAFTA," Brian Mulroney recalled in a conversation moderated by *Globe and Mail* editor David Walmsley, "it quickly became clear to us that this was going to happen."

No way, the former prime minister recounted. He flew to Washington to have it out with his friend Bush at the White House.

"I said, 'George, look, we have an FTA with you. This has to be a trilateral.'"

Bush replied that Hills thought a bilateral was the better way for the Americans to go.

"George, I don't give a damn what Carla thinks," Mulroney replied. "I'm interested in your opinion."

Which is how the NAFTA became a trilateral conversation in 1991, with Mulroney's insistence that Canada be at the table. In effect, Canada crashed the party.

"George Bush deserves enormous credit for that," Mulroney said, with Canada and the U.S. becoming the first G7 nations to do a free trade deal with a developing country, "modernizing the economy of Mexico."

The trade facts speak eloquently for themselves in a 2015 NAFTA study by the U.S. Congressional Service. U.S. merchandise exports to Mexico increased from US$46 billion in 1993 to $240 billion in 2014, while U.S. imports from Mexico increased from $40 billion to $294 billion over the same period.

Sorry, President Trump, the facts do not support your claims that NAFTA has been "disastrous" for the U.S. Even in the automotive sector, Trump's primary target, U.S. exports to Mexico increased by 250 per cent over the period, while imports admittedly spiked by 680 per cent.

In terms in the U.S. manufacturing sector, a report released at the Davos conference last month attributes 86 per cent of job losses to productivity gains through new technologies, and only 14 per cent to plants leaving the country. As Mulroney pointed out, the U.S. unemployment rate of 4.8 per cent last month is only slightly above a nine-year low of 4.6 per cent last

November. Trump did not "inherit a mess" as he claimed last week, but a very strong economy. He can certainly take some credit for the stock market soaring to record territory since his election, with the Dow above 20,000 for the first time in history. Wall Street likes his talk of deregulation and tax cuts, and Bay Street has also gone along for the ride, with the TSX also setting record highs.

On the matter of a bilateral or trilateral NAFTA engagement, Mulroney said there could be no question of "throwing Mexico under the bus," adding that's "what losers do," and Canada is a country "of winners."

And Foreign Affairs Minister Chrystia Freeland, in a conversation with her Mexican counterpart Luis Videgaray, pointed out that their American interlocutors, incoming Secretary of Commerce Wilbur Ross and United States Trade Representative Bob Lightizer, "have yet to be confirmed."

Added Freeland, who remains in charge of NAFTA: "We are quite far away from discussing our trilateral relationship, which is NAFTA. If and when that discussion happens, we are absolutely prepared to take part in it."

When that comes, the Americans will have two re-openers, one on rules of origin and the other on dispute settlement, both of which date from the Canada-U.S. FTA. As Mulroney reminded the symposium, the dispute settlement mechanism was Canada's deal-breaker when they stopped the clock at five minutes to midnight on October 3, 1987, before the expiration of Ronald Reagan's fast-track authority to negotiate a deal "up or down" without amendments by Congress. And under the rules of origin, foreign materials are regarded as North American up to 37.5 per cent of content. In the clothing industry, for example, foreign fabrics have helped made Canadian companies big winners under free trade. Mulroney's advice to Freeland and Justin Trudeau is that Canada should hold the line on both issues.

The PM is coming off a big week, maybe his best in terms of substance as well as style since taking office, first having a working visit to Washington that went off without a hitch, among other things giving Team Trump one of their few chaos-free days in the White House. Then in visits to the EU and Germany, Trudeau was treated as an interlocutor explaining the new American administration to the Europeans. His speeches to the EU Parliament and Hamburg were free of platitudes and quite thought provoking.

Mulroney said he could attest to the success of Trudeau's Washington visit, having discussed it with Trump at a charity ball Saturday in Palm Beach. He said he knew this to be the case "because President Trump told me so." Trump's son-in-law and close adviser Jared Kushner has also said Trudeau's team of advisers were the best and most professional foreign delegation they had dealt with to date.

"He got high marks," Mulroney said of Trudeau, "let me just leave it at that, and that Canada's case was advanced enormously."

It is no secret that Trudeau and his team have been seeking Mulroney's advice as an elder statesman and well-connected adviser on the Canada-U.S. trade file.

This seems to have been met with general approval by Canadians. They evidently like it that a prime minister of one generation and one party, has reached out to one of another generation and another party.

February 2017

NOTHING BUT BAD DAYS

In an abbreviated fall sitting, the House of Commons sat for just 34 days. Every one of them was a bad day for the Conservative government, except for the throne speech opening the new session, when there was no question period.

It's not that the government didn't set an agenda in the throne speech, one driven by consumer issues such as the cost of wireless phones. It even announced a significant achievement on the second day of the sitting – the Canada-Europe Trade Agreement, which is a very big deal.

But on the same day, the Conservatives stepped on their own message by turning the Senate into a star chamber rather than one of sober second thought.

At issue were the ineligible travel and housing expenses of three senators appointed by Stephen Harper – Mike Duffy, Pamela Wallin and Patrick Brazeau.

Rather than waiting for internal and outside audits, the Prime Minister's Office suspended the presumption of innocence by having their Senate majority vote to suspend the three senators without pay. But not before giving them a microphone, as if longtime broadcasters Duffy and Wallin didn't know how to use one.

Had the PMO left well enough alone, the first two weeks of the sitting, in the second half of October, would have been a walk-up to the party's convention in Calgary. Instead, the Senate

6

THE SENATE EXPENSE SCANDAL

expense scandal dominated the news cycle. The convention itself is remembered for two things – Jason Kenney saying Nigel Wright was a person of good character, and the party bagman, Sen. Irving Gerstein, giving a speech in which he said he never authorized any reimbursements of Duffy's expenses from the party, which turned out not to be the case. Imagine, a party bagman giving an on-camera keynote speech.

The RCMP, investigating the Wright-Duffy affair, would have been heard from soon enough, and they certainly were, with an affidavit which blew up the story line that Wright signed a personal cheque to Duffy for $90,000, without anyone else knowing about it.

It turned out that several other PMO and Conservative party insiders did, so then the question became what the PM knew and when. For his part, Stephen Harper maintained that he'd been kept in the dark all along. As for Wright, his former chief of staff, whose resignation he had accepted with regret in the spring, Harper said in the fall that Wright had been terminated, and that only his actions and Duffy's were being investigated by the RCMP. In other words, no one else in PMO was a target.

In question period, no one was buying it. In the role of grand inquisitor he was born to play, Opposition Leader Tom Mulcair totally dominated question period every day of the sitting. In his own behavioural terms, he's done a very good job of holding his famous temper in check, and even revealed a wicked sense of humour. But it's interesting that Justin Trudeau and the Liberals, rather than Mulcair and the NDP, seem to have got a bounce in the polls. That may be because Mulcair is playing a hit man, and Canadians may not be inclined to vote for the guy with the gun.

It may also be because of the inherent value of the Liberal brand, as well as the Trudeau family one. It certainly isn't because of anything Trudeau has done in the House, where he's not very good, and where as the third party the Liberals only get a couple of questions per day. Trudeau's job isn't in the House anyway, it's in the country, where his strong retail game is very much in evidence. He's personable and authentic. And remarkably, he's brought the Liberal party's 10-year civil war, between the Chrétien and Martin camps, to an end.

Inside the Conservative party, there's something else going on. For the first time, MPs and the rank and file are beginning to look past Harper. Not that he's in a hurry to go anywhere. He's announced his intention to run again in 2015, and in case anyone didn't get that, he made the point two weeks ago by bringing back his former communications director, Dimitri Soudas, to be executive director of the Conservative party. He's now surrounded by ultra-loyalists in both PMO and the party.

But PMO has badly mismanaged the Senate expense file, and Tory MPs are tired of being taken for granted by the kids in the hall at the Langevin Block. There is significant support on the Tory backbench for Michael Chong's private member's bill, the Reform Act, which would give significant powers to party caucuses.

In all, the fall sitting was utterly wretched for the Conservatives and the PM. In fairness, he did sound a lovely and appropriate grace note last week, on the death of Nelson Mandela. He invited former prime ministers Mulroney, and Campbell, as well as Mulcair, Liberal MP Irwin Cotler, and First Nations Chief Shawn Atleo, to join him on the long flight to South Africa. By all accounts, everyone got along famously.

There was a shared sense of occasion, for which Harper deserves full credit.

December 2013

THE $90,000 CHEQUE

Nigel Wright did the right and honourable thing in resigning as Stephen Harper's chief of staff for writing a personal cheque for $90,000 to Sen. Mike Duffy so Duffy could reimburse the government for disallowed travel expenses.

It's never a good thing when staff becomes the story, least of all the head of the Prime Minister's Office. In jumping on this grenade, Wright was observing a code of honour in accepting responsibility for his own actions. He was also doing his job: protecting the king.

As someone who has known Wright for more than 25 years, I can attest that his lapse of judgment in this matter was entirely out of character. In both the public and private sector, he has led a life above reproach. He was always more interested in policy than power, and his only motive was to serve.

But while his resignation removes him from the line of fire, it does not end the story of the Senate expense scandal, the whiff of which has now reached the highest office in the land.

And here begins the tick-tock, of who knew what and when; of what the prime minister knew and when he knew it.

Wright himself raises this, somewhat obliquely, in his statement of resignation, released on the Sunday morning of a long weekend.

He says he "did not advise the prime minister of the means by which Sen. Duffy's expenses were repaid, either before or after the fact."

Well, to paraphrase Bill Clinton, that depends on what the word "means" means.

There are some things a prime minister shouldn't know. It's another way of protecting the king: providing plausible deniability.

But CTV has also reported that lawyers were involved in drafting an agreement with Duffy before the cheque was cut.

This would be back in February, when the Senate expense story was breaking around three Harper appointees – Duffy, Pamela Wallin and Patrick Brazeau – and Liberal Mac Harb, all of whom have left their respective caucuses over contested travel and housing claims.

CTV also reported that there are before-and-after versions of a Senate internal board of economy report as it relates to Duffy – that is before and after the cheque was cut. Moreover, the cheque was written during a forensic outside audit by Deloitte.

All of which just raises more questions about who knew what and when, and of whose idea it was to make it all go away by writing a cheque for $90,000. While it may have been legal, it wasn't right.

Stephen Harper tried to hit the reset button when the Conservatives allowed cameras into their caucus while he tried to rally the troops. Exceptionally, the caucus met a day early because the prime minister was leaving in the afternoon on a scheduled trade mission to South America, which allowed him to skip facing the music in question period.

Harper did get the sound bite of the day. He declared: "I'm very upset about the conduct we have witnessed, the conduct of some parliamentarians, and the conduct of my own office."

But Harper is ultimately responsible for the conduct of his own office, and he missed an opportunity to apologize for it. He then went on to reiterate that the Conservatives are the party proposing reform through an elected Senate, that they came to office promising to clean up Ottawa, and that they were the authors of the Accountability Act, "the toughest accountability legislation in the history of this country."

Which is kind of the point. There are two fundamental pillars to the Conservative brand. The first is the economy, which is a very good story. And the second is accountability, which is now a very bad story.

And don't think the Conservatives don't know it. A political party is an extended family, and the Conservative family gathered at the National Arts Centre in Ottawa Monday evening for a memorial service to Senator Doug Finley, the party's former campaign director who died last week of cancer.

The evening was an upbeat celebration of a man whose organizational skills played an important role in bringing the Conservatives from opposition to government. Harper himself delivered a classy tribute that was full of good humour.

But the other topic of conversation was about the Senate expense scandal, and how the stain had now spread to the centre. In their ridings and districts last week, MPs and senators got an earful.

This is not a one-off story about an expensive glass of orange juice or an airport-limo charge. It's about character and judgment in government. Which, in the end, is a test for the prime minister. To be continued.

May 2013

A REPUTATIONAL HIT

One of the unintended consequences of the Senate expense scandal is that it brings the Upper House itself into disrepute. And that's a pity because the Senate does some very good and important work, particularly in its committees.

The Senate banking, trade and commerce committee, for example, has for many years been known as the best on Parliament Hill. When Leo Kolber was chair back in 2002, the committee turned out an outstanding report recommending large bank mergers in record time of only two months. The financial services industry and the Department of Finance itself both regarded the Kolber committee as a much more serious operation than the Commons finance committee.

It was no mystery – many senators on the banking committee had been executives or directors of banks, and knew how they worked. There was a civility and a degree of collegiality about their hearings that's rarely seen on the House side, where the idea is to score partisan points, even in committee. That's no mystery, either – senators don't have to face the voters as elected members of Parliament do, and can take a long view.

The 2006 Senate report on mental health, Out of the Shadows at Last, was the first of its kind in Canada, or North America for that matter. Thousands of Canadians came forward to tell their stories, and their voices were heard in the report, which was a milestone that led to the creation of the Mental Health Commission of Canada. It was greatly to the credit of its Liberal chair, Michael Kirby, Conservative vice-chair Dr. Wilbert Keon and members on both sides. In all, 30 senators participated in the hearings at one point or another.

Previously, in 2003, Kirby had teamed up with Conservative Marjory LeBreton on the landmark Senate report on health care. They recommended a health care guarantee as a remedy for waiting times in the public health-care system – that if patients couldn't receive timely treatment within the public system, they could go outside it.

The Conservatives later ran on the health care guarantee, as one of their five priorities in the 2006 election. The Kirby report on health care was much more solution-oriented than Roy Romanow's royal commission. It was Kirby who sounded the alarm that public health care as unsustainable without new investments from Ottawa and the provinces. This clarion call became the policy template that ultimately led to the 10-year, $41-billion 2004 Health Accord, being renewed by the Conservatives for an additional three years past 2014.

More recently, in February of this year, the Senate national finance committee, chaired by Liberal Joseph Day, put out an important report, The Canada-USA Price Gap. "Large price gaps remain even when the Canadian dollar is at or above par," the committee reported. "Even some automobiles made in Canada are priced significantly higher than in the United States." It's called tariffs, and it's why the same book that costs $25 in the U.S. can cost $35 in Canada. As Conservative vice-chair Larry Smith said: "Canadians feel ripped off." Well, this is why we have cross-border shopping.

Not to mention drive-and-fly cross-border travel. The Senate transport and communications committee, chaired by Liberal Dennis Dawson, last month issued a report, The Future Growth and Competitiveness of Canadian Air Travel, a $45-billion industry. From the time it started its work to completion, the committee found the number of Canadians driving to a U.S. city to catch a flight increased from 4.2 million to five million, "in order to take advantage of cheaper flights."

This is no surprise, either, what with airport-departure or improvement taxes, not to mention security fees and sales taxes. So even as airports are upgraded in this country, Canadians by the millions are taking flights from places like Plattsburgh, NY, rather than Montreal, to avoid the high cost of leaving the country, to say nothing of lower costs on such carriers as Southwest Airlines.

You didn't hear that from the House of Commons, but from the Senate.

Many senators have carved out niches for themselves, like Hugh Segal on the Commonwealth, and his Conservative colleague Janis Johnson on the foreign affairs committee. And former chairs, Liberal Colin Kenny and Conservative Pam Wallin – yes, that Pam Wallin – have done very good work on the Senate national security and defence committee.

None of which is to excuse the Senate shenanigans over travel expenses and housing allowances, a scandal that went from bad to worse last week with the resignation of Nigel Wright as chief of staff to the prime minister for writing a personal cheque to Senator Mike Duffy for reimbursing $90,000 he owed the government.

But it's precisely the diligent and financially upright senators who are most annoyed by the scandal in their midst, in that they've all taken a reputational hit. So they should be.

May 2013

∞

GOOD MONEY AFTER BAD

Now comes the reckoning – not just for the Senate, but also for Auditor General Michael Ferguson, who spent $23.6 million investigating its travel and living expenses.

And what do we have to show for two years of work by Ferguson's own team and numerous outside auditors looking into everything from flights to cab slips and coffee? A grand total of $975,600 of alleged ineligible expenses – more than half of them incurred by five senators who are now retired and no longer sitting in the Red Chamber.

The key word here is "alleged." Nothing has been proven. Our system is based on such concepts as the presumption of innocence and the rule of law. In the age of 24/7 news and social media, it's important to remember that – even if the media don't.

Seven former and two sitting senators have seen their expense claims referred to the RCMP. Another 21 members of the Upper House have been named in the report, and all 30 of them have the option of making their cases directly to Ian Binnie, the former Supreme Court justice named last month as the independent arbiter in disputes between the auditor-general and senators.

Binnie was brought in by the Senate leadership – Speaker Leo Housakos, Conservative Leader Claude Carignan and Liberal Leader James Cowan – who were themselves named among the Senate 21. To avoid the appearance of benefiting from a process they created, they're deferring on arbitration and have repaid what they're alleged to owe.

In Carignan's case, it was $3,650 in mileage claims by a staffer. In Cowan's it was $10,000 for travel deemed personal. In the case of Housakos, it was $6,000 for a contractor he brought in rather than hiring someone full time, as he could have done. He probably saved the Senate at least $50,000, but … never mind, Alice. Welcome to the tea party.

A fourth Senate leader, Deputy Speaker Nicole Eaton, decided to reimburse the Senate $3,600 for flights to her hometown of Toronto for meetings of voluntary boards on which she sits, including the St. Michael's Hospital Foundation, the National Ballet of Canada, the Pontifical Institute of Medieval Studies and the Gardiner Museum. The AG found these trips were for "personal interests." But as the Canadian Press reported: "Eaton points out that the ethics and conflict of interest code for senators specifically declares that senators are expected to continue their activities in their communities and regions while serving the public." No kidding.

Senators on both sides of the aisle, Conservatives and Liberals alike, will avail themselves of the opportunity to make their case to Binnie. They're very angry that their reputations have been sullied by the AG, and furious at how their staffs have been treated by Ferguson's hired help – in some cases kids recently out of accounting school who wouldn't know Parliament Hill from third base.

For example, Manitoba Senator Don Plett was on holiday in Calgary in 2011 when he received a call from then-Public Safety Minister Vic Toews asking him to fly to Ottawa to meet the commissioner of Correctional Services. He flew direct from Calgary; the AG maintains he should have paid his own way home to Winnipeg first and caught a flight back from there, and says he owes a $700 differential in airfare. I'm not making this up.

Plett has repaid about $3,000 in other expenses he and his staff flagged for the auditors, but will take the $700 in disputed airfare to Binnie. "I feel very strongly," he said, "that travel at the request of a minister of the crown is Senate business." He's got a point.

Manitoba Senator Janis Johnson is looking at $22,000 in contested travel claims, some of it involving her role as founder of the non-profit Gimli Film Festival, which is a cultural and tourism magnet in her community. Last summer, she said, 12,000 people attended the weeklong festival in July on the shores of Lake Winnipeg. It has also, she said, "created five full-time jobs in the community."

Among other things, during uncounted hours of grillings by outside auditors, she was once asked why she took a cab back to her hotel at night in Halifax from a hearing she was chairing on Canada-U.S. relations. She was also asked about postage for greeting cards sent to colleagues in the U.S. Senate. While the auditors were nickel-and-diming her, their own metres were ticking.

It isn't just senators' reputations that are on the line – it's Ferguson's as well. Leave aside for a moment the nine senators referred to the RCMP; should Binnie dismiss his conclusions about many or most of the Senate 21, Ferguson's reputation for competence – not to mention that of his consultants – would be in trouble. He'd need to consider his own future at that point, if only for the integrity and standing of the AG's office.

As for the Senate, there's no question that, in reputational and collective terms, this has been a terrible time for the Red Chamber.

What is to be done for it?

No one is going to say, "Senate, heal thyself." We're way beyond that now; the public sees the Senate as fundamentally dysfunctional. But to borrow another phrase from the medical profession, it isn't too late to say, "Above all, do no more harm."

This applies not only to the Senate, but to leaders in the Commons. In this regard, the Supreme Court's 2014 decision on the Senate reference is required reading.

In its landmark decision, the court found that the Senate "is one of Canada's foundational political institutions." The court was clearly guided by "the intent of the framers." As they wrote: "The contrast between election for members of the House of Commons and executive appointment is not an accident of history. The framers of the Constitution Act 1867 deliberately chose executive appointment of Senators in order to play the specific role of a complementary body of 'sober second thought.'"

Reforming the executive appointment process requires a constitutional amendment under the 7/50 general amending of Parliament and seven provinces representing 50 per cent of the population. Abolishing the Senate requires the unanimous consent of Ottawa and the provinces.

Opposition Leader Tom Mulcair says he would begin consulting the premiers with a view to abolishing the Senate soon after forming a government. Sure, Tom, just ask the premier of Prince Edward Island to give up his province's four seats in the Senate. Just ask the premiers of New Brunswick and Nova Scotia to give up their 10 seats.

Ask the premier of Quebec to give up his province's 24 Senate seats. (Actually, Philippe Couillard is open to a constitutional conversation, provided it includes a Quebec Round. As Stephen Harper pointed out from the G7 meeting, a constitutional round is a complete non-starter.)

But neither can the Senate be abolished by attrition. There are now 20 vacancies in the 105 seat Senate, and there's going to be a court case on whether the PM should be obliged to fill vacancies within a reasonable period. Reading the Supreme Court's 2014 Senate reference case, it's pretty clear the government would lose in the high court. Again. Justin Trudeau has suggested Senate nominations by an eminent persons panel and as long as they were confirmed by executive appointment, this would fit perfectly within constitutional bounds. Former prime minister Brian Mulroney has suggested appointments by the PM from ranked lists furnished by the provinces, as was the case under the Meech Lake Accord.

Whatever way forward we take on the Senate, we ought to be guided by two rules – decency and common sense – both of which appear to have gone missing.

June 2015

∞

DUFFY: CASE DISMISSED

Mike Duffy wasn't just acquitted, he was vindicated. As much as he was exonerated in court, the Conservative leadership in the Senate was excoriated and the former PMO eviscerated in the scathing verdict of Ontario Justice Charles Vaillancourt.

While Duffy was acquitted of 31 charges of fraud, breach of trust and bribery, Stephen Harper and his former PMO were convicted *in absentia* of abuse of power.

Vaillancourt was also quite unsparing in his criticism of the Crown and the RCMP for bringing such a weak case to court. Absent evidence of criminal intent, the Crown rolled a lot of counts together into one big ball of mud, hoping some of it would stick. In the judge's considered view, none of it did.

It should be also said that Duffy was brilliantly represented by his defence lawyer, Don Bayne. Over more than 60 days in court, one government witness after another was turned into a witness for the defence, particularly on the rules, or lack of them, on senators' expenses, office budgets and residency. It is hard to interpret the rules where there are none to be read.

A disclosure here, that I was paid to write a speech for Duffy, and briefly testified to that effect at his trial a year to the day before his acquittal. I've also known Duffy for more than four decades, as a friend in all circumstances.

Over the last three years, Duffy was tried in the court of public opinion, where the presumption of innocence was suspended, both in mainstream and social media. Vaillancourt's judgment is a reminder that it's quite different in a court of law, where presumed innocence is the starting point and guilt must be proven beyond a reasonable doubt. For the judge, it wasn't even close.

"I don't think I've ever been witness to such a resounding acquittal," Bayne said of his 44-year career in court. "There are near misses and close calls. Justice Vaillancourt made plain, this was a resounding not guilty."

Bayne also pointed out that public figures "are also entitled to due process," adding that his client "has been subjected for the last two-and-a-half to three years to more public humiliation than probably any Canadian in history."

That's a bit of a rhetorical flight of fancy, but the important thing is that the judge wasn't buying any of the shaming of Duffy. Nor was he buying any of the Crown's case.

Vaillancourt wondered, for example, how the Crown could fail to call Senator David Tkachuk, the former head of the Senate Board of Economy who had advised Duffy on residency rules and eligible expenses. He also wondered why the Crown, when it had Duffy on the stand, neglected to ask him about the $90,000 personal cheque he received from Nigel Wright to cover his ineligible expenses.

One might add that if Duffy was to be accused of accepting a bribe as a public official, wasn't Wright, then PMO chief of staff, offering one?

As for the cheque, the judge found that Duffy was coerced into accepting it by "Nigel Wright and his crew" at PMO. In effect, they were buying Duffy's silence and making the story go away. "This was damage control at its finest," Vaillancourt wrote.

As for the Conservative leadership in the Senate, the judge found they turned the Red Chamber into a kangaroo court by voting to suspend Duffy without pay, and in doing so suspending the presumption of innocence. They also allowed the Upper House, part of the legislative branch of government, to be pushed around and manipulated by the executive in PMO.

"Was Nigel Wright actually ordering senior members of the Senate around as if they were pawns on a chess board?" the judge asks incredulously. "Were those same senior members of the Senate meekly acquiescing to Mr. Wright's orders? Were those same senior members of the Senate robotically marching to recite their scripted lines?"

The judge also noted disapprovingly of Wright asking Senator Irv Gerstein, then the Tory bagman, to see if a friend at Deloitte could give them a heads up on the firm's 2013 audit of Senate expenses. The judge asks: "Did Nigel Wright really direct the senator to approach a senior member of an accounting firm that was conducting an independent audit of the Senate to get a peek at its report ... or to influence that report in any way?"

In the Crown and RCMP singling out Duffy as "driven by deceit, manipulations and carried out in a clandestine manner," the judge ironically suggested "if one were to substitute the PMO, Nigel Wright and others for Senator Duffy ... you would have a more accurate statement."

Overall, on the Harper PMO, the judge's verdict is devastating.

"The political, covert, relentless unfolding of events is mind-boggling and shocking," he wrote. "The precision and planning of the exercise would make any military commander proud. However, in the context of a democratic society, the plotting as revealed in the emails can only be described as unacceptable."

You don't hear that every day in court. There's more: "Could Hollywood match their creativity? It is interesting that no one suggested doing the legal thing."

And: "If anyone was under the impression that this organization was a benign group of bureaucrats taking care of the day-to-day tasks associated with the prime minister, they would be mistaken."

Actually, the benign bureaucrats are in the Privy Council Office, the prime minister's department on the top two floors of the Langevin Block and the Blackburn and Post Office buildings behind it on Sparks Street.

The PMO, on the first two floors of Langevin, is a political office with exempt staff. But PMO staff are supposed to be there for a higher purpose, of crafting and implementing the government's agenda, and getting out the PM's message, not running cover-ups and abusing the power of the PM's office.

In only six months, the Harper legacy has already been significantly dismantled by the Liberals, especially in their budget, and by the Supreme Court in its rulings last week disallowing Conservative criminal justice system laws on time served and minimum sentencing.

The Vaillancourt ruling makes the Harper PMO look like the Nixon White House, a place full of unindicted co-conspirators.

As for Duffy, he gets the last laugh on Harper and his PMO team, who ruthlessly threw him under the bus. He is reinstated in the Senate, with salary and staff restored. He can serve Prince Edward Island and Canada for another five years as an independent, the new political colour in the Red Chamber. Most of all, he has re-gained his reputation and his good name, thanks to an eloquent judge with a fierce sense of decency.

April 2016

7

THE FISC AND THE ECONOMY

WHY JIM FLAHERTY WAS SMILING

In every government known for its competence, there's a strong number two standing behind the prime minister. Brian Mulroney had Don Mazankowski, known as his chief operating officer. Jean Chrétien had Paul Martin, and together they balanced Canada's books. When they famously split up, it was the beginning of the end for the Liberals.

In the present government of Stephen Harper, the number two is Jim Flaherty, the finance minister. Flaherty's influence in the government is unique. Only Foreign Affairs Minister John Baird and Immigration Minister Jason Kenney even come close.

Flaherty's standing is partly a function of his length of service – he's been finance minister since the Conservatives took office. Flaherty is also the ranking finance minister in the G7 and G20. Flaherty and Bank of Canada Governor Mark Carney get much of the credit for steering Canada through the shoals of the Great Recession to the shores of the recovery. At international conferences, they are treated like rock stars, because Canada has such a good story to tell.

Flaherty was telling it again the other day to an attentive audience of CEOs at the Canadian Council of Chief Executives in Ottawa for their conference, Canada in the Pacific Century.

There are two elements to strategic communications – the messenger and the message. And in Flaherty, the government has both. He is a happy warrior, and a congenial spirit.

And his narrative is clear and clean. Quite simply, it's the Canadian Advantage.

Consider: Canada's banking system has been ranked the strongest in the world by the World Economic Forum for the last five years in a row. Five of Canada's banks have been named to Bloomberg's list of the world's strongest banks. And the Big Five banks are among the top 10 in terms of assets in North America.

Then on fiscal frameworks, Canada has the lowest deficit as a percentage of GDP of any G7 country and will return to balance by 2015. Canada's debt to GDP ratio is also the lowest in the G7, and by a considerable margin.

It was Flaherty, with then Industry Minister Tony Clement, who organized Canada's 20 per cent share of the bailout of General Motors and Chrysler. Without which, as he later said, "they would have left Canada," including his own riding of Whitby-Oshawa.

The stimulus and auto bailout worked.

"Since the end of the recession in July 2009, almost 770,000 new jobs have been created," Flaherty told his audience of CEOs. "The Canadian unemployment rate has dropped to 7.3 per cent, 1.4 per cent lower than the recession peak in August 2009, lower than the American unemployment rate, which hasn't happened since the 1970s."

If Canadian unemployment were measured the same as in the U.S., our unemployment rate would actually be 6.3 per cent, nearly two points lower than in the U.S.

As Flaherty said: "We're now close to 340,000 jobs above the pre-recession peak."

Other fundamentals of the Canadian economy are strong.

U.S. foreign direct investment alone in Canada stands at $275 billion, or nearly 20 per cent of GOP. There are several reasons for this, but one of them is Flaherty lowering the corporate tax rate to 15 per cent, down from 28 per cent a decade ago. The U.S. corporate tax rate is 35 per cent. Money goes where it's well treated.

Canada is also seen as a good place to invest precisely because of our fiscal frameworks, and the soundness of our banking system.

Not to mention that Canada has a lot of what the world needs, notably in commodities such as oil and gas, potash, gold, silver and uranium. Our proven oil reserves of 170 billion barrels are the third largest in the world.

For example, our oil and gas exports last year, when refined products were included with crude, were $102 billion, or 22 per cent of all our merchandise exports, according to BMO Economics.

All of which makes Flaherty's narrative a positive one. There are things that keep him up at night, as he told the crowd from Canada Inc. The currency and sovereign debt crisis in the eurozone. Systemic gridlock in Washington, a town where they can't even pass a budget, much less get a grip on their deficit and debt.

But the Canadian story is all about comparative advantage and Flaherty clearly enjoys telling it.

September 2012

∽

BORING IS GOOD, BORING WORKS

The essential takeaway in Jim Flaherty's 2014 budget can be found in the title: "The Road to Balance." Then, reading on to the subtitle: "Creating Jobs and Opportunities."

That's the top line – the government will balance the books next year, going into the October 2015 election with a forecast surplus of $6.4 billion that will be available for promises in the Conservative campaign platform.

The deficit for the current fiscal year is now forecast at $16.6 billion, down from $17.9 billion only three months ago in the fall update. That's less than one per cent of GDP.

In the next FY beginning April 1, Ottawa sees a deficit of $2.9 billion, including "a $3 billion annual adjustment for risk." This is the contingency reserve, and it's also included in the forecast surplus of $6.4 billion for 2015–16.

The $2.9 billion deficit number represents only 0.2 per cent of GDP, a rounding number. This is a balanced budget in all but name, and if the contingency reserve were excluded, it would be. Some economists think balance could be achieved in the coming FY rather than the following one. Flaherty doesn't think so, but you never know.

If the economy grows at a forecast rate of 2.3 per cent (up from 1.8 per cent last year), and the U.S. grows at a forecast 2.7 per cent (up from 1.9 per cent), then Canada should see modest economic and employment growth going into an election year.

U.S. growth and the decline of the loonie should be drivers of increased exports, particularly from the manufacturing heartland of southern Ontario.

And if you don't think the Tories are focused on vote rich southern Ontario, consider the announcement of "an additional $500 million over two years to the Automotive Innovation Fund." This could also be called the Chrysler Fund. Chrysler has threatened to close its Windsor plant unless governments subsidize modernization costs. General Motors might also have an ask for its Oshawa assembly plant.

And for those who'd like to work there, Flaherty is introducing the Canada Apprentice Loan to "help registered apprentices in Red Seal trade with the cost of training." It also "promises to create thousands of new paid internships for young Canadians entering the work force." It even says Ottawa will "eliminate the value of student-owned vehicles" from the assessment process "of the Canadian Student Loan Program to better reflect the needs of students to commute." You could call this 905 program, after the sprawling area 905 suburban belt around Toronto, where many post-secondary students have to drive to campuses such as Humber College, in Flaherty's riding of Whitby-Oshawa.

And here begins the "Jobs and Opportunities" part of the budget, with a focus on labour markets and training, including First Nations' education and the $1.9 billion in Ottawa's partnership with the Assembly of First Nations. In case there was any doubt who will be in charge of reserve schools, the legislation will be called the "First Nations Control of First Nations Education Act." The $1.9 billion will be in the pipeline in 2016. The trade-off is First Nations control the reserve schools, but insure accredited teachers and better attendance. The dropout rate in reserve schools is a shocking 62 per cent, as compared to 26 per cent Aboriginal dropout levels in non-reserve schools, which in turn is three times the dropout rate of non-Aboriginal students.

Flaherty also announced new "Labour Market Agreements for Persons with Disabilities," with Ottawa putting in $222 million annually over four years "to be matched by the provinces and territories."

The budget also "supports the creation of vocational training centres for persons with Autism Spectrum Disorders (ASD)." Specifically, Ottawa will fund $11.4 million to the Sinneave Family Foundation and Autism Speaks Canada for vocational training programs that when fully operational will benefit 1,200 youth per year. In terms of the therapeutic needs for children with ASD, this is a very modest initiative. In terms of visibility for autism, it's very important for stakeholders – one in 68 Canadian children and their families. The budget papers devote two pages and nine references to persons with ASD, and that's highly unusual.

On the R&D side of economic development, Flaherty is creating the Canada Research Excellence Fund, with $1.5 billion of funding over 10 years. This continues in Canada's commendable tradition of endowing university research, though we face a deficit of private sector innovation compared to most developed economies.

For the rest, Flaherty said at a press briefing Tuesday, if Canadians found the budget boring, he took that as a compliment. "Boring is good," he quoted a mentor, former Ontario premier Bill Davis, who had 14 consecutive boring years in office.

Referring to his upcoming trip to Australia for a G20 finance ministers meeting next week, Flaherty said Canada is regarded as "the envy of the world – virtuous Canada."

Which is where his narrative of success kicked in – one million new jobs since the end of the recession, two-thirds in high wage industries, 80 per cent of them in the private sector. A 5.2 per cent investment growth rate since before the recession, compared to 0.8 per cent in the U.S. The highest foreign direct investment rate in the G7 since the recession. The best employment and GDP growth rates in the G7 over the period. The second best place in the world, in the Bloomberg ranking, in which to do business. And never to be left out of Flaherty's litany, the strongest banking system in the world for the last six years, as ranked by the World Economic Forum.

Yes, boring is good. Boring works.

February 2014

OLD MONEY CHASING NEW VOTES:
HARPER'S INFRASTRUCTURE SHUFFLE

In October 1986, the Mulroney government announced a $1 billion deficiency payment to Western grain farmers, then on the losing end of an international price war over wheat.

Brian Mulroney himself made the announcement in a speech to the National Farmers Union, who were meeting at the National Conference Centre in Ottawa. The farmers were very happy, as was Saskatchewan Premier Grant Devine – who, by no coincidence, went on to win re-election a few days later.

Mulroney was on his way to give the speech when the phone rang in my office in the Langevin Building. It was a senior adviser to the Finance minister, calling with several colleagues on the line.

"We have changes for the PM's speech," she announced. "He can't say that the $1 billion is new money. It has to be re-profiled money." Announcing the money as new money, she explained, would change the fiscal framework.

"What assurance can you give us," she continued, "that the speech will be delivered exactly with the changes as we have dictated them to you?"

"There must be some mistake," I replied. "This isn't the Ministry of Youth. This is the PM's office. We don't work for you. *You* work for *us*."

Which ended the conversation.

But Imperial Finance has always been very good at protecting its interests, which begins with protecting the integrity of the 'FISC' – the fiscal framework, the whole budget plan, from taxes to programs. And the integrity of the FISC in Joe Oliver's coming budget depends on the Conservative government keeping its promise to balance the books in this fiscal year, as it did last year or the first time since the downturn of 2008–09.

The government already has preannounced $5 billion a year in spending on enhanced child care benefits, childcare cost deductions, the child fitness tax credit and income-splitting. Oliver hasn't forgotten the government's promise to double the Tax Free Savings Account contribution cap, which would take it up to at least $10,000 per year. Eleven million Canadians have set up TFSAs since Flaherty established them in 2009.

All this retail stuff works very well in suburban ridings where the October election will be decided. The $5 billion in pre-announced family benefits were priced into the fall update. No one has mentioned the cost of doubling the TFSA limit to the government in foregone revenues.

In the fall update, Oliver forecast a surplus of $1.9 billion – but that was when oil was US$81 a barrel, $30 above where it is today. Bearing in mind that every $5 drop in oil prices costs Ottawa $1 billion, that would leave Ottawa short $6 billion, with a deficit of $4 billion.

Not a problem. Oliver just spends down the $3 billion contingency reserve, sells off Ottawa's shares in General Motors for another $3.3 billion, and he's at least $2 billion to the good, with TFSA head room to spare. No worries about the FISC.

Anyway, all of this is to point out that Oliver can get to balance while keeping the FISC intact. So what on earth was Industry Minister James Moore doing on CTV's Question Period on Sunday, talking about new infrastructure spending?

"This budget," he told CTV's Bob Fife, "will reaffirm our commitment to infrastructure spending ... on a very large scale in every part of the country to the benefit of productivity, to the benefit of infrastructure and to the benefit of the quality of life of everyday Canadians."

Wouldn't this blow up the FISC? It surely would – if it were new money. In fact, the money's coming out of a $75 billion pool Ottawa earmarked to be spent over 10 years – in the 2013 budget. That includes $52 billion for the New Building Canada Plan.

So it's not new money – not a thin dime of it. It's re-announced money, allocated for the current year. The only thing new about it will be the press releases.

And it will work. Here's the thing – nobody in the real world talks about infrastructure. You never hear anyone on the bus say, "I'm really worried about our infrastructure." But voters may notice photo ops about bridges, interchanges or subway stops coming to their neighbourhood. For an incumbent government facing a tough election, previously-announced infrastructure spending is the gift that keeps on giving.

All the announcements Oliver and Moore have made over the last few days confirm the Conservatives are hard at work changing their message track: away from scary stories from terrorism, towards a more positive narrative that works for them in the suburbs. As for the FISC – Finance still has it covered. Not new money, but re-profiled money.

Welcome to a Groundhog Day moment.

April 2015

A DEFICIT MANDATE

What's in a deficit? It depends how you look at it. Justin Trudeau promised in the election campaign to run a $10 billion deficit in his first fiscal year in office. But in the run-up to the budget, senior officials playing the managing expectations game have already leaked that the deficit will be more like $30 billion.

North of $30 billion, the Liberals would be crossing a psychological barrier with both political and economic markets. So, don't be surprised if the deficit number is $29.5 billion, just below that threshold where the Liberals' economic competence could become an issue. At $10 billion, the deficit would have been 0.5 per cent of GDP. At $30 billion, it will be 1.5 per cent of Canada's annual output. That's still on track to be the second best deficit to GDP number in the G7, with only Germany doing better at 0.2 per cent in 2015, but that's not a conversation Canadians will have on the subway.

The point is, Trudeau said he would run a deficit, and got his permission slip from the voters. By his own account in a Q&A with Bloomberg TV in New York, his deficit promise was the game-changer in last October's election.

"On that night last August 27 when I got home to my wife, I said 'I'm pretty sure we just won the election,'" he recalled. "And of course the next morning she opened up the newspaper, and she said: 'Well, it doesn't say anything about that, that you just won the election.' And I said, 'it's going to take a while to figure that out.'"

Also in New York, Trudeau showed some budget leg of his own, revealing that the eligible age for receiving Old Age Security will remain at 65, instead of being raised to 67 by 2023 as announced by the previous Conservative government. Stephen Harper was criticized at the time for making the announcement outside the country, at the Davos Conference in 2012. Trudeau was also outside Canada, but in fairness he was answering a question from Bloomberg's editor, not making a policy speech. "It was a mistake to bounce it up to 67," Trudeau said, and just like that, another one of Harper's legacy items was undone.

Trudeau's decision to keep OAS eligibility at 65, may have a real economic cost over decades, as older Canadians stay in the work force, with decreasing compulsory retirement. But there's no doubt that it will be very popular with older voters who would have given up two years of income supplement to their Canada/Quebec Pension Plans. Moreover, Trudeau campaigned on this, so it's a promise made, promise kept.

At the other end of the demographic scale, the Liberals will be bringing in a Canada Child Benefit to replace the Universal Child Care Benefit and other family entitlements for children under 18 adopted by the Conservatives. In their campaign platform, the Liberals projected $1.8 billion of new costs in a CCB that "invests $21.7 billion in 2016–17, the savings from cancelling income splitting" and replacing other programs.

We'll see how that comes out in the budget wash. But it's yet another "undo" moment for the Harper legacy.

Then there's infrastructure spending, much awaited by municipalities, which are looking for relief from the one-third, one-third, one-third funding formula by the three levels of government. Cities and towns are hoping Ottawa will step its share up to half of costs, while keeping the provinces' shares at one-third, and bringing cities in around 20 per cent.

Then the petroleum producing provinces of Alberta, Saskatchewan and Newfoundland and Labrador are expecting funding from the feds to help them through the numbing economic shock of the oil crash. For example, Finance Minister Bill Morneau has said Alberta could be eligible for about $250 million from a federal fiscal stablization program. With Alberta looking at a stunning $10 billion deficit, that would just be a drop in the bucket. With an unemployment rate of 7.9 per cent, compared to the national average of 7.3 per cent (even higher than Quebec at 7.6 per cent), Alberta is also looking for some relief on employment insurance eligibility and duration of benefits.

Western sensibilities may be one of the reasons that Trudeau won't be doing an announcement on investing $1.3 billion in Bombardier's CSeries passenger jet in the budget, though he made clear in New York that he regarded it as a great aircraft, pointedly noting that aerospace industries are subsidized by governments around the word. The Bombardier announcement will come after the budget.

Trudeau was also asked about the loonie, and while the prime minister should never discuss exchange rates, he seemed unperturbed by the question. "The Canadian dollar has bounced around a bit," he said. "There's a range in which it is comfortable" and it seems to be "in that now."

As he was speaking, the loonie moved over 77 cents to the greenback from a January low of 68 cents, and oil was back over $40 a barrel, from a low of $26 two months ago. Some fundamentals may be moving in the right direction again.

Trudeau also appeared to be in a comfort zone in the New York financial district. He sounded like he knew what he was talking about. And he looked like he belonged.

March 2016

CREATIVE ACCOUNTING 101

In its latest monthly Fiscal Monitor, the Finance department reports a $4.3 billion surplus in the current fiscal year to the end of January.

Looking ahead, Finance forecasts that a surplus is also expected in February. But then in March, the last month of the fiscal year, "Budget 2016 projects that the cumulative budgetary balance will deteriorate to reach a year-end deficit of $5.4 billion."

That means an operating deficit of $9.1 billion in the month of March alone. Some of it is in year-end costs and adjustments – the average March deficit running $6.5 billion per year from 2009–14, and $3 billion in the last fiscal year.

That's a huge swing. What accounts for it? "That's a very good question," says Kevin Page, the former parliamentary budget officer.

It turns out that part of the March shortfall is "the cost of measures undertaken to improve benefits for veterans in Budget 2016." And there it is in the budget – $3.7 billion in future spending on veterans, but booked in the current fiscal year, which ends next Thursday.

Welcome to Creative Accounting 101.

By the sleight of hand of booking the veterans' benefits as a year-end expense, the Liberals get to keep their first deficit under $30 billion, an important psychological threshold. Instead of a deficit of $33.1 billion, it comes in at $29.4 billion for 2016–17. Going forward, the budget projects a deficit of $29 billion in 2017–18, $22.8 billion in 2018–19, and $17.7 billion in 2019–20.

That's $98.9 billion in deficit spending over the Liberals' four-year mandate. So much for their campaign promise to return to budgetary balance by 2019, after running deficits of no more than $10 billion in the first two years of their mandate. And looking forward to 2020–21, the Liberals forecast a further deficit of $14.3 billion, for a five-year total of $113 billion in the red. At his news conference before the budget speech, Finance Minister Bill Morneau said he hoped to achieve balance over five years. But his words were contradicted by his own five-year forecast.

The Conservatives were certain to be all over the fiscal monitor and deficit numbers.

Their position is that they left office with the fiscal framework in balance, and even slightly in the black. The fiscal monitor numbers support their claim. Even allowing for the five-year average deficit of $6.5 billion in the month of March, FY 2015–16 would be virtually in balance without the charges booked for veterans' benefits.

As for the deficit in the coming fiscal year, it amounts to nearly 10 per cent of federal government spending of $317 billion. That's up from $280 billion in 2014–15, when the late Jim Flaherty balanced the books in his last budget, leaving a surplus of $1.9 billion. In the last interview of his life, asked about the budget being nearly in balance, he said: "We're almost there." It turned out that he was already there.

Of course, Flaherty ran up more than $150 billion in debt from 2009–14, beginning with a $56 billion deficit in the midst of the Great Recession of 2008–09, the steepest economic downturn since the end of the Second World War. But those were cyclical deficits, whose purpose was to get the economy growing again, as it did from the third quarter of 2009, and as it has ever since, with the exception only of the first two quarters of 2015, which were technically a recession.

It remains to be seen whether the Liberal deficits prove to be cyclical or structural. One thing is certain – the Liberals are projecting five years of deficits, with no prospect of balancing the books before 2022, or not before the middle of a second majority mandate.

The Liberals prefer to refer to their deficit spending as investments in the future of Canadians. Or as they call it on the title page of the budget, "Growing the Middle Class" (in the cover image, a mother and daughter are walking down a yellow brick road, or a street paved with gold).

Or as Morneau put it in the opening words of his first budget speech: "Today, we begin to restore hope for the middle class." He then waxed nostalgic about a time when Canadians "could hope that their children would do even better than they did."

Referring to the post-war Liberal era, he said: "Canadians built the St. Lawrence Seaway and the Trans-Canada Highway. They constructed new airports, subways, pipelines and communication networks. They created new colleges and universities – and parents sent their children to those institutions in record numbers."

Fast forwarding to the Chrétien-Martin years, Morneau noted that "wise management of the nation's finances back in the 1990s restored Canada's fiscal health, leaving us with a debt-to-GDP ratio that is by far the lowest of any G7 country."

Speaking of which, the Liberals in their campaign platform promised to reduce the debt-to-GDP ratio from the 30 per cent they inherited from the Conservatives to 27 per cent by 2019. So, while tripling the deficit promised for 2016–17, and ruling out a return to balance as promised by 2019, the Liberals still hope to reduce the debt-to-GDP ratio by then, even while running up $113 billion in new debt.

Good luck with that, in an economy growing by a consensus forecast of less than 2 per cent per year.

Sunny ways.

March 2016

RED INK

Then there's the story, right out of *Yes, Minister*, of the new Ontario finance minister who was being briefed by his deputy minister on the province's fiscal outlook.

"How bad is it?" the minister asked.

"How bad would you like it to be, sir?" the deputy replied.

That's kind of where we are now with the numbers in the federal budget. This is a FISC with flexibility, and huge margins of error, built into the budget assumptions and forecasts.

For example, the $29.4 billion deficit in 2016–17 includes a $6 billion contingency reserve, twice the amount set aside as under the Conservatives in Jim Flaherty's last budget only two years ago. What's happened since then for the Liberals to double the contingency reserve? Nothing, except for the collapse of oil and other commodity prices.

But the Liberals are also allowing for that in their deficit projection, forecasting oil at a rock bottom price of $25 a barrel, when it has recently recovered to $40, which happens to be the consensus forecast for this year. Every $5 drop in the price of oil costs the federal treasury $1 billion. Oil at $40 rather than $25 would mean $3 billion more in cold cash.

As BMO economists Douglas Porter and Robert Kavcic note in their budget analysis: "The consensus expects that WTI oil prices have found a bottom and will average around $40 this year before rising to $52 in 2017."

By assuming the worst, the Liberals may be overstating the deficit in a way that redounds to their political credit. If it turns that only $3 billion of the contingency reserve is needed, and oil stays at $40 over the year, that would bring the deficit in at only $23 billion. If the Liberals then re-allocated $2 billion for new spending, the deficit would still be only $25 billion, $4 billion below forecast. And Finance Minister Bill Morneau would look like a very smart manager of your money.

As Porter and Kavcic note: "We might see a page taken from the Ontario playbook – that is, part of the cushion gets back-filled with more spending, while the finance minister still reports better-than-expected bottom lines through the forecast horizon." Well, the same people who were advising Dalton McGuinty and Kathleen Wynne at Queen's Park are now advising Justin Trudeau in Ottawa. Noted in passing – Ontario's debt has more than doubled to $300 billion during the McGuinty-Wynne years, or nearly 40 per cent of GDP.

Then there are Ottawa's deficit numbers themselves over the next four years. At $29.4 billion for 2016–17 and $99 billion over four years, this is a political calculation, not just a mathematical one.

The Liberals were clearly determined to keep the current deficit below $30 billion, and the accumulated deficit over their four-year term to less than $100 billion. The deficit for the current year isn't $29.5 billion, which can be rounded to $30 billion, it's $29.4 billion, which can't. The deficit to 2019 isn't $100 billion, it's $98.9 billion, which can be rounded to $99 billion. So, $30 billion and $100 billion headlines were barely avoided, and an important psychological barrier of fiscal prudence was not crossed. There are no coincidences in politics.

The direct means the Liberals used to avoid the $30 billion deficit threshold was to book $3.7 billion in future veterans' benefits in the fiscal year ending next Thursday, rather than the next one.

This is typical of the first Liberal budget in that it is re-distributive, but not very transparent. A fiscal year that was on track to end in a surplus when the Conservatives were in office, is ending with a $5.4 billion forecast deficit on the Liberals' watch. It will be interesting to see the final numbers in the Fiscal Monitor, now in $4.3 billion surplus territory through January, with another surplus forecast for February, before an eye-popping $9.1 billion of adjustments and costs booked by the Liberals in March. We'll only know the final numbers for FY 15–16 at the end of May.

There are obvious winners in this budget, from Indigenous peoples with $8.4 billion over five years for education, housing and clean water on reserves; to students, whose Canada Student Grants are increased by 50 per cent to $3,000 a year; to universities, the main beneficiaries of a $2.2 billion three-year program for infrastructure upgrades to aging campus facilities.

Not to mention growing the middle class, with the middle class tax cut and new child care benefits, as well as the Old Age Security eligibility threshold being lowered back from 67 to 65 years of age. This may not be actuarially sound over the long term, given the costs of supporting an aging population. Economist Jack Mintz also observes that lower marginal tax rates and a lowered OAS eligibility level, "and other various benefits have resulted in negative taxes (taxes net of transfers paid) on seniors for incomes up to $60,000."

As Mintz writes in *Policy* magazine's budget issue: "This leads to significant income redistribution from workers to retirees, and is therefore a critical issue as to how to target support to help low-income seniors as the population ages."

At the other end of the tax scale, the increased top marginal rate from 29 to 33 per cent for "the one per cent" earning over $200,000, brings the combined federal and provincial top rates for Ontario and Quebec to 53 per cent. As the Fraser Institute noted in a study last week, that's seven points higher than the top marginal rate in the U.S., and the second highest in the G7 after France at 54.5 per cent.

Morneau and the Liberals speak of program spending as "investments" in the future, and some important brain gains may result in areas such as university research. But the Liberals should also be wary of creating uncompetitive tax rates for business people and professionals who can vote with their feet.

Overall, there's a question of whether the Liberals can hit their deficit numbers, or improve on them. How good would you like it to be, minister?

March 2016

A DEFICIT SLEIGHT OF HAND

Under intense opposition fire the other day on whether the government was running a deficit or in a surplus as the fiscal year comes to a close, Finance Minister Bill Morneau finally lost it. "Clearly," he snapped, "the members from the other side are still stuck in this balanced budget thing."

This obviously wasn't one of Morneau's talking points or part of his prep for question period. The Conservatives have been throwing the quote back at him ever since.

Does it matter whether the books are in the red or in the black by a few billion dollars at the end of the fiscal year?

Well, it matters to the Conservatives, who managed to eke out a $1.9 billion surplus in the previous year, after forecasting a $2.9 billion deficit in the 2014–15 budget, which was Jim Flaherty's last one.

In Joe Oliver's first and what proved to be his last budget, the Conservatives forecast a $1.4 billion surplus for 2015–16, and in their view they handed over the books to the Liberals in the black.

In this, they are supported by the Parliamentary Budget Officer, who in his annual fiscal outlook last month forecast a small surplus of $700 million in the year ending March 31. And this includes $3.7 billion in future veterans' benefits put retroactively on the books for 2015–16 by the Liberals in their March 22 budget.

The enhanced veterans' funding was one of two important numbers driving the Liberal forecast of a $5.4 billion deficit for the 2015–16 fiscal exercise, the other being the Liberals' doubling the contingency reserve from $3 billion to $6 billion.

The Department of Finance's Fiscal Monitor tracks the FISC on a monthly basis, and a February surplus of $3.2 billion increases the budgetary surplus to $7.5 billion through the first 11 months of the fiscal year.

There are always year-end costs in March – in the budget papers, Finance noted the average deficit for the final month of the fiscal year was $6.5 billion over the six previous years.

We won't know the deficit number until the end of May, but the PBO still sees a surplus, because of "higher monthly receipts offsetting additional Budget 2016 spending measures" such as the enhanced veterans' benefits.

Why was Morneau back-booking $3.7 billion of veterans costs going forward? Quite simply, this sleight of hand allowed him to bring the 2016–17 deficit in at $29.4 billion rather than $33.1 billion. In doing so, he avoided headlines of the deficit being north of $30 billion, an important psychological barrier for markets and voters alike.

The PBO doesn't share Morneau's pessimistic forecast for the new fiscal year. PBO Jean-Denis Fréchette projects a deficit of $20.5 billion this year, $8.9 billion below the Finance projection. While the budget projects a cumulative deficit of $99 billion to 2019, the PBO sees it at $78 billion over the Liberals' four-year mandate.

Clearly, there was a lot of downside prudence built into Morneau's deficit forecast. One of the reasons for doubling the contingency reserve to $6 billion was to cover the possibility of the world price of oil falling to as low as $25 a barrel rather than the $40 forecast in the budget. Every $5 drop in the price of oil costs Ottawa $1 billion, so the additional $3 billion contingency reserves covers that grim possibility.

In the event, oil has bounced back to the $45 range, recovering from a low of $26 in January. And it has brought the Canadian dollar back with it, from a 12-year low below US70 cents in January to recent levels closer to US80 cents.

But other events have intervened that do not bode well for the fiscal framework.

The wildfire at Fort McMurray has caused the evacuation of nearly 100,000 people and temporarily shut down the oil sands, taking 1 million barrels a day out of production.

Nearly 2,500 homes and businesses have been destroyed, though it turns out that the great work of first responders has saved Fort Mac's public infrastructure such as schools, municipal buildings and the local hospital. The mass evacuation without incident, in the midst of a ravaging fire storm, was a very Canadian response. So was the way Albertans opened their homes, as was the generous response of Canadians in other regions of the country.

In financial terms, as well as the ravaging sweep of the firestorm, the cost will be unprecedented. Moody's Investor Services, the credit rating agency, estimates the cost to insurers at $5 billion, which would make the Fort Mac wildfire the costliest natural disaster in Canadian history.

And in terms of the economic slowdown in the energy patch, BMO chief economist Doug Porter, who was already trimming his 1.5 per cent GDP growth for the second quarter, writes that "based on what we know at this point on production curtailments, we have cut our Q2 GDP estimate to zero."

But in terms of what Ottawa should do to help Fort Mac and Alberta, the answer is obvious – whatever it takes. As Flaherty said of the contingency reserve in what turned out to be the last interview of his life: "You never know when we will need extra millions to help out."

Or in this case, extra billions.

May 2016

∞

BUDGET 2017: MORNEAU RAGS THE PUCK

Sometimes you can tell a book by its cover.

Bill Morneau's first budget in 2016 featured a cover image of a mother and daughter holding hands as they walked down a yellow brick road on their way to prosperity. The title of the book was "Growing the Middle Class." The message was crisp, clean and clear.

The title of Morneau's second budget is a sequel: "Building a Strong Middle Class." But there are four images rather than one, with line drawings over the pictures.

The largest one is on the theme of innovation, with a young woman working on her laptop, while a lightbulb goes on over her head. We are not making this up.

In the second image on continuous learning, a young student is playing a line drawing of her guitar, with musical notes filling the air. In the third image on infrastructure, a young man is pictured standing in front of a city, with a line drawing of a bridge and a highway with a city bus on it, and construction cranes in the background skyline. Finally, on health care and home care, there's a man sitting in his den, with a drawing of blood being pumped into his arm.

Like the cover, Budget 2017 is a veritable hodge-podge of themes, none of them really going anywhere.

And then there's the fiscal framework, buckling under deficits as far as the eye can see, with no pathway to balance.

In the coming fiscal year, the deficit is forecast at $28.5 billion, up from $26.9 billion predicted in last fall budget update.

Then Ottawa is looking at a $27.4 billion deficit in FY 2018–19, up from $23.5 billion in the fall economic statement. For FY 2019–20, Finance now forecasts a deficit of $23.4 billion, up from $18.2 billion in the fall update.

Those are real misses, especially at a time when all the economic indicators, from employment to GDP growth, are moving in the right direction.

Part of the miss can be explained by the decision to restore the $3 billion per year contingency reserve that had been dropped in the fall statement.

But the contingency reserve is back in the FISC for the next five years going forward as a line item called "adjustment for risk."

"There it is," said a senior adviser to Morneau. "It's back."

It's because Finance persuaded PMO that in the real world, the FISC needs a contingency reserve.

Jim Flaherty once explained why in a Q&A with *Policy* magazine after tabling his last budget in 2014. He forecast a deficit of $2.9 billion, including the $3 billion contingency reserve. Without the reserve, he was reminded, he would have balanced the books. "We can't do that," he replied, adding they needed it for emergencies such as natural disasters. In the event, the Alberta floods of 2014, and the wildfires of 2016, would provide evidence of that.

While the deficit numbers are moving up from last fall's forecast, the budget points out that the debt-to-GDP ratio is holding steady at 31.6 per cent, and "is projected to decline gradually to the end of the (five-year) fiscal horizon, reaching 30.9 per cent in 2021–22."

The Liberals maintain the debt-to-GDP percentage is a more important indicator of managing the FISC than the deficit and debt. But the limpid fact remains that in Finance's own long-term forecast, released two days before Christmas when no one was paying attention, Ottawa doesn't expect to balance the books until 2055, running up another $1 trillion of debt in the meantime. This would be in addition to the $665 billion on the books for FY 2017–18, expected to rise to $716 by the end of the Trudeau government's first term in 2019, and $757 billion by the end of the horizon in 2022. In its first term alone, the Trudeau government is taking on another $100 billion in debt, sustainable only because money is so cheap, with a central bank rate of 0.5 per cent.

As for new ideas and program spending the government kicked a lot of things down the road. For example, last fall the Liberals announced the creation of the Canada Infrastructure Bank for $15 billion of funding and another $20 billion in equity investments in infrastructure projects. But the enabling legislation creating the bank has yet to be tabled in the House, and there was no mention of it in the budget or Morneau's speech, even though there was a section on infrastructure.

In a budget speech in which soundbites were notably absent, Morneau mostly ragged the puck.

On tax avoidance, Morneau said: "Our government is committed to taking action on this issue … Going forward, we will close loopholes that result in unfair tax advantages for some at the expense of others."

Translation: Ottawa will consult with the financial services industry and other stakeholders.

On defence, there's no new money in the budget, despite pressure from Washington for Canada to increase spending above the present level of 1 per cent of GDP, and closer to the NATO target of 2 per cent. Canada is a laggard on this, ranking 23rd out of 28 NATO countries. But pending a defence review, Morneau said the government would "support our men and women in increasingly complex and unpredictable times, our government will soon release a new defence policy for Canada, following extensive consultation and analysis."

Stay tuned.

Morneau did have one interesting section of his speech on gender equality and empowering women, announcing the government's "first ever Gender Statement … to help advance the goals of fairness, workforce participation and gender equality."

"As a first step," he said, "we've asked the Canada-United States Council for Advancement of Women Entrepreneurs and Business Leaders on how we can better empower women entrepreneurs and remove barriers for women in business."

This is the council whose creation was announced during Justin Trudeau's February trip to the White House, led on the American side by Ivanka Trump.

So while Donald Trump may have cast a shadow of economic uncertainty over the budget, his daughter Ivanka is actually in it in a rather positive sense.

March 2017

8

ENERGY AND PIPELINES

NEXEN: WELL-PLAYED, HARPER

Usually when the government puts out an announcement at 5 o'clock on a Friday afternoon, they'd rather not talk about it and would really prefer if you didn't hear about it, much less care about it.

Such was not the case last Friday when, as markets closed, Industry Canada hosted a lockup for reporters on Ottawa's decision on the friendly takeover bids of Nexen and Progress Energy Resources by Chinese and Malaysian state-owned enterprises (SOEs).

An hour later, the prime minister himself appeared on Parliament Hill to announce that while the government was approving these big deals, $15.1 billion for Nexen and $6 billion for Progress, the takeover party was over for SOEs.

Or as Harper put it: "These decisions are not the beginning of a trend, but rather the end of a trend."

And then, in what became the sound bite of the week: "To be blunt, Canadians have not spent years reducing the ownership of the economy by our own governments only to see them bought and controlled by foreign governments instead."

Harper's logic was impeccable. Why would Ottawa have sold off Petro-Canada, its own SOE in the oilpatch, only to allow the Chinese to take it over through CNOOC, the China National Offshore Oil Corporation?

To be clear, Harper added that going forward, the government would approve "the acquisition of control of a Canadian oil sands business by a foreign state-owned enterprise to be of net benefit (to Canada) only in exceptional circumstances."

In other words, the oil sands are a strategic national resource. And they are not for sale. Or as Harper said: "When we say Canada is open for business, we do not mean that Canada is for sale to foreign governments."

Nothing prevents the Chinese from being investors in the oil sands, notably in joint ventures or through the stock market; they just can't be owners in the future.

Just to be sure SOEs got the message, Harper said the threshold for foreign takeovers to meet the net-benefit test would rise to $1 billion over the next five years, but for SOEs, it would remain at $330 million.

And make no mistake, we need foreign investment to develop the oil sands, because we simply don't have the capital to do it alone. The energy space has been a huge beneficiary of foreign direct investment under the Canada-U.S. Free Trade Agreement and liberalized rules of investment Canada, created by the Mulroney government in 1985 to replace the Foreign Investment Review Act.

A study by BMO Economics concluded that U.S. direct investment in Canada "jumped from $76 billion at the end of 1988, to $326 billion by the end of 2011." The report said: "The share of U.S. FDI in Canada has thus risen from just over 10 per cent of Canadian GDP before the FTA to almost 19 per cent now." Half of that investment, wrote BMO deputy chief economist Douglas Porter, has been in the energy and financial services sectors.

Natural Resources Minister Joe Oliver estimates Canada will need $650 billion of investment over the next decade in order to develop the oil sands.

The Progress sale to Petronas is a good example of our need for foreign capital. The two companies are going to build a liquefied natural gas terminal in Prince Rupert, BC, at a cost of $9 billion.

And while there won't be any more Canadian oil companies selling themselves to the Chinese at a premium price, the energy index was actually up one per cent on the TSX on Monday, confounding predictions that oil stocks would take a hit.

In the meantime, Nexen shareholders will receive a 61-per-cent premium to the stock price when the offer was announced at $27.50 per share. Progress shareholders, at a sweetened offer of $22 per share, will receive a premium double the closing price when the deal was announced. This is only fair in terms of upholding the core corporate governance attribute of shareholder value.

While the government is changing the rules for SOEs after the game, at least it didn't change them in the middle of the game, by turning down the two takeover bids on the grounds they didn't meet the net benefit test.

That's where the public was coming out on the Nexen deal – three Canadians in four in one poll were concerned about ownership of the resource. And as many as two in three in other polls were against the deal. And those opposed to the deal were probably a lot less concerned about CNOOC being an SOE than they were about it being a Chinese SOE. There was definitely Sinophobia in the air.

Harper has clearly worked hard on this file to achieve a balanced economic and political outcome.

And it showed in his clean delivery of a crisp message.

December 2012

STONEWALLING ON KEYSTONE

In an interview published in the *New York Times*, U.S. President Barack Obama made his most extensive comments to date on the Keystone XL pipeline project, saying Canada could "potentially be doing more" to mitigate emissions from what he pointedly called the "tar sands," adding for good measure that the project would create "maybe 2,000 jobs" during construction.

This does not bode well for approval of the $7.6 billion TransCanada project to carry 830,000 barrels a day from the Alberta oil sands to refineries on the Gulf Coast of Texas.

That's oil sands, Mr. President, not tar sands. The Canadian oilpatch, as well as the Alberta and federal government, have spent a fortune rebranding and even the *New York Times* now refers to bitumen from the Canadian "oil sands." Only the environmental lobby in the U.S. still uses the tar sands nomenclature, so Obama was simply playing to his eco base.

But it's Obama's comments downplaying job creation that are astonishingly inaccurate.

Here's the full quote from the *Times* interview: "My hope would be that any reporter who is looking at the facts would take the time to confirm the most realistic estimates are that this might create maybe 2,000 jobs during the construction of the pipeline – which might take a year or two – and after that we're talking about somewhere between 50 and 100 jobs in an economy of 150 million working people."

No one has ever heard of a $7.6 billion construction project that would create only 2,000 jobs at most. TransCanada has a very different number of eight times that – 9,000 jobs in construction and another 7,000 in manufacturing.

"We have and can factually rebut each point the president has made," TransCanada spokesman James Millar wrote in a weekend e-mail to the media.

While there's not much percentage in publicly taking on the president of the United States, Millar has a point when he says TransCanada's not pulling its numbers out of thin air. "There is no reason for us to overinflate our numbers," Millar said. "We have to answer to our board. We have to answer to shareholders." It's called corporate governance. Markets and regulators expect transparency and accuracy in the forecasting of publicly traded companies.

Obama had only to read or be briefed on the environmental impact statement of the U.S. State Department, which last March found Keystone would have virtually no effect on oil sands production, since the Canadians would find other markets. And on job creation, the report stated: "Including direct, indirect and induced effects, the proposed project would potentially support approximately 42,100 annual jobs across the United States over a one-to-two year construction period." While the State Department forecast of 3,900 construction jobs is much lower than TransCanada's, it's twice as many job as Obama is talking about.

So why was Obama talking down Keystone as a creator of jobs? Here's the answer, in his own words: "Republicans have said that this would be a big jobs generator. There's no evidence that that's true." Yes, there is, from his own State Department.

Obama did acknowledge one "potential benefit for us integrating further with a reliable ally to the north on our energy supplies." Which is to say Canada, not Venezuela, Nigeria or Saudi Arabia.

As for Canada doing more on emissions reductions, Obama said: "We haven't seen any specific ideas or plans." He added that "would go into the mix in terms of (Secretary of State) John Kerry's decision or recommendation on this issue."

And here's where Alberta has a story to tell. Back in 2008 it was the first jurisdiction in North America to require industry to reduce GHG emissions and also has a $15 per tonne price on carbon. It has invested more than $1 billion in carbon capture and storage, and created a fund helping to finance more than 40 clean energy projects. On the R&D side, the industry is working to reduce emissions intensity and making improvements. As Alberta Premier Alison Redford put it in a Q&A with *Policy* magazine: "We know that what industry is doing right now is reducing the intensity of emissions with respect to production on a per-barrel basis."

Then there's the sheer hypocrisy of the Americans lecturing Canadians on climate change when the oil sands account for just over 0.1 per cent of the world's GHG emissions, while the U.S. coal-fired electricity industry accounts for more than 40 times that.

Finally, as a lawyer, Obama might take time to read the energy chapter of the Canada-U.S. Free Trade Agreement, in which we gave them security of supply in return for security of access. Or as Redford has put it: "We promised to be good suppliers if they promised to be good customers."

We ought to be right in their face in reminding the Americans of that.

July 2013

AN INCONVENIENT TRUTH

In an interview with *The Globe and Mail*, former U.S. vice-president Al Gore referred to Canada's oil and gas riches as a "resource curse" and said the Alberta oil sands add "to the reckless spewing of pollution into the Earth's atmosphere as if it's an open sewer."

Gore speaks as winner of the Nobel Peace Prize in 2007 for his efforts to educate the world on climate change. This would be the same Al Gore who recently sold his cable-TV network, Current, to Al Jazeera for $500 million. Al Jazeera, of course, would be the network owned by Qatar, which produces and exports oil.

As an environmentalist, Gore is undoubtedly aware that the greenhouse-gas emissions from coal-fired electricity stations in the U.S. are 40 times those from the Canadian oil sands. As for Europe, according to Natural Resources Canada, emissions from electrical installations are nearly 30 times those of the oil sands. This is, for Gore, an inconvenient truth.

According to Energy Alberta, the oil sands are responsible for only 6.8 per cent of emissions in Canada, and only 0.15 per cent of emissions worldwide.

There's no doubt that extracting bitumen takes an environmental toll, but it's also true that industry is doing a better job on issues like water and land reclamation. Alberta also monitors the intensity of emissions, and industry is doing a better job there, too, through research and development and new technology.

As Alberta Premier Alison Redford notes in an interview with *Policy* magazine: "When you're having a climate change discussion and you're talking about emissions, we know that what industry is doing right now is reducing the intensity of emissions with respect to production on a per-barrel basis."

But as she also notes, while intensity is decreasing, production is increasing to meet demand and "therefore you don't always see a net reduction in the emissions, even though, based on intensity, there is a reduction."

As the *New York Times*'s Joe Nocera observed: "Extraction technology has improved to the point where there is almost no difference, in terms of greenhouse-gas emissions, between sands oil and old-fashioned oil drilling. The government insists that companies extracting the oil return the land to its original state when the mining is completed. Indeed, for all the hysteria over the environmental consequences of the oil sands, there is oil in California that is actually dirtier than the oil from the sands."

That would be California, home to Hollywood-celebrity eco-activists, where Al Gore also has a residence.

All in, the U.S. accounts for 22 per cent of global greenhouse-gas emissions, according to Natural Resources Canada, while Canada is responsible for 2 per cent. The U.S. population is nine times that of Canada, while its greenhouse-gas emissions are 11 times higher than ours. And Canada is a much colder country, with higher home-heating requirements.

Everyone understands that the environmental movement in the U.S. is using the oil sands and the Keystone XL pipeline project as leverage for a larger conversation on climate change.

And in politics, you have to make the usual allowances for hypocrisy.

But there are limits, especially from advocates like Gore, who has been on this issue since before he invented the Internet, and should know better than to accuse Canada of treating the atmosphere like an "open sewer." Not only is it insulting; it's untrue.

Nor do these activists take account of the importance of energy exports to the Canadian economy, the importance of Canadian energy imports to the U.S. economy and the political importance of Keystone to the relationship between the two principals – the U.S. president and the Canadian prime minister.

Energy is now far and away the largest segment of Canadian exports, and the U.S. accounts for more than 99 per cent of our exports of oil and gas. Since 1992, according to BMO Economics, Canada's oil and gas exports to the U.S. have increased from $17 billion to $102 billion, from 11 per cent of Canada's world exports to 22 per cent.

As U.S. ambassador David Jacobson has said: "Canada is the largest supplier of every form of energy to the United States."

As he noted, Canada supplies the U.S. with 100 per cent of its imported electricity, 85 per cent of its natural gas imports and 27 per cent of its oil imports – more than twice as much as the 12 per cent of U.S. oil imports supplied by Saudi Arabia.

Moreover, in the energy chapter of the free trade agreement, we guaranteed the Americans security of supply in return for security of access. It's the considered view of Brian Mulroney, the father of free trade, and Derek Burney, who negotiated it, that the U.S. is violating the spirit if not the letter of the agreement in delaying approval of Keystone.

May 2013

∞

KEYSTONE: NOT A "NO BRAINER"

The controversies surrounding the Keystone XL project have never been about the pipeline itself – except in Nebraska, where it was about water and grazing rights, two issues that have always resonated back in Washington.

For the rest, opposition to Keystone in the U.S. has always been about the oil sands and climate change. And now in 2015, with Republicans in charge of both houses of Congress and with a Democrat in the White House, it's become a purely political play.

As first proposed by TransCanada in 2008, the pipeline from Alberta to the Gulf Coast of Texas would have crossed an aquifer that's Nebraska's largest source of water, with a right of way through ranching and farm country. Only when TransCanada modified the route was the project approved by the state's governor in 2012.

But a group of ranchers successfully made a case in a state court that the governor was exceeding his constitutional authority. Only last Friday did the state supreme court overrule the lower court. While four out of seven judges sided with the ranchers, the other three were silent, and as a "super majority" of five judges was required to overturn the governor's power to approve Keystone, the petitioners had no standing before the court. Case dismissed.

"So, in terms of process," as Barack Obama had told a year-end White House news conference, "you've got a Nebraska (court) that's still determining whether the new path for this pipeline is appropriate. Once that is resolved, then the State Department will have all the information it needs to make a decision."

So – according to what Obama said then – once the State Department recommended the project, the U.S. president would then approve it.

Or not exactly. Actually, not at all.

If anything, the president is likely to veto a congressional bill approving Keystone on the grounds that it usurps the presidential prerogatives of the executive branch. That argument, as a White House spokesman put it last week, holds that the "bill still conflicts with long-standing executive branch procedures regarding the authority of the president and prevents the thorough consideration of complex issues that could bear on U.S. national interests."

So there. That argument isn't even about politics – it's about the separation of powers between the executive and legislative branches of the U.S. government.

On that pretext, Obama would veto the Keystone bill in a heartbeat. It's already passed in the House of Representatives by a large margin of 266–153. And in a preliminary Senate vote on Monday, it passed by a super-majority of 63–32, 60 votes being required to make a bill filibuster-proof. But clearly, there aren't enough votes to meet the required two-thirds of both houses to override a presidential veto.

Stephen Harper once called Keystone a "no-brainer" and still maintains that it will be built ... eventually. But it doesn't matter what the prime minister says. What matters is what the president thinks.

And according to all the evidence – his comments and actions since the 2012 presidential campaign – Obama will never approve Keystone.

Consider his most recent remarks at his year-end newser. "At issue is not American oil," he said. "It is Canadian oil that is drawn out of tar sands in Canada."

And anyway, would another 830,000 barrels a day of oil supply benefit American consumers at the pump? "It's good for the Canadian oil companies," Obama said, "but it's not going to be a huge benefit to U.S. consumers. It's not even going to be a nominal benefit to U.S. consumers." He's not wrong about that. Gas prices have fallen by as much as half at U.S. pumps because the world price of oil has plunged by half since last September.

What about the jobs the pipeline is supposed to offer? Obama conceded that "construction of the pipeline itself will probably create a couple thousand jobs." That's a pretty grudging assessment: The State Department's own estimate of last year was that Keystone would create 42,000 direct and indirect jobs in the U.S. – high-paying jobs for skilled tradespeople such as welders and pipefitters. Which is why the American trade unions, a key Democratic constituency, are strong supporters of Keystone.

"If that's the argument," Obama said, "there are a lot more ways to create well-paying American construction jobs."

It's not every day that a Democratic president blows off a core constituency of his own party. But then, Obama is playing to a larger gallery – the environmental movement. He's also looking for a legacy on climate change, and Keystone has become highly symbolic of that quest.

The Canadians, through countless interventions, have also made it clear that Keystone is important to us. It may not be a litmus test of Canada-U.S. relations, but it's not a positive aspect of the narrative right now. We're not going to get Keystone as a tradeoff for participating in the U.S.-led coalition against the Islamic State, or for quietly hosting the secret talks that led to the U.S.-Cuban detente.

But it might be a good time to remind the Americans that we are by far their most important foreign supplier of energy – for 27 per cent of their imported oil, 85 per cent of their imported natural gas and 100 per cent of their imported electricity. And in the Canada-U.S. Free Trade Agreement, we gave them security of supply in return for security of demand to their market. Oh, well.

January 2015

PIPELINES STYMIED BY SPILLS

An oil leak right in Vancouver harbour, with slicks washing up on the pristine shores of English Bay and Stanley Park – that certainly gets voters paying attention to the environment in an election year.

Last week's spill from a cargo ship's own fuel tank was small as these things go – less than 3,000 litres, 80 per cent of which was cleaned up within a few days. The point is that it happened not at sea or in a remote northern inlet, but within sight of downtown Vancouver, one of the most celebrated cityscapes in the world. Vancouver's famous beaches were closed until further notice.

Federal, provincial and municipal politicians subsequently engaged in an unseemly blame game over the Coast Guard spending six hours getting booms in place to contain the leak – and allegedly waiting 12 hours before notifying the City of Vancouver. It also happens that the Harper government closed the nearby Kitsilano Coast Guard station, minutes away from the spill scene, as well as an Environment Canada emergency station and a Fisheries and Oceans marine mammal contaminants program. No one has brought up the Port of Vancouver's role in the response.

What does this incident have to do with the oil sands and pipelines? Nothing and everything. Much of the controversy has been about the speed of the response to the spill. Premier Christy Clark made efficient spill response one of her five conditions for supporting new pipelines through British

Columbia to tidewater on the West Coast. BC, she said at the time, demands a "world-leading oil response prevention and recover systems."

Well, this wasn't exactly world-leading, was it? Which is where the pipeline companies come in – through no fault of their own. Kinder Morgan comes to mind first.

The $5 billion twinning of Kinder Morgan's Trans-Mountain pipeline would increase its capacity from 300,000 barrels per day to 850,000 barrels. All that extra oil sands capacity would flow through lower BC to an expanded marine terminal in – you guessed it – Vancouver harbour. Large tankers would carry the heavy crude from Vancouver to refineries in Asia.

Then there's Enbridge, with its $8 billion Northern Gateway project to run a pipeline from the oilsands to Kitimat in northern BC That's another 525,000 barrels per day through 45 First Nations communities along the way – some of which have endorsed it, some of which oppose it. And Clark wants those world-class spill response times for the pristine Douglas Channel as well.

Next comes TransCanada, with its $15.7 billion Energy East pipeline project that would carry 1.1 million barrels per day through six provinces from Alberta to refineries in Quebec and New Brunswick. There's fierce opposition to it in Quebec – not just from environmental activists but from residents farmers who want to know what it means for their back yards and fields.

And let's not forget Keystone XL, TransCanada's stymied $8 billion project to transport 800,000 barrels from Alberta to Texas refineries on the Gulf Coast, long delayed in the courts and by President Barack Obama's clear opposition.

Altogether, we're talking about nearly 3 million barrels a day of new pipeline capacity in political limbo – and the question is whether there's that much demand for the product, to say nothing of the collapse in world oil prices. The Canadian Association of Petroleum Producers estimated last year that current light crude and oil sands production of 3.5 million barrels per day would virtually double to 6.5 million barrels per day by 2030. That was in another era, when the world price of oil was over US$100 per barrel – twice what it is today.

And then there are the environmental issues, which would have come up at Tuesday's Climate Summit of provincial and territorial premiers in Quebec City. Canada accounts for just two per cent of the world's greenhouse gas emissions; the oil sands are responsible for only 0.15 per cent of global GHG emissions. That compares quite favourably to the U.S. coal industry, which accounts for about 40 times that level.

But nobody can pretend Canada is a world leader on fighting climate change. We signed on to the 2009 Copenhagen target of reducing emissions to 17 per cent below 2005 levels by 2020. We're on course to miss that target ... by a lot. As David McLaughlin, former head of the National Round Table on the Environment and the Economy, wrote in *Policy* magazine: "Without additional measures, Canada will miss its target by ... almost 50 per cent."

Meanwhile, the U.S. and China came to an agreement announced by Obama last November which would see the Americans cut their GHG emissions by 28 per cent below 2005 levels by 2030, with the Chinese targets kicking in only then.

And with that, Obama basically hijacked the agenda of the UN climate conference in Paris this coming November. Canada missed a March 31 deadline for proposing its GHG reduction numbers – because it says it hasn't heard back from the provinces. "Obviously we will be moving forward with our partners," Stephen Harper said last weekend on the margins of the Summit of the Americas in Panama, adding he would have the targets set in time for the G7 Summit in June.

It's interesting that the European Union – made up of 28 sovereign states – managed to meet that deadline but Canada – with one federal government and 13 provinces and territories – didn't.

The provinces have taken over the climate change and energy file from Ottawa. That Quebec City meeting was organized and hosted by Premier Philippe Couillard. He's not just at the table of the federation – he intends to lead it. It's easy to take issue with the cap-and-trade agreement he announced with Ontario Premier Kathleen Wynne. But the important thing is that Ontario and Quebec are close partners again, and the Canadian federation will work better for that.

Paging Ottawa.

April 2015

PIPELINES AND THE CONSTITUTION

With an NDP-Green coalition government forming up in British Columbia, a legal and constitutional crunch is looming over Kinder Morgan's $7.4 billion project to twin its Trans Mountain pipeline from Alberta to Vancouver, tripling its capacity to 900,000 barrels a day.

With 41 and three seats respectively in the provincial legislature, both B.C. NDP Leader John Horgan and Green Leader Andrew Weaver have signalled their intention to join court challenges of the pipeline, particularly two filed by B.C First Nations. (First, of course, they must elect a Speaker, reducing them to a 43-member tie with Christy Clark's Liberals – then the Speaker would have to break the tie to defeat Clark on her throne speech.)

So the big question here is: What will Ottawa do? How can it respond to political opposition in BC to the pipeline, which could also extend to delays in issuing construction permits at the municipal level?

Asked about this in Rome last week, Prime Minister Justin Trudeau insisted that his government's approval of the Kinder Morgan expansion was evidence-based and recommended by the National Energy Board.

"The decision we took on Kinder Morgan was based on facts and evidence on what is in the best interests of Canadians and, indeed, all of Canada," he said. "Regardless of the change of government in British Columbia or anywhere, the facts and evidence don't change."

Approval of Kinder Morgan was the clincher in Trudeau's talks with Alberta Premier Rachel Notley on getting the province to set a price on carbon emissions. Forget for a moment that Notley leads an NDP government: Alberta desperately needs to get its oil to tidewater and Asian markets to break the American stranglehold on Canadian exports. The U.S. accounts for over 99 per cent of Canadian crude exports, and imposes a discount of about $15 a barrel below the world price. Both Ottawa and Edmonton need to diversify the oilpatch's international markets.

And Ottawa has the constitutional tools to make it happen. First of all, let's remember that interprovincial and international trade are federal jurisdictions.

"On top of all that," the *Globe and Mail* noted in a lead editorial Monday, "there is a clause in the Constitution that gives Ottawa jurisdiction over projects that are 'declared by the Parliament to be for the general Advantage of Canada.'"

This has led to a century of provincial protectionism, particularly when it comes to transporting beer and wine across provincial lines. These are called BITS – barriers to interprovincial trade – and the existence of BITS was the reason beer was excluded from the 1987 Canada-U.S Free Trade Agreement.

But now the Supreme Court has agreed to hear a case on New Brunswick limiting alcohol imports to a case of 12 beers, or one bottle of wine or liquor. A New Brunswick judge has ruled the restriction is unconstitutional, citing Section 121. And it will now be up to the Supremes to uphold or overturn the Court's 1921 ruling.

As for the declaratory power in Section 92 (10), the Trudeau government has a high-profile opportunity coming up to use it. The House rises for the summer on June 23; normally that would mark the end of the first session of this Parliament, with a throne speech to begin a second session in October – mid-mandate for the Liberals.

Trudeau could announce the plan to use the declaratory power in the throne speech, and bring it to the House as Bill 1. It's called leadership.

June 2017

9

THE MISSION AGAINST ISIS

AN AIR MISSION

By any standard, Canada's contribution to the allied air mission against Islamic State is a modest one. We're talking about six CF-18 fighter jets, a refueling plane and two surveillance aircraft that will be flying over northern Iraq in support of Kurdish resistance to Islamic State terrorists on the ground.

Only in Canada would we make this all about us.

Are we putting boots on the ground? Nope. Are we putting our pilots in harm's way? Hardly.

CF-18s flew bombing missions in the First Gulf War of 1991, over Kosovo in 1999, and over Libya in 2011. In those three campaigns, no Canadian planes were lost and there were no Canadian casualties.

The pilots and their support teams will be based hundreds of miles away, probably in Kuwait. CF-18 pilots should be in no more danger than they would on be manoeuvres at home. Several dozen elite Canadian Forces members may be on the ground in northern Iraq as advisers and trainers to the Kurds, and could be in harm's way in an ISIS offensive, but they will have no combat role. This is not Afghanistan.

So the Canadians are finally on their way. The United States, Britain, France, Australia, Belgium, Denmark and the Netherlands are already there.

While it might be difficult to make the case that Canada should do more, it's harder still to argue that we should do less. The New Democrats have argued that Norway, Germany and Italy aren't participating in the air mission, but are making value-in-kind contributions in aid and equipment.

On the question of humanitarian aid, Foreign Affairs Minister John Baird aimed for the moral high ground in the House debate, when he announced $10 million to help women victims of Islamic State sexual violence.

However, no one in his right mind would advocate sending in Canadian aid workers. As with journalists, the westerners with no military protection are the people Islamic State has been targeting for public decapitation. Its other crimes against humanity include torture, mass executions, selling women and girls into sexual bondage and persecution of religious minorities – including Islamic minorities. As Baird aptly put it, Islamic State's "brutality is matched only by its depravity."

No one is suggesting that Islamic State can be "degraded and defeated," in Barack Obama's words, by air power alone. Indeed, Stephen Harper has been careful to use only the word "degraded." It took the prime minister a while to get there – the debate in the House began ten days after the one at Westminster – but in the end Harper struck a balance between participating in the mission and not playing any part at all.

Of course, Canada's role in the mission must be viewed through the prism of the corning 2015 election campaign, which has already started.

This was clear from a prepared text delivered last week by Liberal Leader Justin Trudeau to the Ottawa conference of Canada 2020, the progressive liberal think tank. "Mr. Harper," Trudeau said, "is intent on taking to Canada to war in Iraq ... Canada's best contribution to this effort is a handful of aging war planes."

Right. Harper as a warmonger. Trudeau's smartass crack about how we shouldn't "whip out our CF-18s and show them how big they are" came in a subsequent Q&A with Don Newman. But when the debate was finally joined in the House over two days, Trudeau's own contribution was limited to a couple of questions. For the rest, Trudeau was M.I.A. for a debate the Liberals demanded. In over 100 pages in Hansard Monday and Tuesday, there are no other remarks by the Liberal leader.

The debate saw the usual posturing and positioning by all parties, but by and large the House rose to the occasion. Baird, for example, can be a highly partisan figure. But he also has a sense of occasion. "Let us debate what needs to be done, but let us be Parliament at its best," he said in leading off the debate on the government's motion. "Let us be Canada at its best."

There was a lot of that in Mulcair's speech. He could have done without reading entire newspaper columns supporting his position into the record. But he also had some relevant warnings about avoiding what Harper himself has called "a quagmire," and drew some pertinent lessons from Canada's decade and more in Afghanistan. "What began as a reconstruction mission quickly transformed into a combat mission," he noted.

And why? Because a reconstruction role in Kabul in 2001 became a combat role in Kandahar in August 2005. At the time, the House was in recess and the Liberal government of the day never brought the re-profiled mission to the House for a debate and vote. The Harper government, on taking office in 2006, continued the Kandahar mission for years. It was in Kandahar, not Kabul, that Canada suffered all but a handful of its casualties.

"A few dozen members in a mission that had a very short time frame became 40,000 Canadian combat soldiers in the longest combat mission in the history of our country," Mulcair said. "We spent at least $30 billion, 160 soldiers were killed, thousands were injured and let us not forget – because we tend to forget them – the thousands of men and women who returned suffering from post-traumatic stress syndrome."

As a closing argument in court, Mulcair's case was irrefutable. Where the parties stand in the court of public opinion after the debate is a good question. The NDP offered an amendment – all aid short of combat – and the Liberals apparently saw no alternative other than to support it. When it was defeated, the Liberals joined the NDP in opposing the government resolution, which easily passed in a majority House.

And then, having opposed the mission, the Liberals then said they supported the troops. Seriously.

People were watching. This was a moment for grown-ups. Make no mistake, the Liberals took a hit this week. And so did their leader.

October 2014

OTTAWA IN LOCKDOWN

Gord Miller and Phil Lamothe saw the shooting at the National War Memorial from the front of the Château Laurier, where they work as doormen.

"There were five shots," said Lamothe.

"I was bringing a car around," said Miller, "and it sounded like the bang of an accident. Phil saw the man shoot four more times. He called 911."

Hours later, both were still shaken by what they had seen. "What kind of person would do something like that?" Miller wondered.

It was 9:52 in the morning. The ceremonial guard of honour, accompanied by a piper, had just assumed their post at the National War Memorial. The soldier, Cpl. Nathan Cirillo, 24, a reservist from a Hamilton regiment, later died in an Ottawa hospital. He was the second Canadian soldier to be killed on Canadian soil in three days.

His presumed assailant then crossed the street to Parliament Hill, entered the Centre Block at the Peace Tower and ran with a large weapon through the Hall of Honour – where he died in a hail of bullets at the entrance to the Parliamentary Library. He was later identified as Michael Zehaf-Bibeau, 32. It wasn't immediately clear whether he was a "radicalized" Canadian jihadist.

This assumes the shooter in the two incidents was one and the same person – a lone gunman. But security forces worked on the assumption that at least one other shooter was at large, keeping most of downtown Ottawa in lockdown until mid-afternoon.

At mid-day, while police carrying semi-automatic weapons ran past the front door of the Château Laurier in the direction of the Rideau Centre, hotel guests were warned it was dangerous to go near doors or windows.

For the rest, hotel employees and guests alike did their best to keep calm and carry on. A large silver urn of coffee was wheeled into the lobby. Bottles of water were distributed. Zoe's lounge was opened so guests could follow the developing story on two giant screens behind the bar.

On Parliament Hill, there was a clearly a sense that it could have been much worse. The shooter was probably unaware that Wednesday is caucus day in Centre Block. The Conservatives and NDP meet in the Reading and Railway rooms just off the Hall of Honour. The shooter ran right past 300 MPs and senators who had just begun their weekly closed-door meetings. The Liberals were in the building, too, in their caucus room one floor below.

Prime Minister Stephen Harper and Opposition Leader Tom Mulcair were both quickly evacuated from the scene. Liberal Leader Justin Trudeau remained in the protective lockdown.

The shooter was taken down by Kevin Vickers, the sergeant-at-arms of the House of Commons, who rushed down the corridor from the Speaker's office. Which makes him the hero of the piece.

In the aftermath of the 9/11 attacks in 2001, only cars with parking access were admitted from the Bank Street entrance, with the other two gates closed to all but parliamentary buses and police cars, which is still the case today. In the aftermath of Wednesday's events, it may become similarly difficult for visitors to enter the Parliamentary precinct on foot. The days of easy access for guests to members' offices and the Parliamentary Restaurant may be over.

In symbolic terms, these events were an affront to our way of life. A soldier was killed while standing guard on hallowed ground – the National War Memorial. One can only imagine how Remembrance Day ceremonies will unfold there next month. And the Centre Block, the central forum of Canadian democracy, came under attack by a man with a gun.

When Parliament is attacked, we are all attacked.

But there is also a balance that needs to be struck between keeping our country safe and maintaining our way of life. There's a distinction to be made between a lockdown and a shutdown.

On Wednesday, Ottawa was virtually shut down. The Ottawa Senators postponed their home game against the Toronto Maple Leafs. Minor league hockey games were cancelled across the city. The Former Parliamentarians Dinner was cancelled at the Château Laurier.

In a three-minute prime time TV statement, Harper looked tense and sounded terse:

"We will not be intimidated," he declared. "We will never be intimidated." That was the heart of his message, and it needed to be said, even though he appeared somewhat shaken by the day's events.

In his own address, Opposition Leader Mulcair reached across the aisle: "I'm here tonight in solidarity." He looked and sounded calm and reassuring, delivering a message that people badly needed to hear Wednesday night – that at moments like these, there are no partisans. Only Canadians.

October 2014

A SHOOTING ON HALLOWED GROUND

Two things have stood out in the days since the shooting at the National War Memorial and the subsequent events on Parliament Hill. One is the importance of a sense of occasion on the part of the leaders and parliamentarians of all parties. And then there's been the response of ordinary citizens, who instinctively knew how to honour a soldier slain while standing guard on what is supposed to be hallowed ground.

Either by coincidence or choice, it was exactly 24 hours after the murder of Cpl. Nathan Cirillo that Stephen and Laureen Harper came to the crime scene at the national cenotaph to lay a wreath in his honour. MPs of all parties were already there. As the CBC reported on its website: "MPs gathered close to the memorial and sang O Canada before hugging and wiping away tears."

It is not difficult to imagine the carnage that might have unfolded in the Hall of Honour Wednesday morning, with the Conservative and NDP caucuses meeting behind closed but unsecured doors in the Reading and Railway rooms. Did the shooter know they were there? What if he had been carrying a semi-automatic weapon? One shudders at the thought, as did many MPs.

We can hope the sense of parliamentary camaraderie on display last week will yet prove to be more than a passing moment in time. MPs and senators on all sides shared a harrowing experience. They have been marked by it and their parliamentary manners may well be improved because of it. The public can hope. Parties can still have their differences in debate, without being so dysfunctional in tone.

As for Canadians, they responded with grace. When the honour guard returned to the War Memorial on Friday, they came by the hundreds to honour Cpl. Cirillo. Nobody asked them to come, but they did, carrying bouquets and hugging their children.

Hundreds more stood at the many overpasses, waving flags and saluting, as the motorcade and hearse carrying his coffin traveled down highways to his home town of Hamilton. For the occasion, the entire route was renamed the Highway of Heroes, though normally it's only the 401 between CFB Trenton and Toronto.

Canadians have a reputation for being undemonstrative, which takes no account of their love of country. No one in Ottawa has ever heard the national anthem sung as it was before football and hockey games there on the weekend.

In Ottawa and across the country, Canadians appeared glad to see soldiers back in uniform, after they'd been advised by the brass to wear civvies when off duty so as not to be targets for murder as were Cpl. Cirillo and Warrant Officer Patrice Vincent, run down in a parking lot in St-Jean-sur-Richelieu only two days earlier. This wasn't so much Canadians feeling protected by the military, as having the opportunity to thank them for their service.

Meanwhile, many questions remain about the Ottawa shooting and the shooter. It appears he had money from his time working in Alberta's oil fields. But how did he get from Ottawa to Mont-Tremblant and back without being stopped by either city or Quebec police for driving a car without a licence plate? And at some point, would he have needed more cash to stop for gas?

Where did he get the antique Winchester rifle and the 30-30 ammo? The guy had a criminal record, which meant he couldn't buy it in a gun shop. Was it already in the car when he left his aunt's place at Mont Tremblant to return to Ottawa on his murderous errand early on Wednesday morning?

Not to mention how he was able to park the car illegally within 50 metres of the PM's office at the Langevin Block, shoot the corporal in the back at the memorial, pull a u-turn on Wellington Street and leave the vehicle in front of the blocked East Block entrance to Parliament. Which is where the questions begin about his commandeering a minister's car in front of the East Block, and rushing the Peace Tower entrance to Centre Block.

This raises the obvious larger questions about security on the Hill, and the prime minister might consider naming a blue-ribbon panel of elders from all parties to report back to Parliament within a few weeks of the OPP finishing its review.

Then, what kind of legislative framework, in addition to what we already have, is needed to combat threats to our security without compromising our liberties? Are the authorities going to round up suspects whose names are on a travel watch list? We went through that in the October Crisis of 1970, and it was not Canada's proudest moment.

October 2014

∞

THE FOG OF WAR

Sgt. Andrew Doiron's death in a friendly fire incident with Kurdish forces underlines the need for a full and frank debate in the House on extending Canada's mission in northern Iraq.

The six-month deployment of CF-18s in the air and special operations advisers on the ground expires on April 7. In terms of parliamentary approval, the clock is already ticking on extending the mission. The House will be on break again next week; it will sit only nine days after that before rising for the Easter break on April 2.

So what is the mission going forward? What are the rules of engagement?

And to what extent are Canadians being put in harm's way?

These are all questions the prime minister would be asking his commanders. It is the loneliest burden a prime minister carries, and Stephen Harper has carried it in all the private calls he has made to the families of Canada's casualties in Afghanistan.

In this regard, it's worth re-reading Harper's speech to the House last October 3, outlining the terms of the mission:

"On September 5, I announced that members of the Canadian army, in a non-combat role, would advise and assist security forces in Iraq," he said. "We are extending the deployment, in a non-combat role of up to 69 members of the Canadian army advising and assisting security forces in Iraq.

"We will strike ISIL where, and only where, Canada has the clear support of the government of the country."

So, Iraq – but not Syria.

He continued: "Let me assure all Canadians the government is seized with the necessity of avoiding a prolonged quagmire in this part of the world."

How has that turned out? Well, certain rhetorical allowances have to be made for ambiguity, and for the fog of war.

Technically, Harper was not being disingenuous when he said there would be "no ground combat mission." Technically, Canadian special ops troops are training and advising Kurdish troops. Technically, our guys are not on the front lines. Technically, Canadians are always at least 200 metres from the front line.

Two hundred metres is the length of a football field, including the end zone. No wonder commanders back in Ottawa have acknowledged that, on several occasions, Canadians have exchanged fire with Islamic State fighters.

Is this a "non-combat role," as described by the PM? Hard to say, since there are no Canadians reporters embedded with the Canadian "advisers" on the ground.

And what of the role of the six CF-18s, based in Kuwait, whose pilots have flown hundreds of sorties against Islamic State fighters or assets? Their mission, Harper said last October, is to "specifically degrade" ISIS. In this, Canada has some success – though ISIS is far from being "on its back heels," as Defence Minister Jason Kenney said in his weekend speech to the Manning Conference. No one else is making that claim – least of all the Americans.

Where do we go from here? And how long are we going to be there? Another six months would take us to November 7, just after the election scheduled on October 19. That seems like an appropriate and politically tenable timeline. But the government hasn't ruled out an indefinite extension.

Foreign Affairs Minister Rob Nicholson, himself a former defence minister, evidently shared some of the government's thinking last week when he said, after a covert visit to Iraq, that Canada is there for the long term.

"Being in this for the long term … it's similar to what we did in Afghanistan, for instance," Nicholson said. "We were in Afghanistan, but we indicated that we would continue our assistance, and we have, in Afghanistan."

Afghanistan? We were there for 13 years, from 2001–2014. The Chrétien government increased our role there mainly because we didn't join George W. Bush's "coalition of the willing" in Iraq in 2003.

So now, ironically, we're in Iraq – having paid a very heavy price to avoid it. Which is one very good reason for having an informed and intelligent debate about extending the mission, one in which all parties rise above the partisan fray.

Perhaps that's asking too much in an election year. But it would be refreshing if the PM began the debate by acknowledging that MPs on all sides love our country. There's been quite enough talk from the government side about "jihadists" bringing "terror to Canada." This debate needs to move to higher ground.

And it's one that Liberal Leader Justin Trudeau – who asked for a debate on the mission last October, then failed to speak in it – needs to show up for this time. As for NDP Leader Tom Mulcair, he needs better lines than Jack Layton had over Afghanistan, when he said he would "support our troops by bringing them home." Please, spare us the NDP boilerplate.

Finally, on the question of our troops and pilots being in harm's way: Our fighter pilots are probably in no more danger than they would be flying manouevres over the Arctic, since ISIS doesn't have anti-aircraft missiles. And our special ops forces are not people Islamic State wants to meet down a dark alley.

And yet, there is always the nightmare scenario of a Canadian pilot having to eject in an emergency, or a soldier being captured on the ground. Given the barbaric behaviour of Islamic State, no one even wants to think about that.

March 2015

MAKING THE CASE

In making his case for extending and expanding Canada's military campaign against the Islamic State, Stephen Harper faces two political tests – in how he presents it, and in how he manages the mission itself.

For the opposition parties, there's only one test – where they stand on the mission. Tom Mulcair and Justin Trudeau made their opposition clear in the House, setting the stage for a good debate with clearly drawn lines; the yeas have it, but the nays will be heard in Parliament. Harper even did the opposition leaders the courtesy of sending them the text of the motion the night before, so they could come to the Commons well prepared.

Harper is asking the House to support extending the mission in northern Iraq by "up to an additional 12 months" and to expand the air campaign against Islamic State across the border into Syria. He is not proposing to send any on-the-ground military advisers into Syria.

That's a careful approach, calibrated to keep the mission from going beyond what Canadians are prepared to accept. The pilots of the six CF-18s and the Aurora surveillance aircraft stationed in Kuwait right now will be in no more danger over Syria than they are over Iraq. ISIS doesn't have anti-aircraft missiles and the Syrians aren't likely to fire on Canadian jets.

As the Americans and other allies have done in attacking ISIS positions in Syria, Canada doubtless will notify Damascus of air attacks, without seeking its permission to enter Syrian airspace. The reason is obvious: Bashar al-Assad is a very bad guy, and we should not be doing business with him. This is one instance where the enemy of our enemy is *not* our friend.

This is a man who wages war on his own people, and uses chemical weapons against them. Over 200,000 people have been killed in Syria's civil war to date; more than three million have become refugees in neighbouring countries, while six million more have been internally displaced.

In short it's an extremely dangerous place and our special forces shouldn't go anywhere near it. They're already in harm's way in Iraq, as the death of Sgt. Andrew Doiron in a friendly fire incident with Kurdish forces reminded us.

It's not clear whether the government will send a second squadron of CF-18s to the region, but with 600 military personnel already on the ground in Kuwait, there would no problem in supporting them as part of an expanded mission. The planes have to be airborne anyway, the pilots have to get their time in – and they might as well be over Syria as over Labrador. But in question period Tuesday, Harper said "the same number" of special forces would be deployed on the ground, with no increase.

The NDP and Liberals, in opposing the extended and expanded mission, predictably proposed that Canada step up its humanitarian aid in both Iraq and Syria. Harper pre-emptively noted that Canada has helped feed 1.7 million Iraqis and has "provided shelter and relief to one and a quarter million people and given some education to at least half a million children," as well as helping 200,000 Syrian refugees in Iraq.

"There is," Harper declared, "no either/or here between military action and humanitarian aid." Evidently Canada is already, in dollar terms, the fifth largest provider of humanitarian aid in the region.

"We don't have to choose between fighting ISIS or helping its victims," Harper said. "We will continue to do both."

For Mulcair, Iraq is "a war that is not ours." He went further: "Mark my words, when the NDP form government, we're going to pull our troops out, we're going to bring them home."

This is NDP boilerplate, and the party's base on the left demands nothing less from Mulcair – though he has left himself no room to manouevre. (He also left himself the best soundbite of the day, accusing Harper of moving Canada "from mission creep to mission leap.")

Part of Mulcair's rationale for rejecting the extension is that, in his words, "it's not a UN mission, it's not even a NATO mission." Well, good luck getting a UN resolution out of the Security Council, where the Russians have a veto.

And while NATO may not be involved in this mission, some 60 countries are – including the Americans, the British and the French, our three closest allies.

Mulcair crossed a rhetorical line when he called it "the prime minister's war." But he was asking the right questions when he demanded the government explain what its intended endgame is, and whether there is "a well-defined exit strategy."

Perhaps the parliamentary debate can shed some light on that. That's one of the lessons we should have learned from Afghanistan. In the summer of 2005, Canada re-deployed from the relative safety of patrolling Kabul to taking on the Taliban in their stronghold of Kandahar province, without the re-profiled mission ever being debated in the House.

That happened under a Liberal prime minister, Paul Martin, who approved the mission shift on the recommendation of the chief of defence staff, Gen. Rick Hillier. And it was in Kandahar that Canada lost most of the 158 soldiers who died during our 12-year mission to Afghanistan.

Here's hoping we learned something from that. Never again.

March 2015

VISITING THE TROOPS

In an aircraft hangar in Kuwait on Sunday, Stephen Harper spoke from the prime ministerial lectern, the one emblazoned with the Canadian coat of arms.

In front of him, dressed in combat fatigues, stood the pilots and support crews deployed there for the Canadian mission against ISIS in Iraq and Syria. Behind him were two CF-18s parked at diagonal angles, and between them was a large Canadian flag.

In a sense – per the infamous Justin Trudeau quote – Harper was whipping out our CF-18s and showing how big they are.

His staff then posted the image to Harper's Twitter feed with the message: "I'm here to show our unconditional support for the troops and the mission they've accepted on behalf of our country."

Earlier, Harper had breakfast with the troops, and dropped a puck at a game of floor hockey. "Honoured to have had breakfast with Canadian troops at Camp Canada in Kuwait," Harper tweeted. "Canada is proud and thankful for their service."

Harper then paid a courtesy call on the Emir of Kuwait, Sheikh Sabah Al-Ahmad Al-Jaber Al-Sabah. There's an image of that on his Twitter account as well, for the information of his 783K followers.

How's your day so far, Prime Minister?

On Friday Harper had flown out of Ottawa, supposedly en route to the Netherlands, to join in ceremonies and celebrations marking the 70th anniversary of V-Day and the end of the Second World War in Europe.

But his Airbus diverted instead to Baghdad for an unannounced visit to Iraq.

In Baghdad's Green Zone, Harper was greeted with military honours and met with Iraqi Prime Minister Haydar al-Abadi, before meeting semiautonomous Kurdish leaders in Erbil in northern Iraq, where nearly 70 members of the Canadian special forces are training Kurdish Peshmerga troops. He also toured a Canadian concrete pre-fab plant, where the host gave him a Habs jersey. Then Harper went out to within a few kilometres of the Kurdish front against ISIS, with the PM's photographer and video unit recording it all.

Welcome to Campaign 2015.

Harper was also understandably reminded by reporters travelling with him of the death two months earlier of Sgt. Andrew Doiron in a friendly fire incident with Kurds near the front. Harper stated the obvious, that it was "a terrible tragedy," but refused to play the blame game with the Kurds who, he said, had done a remarkable job of liberating a large part of northern Iraq in a short period of time.

While he was in Iraq, Harper announced $139 million in Canadian aid to Iraq, Syria and Jordan, in addition to $67 million previously committed. For opposition critics asking that Canada do more on the aid front and less on the military mission, this was Harper's way of saying shut up.

These images and announcements were all very awkward for the opposition parties, both of which voted against extending the mission against ISIS in Iraq and expanding it to Syria.

The NDP, with its pacifist base, wasn't going to vote for it anyway. But Tom Mulcair had rational cover in saying the mission was neither sanctioned by the UN, as Operation Desert Storm was in liberating Kuwait in 1991, nor was it a NATO operation as was Libya in 2011. Never mind that the Americans, the British and the French, historically Canada's three strongest allies, are all involved in the mission. At least Mulcair's position is logically sustainable.

The Liberal position is that they oppose the mission but support the troops, which has proved difficult for Justin Trudeau to explain, and left his party somewhat divided.

The visuals and messaging from Harper's tour of Iraq, and visit with Canadian troops in Kuwait, obviously reinforced his ownership of the pro-mission side of the debate. He's for it, and the other two guys are splitting the vote against it.

Harper's excellent adventure will continue in the Netherlands. He'll be joining Canadian veterans in their 80s and 90s, who will be cheered to the echo. Some of them have already flown in with Laureen Harper, who served them snacks on the plane. On Sunday they joined her and Veterans' Affairs Minister Erin O'Toole in a ceremony at the Canadian War Cemetery in Groesbeek, where more than 2,300 Canadians are buried. Some 7,600 Canadian soldiers lost their lives in the liberation of the Netherlands.

This is why, 70 years after war's end, Canadians still can't pay for their own drinks in the Netherlands.

May 2015

POLICY CHOICES

If a government is looking for a full suite of policy options, there's no better place to shop in Ottawa than the Department of National Defence.

The Trudeau government's imminent reconfiguring of the mission against ISIS is a case in point. The Liberals are poised to do both more and less at the same time. Only DND could offer such a diversified menu of policy choices.

The re-profiled mission will be announced ahead of a NATO defence ministers' meeting in Brussels. Justin Trudeau is expected to recall the squadron of six CF-18 fighter jets from the Middle East.

So this is one thing that President Barack Obama won't be asking Trudeau about during his working visit and state dinner at the White House next month, since Trudeau is taking an extended CF-18 deployment off the table.

If ever there was a campaign promise made to be broken, it's Trudeau's pledge to recall the CF-18s from the ISIS mission. It's not as if there's any great groundswell of voices across the land demanding their return.

The jets have flown some 1,350 sorties from their base in Kuwait, where they are supported by hundreds of Canadian Armed Forces personnel. Neither the pilots nor the support staff are in harm's way. ISIS doesn't have surface-to-air missiles as far as we know, and Kuwait is hundreds of miles from the front lines in northern Iraq and Syria.

As DND puts it on its website: "The use of air power contributes to the destruction of ISIL infrastructure and equipment, denying them the military means to attack Iraq security forces or coalition assets."

The DND post also claims that ISIS "has lost the ability to operate freely in roughly 25 to 30 per cent of populated Iraq territory it previously controlled."

So the allied air campaign apparently is achieving its goal of pushing back ISIS on the ground. But Trudeau is bound and determined to bring the planes home, and at DND they know how to salute and say, "Yes, Prime Minister."

Or rather, "Yes, Minister": Defence Minister Harjit Sajjan is one of their own, a former colonel in the reserves who served on the ground in the Afghanistan campaign against the Taliban.

Sajjan will inform his NATO colleagues that Canada will keep two Aurora reconnaissance aircraft in the region, as well as one Polaris refueling aircraft that has flown 400 sorties and delivered more than 20 million pounds of fuel to allied planes. It seems like a token contribution, and begs the question of how many ground personnel will remain in Kuwait to support three planes.

That's the doing-less part of the Canadian contribution to the U.S.-led campaign. The doing-more part is that Canada is expected to triple the 69 Special Forces troops on the ground training Kurdish fighters in northern Iraq.

This, of course, could put Canadian troops in harm's way, depending on how close they are to the front. The one Canadian casualty in northern Iraq was a soldier killed in a friendly fire incident a year ago. With his experience in Afghanistan, Sajjan will need no briefing or risk assessment on the danger to Canadian forces on the ground.

Another part of the doing-more component is that Canada is expected to join an out-of-theatre NATO-led training mission to be established in Jordan and Turkey. The *Globe and Mail* reported the Canadian contingent would be battalion-sized, quoting one source saying "it could be anywhere between 500 to 1,000 troops."

This is not like summer manouevres at an army camp. It means military transports will be required to fly hundreds of troops and their equipment to the Middle East.

The Liberals also are planning to announce cash and humanitarian assistance, notably for Syria, as part of a United Nations relief effort for a war-torn nation where virtually half the entire population is homeless, and millions more have fled to refugee camps in neighbouring countries. More than a million of those refugees have sought refuge in Europe, not to mention the 25,000 destined for Canada.

There's no question about how the re-tooled mission will play out in Parliament. The Conservatives and their interim leader, Rona Ambrose, have strongly urged the government to maintain the CF-18s' presence as a vital part of the mission against ISIS. This is one time the Conservatives appear to be lined up with public opinion.

As for the NDP, they can be relied upon, in Jack Layton's words, to "support our troops by bringing them home."

One thing is clear: The Liberals should commit to a debate in the House and a resolution authorizing the re-defined mission. Even the Harper Conservatives, never the most democratic gang in town, did that much.

February 2016

IT'S TRUDEAU'S MISSION NOW

Whether Canada's re-profiled role in the allied campaign against ISIS is a combat or non-combat mission, one thing is clear – Justin Trudeau owns it.

He inherited a very different operation from the previous Conservative government, one led by six CF-18 fighter jets, and 69 Special Forces members training Kurdish resistance fighters on the ground in northern Iraq.

Trudeau is recalling the CF-18s, but tripling the number of Canadian trainers in Iraq, saying the reconfigured mission "should better reflect what Canada is all about."

Actually, deploying CF-18s to combat missions is what Canada has been "all about" since Operation Desert Storm in 1991, when Brian Mulroney sent 24 CF-18s to help liberate Kuwait in the first Gulf War. Stephen Harper sent seven CF-18s to help coalition forces overthrow Libyan dictator Moammar Gadhafi in 2011. A Canadian general, Charles Bouchard, commanded the successful allied campaign.

In Kuwait and Libya, not a single Canadian plane was shot down, nor were there any Canadian casualties, just as there have been none over Iraq and Syria.

The one Canadian casualty in Iraq has been a trainer killed in a friendly fire incident nearly a year ago. There is no doubt that in tripling the Canadian trainer contingent on the ground in northern Iraq to 207 Special Forces members, they will be in a theatre of combat, even as non-combatants.

Which is how the prime minister insisted on framing their role in his Monday morning announcement.

"This is an advise and assist mission that our trainers will be engaged in," he said. "And as I said many times during the campaign, and my commitment to Canadians, this is a non-combat mission."

Right.

General Jonathan Vance, Chief of Defence Staff, had a more nuanced explanation at the briefing following Trudeau's news conference with three of his cabinet colleagues.

"We want Canadians to know that we will be involved in engagements as we defend ourselves and those partners we are working with," the CDS clarified. "You put a lot more people on the ground in a dangerous place, it is riskier overall."

No kidding.

But Vance wouldn't allow the suggestion that he was contradicting the PM.

"The prime minister has clearly described it as non-combat," Vance acknowledged. "In my view, it's a non-combat mission in that we are not the principal combatants here." Got it.

Defence Minister Harjit Sajjan is well aware of the risks, having served a reserve colonel in Afghanistan during the deployment against al-Qaida.

"This is a conflict zone, it comes with risk," Sajjan told CTV. "We can't obviously mitigate the risks to zero."

And they can't, equally obviously, call in Canada's own CF-18s in the event the trainers get caught in a firefight.

Trudeau may be keeping a campaign promise in recalling the jets, but he has missed an opportunity to change his mind.

PMs have been known to do this. His own father ran against wage and price controls in the 1974 election, famously shouting "Zap! You're frozen!" all along the way. Graduating from a minority to majority government as a result, Pierre Trudeau imposed wage and price controls.

In the 1983 Conservative leadership campaign, one of Mulroney's opponents, John Crosbie, strongly advocated free trade with the United States. "We will have none of it," Mulroney declared. Three years later as prime minister, Mulroney began free trade talks with the United States. The 1988 election was transformed into a referendum on the deal with the Americans, later leading to the NAFTA in 1992, both signature achievements of Mulroney's government.

Some promises are made to be broken. Trudeau's promise to withdraw the CF-18s was before the terror attacks in Paris and San Bernadino in California, to say nothing of the terrorist attack in Burkina Faso last month, in which six Canadians were killed.

It would have been very easy for Trudeau to say, that was then, this is now. However, the Trudeau government was careful to solicit endorsements from the White House, State Department and Pentagon in Washington. Trudeau had a conversation with U.S. President Barack Obama before his announcement, and spokespersons at daily Washington press briefings went out of their way to thank Canada for expanding its training role in Iraq.

However, White House press secretary Josh Earnest pointedly said the Americans might be looking for more. "We're going to have continuing discussions with the Canadians about additional steps they can take to further enhance our efforts," he told the morning White House briefing. "Those new commitments are indicative of the kind of close relationship that Canada and the United States enjoy, particularly when it comes to our mutual national security."

Apart from the expanded training mission in Iraq, another 100 or so Canadian soldiers will be deployed to Jordan and Lebanon to train anti-ISIS soldiers out of theatre. In all, the Canadian deployment will increase from 650 to 830 military personnel.

Moreover, two Canadian Aurora surveillance aircraft will remain based in Kuwait, as will one Polaris airborne refueling plane.

So, the Auroras will gather intel on ISIS on the ground in Iraq and Syria, the Polaris will re-fuel allied planes, and Canadian trainers will paint ISIS targets on the ground. But it's a non-combat mission.

In an authentically non-combat role, Canada is pledging $1.1 billion in humanitarian and development aid over three years for Middle East countries overwhelmed by the exodus of millions of refugees from Syria. It's the right thing to do, but also strikes a Canadian feel-good reflex.

In all, Trudeau said, "we are for what will be effective, not for what will make us feel good to say at any given moment." Meaning, any rush that might come from a bombing campaign, though he acknowledged "there is a role for bombing." Just not by Canada under his government.

Closing his news conference, Trudeau referred to notes for "one more thing I want to say."

He said: "There are those who think we should engage in heated over-the-top rhetoric when speaking about ISIL and terror groups like them. We see things in a different way. The enemy of barbarism isn't hatred, it's reason."

It's not really clear what he meant by that. Perhaps he will elaborate in the coming debate in the House. But one thing is clear – it's Trudeau mission now, on his watch as prime minister.

February 2016

10

THE 2012 QUEBEC ELECTION

Unless Jean Charest changes his mind, he's on track to send voters to the polls on September 4, the day after Labour Day, a Tuesday. That would see him calling the election on August 1, following a cabinet meeting.

It's a narrow window of opportunity. A writ for the following Monday, would leave the advance poll over Labour Day week-end, when many voters are away, and the Liberals count heavily on advance polls. The following Monday, September 17, is a non-starter because it falls on the Jewish holiday, Rosh Hashanah.

Beyond that, the Charbonneau Commission will resume its televised hearings into the construction industry, and that's not a narrative that plays into Charest's election scenario.

If he walks away from an election now, don't expect one until the fall of next year, after the inquiry's findings are released.

In effect, it's the day after Labour Day or the fall of 2013, when the turmoil of the student revolt, and the churn of the construction inquiry, will be in the rear-view mirror. But fall 2013 is at the end of the five-year mandate, whereas the normal accounting to voters is after four years. At four months short of four years, Charest can't be accused of calling a snap election.

Even so, there are voices of caution in the cabinet, caucus and campaign, those who remember what happened the last time a Liberal premier called an early election, in 1976: the Parti Québécois came into power. All things considered, they would rather wait.

But this is Charest's call, and his alone. And he's inclined to go.

First of all, the Liberals have moved back ahead of the PQ in their internal polling. Not by a lot, but by enough to form a minority government, with the opportunity of breaking into majority territory during the campaign.

The splits of the opposition vote appear to be breaking in Charest's favour, according to a senior Liberal source.

For example, François Legault and the Coalition Avenir Québec are polling close to 20 per cent, and at that level more of those votes come from the PQ than the Liberals, the source says. Amir Khadir and Québec solidaire are hovering around 10 per cent, and every one of those votes comes at the expense of the PQ. Since Khadir already has a seat in the legislature, that should be enough to get him into the leaders' debate, by definition a level playing field. The PQ will not be happy about that.

Normally, after three terms in office, an election would be about change, but Charest has the opportunity to make it about continuity instead.

His ballot question is simple: Who's in charge, the democratically elected government, or a mob?

That the mob of students and anarchists would disrupt his meetings would only make his point.

And Charest has a deeper ballot question: What kind of Quebec do you want?

This poses a dilemma for Pauline Marois. There's an alignment of forces on the left – the students, trade unions, Québec solidaire voters – with whom she's already allied. That was her wearing the red square in the legislature in solidarity with the students.

In other words, while there are plenty of votes on the left in Quebec, they're not middle class votes. And that's where elections are won.

Then Marois carries the burden of the PQ's fundamental option of sovereignty. Voters remember the last referendum in 1995, and most don't want to live through another one. For her part, Marois promises not a big referendum on a question of country, but a series of sectoral ones on issues such as culture. The referendum of the month club. Great.

Then there are the issues of fiscal frameworks and the economy. Charest's finance minister, Raymond Bachand, is on track to balance the provincial budget in the next fiscal year, no mean feat coming out of the worst recession in 60 years. On the economy, unemployment of 7.7 per cent is just half a point above the national average of 7.2 per cent, when the historic spread can be as much as three or four points. Quebec's unemployment is actually half a point lower than the United States, at 8.2 per cent.

In fact, the uncertainty of the U.S. economy, and the continuing euro crisis, may give Charest his closing argument for a campaign – that it's no time to change government. This was precisely how he closed the deal for a majority in 2008.

But this will be a very different campaign, one in which big societal choices are on the ballot. As the leader calling this election, Charest's job is to articulate and frame them.

July 2012

WELCOME TO TWITTER

The opening and closing arguments of every election are about the framing of the ballot question. Each party has a different one and struggles for control of the message with the media. And nowadays, not just mainstream media, but social media. Campaign 2.0.

Welcome to Quebec's first Twitter election. François Legault, leader of the Coalition Avenir Québec, already has a very active Twitter feed, sometimes to the point where it seems he has nothing else to do. The other day, when Jean Charest announced three former MNAs from Action démocratique du Québec were running for the Liberals, Legault posted bitter and twisted comments to Twitter.

Twitter can be a very dangerous place, but also a very useful one for making mid-course adjustments, as well as rallying and thanking the base. We saw both in the Alberta election last spring, when one of Alison Redford's young Progressive Conservative campaign workers posted a tweet alleging that childless Wildrose leader Danielle Smith was unfit to be a mother. Redford immediately apologized to Smith, but lost three days in damage control.

On the other hand, as she pulled away in the closing days of the campaign, Redford used her Twitter feed as a momentum builder, before during and after each event. If she had a great event in Vegreville, she thanked the crowd and told you about it in 140 characters or less.

Up to now, Premier Charest and Parti Québécois leader Pauline Marois haven't been on Twitter, but you can be sure someone will be tweeting from his and her bus. It's pretty hard to ignore.

Barack Obama, for example, has 17 million followers on Twitter, which gives him a big advantage in that department over Mitt Romney, who has only 750,000 followers. Not that the president of the United States has time to tweet, but someone in his Chicago headquarters or the White House does so several times a day in his name. While he's preaching to the converted, he is rallying the troops, as well as getting messages out for fundraising.

Until recently, the Quebec Liberals didn't do social media very well, but they're getting better at it. Their video of Marois banging casseroles at the Argenteuil byelection went viral on YouTube, and got lots of earned media on broadcast news and in print. And they've put together hundreds of social networkers for the campaign.

As for the mainstream media, and the ballot question, it depends on each party's message. For the PQ the ballot question is change and corruption. For the Liberals, it's continuity or chaos. For the CAQ, it's somewhere in between – change without sovereignty, change you can trust.

The next 33 days will be about which party has the best message, and the best messenger. And make no mistake, it is all on the shoulders of the leaders. The PQ can talk all they want about building a team around Marois, but she will be the only one on stage at the leaders' debate.

When the campaign is built on the team, some of them talk too much, as the PQ's Bernard Drainville did in the *Globe and Mail*, talking about building support for sovereignty by picking fights with Ottawa. At a conference of New England governors and Eastern premiers in Burlington, Vermont, Charest jumped all over it. "The strategy of the Parti Québécois," he said, "will be to start fights with Ottawa to promote their option, and to hold a referendum as soon as possible. And that's the priority of Pauline Marois."

There it is again, the hidden ballot question in the prospect of another referendum, what Robert Bourassa used to call "the ballot box bonus," which he always thought was worth at least five points for the Liberals on election day.

Elsewhere on the PQ team, there's student leader Léo Bureau-Blouin, who's trading in his red square for a PQ membership card as a candidate in Laval.

Which kind of frames the Liberal ballot question of continuity or chaos. The Liberals would raise university tuition fees by $254 a year over seven years, already a compromise from their initial five-year plan. The PQ would freeze tuition fees pending an education summit, while CAQ would raise them $200 a year over five years.

But this is really about who's in charge in Quebec, the government or a street mob. Continuity or chaos.

As the campaign begins, the election is too close to call. The Liberals and PQ appear to be tied within the margin of error in the low 30s, with CAQ in the low 20s, and Québec solidaire in high single digits. Those splits should work to Charest's advantage.

One thing's for sure – he wouldn't be calling this election if he thought he was going in behind.

August 2012

∽

THE POLITICS OF FEAR

It's morbidly fascinating that Pauline Marois has chosen to take a hard line on language, making it the centrepiece of the Parti Québécois campaign, at a time when hardly anyone is talking about it.

It's not as if students and the unions have been rioting about the language issue; they've been rioting about tuition fees. It's not as if language rates anywhere near the top of voters' concerns in any of the polls. Health care, the economy, the environment, entitlements, corruption and change are all more important.

But Marois says that if she forms a government, a new Bill 101 will be the signature legislation of her first 100 days in office. Apparently she sees herself as Franklin D. Roosevelt – only instead of proposing "nothing to fear but fear itself," she has nothing to sell but fear itself.

Under her proposal, the restrictions on francophones and allophones attending English language high schools would be extended to non-anglophone college students, preventing them from attending CEGEP at English-language colleges.

And Bill 101 regulations on French as the language of business in Quebec, which now begin with companies of 50 employees or more, would begin applying to firms with more than 10 employees.

In their second year of CEGEP, students are old enough to vote and old enough to pay taxes on their summer jobs. But according to Marois, they are not old enough to decide the language of study in their college education.

"Currently half the enrolments in English-language colleges are students whose mother tongue is other than English," Marois said at the rollout of her language policy on Sunday. "Of all the students whose mother tongue is neither French nor English, half chose English-language colleges. This situation must be remedied."

Aha, those allophones again! The enrolment level of francophones in English-language CEGEPs is only about five per cent. Maybe some of them chose Dawson College for its strong fine-arts program, which leads to the world-renowned Fine Arts faculty at Concordia University. Maybe Concordia and McGill are next on Marois' hit list. To pursue the absurd logic of her argument, they would be.

Maybe these kids, children of the internet, don't want to live in a linguistic ghetto but want to go out into a bigger world beyond the parochial one of Quebec. That should be a choice for them, and their families, to make. If she sat down with her star recruit, Léo Bureau-Blouin, he would tell her this policy didn't fly when he was president of the CEGEP student federation.

As for small businesses, both established and startups, they are the motor of economic growth. And in the global economy, English is the common language of international trade and commerce. At a time when Quebec desperately needs new jobs, Marois would drive new investment and jobs out by increasing the number of doors knocked on by the language police.

"The message has to be clear," she said. "In Quebec, we live in French, we work in French, we communicate in French."

Would someone please tell this woman about Twitter, so she can look at #qc2012, where Quebecers are communicating with each other in both languages? Why not censor the internet, as they do in China? Let's shut down Facebook, and tell kids they can only post YouTube videos in French. After the language police, the thought police.

The question is why Marois would propose these ideas, which would be laughable if they weren't so dangerous to the social peace and economic prospects of Quebec.

And the answer is pretty obvious. The PQ, in a competitive election, is trying to consolidate its base. Its old base. It is calling home the hardline separatist and leftist voters who have left it for Québec solidaire. If the PQ could reduce the QS vote from eight per cent in recent polls to four per cent on election day, that might make all the difference.

Similarly, Marois is talking out of both sides of her mouth on sovereignty and a referendum. On Radio-Canada's flagship *Coulisses du Pouvoir* show on Sunday, she was asked about the prospect of a referendum in a first mandate.

Her reply: "I want one, as quickly as possible, but I won't announce when there will be a referendum." She added she wouldn't call one until the PQ had a chance of winning. Ah, winning conditions again, a page from the Lucien Bouchard playbook.

The language issue and a referendum might mobilize the old PQ base, but what she is proposing is socially reckless and economically irresponsible. It's not only intellectually dishonest, it's morally reprehensible.

She sounds like someone from the 1970s. In fact, that's exactly where she's from.

August 2012

CLEAR CHOICES

Quebec elections are different than those in other provinces in one important respect: They are the only ones in which the future of the country itself is at stake.

Seldom in the modern era have the choices been more clearly presented by the parties and their leaders. Seldom has more been at stake, beginning with the social peace and economic prosperity of Quebec.

In the Quebec proposed by Pauline Marois and the Parti Québécois, a petition signed by 15 per cent of the population could trigger a referendum on independence. Or maybe not. Marois, and Marois alone, would determine the calling of a referendum. Check.

Citizens would be required to speak French as a condition of seeking public office. Or maybe this restriction would only apply to newcomers – as if anyone would move to Quebec under such conditions.

Voters of the Muslim faith would be banned from wearing hijabs if they worked for the Quebec public service – as if any of them would want to work there under those conditions.

A PQ government would also issue citizenship cards, with newcomers required to have a working knowledge of French. So there would be two classes of citizens, first and second.

Francophone and allophone college students of voting age would not be permitted to attend English-language CEGEPs, as a new Bill 101 would extend the restrictions now in place for primary and secondary schools.

And under this legislation, to be passed within 100 days of taking office, Marois would require French as the language of work in businesses with more than 10 employees, rather than the current threshold of 50 employees. So much for new investment and startups.

Marois even has the temerity to lecture Robert Card, the new chief executive officer of SNC-Lavalin and an American, that he must become "at least bilingual." Actually, his job is to clean house after a major governance scandal, in which $56 million disappeared from the company's balance sheet, some of it to Moammar Gadhafi's Libya.

In laying down these hard line markers on the language issue, Marois is said by political commentators to be playing "the identity card." Maybe it's time to call it what it is: the race card.

The PQ's founding father, René Lévesque, would be ashamed of a party that has become so narrow-minded, bigoted and xenophobic. He used to define a Quebecer as "someone who lives here."

Marois is the worst kind of demagogue, one who will say and do anything to get elected, with no regard for the higher public interest. It's all about consolidating the PQ's separatist base. And to all appearances, it is working.

Then there is the Coalition Avenir Québec and François Legault, who will campaign neither for a sovereign Quebec nor a united Canada – as if a responsible leader can simply sit on the sidelines. This is the same guy who, as a PQ minister, used to talk about "the tools" of sovereignty. But it's working for him, too; the CAQ has the upper hand over the PQ in the struggle for ownership of the opposition ballot question of change and corruption. If he has really moved into second place, as Léger and CROP polls suggest, there's a possibility that strategic federalist voters could move to him to stop the PQ.

At least Amir Khadir, Françoise David and Québec solidaire are intellectually honest. They are separatists and socialists, and it's working for them, moving their support to near double-digit territory at the expense of the PQ, mostly in east-end Montreal.

There's only one party in this race whose Quebec clearly includes Canada: the Liberals and Jean Charest.

In the closing days of the campaign, Charest retains a comparative advantage over his opponents on two issues: a Canadian Quebec and the economy. The Liberals own both issues, but they haven't found a way to frame and leverage them over the cries of scandal from the opposition parties.

I've known Jean Charest since he first went to Ottawa as a 26-year-old freshman MP in 1984. He's spent his entire adult life in the service of Canada and Quebec. While his government could do a better job on the ethics files, no one has ever questioned his personal integrity.

And he remains the best campaigner of his generation, one with a history of finishing strong in the home stretch. That's just what he needs now in what is, at the end of the day, a question of country.

September 2012

CHAREST AND THE CANADIAN CARD

Late in the afternoon on election day, Jean Charest's chief of staff, Dan Gagnier, was on the phone with an old friend.

"What does it look like?" he was asked.

"We've got 50 seats," he replied. "It's either a PQ or a Liberal minority. The only thing we don't know is whether the CAQ vote will turn out. If they come out in the 450 (region) to stop the PQ, we'll form a government."

He went on: "The one thing I don't know is whether Legault can deliver his vote. But that's not my problem."

He called it exactly right. The pollsters and the pundits were wrong. Again.

The polls were wrong because they failed once again to measure the hidden Liberal vote, the discreet and undecideds, who broke to Charest in a big way. Robert Bourassa used to call it "the ballot box bonus." Gagnier called it "the Liberal premium" and in all their internal tracking, the Liberals gave themselves an extra four points.

It's not scientific, but it is historically accurate, and that's exactly how it came out. Instead of finishing third at 27 per cent as predicted by the polls, the Liberals finished a close second at 31 per cent, within one percentage point of the Parti Québécois and only four seats behind in the seat count at 54–50. If only two seats had gone to the Liberals rather than the PQ. Including Charest's own seat of Sherbrooke, the Liberals would have tied and formed a minority government. Or if Legault had shown up with a ground game in the 450 belt around Montreal, Charest would have run up the middle.

In the event, the Coalition Avenir Québec won no seats in Montreal and Laval, and only seven on the north and south shores of the city, where the PQ won 19 seats and the Liberals won eight. That was the PQ margin of victory in both the popular vote and the seat count.

So Charest very nearly pulled off a major upset in an election where the pollsters and pundits had relegated him to third place. On the final weekend of the campaign, pollster Jean-Marc Léger even gave an interview to *Le Journal de Montréal* in which he said the PQ was only one point away from a majority. Some majority.

As for the pundits, they missed the late-breaking Liberal trend, just as they missed the story of the emerging Conservative majority in last year's federal election, and just as they missed the Progressive Conservative majority of Alison Redford in Alberta last April.

This is because reporters spend far too much time talking to each other on Twitter all day. It's not journalism; it's gossip and opinion reinforcement.

Charest's problem at the outset of the campaign was that he lost his ballot question when the students failed to show up for it. In retrospect, the time for an election on the rioting students and the tuition issue was in the spring, when they were in the street. Then Legault won the opposition ballot question of change and corruption. And in the closing days of the campaign, Charest had to sail against the wind created by negative polls that almost became a self-fulfilling prophecy.

Fortunately for the Liberals, Charest campaigned brilliantly in the closing week, with undecided francophones breaking to him, and non-francophones returning to the Liberal fold. In future Quebec elections pollsters and pundits alike would do well to remember the strength of the Liberal brand as the only clear federalist party on the ballot.

In the meantime, Charest did much more than save the Liberal furniture last week. He may well have saved the country, just as he did in the 1995 referendum. In that very close campaign, he emerged as the champion of Canada. In this one, in thwarting a PQ majority, he made sure there will be no third referendum during the life of a minority legislature.

There are lots of other things Pauline Marois can't do with a minority government. She can't prevent students of voting age from attending CEGEP in English, and she can't send the language inspectors to small businesses with as few as 11 employees. Not without amending Bill 101, as she promised during the campaign. Only she doesn't have the votes for either. She can raise the top marginal tax rates to 55 per cent from 48 per cent in her budget next spring, but the budget would be defeated on that alone, and her government would fall.

As for the Liberals, they get to choose a new leader who won't be weighed down by the construction inquiry. And Charest gets to walk away, with his head high.

His legacy? That's easy. Canada is still one country.

September 2012

11

LANGUAGE AND IDENTITY POLITICS

PASTAGATE

Every now and then in Quebec's language debate there comes a tipping point of silliness.

We're there now, with Pastagate, and the furor over the lack of French on menus in an Italian restaurant: It's not pasta, it's pates. Seldom has Quebec been subjected to such ridicule and derision beyond its provincial borders. The story got picked up on CNN, which means it was broadcast worldwide. Social media went viral.

Inspector Clouseau never had such hilarious material.

Jean-François Lisée, the Parti Québécois cabinet minister responsible for Montreal and the English-speaking community, put it down to an excess of zeal on the part of the language inspector from the Office Québécois de la langue française.

Apart from the language of menus and signs, there's a question of customers in restaurants and stores being served in French first: the "hi/bonjour" versus "bonjour/hi" issue. Seriously.

Lisée and his PQ colleagues may dismiss the pasta incident as overdone, but subsequent reports in *The Gazette* and *La Presse* make it clear that it was not a one-off at Buonanotte, but more like the language police out of control.

Moreover, it was the PQ that rekindled the language issue in last summer's election campaign, when Pauline Marois played the identity card at every turn. The last thing Quebecers needed or wanted was another language debate, but Marois cynically stirred one up to consolidate her base, which had been bleeding votes to Québec solidaire on the left.

Marois promised to extend the student-enrolment restrictions of Bill 101 from the kindergarten-to-Grade-11 system to CEGEPs, which would have excluded francophones and allophones from English-language colleges. She pledged that companies with as few as 11 employees would have to comply with Bill 101, when the present requirements begin at 50 employees.

Elected with a weak minority government, she had no choice but to step back from those promises. She would never have got them past the Liberals and Coalition Avenir Québec in the legislature.

Instead, she has proposed Bill 14, amendments to the language law and provincial charter of rights. CEGEPs are left alone and businesses with more than 25 employees will have to comply with the linguistic regime. Which continues to miss the point: why would anyone in his or her right mind buy a small company or start one in Quebec, when he/she would spend all that time filling out forms, and when as a resident he/she would be looking at the highest marginal tax rates in North America?

The election campaign behind her, Marois urged Quebecers to be "sentinels of the language."

Echoing her boss when introducing Bill 14, the minister responsible for the language law, Diane De Courcy, said that while there was no money for more language police, "what is possible for all citizens is to become language sentries."

In other words: snitches, filing anonymous complaints to the OQLF, which then sends its inspectors swooping down on restaurants, stores and businesses dealing with the public. This is where it the script becomes less like Peter Sellers and more like George Orwell.

Is there reason to be vigilant in protecting French? Sure. But it's not by persecuting English and other languages that Quebec will promote the use of French.

A test of tolerance will come if some of Quebec's bilingual municipalities lose their bilingual status because of their English-speaking share of the population falling below 50 per cent. That's what is currently proposed in Bill 14, and it's already sparked an uproar in Montreal and the Eastern Townships.

In terms of language demographics, the latest census data are quite intriguing. The percentage of francophones in the Montreal area fell from 49.8 per cent in 2006 to 48.5 per cent in 2011. Cause for alarm? Nope. Because in that period, the number of Montreal residents speaking French and another language at home increased by 37 per cent or 90,000 people. As Celine Cooper noted in a recent *Policy* magazine piece: "The statistics show that across Quebec, including Montreal, an increasing number of allophones are speaking French at home, indicating that French has surpassed English as the language to which newcomers are turning." Moreover, linguistic and cultural diversity are an important source of comparative advantage for Canada and Quebec in the global economy.

Finally, Pastagate symbolizes a retrograde movement dating to the late 1970s, when Bill 101 was born. It was a different era, before laptops, cellphones, the Internet, smartphones and social media. Today, people converse back and forth on Twitter and Facebook in the language of their choice.

This revival of language tensions is completely disconnected from the reality of the street, where students riding the No. 24 bus on Sherbrooke Street effortlessly switch back and forth in several languages, and where people in downtown bars and restaurants do the same.

The other day I was at the meat counter at Metro chatting with the butcher in French. Eventually he switched into English, which is how the conversation ended as we wished each other a good week.

Only in Montreal. And tonight is pasta night.

February 2013

THE CHARTER OF QUEBEC VALUES

Sovereignty can't be sold and the language issue evidently doesn't move the numbers for the Parti Québécois, so the Marois government decided to play the identity card instead with its proposed Charter of Quebec Values.

Maybe it's time to call it what it is – the race card. Banning head wear and the wearing of religious symbols by government employees-including educators and healthcare workers – is conformist, discriminatory and intolerant. Not to mention racial profiling. There would be a five-year exemption period for municipalities, hospitals and post-secondary education institutions.

All of this in the name of promoting a secular state, while leaving the crucifix in place over the speaker's chair in the legislature because, after all, it's part of our cultural heritage.

Not content to exploit a linguistic divide, the PQ would create second class citizens along religious lines.

Enough, already!

That the proposed Quebec charter is unconstitutional is an open and shut case. It clearly violates the Canadian Charter of Rights and Freedoms in the 1982 Constitution Act, as well as the Quebec Charter of Human Rights and Freedoms of 1975.

In fact, on fundamental freedoms, the two charters are virtually word for word identical.

Article 2 of the federal charter stipulates: "Everyone has the following fundamental freedoms: freedom of conscience and religion; freedom of thought, belief, opinion and expression; freedom of peaceful assembly; freedom of association."

The same words appear in Article 3 of the Quebec charter, enacted by the Bourassa government in 1975, in the wake of a bitter language debate over adopting Bill 22 as Quebec's official language in 1974.

Yes, we've been in this movie before.

Moreover, the proposed Charter of Quebec Values offends Canadian constitutional convention going all the way back to the Quebec Act of 1774.

The Quebec Act guaranteed Quebecers the freedom to practise the Catholic religion, as well as restoring French civil law alongside British common law. It also allowed Catholics to hold public office and removed a reference to the Protestant denomination in office holders' oath of allegiance to the Crown.

The Quebec Act later served as the model for asymmetrical federalism in the British North America Act, now styled the Constitution Act of 1867.

Section 93 of the 1867 Constitution Act specifically entrenched the right to denominational education in Quebec. It stated that nothing in the provincial jurisdiction of education "shall prejudicially affect the right and privilege to denominational schools ... extended to the dissentient schools of the Queen's Protestant and Catholic subjects in Quebec."

It required nothing less than a bilateral constitutional amendment between the Chrétien and Bouchard governments to change Quebec's school boards from denominational to linguistic-based.

Section 133 entrenched both French and English as the recognized languages of the legislature and courts of Quebec, a constitutional provision which prevails to this day. The constitutional heritage of Sections 93 and 133 is one of a tolerant society that protected both its religious and linguistic minority communities. Along with the division of powers, they were dealmakers in the bargain of Confederation.

And the federal Charter of Rights explicitly entrenches the fundamental freedoms of conscience and religion.

So, Pauline Marois thinks her bill will pass constitutional muster? Any first year law student could tell her otherwise. She does have the constitutional override of the notwithstanding clause in the federal charter, which would allow her to set it aside for five years, but she's already said she wouldn't do that.

Instead of proposing a generous society, open to the world, this is how Marois sees a sovereign Quebec. Her national project is narrow, parochial and bigoted.

Quite apart from the odious and offensive nature of her values charter, it exposes Quebec to derision and ridicule on the national and world stage.

Naheed Nenshi, the popular Muslim mayor of Calgary, invited anyone who had an issue with the Quebec values charter to move there. An Oshawa hospital, recruiting McGill med students, put up an ad of a young woman doctor wearing headgear, saying it wanted what was in her head, not what was on it. In Britain, the *Guardian* website ran the Quebec government's pictographs of what was acceptable to wear to work and what was not. "Almost Monty Pythonesque in its absurdity," as Employment Minister Jason Kenney aptly put it.

If this weren't so serious, it would be hilarious. It will be permissible to wear a small cross on a necklace but not a large one. The Star of David will be allowed on a ring, not something you see every day, as will the Muslim crescent on earrings. But turbans, hijabs and yarmulkes will not be permitted.

Previously, Marois proposed Bill 14, amending Bill 101 to end the bilingual status of municipalities whose non-francophone population fell below 50 per cent. Small businesses with 26 or more employees would have been obliged to operate in French. English-language CEGEPs would have been required to prioritize anglophone applicants, forcing francophone students into French-language CEGEPs. And so on.

Marois evidently realized she didn't have the votes to pass the bill on third reading in the minority legislature, with both the Liberals and Coalition Avenir Québec opposed to it. She may not have the votes for the charter, either, but maybe what she wants is an election on it.

She's doing identity politics, which apparently plays well outside the Montreal region, as it did for Mario Dumont in the 2007 election, and for the CAQ in the 2012 campaign. It isn't governing, it's playing to the crowd.

This is not only shameless, it's immoral. Fortunately for us all, it's also totally unconstitutional.

April 2013

A NO MANDATE MINORITY

Every government has a limited amount of political capital, and limited time in which to spend it. This is particularly the case for minority governments, and none more so than the present government of Quebec.

Pauline Marois and the Parti Québécois won the 2012 election with just 32 per cent of the popular vote and only 54 seats in the 125-member Quebec

National Assembly, nine short of a majority. The Liberals won 31 per cent of the vote and 50 seats. The Coalition Avenir Québec won 27 per cent of the vote and 18 seats.

Marois formed a government with no mandate, least of all for another referendum on sovereignty. She could not have got a referendum question adopted by the legislature.

Nor has she been able to enact her amendments to Quebec's Charter of the French Language, Bill 101. Her government's Bill 14 is being allowed to die on the order paper. It would have repealed the bilingual status of municipalities whose non-francophone population fell below 50 per cent, forced small businesses with only 26 employees to work in French, and required English-language junior colleges to admit anglophone students in preference to francophones and allophones with higher marks.

Instead, Marois has decided to spend what political equity she has on the Charter of Quebec Values, telling government employees what to wear to work in the morning.

All government workers – including municipal employees, health care and education providers – would be covered by a religious dress code that would allow small crosses but not large ones on necklaces, while banning yarmulkes, turbans and hijabs.

Municipalities, hospitals and post-secondary education institutions would have a five-year exemption. The opting out might be a renewable escape clause, according to Jean-François Lisée, the minister responsible for the Montreal region, home to most of Quebec's non-francophone and multicultural residents.

There's broad support for the proposition of a secular state. The dress code, complete with pictographs of what's permissible and what isn't, is another matter. It's racial profiling, pure and simple.

If Marois was looking for a channel changer, she certainly got one. No one in Quebec is talking about the economy, and how Quebec lost 5,000 jobs last month, and more than 30,000 the month before that. Quebec's unemployment rate of 7.9 per cent is nearly a full point above the national average of 7.1 per cent. In the context of the charter debate, no new jobs will be created in Quebec. Why would anyone move there, or locate a new business in such an inhospitable place?

The proposed dress code is clearly unconstitutional – Article 2 of the Canadian Charter of Rights and Freedoms in the 1982 Constitution Act entrenches freedom of conscience and religion, as well as freedom of speech and association. So does the 1975 Quebec Charter of Rights, in identical words. Marois has evidently received this opinion from her own legal advisers, but decided to play the identity card anyway.

What's interesting is the lack of third-party endorsements from the sovereignty camp, especially among the progressive left in the Montreal area. In just a week since its release, support for a charter of values dropped from 57 per cent to 43 per cent in one poll, with 42 per cent opposed.

To say nothing of the vocal opposition from everyone else. All 15 municipalities on the island of Montreal oppose the charter. As do the Jewish General Hospital and the McGill University Health Centre. As does McGill itself. Not to mention other stakeholders.

And within the sovereignty family the charter has created a split among the separatist cousins, the Bloc Québécois' Marie Mourani, the only Bloc MP from Montreal, was expelled from caucus and then quit the party for opposing the charter. She's a member of Montreal's large Lebanese community. So much for sovereignist outreach to multicultural communities. Even Québec solidaire, a pro-sovereignty movement with two MNAs from Montreal, is uncomfortable with the charter. It's no mystery – both MNAs are from ridings with significant multicultural populations.

If Marois is seeking to polarize voters, and marginalize third party support for the CAQ, she may succeed to that extent. But she has also introduced a profoundly divisive question. And she is proposing a solution to a problem that doesn't exist. And so far as that goes, she is spending what little political capital she has for nothing.

September 2013

WHAT NUMBER FOR SOVEREIGNTY?

The Quebec referendum of October 30, 1995 was a very close call for Canada, with political ramifications that resonate to this day.

Ottawa joining the legal challenge to Quebec's Bill 99, affirming a 50 per cent plus one vote enough to declare independence, is the latest echo.

The referendum, on this day 18 years ago, was a one-point game, with the no side prevailing by 50.58 to 49.42 per cent. Had only 27,000 votes gone the other way, we might have lost our country. Jacques Parizeau had made it very clear that in the event of no negotiations for a partnership with Canada, he would unilaterally declare Quebec's independence.

As a result, the Chrétien government referred the whole secession question to the Supreme Court, which in 1998 ruled that there must be a clear majority to a clear question, in which case Ottawa would be obliged to negotiate the break-up of the country.

Bill 99 was Quebec's response in 2000 to the Clarity Act, which implemented the Supreme Court judgment. English-rights activist Keith Henderson then filed a legal challenge, which has been in limbo for 13 years. But the challenge will finally be heard in Quebec Superior Court, and the news that Ottawa quietly joined the case, two weeks ago, set off a fire storm.

Quebec Intergovernmental Affairs Minister Alexandre Cloutier called a rare Sunday morning news conference to denounce the "direct" and "devious" attack on Quebecers' right to determine their future.

Predictably, all parties in the National Assembly approved a motion supporting Bill 99, although the Liberals reminded the legislature that Jean Charest had warned, back in the day, it would be susceptible to a constitutional challenge that could weaken Quebec.

In the midst of all this noise, Denis Lebel had the misfortune to be in Montreal for a speech, around which he had some media interviews. Since he is minister of intergovernmental affairs and Stephen Harper's Quebec lieutenant, the radio and TV hosts wanted to know whether he thought 50 per cent plus one was enough. He tried to avoid the question in one interview, but when the host persisted, he finally replied: "We've always said we'd leave that to Quebecers, but, yes, it is for me."

The words were scarcely out of his mouth before Canadian Press filed the following lead: "A split has emerged in the Harper government over a fundamental principle: the rules governing the potential breakup of Canada."

Lebel's seatmate in the House of Commons, Prime Minister Harper, had a different interpretation when it came up in question period the following day.

"The fact of the matter is we believe, on this side, that debates on the process for dividing the country are best left to the courts," he said. "Everybody on this side, including the minister of intergovernmental affairs, is an unconditional supporter of the unity of this country. I believe that Quebecers, as much as anyone else, do not want another referendum. They do not want to be arguing about this. They want to be taking this country, united together, forward into the future."

Lebel's office then issued a terse statement: "The federal government did not initiate these proceedings. No one wants another referendum. It is completely normal for the federal government to defend Canadian law. As the case is before the courts, we will have no further comment."

For their part, the NDP were delighted by Lebel's quotes, which they gleefully shared with parliamentary media. Their position, since the Sherbrooke Declaration of 2005, has been clearly in favour of 50 per cent plus one being enough. Tom Mulcair added a nuance last winter when he added that the NDP would make sure the question was a clear one.

But from the time of the 1980 referendum, there has been consensus among all parties in Quebec on two points. First, the question would be written by the National Assembly. Second, 50 per cent plus one would be enough.

The Supreme Court ruling and the Clarity Act changed that, which is what brought on Bill 99 in the first place.

No one wants another referendum any time soon. The last one was a bruising experience, that saw broken friendships and bitterly divided families.

Both the 1980 referendum on sovereignty association, and the 1995 referendum on an economic partnership with Canada, were ambiguous questions.

A clear question, as the Liberals reminded the Parti Québécois in the legislature, would be along the lines of next September's Scottish referendum: "Should Scotland be an independent country."

Absent a PQ majority in the next election, there will be no referendum in the foreseeable future. And no election before next spring, either. Pauline Marois ruled that out last weekend. After using the proposed Charter of Quebec values as a wedge issue with rural voters, the PQ was still four points behind the Liberals, 38–34, in a CROP poll last week.

There's no majority, and no referendum, in numbers like that.

October 2013

12

THE 2014 QUEBEC ELECTION

THE PKP EFFECT

From a fist pump calling "to make Quebec a country," to being shoved aside by his own leader at a news conference, Pierre Karl Péladeau's coming out as a Parti Québécois candidate dominated the campaign's first week.

But not in the way the PQ was hoping for when it recruited the media magnate as a star candidate in St. Jérôme, where his opening statement on independence became the sound bite of the week.

At least it was until Thursday, when it was twinned with "*le shove*," with PQ leader Pauline Marois gently pushing him aside at a news conference where a reporter from one of his own Quebecor papers asked him about a possible conflict of interest from another division of his company doing $13 million a year of IT work for the government.

"I'll answer that," said Marois, as she pushed him away from the podium.

"*Le shove*" went viral on social media and led all the French-language '"' newscasts for the rest of the day, playing on into the weekend. On its flagship news program, *Le Teléjournal*, Radio-Canada showed it several times off the top. By Friday, Péladeau was no longer campaigning with Marois, but instead attracted a small group of demonstrators to a lightly attended event in Quebec City. On Saturday, as he was putting up posters in his riding, a woman on a sidewalk was yelling at him.

The angry shout out at Péladeau marked the end of a very bad week for him and Marois, one in which the PQ was knocked completely off message and unable to get back on track.

After Péladeau's fist-pumping for sovereignty, he gave a Q&A to *La Presse on* Monday in which he said: "The independence of Quebec is a must. A people, a nation, has a legitimate right to become a country."

Péladeau's opening and subsequent declarations about making Quebec a country had the immediate effect of transforming the campaign into a referendum on a referendum. A Léger poll in the Quebec City region, taken Monday and Tuesday, showed the Liberals ahead of the PQ by 39–32 per cent, where the previous week the red team had led by only 32–31 per cent.

The Liberal surge, in a region that's at least 95 per cent French-speaking, was directly attributable to the fist pump moment.

A province-wide Léger poll for *Le Devoir* showed the PQ and Liberals tied at 37 per cent. Where the PQ previously enjoyed a 44–22 lead among francophone voters, the weekend Léger poll, conducted Tuesday through Thursday, showed the Liberals closing the gap to 17 points, 44 to 27 per cent.

Where the PQ entered the campaign comfortably in majority territory, they ended the week back where they were in the legislature, in minority land.

In other words, Péladeau's statements about independence have polarized the campaign, firming up the Liberal vote at the expense of François Legault and the Coalition Avenir Québec, which Léger polled at only 14-per cent.

All of Péladeau's talk about sovereignty, and ethical questions on whether he should sell his Quebecor stock, followed him and Marois around all week. There was also the underlying issue of a free press, and reporters were not rolling over for Marois or Péladeau, least of all those from his own TVA network and Quebecor tabloids.

In response to persistent questioning, Marois ended up musing there would be no borders and no tolls in an independent Quebec. Quebecers would still be able to visit the Rockies and the beaches of Prince Edward Island.

Quebec would use the Canadian dollar as it currency, she later said and would ask for a seat on the board of the Bank of Canada. Nothing prevents Quebec from adopting the loonie. As Jacques Parizeau once said during a debate on the dollar with Robert Bourassa in the 1980 referendum: "You'll still have the queen on your dollar for a few more years."

The debate on the dollar is the Groundhog Day moment of this campaign. Marois ignores the fact that a country's control of monetary policy is a fundamental attribute of sovereignty.

Wait until the media ask Marois if an independent Quebec would have automatic membership in the North American Free Trade Agreement. The advice to then-U.S. President Bill Clinton at the time of the 1995 referendum, just released by the Clinton Library, was that "nothing is automatic." In fact, there is no succession clause in the NAFTA, so it's not clear how and when Quebec would join NAFTA.

No one would be surprised if Marois said an independent Quebec would continue to receive equalization payments from Ottawa. But apparently, she doesn't even know how much that is. In a fun quiz of the leaders published on Friday, *La Presse* asked a multiple choice question of whether the amount of equalization was $5.1 billion, $9.3 billion, $16.8 billion or $22.1 billion. Liberal leader Philippe Couillard got it right at $9.3 billion, while Marois got it wrong at $16.6 billion. Which is only a $7.5 billion miss in her fiscal framework.

Confronted with more questions about sovereignty on Thursday, Marois said the media could ask as many questions as they wanted, but she wouldn't answer them. "We are in an election campaign," she said dismissively. "We are not in a campaign for the future of Quebec."

Well, it's a little late for that. And then came *"le shove."*

March 2014

THE GAME CHANGER

There's no doubt that Pierre-Karl Péladeau could be a game changer in the Quebec election, but not in the sense Pauline Marois had in mind when she recruited him as a star candidate for the Parti Québécois.

One thing is certain – it will be all about him. It already has been since Sunday's announcement of his candidacy Saint-Jérôme. Making a clenched fist as he looked into the cameras, Péladeau declared his goal "to make Quebec a country."

Well, if sovereignty and the prospect of another referendum weren't on the ballot last week, they certainly are this week. Liberal leader Philippe Couillard now has the perfect pretext to campaign flat out against another referendum.

Speaking of which, Péladeau told Radio-Canada Monday that the 1995 referendum "was stolen, pure and simple," by the No side.

That would be the referendum won by the No by a margin of 50.6 to 49.4 per cent. The winning margin was 54,000 votes. If 27,000 votes had gone the other way, Canada would have been lost. As it was, thousands of votes were disqualified in federalist strongholds such as Chomedey. You could ask Tom Mulcair about that – he was the MNA for that riding at the time. He might actually agree with PKP about the referendum almost being stolen, but by the Yes side.

There are people voting in this election who weren't born in 1995, but the memories linger of broken friendships and divided families. Thanks for reminding us of that, PKP. Campaigning with Marois on Monday, Péladeau was asked if he would sell his controlling shares in Quebecor, if ordered to do so by Quebec's ethics commissioner.

"I have no intention of selling my shares," said Péladeau, who has said he'll place his shares in a blind trust. So he'd still be the controlling shareholder, with 28 per cent of Quebecor shares and 74 per cent of the voting rights. This position is firm, he said, "and won't change." He said he wanted to make sure Quebecor's head office remained in Quebec. As if it's moving to Toronto anytime soon.

But Marois later said at a news conference with Péladeau he'd have to abide by whatever the ethics commissioner decides. Péladeau later put out a statement saying he would respect "the law, and the code of ethics and conduct of the National Assembly."

So there wouldn't be two laws, one for Péladeau, and one for everyone else. Péladeau's day wasn't over. He gave a Q&A to *La Presse*, whose reporter asked very leading questions about whether he "might play a role similar (to that of Lucien Bouchard) if there were another referendum."

Péladeau allowed as how "it might be interesting to note what my CV can offer" but it would be up to the premier to determine his role. The headline over the story: "Péladeau, negotiator for Quebec?" The front page headline was even more startling: "A CV to negotiate with Ottawa."

Asked whether independence would be advantageous to the economy, Péladeau replied: "The independence of Quebec is a must. A people, a nation has a legitimate right to become a country."

As for the economy: "It will be advantageous in the sense that we could have all the powers and attributes of a state, that power wouldn't be shared between two orders of government, between the federal government and Quebec."

Speaking to other reporters about the strong pro-Canadian bias of his Sun newspaper and TV properties, Péladeau allowed: "I've always been a sovereignist and I will remain one. But business is business."

The fact is that Péladeau, as head of Quebecor, has been very good at playing both sides of the street.

At the launch of Sun TV in 2010, he said in Toronto: "This is a great day for Canada." Dubbed Fox News North, Sun has struggled in remote channels on the TV spectrum, while Péladeau campaigned for must-carry status with the Canadian Radio-television and Telecommunications Commission.

But otherwise, Quebecor has done very well in federal jurisdiction. Its Videotron cable and Internet unit is a licence to print money. And through Videotron, Quebecor emerged last month as the fourth player after the Big Three of Rogers, Bell, and Telus in the federal wireless spectrum auction. In the event of Quebec independence, would Quebecor still be a Canadian company?

It's too soon to measure Péladeau's impact on the campaign. But this much is evident – he's certain to drive some trade union votes from the PQ to Québec solidaire. He ran lockouts, hired scabs and broke the unions at his Quebec tabloids. Québec solidaire co-leader Françoise David called his candidacy "a gift."

The race is now as unpredictable as Péladeau himself.

March 2014

∽

THE REFERENDUM STRAITJACKET

Pauline Marois is in a political straightjacket, and there seems no way out of it.

One arm is in a sleeve that says two-thirds of Quebecers in a CROP poll don't want another referendum on independence. Her other arm is in a sleeve that says two-thirds of Quebecers think there will be another referendum if the Parti Québécois wins a majority on April 7.

In others words, she has a trust deficit that can't be erased on what has become the ballot question of a campaign that's been transformed into a referendum on a referendum.

She did her best to talk her way around it in last Thursday's debate, and failed to take the referendum question off the table. At one point, she said there would be no referendum "as long as Quebecers are not ready." At another, she said there would be no referendum "as long as Quebecers don't want one." She was trying to talk down a referendum without demobilizing her base.

In a CBC/Radio-Canada Vote Compass with more than 5,000 participants at the network's websites, 33 per cent said Liberal leader Philippe Couillard won the debate, to 22 per cent who said Marois won. Couillard also won every demographic group and every region of the province.

The next day, Marois appeared at her daily media availability with star candidate Pierre Karl Péladeau and Bernard Drainville, the minister responsible for the PQ's charter of secular values. The entire half hour of questions was about the referendum. At one point Péladeau was asked if he would see a sovereign Quebec in his lifetime. He sheepishly replied that he was there to talk about the economy.

This was a far cry from the Péladeau who, in his debut appearance on March 9, pumped his fist and declared his political purpose was "to make a country."

Overnight, the campaign was transformed into a referendum election, not unlike the free trade election of 1988. The fist pump is one of two indelible images of the campaign. The other one is *"le shove"* which came just four days later, with Marois pushing Péladeau away from the podium, saying "I'll take this" in response to a question about whether the media mogul was in a conflict of interest in one of his IT companies having millions of dollars in government contracts.

The damage from the fist pump was compounded in the early going by Marois musing that an independent Quebec would have no borders with Canada, that Quebecers could retain their Canadian passports, and that Quebec would use the loonie and ask for a seat on the board of the Bank of Canada.

Ever since *"le shove,"* the PQ has tried every day to change the channel from the referendum issue, without any success whatsoever.

On the economy and Quebec's fiscal framework, the PQ doesn't have a very good narrative, with unemployment spiking from 7.5 to 7.8 per cent in February, with 25,500 jobs lost in a single month. On the fiscal framework, Quebec continues to run deficits, with a provincial debt of $175 billion, nearly 50 per cent of GDP.

Couillard has recruited three senior bank economists as the face of his economic team, and on Saturday, they were all under attack by Péladeau. "How many jobs have economists created?" he asked. "They publish studies, they fly around to international conferences. But that creates how many jobs? Zero."

His own newspaper, *Le Journal de Montréal,* pointed out in a big headline that he overlooked Finance Minister Nicolas Marceau, an economist from Université de Montréal. Oops!

When the pivot to the economy didn't work, Marois turned her sights on Couillard, with personal attacks on his character and integrity, citing his past association with Dr. Arthur Porter, the ousted head of the McGill University Health Centre, now in a Panamanian jail. That just raised questions about her husband, Claude Blanchet, and his dealings with labour leaders whose names have up at the Charbonneau Commission on corruption in the Quebec construction industry.

It's a safe bet that is why she didn't go there in the debate.

When casting aspersion on Couillard's character failed her, Marois played the corruption card, saying he was the inheritor of the failed legacy of Jean Charest, whose name has been mentioned so many times in the last week you'd think he was still leading the Liberals. Which is what Marois wants voters to think.

"There's nothing more distressing than watching a general re-fight the last war," Couillard replied on Sunday. "I proudly carry the heritage of the Quebec Liberal Party. It's the entire heritage that I carry." As for Charest: "He traversed the financial crisis in a very elegant manner."

Finally over the weekend, Marois and the PQ jumped all over a story in Saturday's *Le Devoir* alleging vote fraud by anglophone and other non-francophone students from other provinces trying to get on the voters list.

"We don't want this election stolen by people from Ontario and the rest of Canada," Justice Minister Bertrand St. Arnaud said Sunday. It turns out to be nothing of the sort. Canadian citizens can vote in Quebec elections after living there for six months – we're at the end of the seventh month of the school year. They also need to declare an intention to live in Quebec permanently. There's no fraud, and no sign of anything more than students becoming politically engaged and seeking their lawful right to vote. They're worried about a referendum, too.

This is what it's come down to for the PQ – accusing McGill and Concordia students of trying to steal the election, when the Péquistes are losing it all on their own.

March 2014

PASSING THE ELECTION TEST

An election campaign is a test of a leader's readiness and ability to govern. And no one can say that Philippe Couillard hasn't been tested in the campaign that ends with next Monday's Quebec election.

The Liberal leader has been tested on his character, integrity, ethics, and personal finances, not to mention his commitment to the French language, culture and identity of Quebec.

Has Couillard been surprised by the personal nature of the attacks?

"No, I was expecting it," he said in a conversation between events the other day. "I'm answering all those questions."

For example, Parti Québécois leader Pauline Marois suggested that Couillard "is truly a risk to our language and culture. When he speaks about language it is to bilingualize Quebec." Of course, Couillard said nothing of the sort, only that bilingualism "is a fantastic asset in life. And it goes the other way, for English-speaking kids to be bilingual in French is a fantastic asset."

He's not wrong about that, even if it isn't politically correct to say so. He added: "Mme. Marois has no lessons to teach anyone in Quebec about patriotism."

This has been the revelation about Couillard in this campaign, that he's able to stand in and give as good as he gets. It helps that he went in with low expectations that he has significantly outperformed.

It isn't just that Couillard knows his files – he's scary smart. But he's also learned how to handle the media, and along the way he's developed a retail game.

And this comes from where he's been for the last year and a half on the road, out of view of the major media outlets and the Quebec press gallery.

"People would keep asking, where is he?" Couillard says. "I was travelling constantly in the regions, meeting people and listening to them."

A lot of what he heard back is reflected in the Liberal program, on everything from forestry to housing. But it's hardly apparent in the coverage of the campaign, which focused in the first half on sovereignty and in the second half on ethics and identity.

For Couillard, the ballot question remains a referendum on a referendum. "The PQ always brings it back to the forefront. It's always about *le pays*. They keep bringing it back." That's certainly what Pierre Karl Péladeau was doing when he announced his candidacy for the PQ with his famous fist pump and call "to make Quebec a country." It's what Marois was doing in response to questions about borders, passports and the Canadian dollar.

Not to mention, Couillard agrees, access to the North American Free Trade Agreement. "The same goes," he adds, "for the Canada-Europe Trade Agreement and eventually, the Trans-Pacific Partnership."

Couillard notes there is neither an accession nor a succession clause in the NAFTA, which was negotiated between Canada, the U.S. and Mexico.

Marois has accused Couillard of running "a fear campaign" on a referendum, but as he says about the PQ, "they keep bringing it up."

At the end of the day, this comes down to whether voters trust a PQ majority government not to hold a referendum.

"It's the usual PQ scenario, that this is not about a referendum but about electing a government," Couillard says. "I just want to call their bluff. This has to be clarified."

It is, he says, a question of trust.

"I keep asking people, 'do you trust her?'" he says. "They say no."

And as he points out, "Article one of the PQ platform is fundamental" on accession to sovereignty.

As the PQ took hits on the referendum issue, they tried to change the channel to integrity and identity. Couillard's integrity and Quebec's identity.

Marois suggested his onetime association with Dr. Arthur Porter, the discredited head of the McGill University Health Centre, was proof of Couillard's bad judgment and showed him unfit to govern. As if Couillard was the only person ever conned by Porter. Couillard's offshore RBC account in Jersey, while he was working in Saudi Arabia, also became an issue last week, when it was perfectly legal and legitimate all along.

In addition to a charter of secular values, Marois proposed to update the Charter of the French Language "for the 21st century," which Couillard says is unnecessary.

"Even more coercion, more negative measures," he says, "when immigrants already accept French as their common language."

As the campaign comes to a close, Couillard is clearly enjoying the test.

"I'm strong, I'm in good shape," he says. "The campaign is 33 days. I look at it as 33 one-day campaigns. We have to win every day."

April 2014

COUILLARD: CHARACTER AND CONVICTION

There are two things to understand about Philippe Couillard. One is character and the other is conviction.

It says a lot about his character that he chose to run in Roberval, a remote Saguenay riding on the western shore of Lac-St-Jean. Hard to get to, and hard to win for any Liberal. But for Couillard, it was home, and he felt he had to go home.

He promised to spend one day a week of the campaign there, and he kept his word. He also had a secret weapon on the ground – his wife, Suzanne Pilot. The reason she was never in the shot on his tour was that she spent the entire campaign in Roberval.

On Monday night, Couillard won Roberval by 22 points over Denis Trottier of the Parti Québécois, who had won the seat by 18 points in 2012. Couillard went home, and offered voters a premier. And they voted massively for a favourite son. It would have been so much easier for him to keep the safe Liberal seat of Outremont, which he won in last December's byelection. This says something very important about Couillard – he knows who he is, and where he comes from. He's authentic.

Then, he is a federalist by conviction, not by convenience. This isn't to say he won't be a strong defender of Quebec's interests within the Canadian federation. If you want to talk about Senate reform, First Nations issues, or building energy pipelines, he'll be at the meeting, but he'll also advocate for Quebec's distinctive role within Canada.

And his vision of Quebec is one in which French is the common language and culture, but recognizes the contribution of anglophones and allophones in a tolerant society that is open to the world. He represents a Quebec that is comfortable in its own skin, and confident of its ability to compete in a global economy.

This is the polar opposite of the paranoid, xenophobic charter of secular values proposed by the PQ. On Monday, Quebecers rejected the charter for what it was – divisive and despicable.

When PQ leader Pauline Marois also proposed a "new Charter of the French Language for the 21st century," Couillard waved it off as "even more coercion." The issue in promoting French, he said, is persuading "newcomers to accept French as the common language of Quebecers." He added there wasn't a parent, francophone or non-francophone, who didn't want their kids to be bilingual, and didn't recognize the advantage of it.

This is what the PQ didn't understand – the diversity and sophistication of modern Quebec. All they had to do was ride the number 24 bus down Sherbrooke Street, and listen to students conversing effortlessly back and forth from French to English and other languages. They live in a BlackBerry, iPad world, posting in unregulated social media.

There was a very revealing demographic in the Léger Marketing polls in this campaign. The only age group the PQ led was 55–64 years olds. These were voters of a certain age, old enough to be nostalgic for the dream of a country, one which dies hard. The Liberals led every other demo, not just seniors over 65. They led the 25 to 34, 35–44 and 45–54 demos by an average of 10 points. This is the middle class demo, the people with kids, mortgages and car payments. And they led the youth emo, the 18–24 year olds, by 2-1 in the last poll. Those are the kids on the number 24 bus.

Not only do they have no interest in the PQ's sovereignty project, they didn't like the charter, because those kids in kippas, scarves and hijabs are their friends.

But even more than the charter, voters rejected the prospect of another referendum under a PQ majority government. This was the other key metric in the polls. A CROP poll found two thirds of Quebecers didn't want another referendum, but two-thirds thought there would be one if the PQ won a majority.

Quebecers hadn't really thought about it until Pierre Karl Péladeau famously pumped his fist and called "to make Quebec a country." His statement was written by Marois' former speechwriter, Stéphane Gobeil, and approved by the PQ leader. What they didn't know about was the fist pump, which became the defining image of the campaign, with Marois in the shot smiling and leading the applause as he said it.

In that moment, the election was transformed into a referendum on a referendum, which Quebecers didn't trust her not to hold. She spent the next three days musing about borders, passports and using the Canadian dollar. Then came "*le shove*," when she decided to take a question directed at Péladeau.

By then, Quebecers had decided that if this was going to be a referendum on a referendum, they would settle this themselves. Once and for all. Or at least, for our lifetime.

April 2014

POSTCRIPT: GOODBYE PKP

In business, politics and his personal life, Pierre Karl Péladeau has always been an impulsive and mercurial figure, ruled by his emotions.

Never was this more apparent than in his hastily called news conference to announce his resignation as Parti Québécois leader Monday afternoon, at which he fought back tears the whole time while explaining he was "forced to make an agonizing choice between my family and my project" of sovereignty and "I chose my family."

What brought that on? Well, like most Quebecers on Sunday night, he watched *Tout le monde en parle,* the wildly popular Radio-Canada talk show. The special guest was his recently estranged wife Julie Snyder, a star on his Quebecor-owned TVA network, and she disclosed they were in a difficult divorce mediation including custody and visitation over their two young children, their 10-year old son and 7-year old daughter. Péladeau also has a teen-aged daughter from a previous marriage.

They were married in a celebrity wedding in Quebec City just last August, but separated less than six months later in January. "We wanted to re-build our family nest, our team," Snyder told TLMEP. "We worked a long time on couple's therapy. My references, my horizons, my country, was Pierre Karl."

Péladeau was evidently devastated by the interview and decided, then and there, that he was quitting politics after less than a year as PQ leader.

The next morning, he went to PQ headquarters in Montreal, informed the staff of his decision, and had them schedule a lunch-hour conference call with the party caucus. Péladeau was apparently extremely emotional on the call, recalling how he and his siblings had been negatively marked by an absent father, Pierre Péladeau, the founder of the tabloid newspaper chain that became the Quebecor media empire.

Péladeau remains Quebecor's controlling shareholder through his multiple-voting shares, but his relationship with the company has been essentially arms-length since his election to the legislature in 2014, and particularly since his accession to the PQ leadership last May. While he pledged to put his shares into a blind trust, he never did.

The Quebecor board happened to be meeting in Montreal Monday and the company put out a statement that it learned of his resignation the same way everyone else did, and offered its support on his personal crisis.

Under CEO Pierre Dion and non-executive chair Brian Mulroney, Quebecor's share price has appreciated by nearly one-third since Péladeau left the company two years ago. Quebecor sold its tabloid Sun newspaper division to Postmedia last year, and closed its money-losing Sun TV, which proved to be a cable news channel without an audience. For an avowed separatist, Péladeau has done very well in federally regulated business space – TVA dominates the Quebec ratings, the Videotron cable division is a highly profitable business, and its wireless network is well positioned for growth.

There is no need for Péladeau to rush back to the office. The business has been running very well without him. He is free to focus full time on his children and family issues.

As for his political legacy, it is certain to be remarkably thin. From the moment he became a PQ candidate in the 2014 campaign, Péladeau has been an incredibly polarizing figure. His opening news conference was a devastating reversal of fortune for the PQ in a single ten-second sound-bite. He said his goal was "to make Quebec a country." And he famously pumped his fist while saying it. The fist-pump became the indelible image and the soundbite the defining moment of the campaign.

Leading in the polls at the start of the campaign, the PQ went into a free fall from which it never recovered. In overnight polling in the Quebec City region that night, the PQ plummeted 10 points. The election was transformed into a referendum on another referendum, something Quebecers had no desire to live through again. Pauline Marois found herself hounded on questions such as a monetary union, seats on the board of the Bank of Canada, borders with Canada and whether Quebecers would continue to carry Canadian passports. For the PQ, leading in the polls at the outset of the election, the campaign was an unrelieved disaster, and it began with PKP's fist-pump.

If the Liberals and Premier Philippe Couillard had every reason to be grateful then, they may be sorry to see the back of him now. As PQ leader, he proved to be a gift that kept on giving to the Liberals and would have been an insurance policy for the federalists in the 2018 election.

The Liberals have had a terrible winter, dogged by a campaign finance scandal left over from the Charest years. It just so happened that the police anti-corruption squad made arrests on the same day as Couillard's budget. That pretty much sums up the spring session of the legislature for the Liberals. But Péladeau was getting no traction in the polls. A CROP poll last week put the Liberals in front at 33 per cent, the PQ at 26 per cent, and Coalition Avenir Québec of François Legault closing fast at 25 per cent.

Péladeau's departure gives the PQ an opportunity to move on from the aging cohort of hardline separatists, or at least to turn the page of generational change. Several MNAs' names are already in the mix: Alexandre Cloutier, who finished second to Péladeau last year, is only 38. Véronique Hivon, who steered Quebec's delicate assisted dying debate, is just 46. Martine Ouellet, a stalwart of the party's left wing, is 47. They belong to the echo generation, the children of the baby boomers.

But the PQ has long been torn between sovereignist, socialist and trade unionist factions, making it what Lucien Bouchard once scornfully called "this ungovernable party." Those centrifugal forces will soon be in play again.

And once again, the Liberals and Couillard will have Péladeau to thank.

May 2016

THE NIGHT QUEBEC CHANGED EVERYTHING

Forty years ago, on November 15, 1976, René Lévesque and the Parti Québécois were elected as Quebec's first separatist government, and everything in Canada changed overnight.

Two generations later, we're still dealing with the consequences of that event.

In Montreal that night, Lévesque took the stage at the Paul Sauvé Arena as the crowd went wild.

"I never thought I would be so proud to be a Quebecer as tonight," Lévesque declared. The audience, numbered in the thousands, chanted: "Le Québec aux Québécois!"

Lévesque spoke of Quebec as "le pays," triggering another delirious response. But then he moved to calm the crowd, and pledged "to work with our fellow citizens of Canada."

And he solemnly reiterated his campaign pledge that sovereignty would be achieved "only by a clear majority in a referendum, as we have promised."

That was Lévesque – he was at once a political provocateur and a calming influence. Two daring steps forward and one cautious step back. That night, he perfectly personified both Quebecers' aspirations and reservations about the sovereignty project and the prospects of a PQ government.

It was the dawn of a tumultuous era, leading to the 1980 Quebec referendum, the 1981 patriation of the Constitution with the Charter of Rights, the 1987 Meech Lake Accord, the 1992 Charlottetown Accord and the 1995 Quebec referendum, which – partly as payback for the death of Meech in 1990 – came within 1.2 percentage points of costing us our country.

And it all began that November night, exactly 40 years ago. Quebec and Canada have since been re-defined in ways no one could have foreseen back then.

The tumult and turmoil divided francophone families around Christmas, Easter and Thanksgiving dinner tables for decades. And it drove non-francophones to vote with their feet.

In 1977 alone, 46,000 people left Quebec and more than 125,000 had left by 1981, according to a 2015 report by the Fraser Institute. It was called "going down the 401." Residential real estate prices plummeted in Montreal.

Sun Life, whose landmark Montreal head office was once the tallest building in the Commonwealth, abruptly packed up and moved to Toronto. The Royal Bank and Bank of Montreal had federal charters that required their head offices to be in Montreal, but they increasingly moved their operating headquarters to Bay Street. The impressive bank towers of the famous Toronto skyline, and the city's unquestioned standing as the heart of Canada's financial services industry, owe much to Lévesque and the PQ.

The Montreal business community has yet to recover from it. Quebec Inc. is fundamentally a defensive economic club.

While Lévesque was dealing with the economic consequences of his election, he was often trying to broker issues between PQ hardliners and moderate voters. He was always proudest of his 1977 campaign finance reform law (the first in Canada), which eliminated corporate and union donations and limited personal donations to $3,000 a year – unheard of in those days.

On the language issue, he was stuck with his minister Camille Laurin and Bill 101, which is controversial to this day. Its restrictive provisions on education and the language of signs, not to mention the creation of l'Office Québécois de la langue française – known to anglos as the "language police" – remain objects of division and derision four decades later.

But Lévesque always defended them, and on Bill 101 pleaded with non-francophones to "give it a chance." Those were his exact words at a synagogue in the West End of Montreal in 1977. You had to admire his courage in going to such a hostile venue, and the audience listened with respect and even a certain amount of affection. No one disliked René Lévesque.

When the referendum was finally held in the spring of 1980, the question was so ambiguous, the language so tortured, it was almost laughable: 114 words in French, 107 in English. It wasn't even a mandate question – it was a mandate question for a mandate question, promising there would be no declaration on sovereignty-association without a second referendum.

Looking back, what seems most remarkable to me about that referendum season is how both sides were represented by great political actors – Lévesque and Pierre Trudeau. They were worthy proponents and great champions. Those of us who were there realized what a privilege it was to cover them.

Without Lévesque, the PQ wouldn't have gotten as far as it had. Without Trudeau, who personified the pride of the Canadian option, Lévesque's side would not have lost by a 60–40 margin. Quebecers were deeply proud of them both.

In the Paul Sauvé Arena, home ice for the PQ, Trudeau and Lévesque both delivered historic speeches in the 1980 referendum campaign. On May 14, six days before the vote, Trudeau gave his famous "Elliott speech" – his answer to Lévesque's taunt that he was not a real Quebecer because of his mother's family name.

"Of course my name is Pierre Elliott Trudeau," he declared. "Elliott était le nom de ma mère, voyez-vous?"

The audience – which had been yelling "Trudeau! Trudeau!" – responded by chanting "Elliott! Elliott!"

On May 20, Lévesque stood on the same stage after his crushing loss and reached out to thank the crowd for their cheers and applause. "If I've understood you well, what you're saying is, 'Until the next time.'"

He added: "It's clear that the ball has just been returned to the federalist court. Quebecers have given them another chance. It's up to them to put content into the promises they've made in the last 35 days." Trudeau put another kind of content into his 1981 constitutional package – but that's part of the narrative that continues today.

And then everyone went home, peacefully. There wasn't a street blocked by protesters, a rock thrown or a window broken in Montreal that night. And it was in some measure due to the exceptional leadership on both sides – two charismatic and socially responsible leaders who represented the best of both options.

The day after the 1976 election, the *Montreal Gazette* published the most famous Canadian political cartoon of the modern era – Aislin's Lévesque, with Robert Bourassa, saying: "OK, everybody take a Valium."

Terry Mosher recalls that evening, taking a drawing without a caption into an editorial board meeting where everyone in the room was stunned by the early results pointing to a possible PQ win.

"I thought I should give them all a Valium," he recalled, as he showed them the two heads with no words. And then he went back to the studio and drew the words that became so famous.

To this day it remains, by his own assessment, Aislin's most famous cartoon – perfectly framing the night that changed the course of modern Quebec and Canadian history.

November 2016

13

AMERICA

SOLOMONIC JUDGEMENT ON U.S. HEALTH CARE

For Canadians, public health care is easily understood. There are three bedrock principles. There's a single insurer: government. It's universal: everyone's covered. And it's portable: you can take it with you to another province.

There may be a shortage of doctors and nurses, there will certainly be unacceptable waiting times for elective procedures, and there is a strong case to be made for private delivery of publicly funded health care to reduce those very shortages and waiting times. Private clinics already do that outside the system.

But no politician or party in Canada, at least not one with any thought of being elected, would propose to dismantle publicly funded and delivered health care as the centrepiece of a caring and compassionate society.

In the United States, it's different, and incredibly confusing, as the U.S. Supreme Court has just demonstrated in its historic ruling on Barack Obama's Affordable Care Act, or Obamacare, as its opponents have derisively branded it.

On the one hand, the Supremes upheld the "mandate" requiring Americans not insured by their employee plans to buy health care insurance or face a penalty or fine. Obama's supporters insist this provision is not a tax, though the court has upheld the mandate on the grounds that it falls within the power of Congress to tax.

On the other hand, the court ruled that Obamacare cannot be justified under the commerce clause of the U.S. Constitution, which has for nearly two centuries been used to expand federal spending power. This is a huge issue, that goes to the division of powers in a federal state, one with which we are very familiar in Canada.

Both parts of the decision were decided by a 5–4 vote, and in both instances the swing vote was Chief Justice John Roberts, siding with four liberal justices to uphold the mandate, and with four conservative colleagues to assert the constitutional division of powers.

As Roberts wrote in the majority opinion on the mandate: "The requirement that certain individuals pay a financial penalty for not obtaining health insurance, may reasonably be characterized as a tax. Because the Constitution permits such a tax, it is not our role to forbid it, or to pass upon its wisdom or fairness."

But as he also wrote for the majority on limiting federal powers: "the commerce clause is not a general licence to regulate an individual from cradle to grave." This is the "broccoli" argument – that theoretically, Washington could invoke the clause regulating interstate commerce, in commodities such as food, to force America to become a vegetarian nation.

On a political level, upholding the mandate was a huge victory for Obama, especially in the run-up to November's presidential election.

He ran on health reform and won on it in 2008, and he got it passed by Congress in 2010, spending a huge amount of political capital to do so, when he probably should have been focused on digging the economy out of the Great Recession.

Obama has now succeeded where every president from Franklin Roosevelt to Bill Clinton failed, in passing public health care in a country whose reliance on private insurance has deprived millions of Americans of any coverage at all, and this in the richest country in the world. This is the signature achievement of his first term, though it is still the economy that will determine whether he receives a second one.

Whether Obamacare is good policy or not, it was supported by the voters in an election where Obama ran as the messenger of "hope and change."

And as Roberts wrote: "It is not our job to protect the people from the consequences of their own political choices."

But while a historic political victory for Obama, the ruling limiting the use of the commerce clause is probably more consequential in the legal and constitutional sense.

It is certainly more problematic in terms of setting precedent on which future cases will be argued and adjudicated.

Moreover, the court also ruled that Washington can't force the states to participate financially in expanding Medicaid, the program that provides health coverage for millions of Americans living below the poverty line. The idea was to cover the poor who would never be able to buy insurance coverage through the mandate.

So while confirming the legitimacy of Obama's health reform, the court has also affirmed a federalist principle that American conservatives have been arguing for decades. In this Solomonic judgment, Roberts is the one who divided the constitutional baby.

July 2012

NEWTOWN

At my daughter's pre K-4 school in suburban Toronto, there's a security system with a code given to parents to open the front door when dropping off their kids and picking them up.

I had been wondering if it wasn't an unnecessary precaution, but not anymore. Not after Newtown, and the loss of 20 children and six educators in the horrific school shooting in Connecticut.

This wasn't a shooting in a mall or a movie theatre or even at a university, but a slaughter of children at a K-4 grade school. A mass murder in a bucolic New England town, the sort of place that Norman Rockwell could have painted on a magazine cover.

Perhaps the unimaginable horror of this event will finally result in some federal legislative limits on guns in the United States, a country with almost as many gun shops as corner stores.

Before Newtown, Gallup reported 50 per cent of Americans were satisfied with the status quo compared with 42 per cent dissatisfied. Nearly seven Americans in 10, 69 per cent, said they had personally fired a gun. Forty-five per cent said they had a gun in their homes.

And 53 per cent, The *New York Times* reported, were opposed to bans on the sale and ownership of semi-automatic weapons "known as assault weapons."

Of course, that was before Newtown, which may prove to be a tipping point for change.

Barack Obama found his voice on this on the weekend, both as the father of two girls and as the president of the United States.

"We cannot tolerate this anymore," he said at Sunday night's prayer service in Newtown. "These tragedies must end, and to end them we must change."

The nation's first priority, he said, must be to protect its children. "I'll use whatever power this office holds to engage my fellow citizens," he said, "in an effort to prevent more tragedies like this."

Well, he does have what Theodore Roosevelt famously called "the Bully Pulpit," namely the moral authority of the office of president of the United States.

At a minimum, a ban on semiautomatics is clearly in order.

A semi-automatic was the weapon the shooter used to shatter the secure door, and kill his 26 victims, before turning one of two handguns on himself. As is well known, semiautomatics are the weapon of choice of mass murderers, not deer hunters. As for concealable handguns, they are a big part of urban crime, especially in troubled neighbourhoods.

All three weapons found at the scene of the crime in Newtown were legally registered by the shooter's mother, who became his first victim before he drove to the school.

Getting meaningful federal gun control on the books in Washington is difficult because the second amendment of the U.S. Constitution entrenches "the right to bear arms."

And that right is ruthlessly defended by the National Rifle Association, one of the most powerful lobby groups in America. Its mantra is that guns don't kill people, people kill people.

No one is saying the problem is as simple as guns, but without semi-automatics, these massacres wouldn't occur.

Mental health is another consideration. How does someone like Adam Lanza slip through the cracks in the system? Some media reported that he was mentally disturbed, and then that he had Asperger's syndrome. Asperger's is not to be confused or compared with mental illness. Rather it is an autism spectrum disorder, often afflicting gifted children at the high performance end of the spectrum. And Asperger's is not linked in any way to violent behaviour.

But mental illness is far more prevalent in society, both in the workplace and at home, than is generally known. For example, Michael Kirby's important 2006 Senate report, Out of the Shadows at Last, was the first serious parliamentary report in Canada on mental health and mental illness.

And then there's Hollywood, and the glorifying of guns and violence in action movies. Not to mention the violent video games that attract teenage boys and young men.

The media are becoming far too good, or predictable, at covering these tragic incidents. First come the reports of the shooting, then the evacuation of the survivors being reunited with their frantic families, then the appearance of the forensic experts, followed by the grief counsellors. Not to mention interviews with people who knew the shooter. He's usually described as a quiet person who kept to himself, maybe a bit of a nerd.

The second and third days feature vigils of grief, with votive candles, flowers and teddy bears. Then the funerals, this time of little girls and boys in small boxes, and the unbearable sorrow borne by their families.

Obama is right. This must stop.

December 2012

A RED LINE

"I didn't set a red line, the world set a red line. My credibility's not on the line. The international community's credibility is on the line. And America and Congress's credibility is on the line."
Barack Obama in Stockholm, September 4

Perhaps the American president was trying to put the squeeze on the international community and the U.S. Congress in his effort to build support for a limited missile strike against Syria for having used chemical weapons against its own people.

But it wasn't exactly his finest leadership moment.

After all, he's the one who said a year ago that it would be crossing "a red line" if Syrian President Basha al-Assad resorted to chemical weapons against rebel forces and civilians in a civil war that has cost more than 100,000 lives and seen at least two million refugees flee their own country.

The Syrian regime crossed that red line last month with a chemical weapons attack that, according to U.S. intelligence, left more than 1,400 dead, including at least 400 children.

Apart from the slaughter of innocents, Assad was also giving the finger to the president of the United States.

Obama was clearly planning a limited air strike, in which Britain and France were to have participated, and he obviously wanted the mission accomplished before this week's G20 summit in Russia, where host Vladimir Putin would lead opposition to any military reprisals against Syria. But then

British Prime Minister David Cameron lost an authorizing vote in the House of Commons, leaving the U.S. without the support of its most reliable ally.

Instead of going ahead with the missile strike, Obama pivoted and asked Congress for a permission slip, making the situation even more complicated.

He didn't have to do that. He didn't in 2011, when the U.S. led from the rear in the NATO air campaign that helped rebel forces oust the Gaddafi regime in Libya. Nor did Bill Clinton seek Congressional approval for the UN sanctioned bombing of Kosovo in 1999.

Congressional approval is no slam dunk, even though Obama made clear it would be a limited missile strike, with no air campaign and "no boots on the ground."

Even in the Senate, it's not clear that Obama can win the 60 votes he needs to make his resolution filibuster-proof. The degree of difficulty was evident in a vote by the Senate Foreign Relations Committee limiting missile strikes against Syria to 60 days, renewable for 30 days, and barring the use of U.S. ground forces. Without the support of leading Republican centrists such as John McCain and Lindsey Graham, Obama would lose a Senate vote, and as McCain said in supporting the president, that would be unthinkable in terms of American leadership in the world.

In the House of Representatives, a coalition of the unwilling is forming among Tea Party and isolationist Republicans, and liberal Democrats. Unlike senators with their six-year terms, members of the House face the voters every two years, and they are sensitive to war-weariness and a degree of skepticism about chemical weapons that can be traced back to the non-existent weapons of mass destruction that are part of the poisoned legacy of the Iraq war in 2003. A *Washington Post*-ABC News poll this week reported that 59 per cent of Americans are opposed to even a limited missile strike.

And then the moment Obama asked for congressional approval, the story line switched from Syria to a Washington soap opera driven by the cable news channels. All Washington all the time, the most narcissistic and dysfunctional town in the world.

Even as Obama courted congressional support, his administration was being mocked by Putin, who brazenly called U.S. Secretary of State John Kerry a liar for telling a House committee there were no Al-Qaeda units among the Syrian rebel forces. Putin has a point, which is the one of the reasons the U.S. wants to put Assad on notice without putting him out.

"They lie beautifully of course ..." Putin said on Russian TV. "Al-Qaeda units are the main military echelon, and they know this ... (Kerry) is lying and he knows he's lying. It's sad."

And then when Air Force One landed in St. Petersburg, the *New York Times* reported that "Obama was welcomed on only his second visit to Russia by the Foreign Ministry's protocol officer, the deputy regional administrator and the vice-governor of St. Petersburg." Not exactly a high-level welcome.

When the summit ended Friday, Obama had won no one over to his plan for a missile strike. The *Times* reported that "the only countries that supported Obama's plan, the Russian leader said, were France, Canada and Saudi Arabia, all nations that were on Obama's side when he arrived on Thursday."

And Canada's support is moral rather than material, except for funding of refugees. Heading back to Washington, Obama announced he would make a TV address. This has now become a test of his leadership on foreign policy. And just as with the red line, he started it.

September 2013

OBAMACARE

In the U.S. constitutional division of powers, the president proposes, the Congress disposes and the Supreme Court decides.

In 2010, Barack Obama proposed the Patient Protection and Affordable Care Act, and Congress passed it. Last year, the Supreme Court upheld Obamacare.

But the Tea Party wing of the Republican majority in the House of Representatives denied funding for Obamacare in the budget standoff with the Democratic majority in the Senate this week.

With no budget authorization, the government ran out of approved money at the end of one fiscal year, and the beginning of another. When the clock struck midnight on Tuesday, the government shut down all non-essential services, and 800,000 federal employees were sent home.

There is a protocol for shutting down the town in Washington. The first thing they do is close all national parks, beginning with the Washington Monument. Members of Congress continue to work, even though Congress is clearly not working, because they are deemed to be essential workers. It's a bit like Alice in Wonderland, at the tea party.

As the U.S. government shut down on Tuesday, registration was beginning for health care "exchanges" for 40 million Americans with no health care insurance. Even Obamacare is a long way short of the Canadian universal public health care. Most health insurance in the U.S. is still provided by employers, with elderly funded by Medicare and low income earners through Medicaid. To say that the U.S. health care system is complex is to understate the case.

But two things are clear in the budget impasse.

First, health reform is a signature piece of legislation for Obama. There is no chance that he would allow himself to be rolled on it by the Republicans.

Second, the Tea Party has broken constitutional convention in terms of the division of powers. They have provoked what amounts to a constitutional crisis.

Such is the significance of the standoff that Obama cancelled an important trip to Asia to attend the APEC summit of heads of government.

But at this point, what is playing out is essentially a Washington blame game, an Inside the Beltway version of reality TV, with Republicans and Democrats voting each other off the island.

The situation will become really serious if Congress doesn't raise the debt ceiling by October 17. If that happens, the U.S. would technically default on its debt. This is a matter involving the good faith and credit of the United States. And since the U.S. dollar is the world's reserve currency, this has implications for the global economy.

The Republican speaker of the House, John Boehner, obviously understands the gravity of the situation, but has lost control of his own caucus.

His spokesperson said Thursday: "The United States will not default on its debt, but if we're going to raise the debt limit, we need to deal with the drivers and of our debt and deficit."

In other words, Boehner is asking the White House for a deal, but he can forget about one with defunding of Obamacare. What Boehner may be looking for is a broader budget deal that includes funding for Obamacare. To do a deal with the Dems, Boehner would have to ditch the Tea Party wing of his caucus. Losing the crazies would be a good thing for the Republican brand, which has taken a big hit in this Washington impasse.

In the circumstances, the stock market hasn't been behaving all that badly. In the last 11 sessions before Friday, the Dow Jones Industrial Average has closed down nine times. While it closed under 15,000 Thursday, it was less than 3 per cent off its all-time high only two weeks ago.

Meanwhile in Ottawa, Opposition Leader Tom Mulcair demanded the House be recalled to debate the shutdown of the U.S. government and its impact on Canada.

In other words, if the House weren't prorogued until after Thanksgiving, the opposition could be grilling the government in question period.

But Mulcair isn't wrong on the substance of it. The furloughing of 800,000 workers will result in a slowdown in the U.S. economy. Unemployment of 7.3 per cent is still higher than the Canadian rate of 7.1 per cent. Any slowdown of the U.S. economy will hurt ours.

Already there's been a flight from the greenback to the loonie. And a higher Canadian dollar hurts exports. Lower exports means lower revenues at both the federal and provincial levels. Which means, among other things, it will be more difficult for Finance Minister Jim Flaherty to achieve his goal of balancing the budget by 2015.

Thanks, Washington, we needed that.

October 2013

TRUMPED

The opening weeks of the American presidential primary season are like the round robin of the world junior hockey championship – they don't decide the winner, but they do determine who gets to play in the medal round.

We're there now – from the Iowa caucuses on the first day in February, to the first-in-the-nation primary in New Hampshire the following Tuesday, to the Republican and Democratic primary and caucus dates in South Carolina and Nevada.

This is the time when the *Des Moines Register* and the *New Hampshire Union Leader* become the two most influential newspapers in America, when scholars from universities you've never heard of show up on cable news channels to explain caucusing in Iowa and independent voters in New Hampshire.

These are the two break-out states – both about 95 per cent Caucasian, with thin populations and northern geographies quite unrepresentative of the United States as a whole. If you can imagine a primary for Canadian leaders being decided by voters in, say, Yukon and Prince Edward Island, you've got a pretty good idea of how presidential campaigns start in the U.S. No country should choose its leaders this way – but that's how it's done in the most powerful democracy in the world.

This cycle to elect the 45th president of the United States is more fascinating than most in that it's the first primary and general election year since 2008 which sees neither the Democrats nor the Republicans running an incumbent president. That said, it comes down in the opening weeks to whether anyone can challenge Hillary Clinton for the Democratic nomination and whether someone – anyone – can turn back the insurgent candidacy of Donald Trump for the Republicans.

Right now, it looks like Clinton versus Trump in November. And what a show that would be, as we've seen in the exchange of insults and accusations between the two contenders in just the last week. The other day, Clinton accused Trump of having "a penchant for sexism." Trump retorted on Twitter: "Be careful Hillary as you play the war on women or women being degraded card." Trump targeted Bill Clinton directly, accusing him of "abuse of women" – a reference to the former president's history of womanizing. (Campaigning for his wife in New Hampshire, Clinton had the good sense to ignore Trump.)

Possibly more problematic for the Clinton campaign are Bill's paid speaking gigs, usually at $500,000 per speech. The *Wall Street Journal* has reported he "collected $1 million for two appearances sponsored by the Abu Dhabi government that were arranged while Mrs. Clinton was secretary of state." Abu Dhabi was then in talks with the State Department on pre-clearance of passengers on flights from its airport to the U.S.

Even Clinton faces a spirited challenge from Bernie Sanders, the socialist senator from Vermont who could well win the neighbouring state of New Hampshire. Right now, Sanders is competitive in Iowa and ahead in the polls in New Hampshire.

Sanders certainly has staked out the territory on the left; he went to New York's financial district and pledged to break up the big banks. "If a bank is too big to fail, it is too big to exist," he declared. He's calling for universal health care and cites the Canadian model as one the most successful systems in the world.

Sanders can't possibly win the Democratic nomination, of course – but if he beats Clinton in the round robin that would present a "winnability" issue for her in the medal round, where she should win easily in South Carolina and Nevada.

As for the Republicans, their run-up to the primary season has featured too many candidates in the televised debates; even after the winnowing-out process was complete, there were still nine on stage at the CNN debate in mid-December

Trump was, of course, the phenomenon nobody in the GOP establishment saw coming. Jeb Bush, the former governor of Florida, came with impeccable family and regional credentials as the successful leader of an important swing state. But eight years out of office, he's proven to be quite rusty and his campaign is mired in single digits in the polls. Senator Marco Rubio, also from Florida, represents generational change and has a compelling personal narrative as the son of Cuban immigrants. Senator Ted Cruz, from Texas, represents the hard-right edge of that same immigrant story, with an American mother and a Cuban father.

So how does Trump end up ahead of the field by double digits? Partly it's because Trump clearly doesn't care what he says – whether it's outrageous or merely offensive. Building a wall on the Mexican border a "total and complete shutdown of Muslims entering the United States" – Trump is running a xenophobic, even racist, campaign.

And it's working – in a nation of immigrants, no less. Trump is connecting with independent and undecided voters, not just as a celebrity candidate but as a sort of "anti-politician." Not content to run just against Washington, he's running against the political class itself. "How can I describe our leaders better than the word 'stupid'?" Trump asked the other day. In small-town New Hampshire, he filled a hall with 1,500 supporters, while hundreds more waited out in the cold. "We're winning big," he shouted, and the crowd cheered him on.

He's also been winning without an ad buy, relying on earned media from interviews and outbursts on social media. The Trump campaign has finally rolled out a 30-second spot in Iowa and New Hampshire in which the narrator repeats his attacks on Mexicans and Muslims and adds for good measure that he would "cut off the head of ISIS."

Trump is not going to be outflanked by Cruz on the right. In an interview with the *Washington Post*, Trump revived the question of Cruz's birth in Calgary, where his parents worked in the oil patch. Elected to the Senate in 2012, he was a dual citizen until 2014, when he renounced his Canadian citizenship. The U.S. constitution stipulates the president must be a "natural born" U.S. citizen, though it's generally agreed this covers children of Americans born abroad.

"A lot of people are talking about it," Trump told the *Post,* "and I know that even some states are looking at it very strongly, the fact that he was born in Canada and has had a double passport. Republicans are going to have to ask themselves the question: 'Do we want a candidate who could be tied up in court for two years?' That'd be a big problem."

Ah, the return of the birthers. But that's Trump – he's impossible to ignore.

January 2016

THE BERNIE EFFECT

The sorting and winnowing of U.S. presidential candidates happens in the space of a week in Iowa and New Hampshire, two of the smallest and least representative states in America.

The Iowa caucuses have reduced the Democratic field to only two candidates, while the Republican contest essentially has been narrowed to three front-runners and a few more who hope to become competitive in New Hampshire.

Both parties are dealing with voters who, like the Peter Finch character in *Network*, are "mad as hell and not going to take it anymore."

Thus, Bernie Sanders, the unlikely challenger to the presumptive Democratic nominee, Hillary Clinton. Trailing Clinton at 45 to 42 per cent in the final *Des Moines Register* poll on Sunday, Sanders tied her on caucus night 49.8 to 49.6 per cent. As Sanders himself put it, a candidate with "no name recognition" and "no money" successfully challenged "the most powerful political organization in the United States of America."

Now Sanders has both money and momentum going into New Hampshire, next door to his home state of Vermont, which he represents in the U.S. Senate as an independent.

A self-described socialist, the 74-year-old Sanders has become a rock star for younger voters – mainly by channeling their rage.

He's running against Wall Street, saying no bank is too big to fail – a very powerful theme on Main Street. Clinton, he maintains, is beholden to Wall Street, not just because she accepts contributions from the banks, but because she and Bill Clinton have taken huge speaking fees – $250,000 in her case, $500,000 in his – from the likes of Goldman Sachs. Ouch!

Sanders doesn't accept corporate donations. His average personal donation is just $27, but in January alone he collected $20 million.

After his showing in Iowa, he'll collect a lot more.

In New Hampshire, he's practically running as a favourite son. In the latest Real Clear Politics poll of polls, Sanders leads Clinton 56–38 per cent. She clearly understands that he's outflanked her on the left, and has been trying to rebrand herself as a "progressive" as well as a "pragmatic" politician, the kind who gets things done.

But Sanders' message resonates with voters when he rails at a U.S. economy "rigged" in favour of the rich, and he would have no hesitation in raising the top marginal tax rate, as the Trudeau government has just done in Canada. Income inequality was a driving theme of the Occupy Movement, which has found an outspoken champion in Sanders.

And in a country where it's not uncommon for students to graduate from university at least $50,000 in debt, Sanders has long advocated reforms to student loans; he once suggested they be pegged at the Federal Reserve's bank rate. No wonder he has the student vote.

Clinton has accused Sanders of wanting to dismantle Obamacare, when what he's really advocating is a single-payer universal health care system of the type Canada's had in place for half a century. Nobody ever called Lester B. Pearson, the father of medicare, a wild-eyed socialist.

Clinton probably can't wait to see the back of New Hampshire, and move on from there to the Nevada caucus on February 20 and the South Carolina primary on February 22. Nevada has a large Hispanic population, while South Carolina has a large number of African Americans – and Clinton has strong support in both groups.

Nevada and South Carolina are supposedly Clinton's "firewall" states. And indeed, she leads Nevada by 50–30 in the RCP polling average, and by 63–30 in North Carolina. After those two states comes Super Tuesday on March 1, with 11 primaries and caucuses. The Clinton campaign had hoped to have the nomination wrapped up by then, but Sanders clearly has the money and the moxie to stay in the game.

On the Republican side, the trio that emerged competitive in Iowa will make the race much more manageable than the one with 10 candidates – and even more on stage for the televised debates. Donald Trump led the last *Des Moines Register* poll with 28 per cent to 23 per cent for Ted Cruz and only 15 per cent for Marco Rubio. But in the event, the evangelical vote propelled Cruz to a winning 28 per cent, with Trump sliding to 24 per cent and Rubio surging to 23 per cent.

For Trump, it was something of a reckoning. He's built his campaign on social and earned media. But in Iowa, Trump was shown to have a weak ground game. Bombast, bluster and big bucks can only take him so far.

Still, he holds a strong lead going into the final week of the campaign in New Hampshire. The RCP average puts him at 33 per cent, with Cruz, Ohio Governor John Kasich and former Florida Governor Jeb Bush all at 11 per cent and Rubio at 10 per cent.

At this point, Bush probably would settle for third place in New Hampshire, a state next door to Maine, where he has roots. Rubio has the most to gain, and the question is whether he can build momentum on his strong showing in Iowa. He represents generational change, has a strong personal narrative as the son of Cuban immigrants, and looks like he could win in November.

For the next week, then, all roads lead to New Hampshire.

February 2016

☙

AMERICA AT ITS BEST, AND WORST

In the last few days we have seen America at its best – at the funeral of former first lady Nancy Reagan – and at its worst in the behaviour of Donald Trump, who takes no responsibility for the incendiary rhetoric of his campaign for the Republican presidential nomination.

Mrs. Reagan's service was dignified and uplifting, a unifying moment across party lines, a moment of which all Americans could be proud. Trump's demeanour on the campaign trail is divisive and disgraceful, fraught with dreadful prospects for American democracy.

Nancy Reagan's service was a state funeral in all but name, a national occasion. Nearly every first family of the modern era, from the Obamas back to the Kennedys, was represented. Even the media played a positive and praiseworthy role, in remarks by former television anchors Tom Brokaw and Diane Sawyer, who covered the Reagan years.

Mrs. Reagan had given her staff a love letter from her husband, with instructions that their friend Brian Mulroney be asked to read it at her funeral. Previously unpublished in the diaries and letters of Ronald Reagan, the letter from their first Christmas in the White House in 1981 spoke volumes about their intimacy and authenticity as a couple. Mulroney also spoke of their exemplary service to their country. "As a first couple, they represented America with great distinction," he said. "They had a magnificent sense of occasion. They had style, and they had grace, and they had class."

The venue for her service, the Reagan Presidential Library on a hilltop overlooking Simi Valley in California, was a reminder of Reagan's high vision of public life – "a shining city upon a hill."

Hours after this uplifting occasion, violence erupted at the site of a Trump rally in Chicago, where thousands of Trump supporters clashed with protesters. Violence broke out at other Trump rallies over the weekend before the Trump campaign finally mustered control of its events by busing in supporters from miles away.

Seething with indignation, Trump predictably blamed the protestors, whom he labelled "disruptors," for the violent incidents. While running on a signature promise to "make America great again," his campaign slogan has become a shout of "get 'em out!"

As of this week, some primaries become winner-take-all contests. The violent incidents of the weekend have apparently worked to Trump's advantage among angry American voters.

But it is Trump whose words and platform have incited violence.

It is Trump who would deport 11 million undocumented U.S. residents to Mexico (though he doesn't say how he would round them up). It is Trump who would build a wall along the Mexican border, and force the Mexicans to pay for it. Good luck with that, Donald.

It is Trump who would ban the immigration of all Muslims to the United States, who would expel Syrian refugees (though only a few thousand have been admitted to the U.S.). It is Trump who took days to distance himself from the endorsement of the former head of the Ku Klux Klan. It is Trump who relentlessly and recklessly insults his Republican opponents, dismissing "little Marco Rubio" and repeatedly calling Ted Cruz "a liar." As for the Democrats, Trump is an equal-opportunity insulter, calling Bernie Sanders "a communist."

Actually, Trump and Sanders have something in common: Both are vociferously opposed to the NAFTA, which the Vermont senator has called "that disastrous piece of trade legislation." His opponent Hillary Clinton, Sanders said the other day, "has supported every piece of disastrous trade legislation that has led to a race to the bottom."

As it happens, Trump, Sanders and Clinton are united in opposing the Trans-Pacific Partnership deal, which the Obama administration has concluded with 11 other countries, including Canada and Mexico.

On NAFTA, all of this is campaign code for jobs being exported to Mexico from the American manufacturing heartland of the Midwest. On the TPP, it's about assembly lines in emerging economies such as Vietnam. Trump also likes to blame China, though it's not a signatory to the TPP.

Two of those heartland states, Ohio and Illinois, hold primaries on the third Super Tuesday in as many weeks, the political equivalent of college basketball's March Madness. There were three other states in play – Florida, North Carolina and Missouri.

On the Real Clear Politics website on Tuesday, Trump was leading in four states and trailing only Governor John Kasich in his home state of Ohio. Trump did not hesitate to use trade as his high card against Kasich. "In Ohio, we have a man who supported NAFTA, and now he's running on TPP," Trump yelled at an Ohio campaign stop.

Kasich's reply was, typically, based on logic and reason. "Thirty-eight million American jobs depend on trade," he retorted. "It's a red herring."

Until Tuesday, Republican delegates were apportioned on a percentage of the popular vote, but as of this week, some primaries become winner-take-all contests. The violent incidents of the weekend have apparently worked to Trump's advantage among angry American voters. The RCP website on primary day had Trump leading Rubio by an average of 18 points in his home state of Florida, and leading Illinois by an average of 6 points over Cruz. Kasich appeared poised to win Ohio, but only by about five points over Trump in the last two polls on Monday.

The anti-Trump forces were desperate to stop him in Ohio at least, with some hope for Illinois to prevent him from effectively clinching the GOP nomination. This appeared to be their last, best hope for a brokered convention to stop Trump from completing his hostile takeover of the party of Lincoln and Reagan.

This is not "a shining city upon a hill."

March 2016

THE BROOKLYN BRAWL

It will be remembered as the Brooklyn Brawl, and neither Hillary Clinton nor Bernie Sanders made any pretense that it was anything other than that.

Each demeaned the character, judgment and veracity of the other in the Democratic debate in the New York presidential primary. The two-hour debate hosted by CNN was a bruising slugfest, acrimonious and riveting from beginning to end.

"If you're both screaming at each other," CNN moderator Wolf Blitzer interjected at one point, "the viewers won't be able to hear either one of you."

Well, it was New York, an in-your-face kind of town. And there was a lot at stake. Not just delegates, but also standing with the voters.

Clinton represented New York in the Senate for eight years, and has her campaign headquarters in Brooklyn. Sanders was born and raised in Brooklyn. She needs a convincing win, somewhere in the double digits. He needs to shrink her margin to single digits, something like five points. And if somehow he were to win New York, well, if he can make it there, he can make it anywhere.

Sanders is the self-described socialist senator from Vermont, and he proposes what he calls a new American revolution. But to many Canadian ears, he doesn't sound like a scary socialist when he points to the Canadian model of single-payer universal health care.

"I live 50 miles from Canada, you know," he declared at one point. "It's not some kind of communist authoritarian country. They're doing okay. They've got a health care system that guarantees health to all people. We can do the same."

At 74, he looks and sounds like a cranky grandfather, but he's a rock star among young and working class voters. The college cohort love it that he's proposing free tuition at public universities so they can be spared crushing debt upon graduation.

In Canada where tuition fees are already quite affordable, and ridiculously low in Quebec, students were big winners in last month's federal Liberal budget. The Canada Student Loans Program is being revamped for students from low and middle income families, while the Canada student grants are being increased by 50 per cent. There's nothing scary or socialist about it. Sanders would be right at home.

He would increase the minimum wage to $15, something Tom Mulcair just ran on in the Canadian election. And Sanders is opposed to any and all trade agreements, from NAFTA to the Trans-Pacific Partnership. This is music to the ears of trade unionists everywhere.

Sanders is the scourge of Wall Street, shouting that banks are not too big to fail, though he's vague on how he would reform the financial services industry.

But where he really differentiates himself from Clinton is on campaign finance reform. He essentially says that she's in the pocket of the banks, having accepted $15 million in campaign donations and another $2 million in speaking fees from Wall Street. Sanders? He doesn't accept corporate donations, attend fund-raisers or charge for speeches. If he wants campaign finance reform in the U.S., he could do worse than consider the Canadian model adopted 10 years ago, which bans corporate and union donations, and limits individual donations to $1,500. But on the home front, he'd have to contend with the 2010 ruling by the U.S. Supreme Court allowing unlimited corporate donations, which led to the proliferation of super PACS.

All of which has given Sanders distance and differentiation from Clinton, and he rolled it all into one sound bite.

"I do question her judgment," he declared. "I question the judgment that voted for the war in Iraq, the worst foreign policy blunder in the history of this country, (which) voted for every disastrous trade agreement, which cost us millions of decent-paying jobs. And I question her judgment about running super PACs which are collecting tens of millions of dollars from special interests, including $15 million from Wall Street."

The live audience loved the red meat.

As for Clinton, she gave as good as she got. In truth, Sanders has forced her to raise her game, and protect her flank on the left of the Democratic Party. Rather than a coronation, she's in a contest, and a better candidate for it.

There's no doubt that the math of a contested convention remains unlikely for Sanders. It takes 2,382 delegates to win the nomination, and Clinton already has 1,758, including 469 automatic super delegates. For his part, Sanders has 1,069 delegates, which includes only 31 super delegates. While he's been on a roll, winning seven of the last eight caucuses and primaries, his odds remain long. Democratic delegates are elected proportionally according to the vote. In New York, for example, there are 247 delegates, plus 44 super delegates, most of whom will support Clinton. But there's four more primary states the following week, and another Super Tuesday on June 7 including primaries in delegate-rich California and New Jersey.

What does Sanders get by staying in all the way to the convention in Philadelphia? He gets a floor fight and a say in the party's platform. He gets to make a speech at the convention. He gets a roll call.

And he can well afford to stay in. Last month, with average personal donations of just $27, he raised $44 million, nearly $15 million more than Clinton.

In Clinton World, this must be making them crazy.

April 2016

TRUMP VS. CLINTON

The best that can be said about Donald Trump is that, in his call to "make America great again," he represents American exceptionalism.

But the basic tenets of Trump's platform are nativism and protectionism. He would, literally and figuratively, build walls around the United States.

He would build a wall along the border with Mexico, and says he would make the Mexicans pay for it, while rounding up and deporting 11 million undocumented residents of the U.S. He would ban Muslim immigrants to America. He would tear up the North American Free Trade Agreement with Canada and Mexico, and kill the Trans-Pacific Partnership deal among 12 countries, including Canada and Mexico. Trump is not alone in his opposition to the TPP. Both remaining Democratic candidates, Hillary Clinton and Bernie Sanders, also oppose it.

At the outset of Trump's presidential campaign last summer, he was regarded as merely a blowhard, denigrating his opponents and degrading public discourse. Yet where there were 17 candidates at the beginning of the race for the Republican nomination, Trump is now the last one standing. It has to be said that, for all his disgraceful and disgusting outbursts, he has won the GOP nomination fair and square.

The Republican establishment had been hoping for a competitive convention, with Trump falling short of the 1237 delegates needed to clinch the nomination. But after his sweep of the Indiana primary, his last two opponents, Texas Senator Ted Cruz and Ohio Governor John Kasich, threw in the towel. There is no longer an ABT candidate, Anyone But Trump, and he is now the presumptive nominee.

While Trump has now completed his hostile takeover, there is no shortage of disgruntled Republican stakeholders. Paul Ryan, for one. He's the Speaker of the House of Representatives, the most powerful Republican figure in the U.S. Congress. He also happens to be chairman of the July convention in Cleveland. On CNN, he said, "I'm just not ready" to endorse Trump "at this point. I'm not there right now." For his part, Trump retorted that he wasn't ready to support Ryan, either. "Perhaps in the future we can work together," Trump added.

Two Republican presidents, both named George Bush, have also declined to close ranks behind Trump. They won't even be attending the convention, and neither will W's brother Jeb. You'll find them at the family compound in Kennebunkport, Maine. Mitt Romney, the party's 2012 nominee, won't be at the convention, either. The 2008 Republican nominee, John McCain, doesn't want his picture taken with Trump, who once demeaned his heroic service as a surviving prisoner of war. After five terms and 30 years in the Senate, McCain is locked in a dead heat for his Arizona seat with a Democratic challenger.

Well, at least they won't need a VIP section at the convention.

Since Trump locked up the nomination, American allies have expressed concern not just about his protectionist impulses on trade, but his views on foreign and defence policy. In several interviews, he has mused about arming Japan and South Korea with nuclear weapons as a deterrent against North Korea's nuclear ambitions, to say nothing of China. As if Japan, of all the countries in the world, would seek or accept nuclear weapons. Have you heard of Hiroshima and Nagasaki, Donald?

Not to worry, say most members of the American political class, Trump has no chance of defeating Clinton in the November general election. Yeah, that's what they were saying when Trump launched his campaign last June – no worries, he can't win the nomination. Wrong.

Derek Burney, a former Canadian ambassador to Washington, doesn't share this reassuring outlook.

"I do not subscribe to the view that Trump will be blown out of the water," says Burney, now an adviser to Norton Rose Fulbright in the international law firm's Ottawa office. "That's what they said last June."

While Clinton usually leads Trump by double digits in run-off polls, the latest composite poll by RealClearPolitics.com has her ahead only 47–41 per cent in the popular vote, though she has a clear but commanding lead in the Electoral College, with 270 votes needed to win out of 538. Most polls have her well over 300 electoral votes.

Both Trump and Clinton have high unfavourables. While he scares people, her problem is trust. For all his bombast and bluster, Trump is at least authentic, while she is not. She's simply not a very good candidate, though she might well make an excellent president.

To make matters more complicated for her, Sanders is still out there, outflanking her on the left, especially among women, working class and younger voters. He beat her in Indiana by six points, and going into the West Virginia primary, he leads her in the RCP composite poll there 51–33 per cent. Her comments about coal mining have not played well in a state whose economy is built on coal. Sanders has hardly any chance of overcoming her lead of 2,205 to 1,401 delegates, with Clinton needing only 2,383 to clinch the nomination. But he has every reason to stay in until the California primary in June, wage a platform fight and make a speech at the convention.

Meanwhile, Trump has already turned his demeaning diatribes on her. Lyin' Ted has already been replaced by Crooked Hillary. He's already served notice that he'll go after Bill Clinton as a womanizer, to which the best response – it takes one to know one – doesn't really work for her. Trump is certain to paint her as being in the pocket of the Wall Street banks which have supported her campaign and paid her handsome $260,000 speaking fees, while Trump has self-financed his campaign.

Anything can happen between now and November.

So what are the prospects of a Trump presidency for Canada?

"I think NAFTA has been a disaster," Trump said at the outset of his campaign. "I think our current deals are a disaster."

Burney, present at the creation of both NAFTA and the Canada-U.S. Free Trade Agreement, thinks Trump would undermine free trade with Mexico by slapping import taxes on goods at the border. His favourite example is Ford closing a plant in Michigan and building one in Mexico.

Trump has said he would impose a 35 per cent tariff on Ford cars and trucks coming into the U.S. from Mexico. He has similar plans for Carrier air conditioners and Oreo cookies made in Mexico.

As for the TPP, there is no prospect that it will pass Congress in the waning months of the Obama presidency, and apparently none that it will be supported next year by either Trump or Clinton.

It stands to reason, then, that Justin Trudeau should not spend any time or political capital on bringing implementing legislation to Parliament. Burney suggests Ottawa should pursue bilateral trade deals with the other TPP signatories. "In other words," he says, "they should come at it from the bottom-up, rather than the top-down."

As it happens, Trudeau will host a Three Amigos summit in late June with Barack Obama and Mexican President Enrique Pena Nieto.

At the end of their trilateral session, they would normally do a joint news conference.

They can be sure that all the questions will be about Donald Trump.

May 2016

CLINTON CLINCHES, SANDERS STAYS IN

Hillary Clinton has clinched the Democratic nomination for president of the United States but Bernie Sanders, true to form, vows to take the race to the convention in Philadelphia in late July.

And why shouldn't he? For one thing, he's earned a significant role at the convention. For another, he's the leader of a movement, and he can't really tell his followers to abandon their hope and hard work for a new American revolution.

What do Sanders and his supporters stand to gain taking his candidacy all the way to Philadelphia?

Well, he'll get to make a keynote speech, repeating the battle cries and hot button issues of his campaign. This is what Ted Kennedy got as a reward for his campaign against Jimmy Carter in 1980, and it was one of the great speeches of his career.

Sanders would get a roll call of delegates state by state, many of which he won. At a certain point, when Clinton is about to go over the top, he could ask for the floor to move a motion to make it unanimous, just as she did for Barack Obama at the 2008 convention.

And throughout the convention conversation, Sanders will demand a say in the Democratic platform. He has issues, such as banks not being too big to fail, campaign finance reform, income inequality, student tuition, and universal health care, that he wants addressed somehow in the platform.

If all of those things happen, the Democrats will leave Philadelphia united and ready to take on Donald Trump in the fall.

The Democrats are already much more united, and in much stronger shape, than they were only a week ago.

First, Clinton mathematically clinched the nomination on Monday, even before her convincing victories on Tuesday in the New Jersey and California primaries. California was particularly important to Sanders, who was heavily invested in the Golden State in both time and money, as kind of his last stand. In the event, Clinton won California easily by 13 points, 56 to 43 per cent.

The delegate numbers speak for themselves. There are 2,382 delegates needed to win, and after the votes were counted Tuesday night, Clinton had 2,903 elected delegates and 577 appointed "super delegates" for a total of 2,780. Sanders had 1,876 elected delegates and only 48 super delegates for a total 1,924. Considering that he's come from nowhere, that's a remarkable showing. But the fact remains that he sits in the Senate from Vermont as an independent, and the super delegates, representing the establishment wing of the Democratic party, are not about to break to him. His argument that he does better against Trump than Clinton in the polls has fallen on deaf Democratic ears. "I can count," Sanders said early in the week.

He is also sounding conciliatory notes. Leaving the White House after a meeting with Barack Obama, Sanders said: "I look forward to meeting her in the near future to see how we can work together to defeat Donald Trump."

As for President Obama, he couldn't have been more effusive in his video endorsement of Clinton. "I don't think there's ever been anyone so qualified to hold this office," he said. For her part, she tweeted his mantra from 2008, that she was "fired up and ready to go!"

There's no doubt that Obama can help Clinton shore up and turn out her vote in November, particularly among African American and Hispanic voters. But she also needs Sanders, not to demobilize his supporters, but to deliver them to her. She has a serious trust deficit with the Sanders coalition of women under 45, the youth vote and white collar voters.

To bring the Sanders voters over, the Clinton campaign needs to allow him a graceful exit. For example, he is still campaigning for the primary in the capital District of Columbia, the last race of the primary season. He has no hope of winning DC, which is heavily black as well as home to much of Washington's Democratic political class, both strong supporters of Clinton. There is no downside for the Clinton team to Sanders staying in the game rather than suspending his campaign.

Clinton and her surrogates have already pivoted to Trump, who in the last week has handed them an incredible gift in his reckless comments on the ethnic background of a judge hearing a civil suit against Trump University. At a campaign speech in San Diego last week, Trump unleashed a vicious tirade against federal court Judge Gonzalo Curiel, saying among other things that he was "Mexican."

The judge, born and raised in the U.S. of immigrant parents, ordered some documents released in an ongoing civil suit against the eponymous Trump University.

"Based on the rulings that I have received in the Trump University civil case, I feel justified in questioning whether I am receiving a fair trial," Trump declared.

He went on: "I have a judge who is a hater of Donald Trump, a hater. He's a hater. His name is Gonzalo Curiel ... I think Judge Curiel should be ashamed of himself ... the judge, who happens to be, we believe, is Mexican, which is great, I think that's fine. You know, I think the Mexicans are going to end up loving Donald Trump when I give all these jobs, okay?"

Trump can't blame the media for distorting something he said, or setting him up in an interview. He said it himself, unprompted at a rally, a totally unforced error. The Republican establishment had a very negative reaction, and have completely disowned Trump on this. House Speaker Paul Ryan, who has been on the verge of endorsing Trump, call the Mexican comment "racist."

Democratic Senator Elizabeth Warren treated Trump to a dose of his own rhetorical excess, saying in a Washington speech that "it's exactly what you'd expect from a thin-skinned, racist bully."

So while Clinton has had an historically successful week, Trump has had a week from hell, totally off message with no one but himself to blame. There's no way that she doesn't get a bump, and no way he doesn't take a hit, in the polls.

June 2016

FEAR OR LOATHING

In the binary choice between two alternatives for the American presidency, it really comes down to the lesser of two evils, untrustworthy Hillary Clinton or scary Donald Trump.

Fear of Trump and loathing of Clinton is about all that unites Democrats and Republicans. This was apparent at last week's GOP convention in Cleveland and again at the Democratic conclave in Philadelphia, where supporters of Bernie Sanders didn't get the memo about being in the City of Brotherly Love.

They served notice on Day One that they weren't party regulars so much as members of a movement that had been denied the nomination by a party establishment which rigged the primaries against their candidate.

Inconveniently for the Clinton campaign, a massive WikiLeaks release of 20,000 Democratic National Committee emails over the weekend made the point that the Sanders camp wasn't paranoid. Cyber security experts, the CIA and FBI confirmed that the DNC server had been hacked by two Russian spy services, one domestic and the other the successor to the former KGB. There's also a question of whether Clinton's own private server, the one with 33,000 unsecure emails when she was secretary of state, may also have been hacked.

All of which only fed the fury of those delegates still feeling the Bern. One email from the DNC's chief financial officer even suggested that whether or not Sanders was an observant Jew could be played to Clinton's advantage in southern primary states. "My southern Baptist peeps draw a big difference between a Jew and an atheist," he wrote.

All of which led to Congresswoman Debbie Wasserman Schultz having to step down as DNC chair on Sunday, and on Monday she was roundly booed at a breakfast of her own Florida delegation. She then stepped aside as convention chair, and did not gavel the proceedings to order, and thus avoided being hooted and hollered down at the podium.

Sanders himself was lustily booed by his own supporters when he endorsed Clinton and her running mate, Virginia Senator Tim Kaine.

"We have to defeat Donald Trump," Sanders shouted, "and we have got to elect Hillary Clinton and Tim Kaine."

When a chorus of boos erupted, Sanders welcomed the crowd to "the real world," to which they replied with chants of "We want Bernie!"

By this time, Team Clinton was installing Donna Brazile as acting DNC chair, and her first act was to issue a "deep and sincere apology" for "inexcusable remarks" about Sanders in the leaked emails. Sanders himself continued to work his own crowd, putting out a statement imploring them against "booing, turning our backs, walking out or similar displays" on the actual convention floor.

The DNC then changed the batting order for the first evening's proceedings in prime time. Sanders had been scheduled to hit lead off, but instead he was the clean-up batter in the closing 10 o'clock hour behind Michelle Obama and Massachusetts Senator Elizabeth Warren. But it was the first lady who hit it out of the park in one of the great convention speeches of modern times.

As parents, she said, the Obamas had taught their daughters that "our motto is, when they go low, we go high." A lovely put down of Trump without ever mentioning him by name. Of a president's responsibility in the Situation

Room she declared: "With the nuclear codes at your fingertips, with the military at your command, you can't make snap decisions."

Obama's elegant and eloquent address was a gift outright to Clinton, and for her part the nominee could not have asked for more from Sanders, who had the hall with him on his call for unity to defeat Trump.

But it will take more than a convention week to deal with Clinton's problems of trust with voters, which have been deepened by her own email issues and highlighted again by the bias in her favour by supposedly neutral DNC officials in the WikiLeaks release.

A *New York Times* poll released Monday found that 54 per cent of Americans had an unfavourable opinion of her, while only 28 per cent viewed her in a favourable light. Even worse, 67 per cent of respondents thought that she was "not honest and trustworthy," while again only 28 per cent thought she was.

Clinton will receive plenty of third party endorsements before her own acceptance address. Bill Clinton was the keynoter in Tuesday prime time. Vice President Joe Biden and Barack Obama are the scheduled headliners on Wednesday evening. And the nominee's daughter, Chelsea Clinton, will introduce her on Thursday.

In this party, unlike the GOP, the political establishment shows up for the candidate. But Clinton can't reply on surrogates to take down Trump, or on her political or personal kin to make the case for her.

And as a presenter, she's got problems arising from her trust deficit – she not very authentic, or at least not very spontaneous.

Trump, in his own way, is authentic in the sense that you can never tell what crazy thing he is going to say next. In one of his improvised outbursts on Monday, he said Clinton never used her middle name of Rodham because it was actually "Hillary Rotten Clinton." Totally lacking in class, but true to himself. Again, of Wasserman Schultz's ouster as DNC chair, his response was his signature TV reality show closer: "You're fired!" That was not only true to form, but actually funny.

For all his own problems at the GOP gathering last week, Trump got a convention bounce. Down seven points in a CNN poll before the convention, he led Clinton 44–39 in a new one taken over the weekend.

While his speech was a dark vision of America, it evidently worked for him among disenchanted swing voters. Clinton needs to bring them back to the Democratic ticket.

July 2016

AMERICA'S LONG NATIONAL NIGHTMARE

Just because this US presidential campaign has been a relentless parade of worst-case scenarios and, if the narrative trajectory holds things will get worse before they get better, here's a look at what would happen if there's no outright winner Tuesday in the previously unthinkable race between Democrat Hillary Clinton and Republican Donald Trump.

In baseball, a tie goes to the runner. In a U.S. presidential race, a tie in the Electoral College goes to Congress.

It takes 270 votes out of 538 in the College to win the presidency. But in the unlikely event of a tie – 269 to 269 – the House of Representatives would choose the president, while the Senate would elect the vice president. This is according to the 12th amendment of the U.S. constitution.

It's happened once before, in 1824, when the House elected John Quincy Adams over Andrew Jackson, who had a higher share of the popular vote and a plurality in the Electoral College of 99 votes but short of the 131 then needed to win. Adams, who had come in second in the college with 84 votes in a four-candidate race, eventually prevailed in Congress.

In the House, each state has one vote that goes to the party that controls its delegation. At present, the Republicans control 33 states in the House, and are likely to remain in the majority after Tuesday – so a deadlock in the college would result in Donald Trump becoming president, even with a smaller share of the popular vote.

We are not making this up.

As mathematically improbable as it seems, a tie cannot be completely ruled out of Electoral College scenarios.

Consider the weekend projection by Real Clear Politics, the polling and aggregator website. As of Sunday morning, RCP had Clinton at 216 votes in the College – 54 short of a majority. They had Trump at 164 solid or leaning votes, 106 shy of the presidency.

RCP has 13 battleground states, and Trump has been closing the gap to the point where he no longer has to run the table of the states that are too close to call – within the margin of error of four points.

From the RCP baseline of 164 votes, if Trump were to win the swing states of Florida (29 votes), Georgia (16), North Carolina (15) Ohio (18) Arizona (11), Nevada (6), Iowa (6) and New Hampshire (4), that would put him at 269 votes.

And if Trump were to win the second congressional district in Maine, that would put him at 270 – Maine's four college votes are allocated at two for the winner of the popular vote and one for each of its two congressional seats.

For her part, starting from 216 votes in the RCP projection, if Clinton were to win the battleground states of Pennsylvania (20), Michigan (16), Colorado (9) New Mexico (5) and Maine's popular vote plus the second congressional district (3), that would also put her at 269. (The other Maine district is in the safe Clinton column.)

Welcome to a very long election night, followed by very long days of recounts and court cases that could make the 2000 Bush-Gore fiasco look simple. In that case, Bush won the Electoral College with 271, but only after a month of Florida recounts, global disbelief and a 5–4 Supreme Court decision stopping the recounts and effectively handing the presidency to Bush. If it comes to that this time, the Supreme Court, being one judge down, could deliver a tie on a tie.

While Trump's path to victory remains a narrow one, it's much more foreseeable and feasible than only two weeks ago, when RCP had Clinton in majority territory at 272, with Trump at only 126, with even the Republican stronghold state of Texas then in play.

What's happened in the meantime? Well, FBI Director James Comey's reopening the file on Clinton's missing emails has underscored her low trust numbers. Trump has also been scoring with a strong 30-second spot on the increase in Obamacare health premiums. He has also been relatively disciplined and on message. Or as he put it, quoting his own interior monologue: "All right Donald, stay on point…stay on point." The message that he's the agent of change resonates outside the Washington-Wall Street axis. In the last few days, he has also been joined on the campaign trail by his wife, Melania, who speaks – however implausibly – of a kinder, gentler side of Trump. Finally, Republican voters are evidently going home in the final days, preparing to hold their noses and vote for him.

All of which has resulted in a considerable tightening of the race in both the College and the pop-vote where, for example, the CNN poll at the weekend had Clinton leading 46–43, within the margin of error.

Looking at the battleground states, Trump must win Florida and its 29 votes, where the RCP average on Sunday had him trailing 47–46, a statistical dead heat. In Georgia, Trump leads by 4.6 points in the RCP average, 48.4 to 43.8 per cent. He should win those 16 votes.

In North Carolina, Trump leads in the RCP average by a narrow 1.5 points, 47.3 to 45.8 per cent. For both Trump and Clinton, North Carolina, with its 15 votes, could be make-or-break. Both appeared there on the weekend, and Barack Obama made two speeches there on Saturday, saying he was "fired up" and was certainly trying to fire up the black vote for Hillary.

New Hampshire, previously leaning to Clinton, is now tied, with Trump leading in the RCP average by 1.6 points, 43.4 to 41.8. That's four more votes now in play.

Ohio is a must-win for Trump – no Republican has ever won the White House without Ohio. Trump appears on track to win it, leading in the RCP average by 3.3 points, 46.3 to 43.

In the swing state of Iowa, with its six votes in the College, Trump leads by three points in the RCP average, 44–41. In Arizona, with its 11 votes, Trump leads the aggregator's average by four points, 46–42. And in Nevada with six votes, Trump leads the average by two points, 46–44.

If he were to win all those states, from a starting point of 164 votes, he would have 269 votes in the College.

On the Clinton side of the College count, she should still win Pennsylvania and its 20 votes, though it has been moved into the battleground column with her average lead shrinking to just 2.4 points, 46 to 43.6. It's no coincidence that she will close her campaign Monday night in Philadelphia, with Barack and Michelle Obama as the headliners.

Similarly, she should still win the industrial state of Michigan, where she leads the aggregate average by four points, 45–41. That's 16 votes. While Colorado has also been moved into the swing state column, she still leads the RCP average by 2.9 points, 43.3 to 40.4. Nine votes there. She also leads by four points in New Mexico, 45.5 to 41.5. Five College votes there. Finally, she's 4.5 points ahead in Maine 44 to 39.5, and should win its two popular votes while the second congressional district is tied, with Trump ahead by half a point, 41.5 to 41.

From a starting point of 216, the 53 votes in those five states would bring her to 269 in the Electoral College.

A tie ball game, with extra innings in Congress.

Or as Yogi Berra famously said: It ain't over 'til it's over.

November 2016

WHEN 'THE DEVIL YOU KNOW' BECAME A NET NEGATIVE

In campaign narratives, the only theme more powerful than "time for a change" is "throw the bums out."

In the U.S. election, Donald Trump played both themes quite effectively, while Hillary Clinton was the candidate not so much of continuity as of the same establishment Barack Obama ran against when he beat her in 2008.

Depending on the economy and the mood of voters, continuity can be a winning theme. It worked for the first George Bush, running for the third term of Ronald Reagan in 1988. It could have worked, it should have worked for Clinton, running for Barack Obama's third term in 2016. Given that Obama's approval rating is at 57 per cent, it probably would have worked for Joe Biden.

Obama took office at the worst moment of the Great Recession in January 2009. U.S. unemployment peaked that year at 10 per cent. In the last jobs report four days before this election, unemployment was just 4.9 per cent. On Obama's watch, the U.S. economy has created some 15 million new jobs.

Normally, those would have been numbers for Clinton to run on, the best argument for retaining the Democrats in the White House. Jobs, jobs, jobs. But she never really made that case, at least not forcefully enough to overcome her own personal negatives.

Throughout the campaign, voters were constantly reminded that in terms of situational ethics, the Clintons hadn't changed since the 1990s: they had two standards, one for themselves and another for other people.

It began with her rather exotic and unjustified email arrangement as Secretary of State whereby crucial and classified diplomatic and security correspondence was routed through a private server in a bathroom closet, presumably to give the Clintons pre-emptive discretion over what would ultimately be accessible to Freedom of Information requests and Congressional subpoenas.

For Trump, this was the gift that kept on giving, right to the final two weeks of the campaign.

Clinton herself, in a conference call with donors, blamed her defeat on FBI Director James Comey's October 28 letter to Congress re-opening the investigation of her emails. "Our analysis," she said, "is that Comey's letter raising doubts that were groundless, baseless…stopped our momentum." Comey's follow-up letter to Congress, putting her in the clear just two days before the election, she said, only made things worse.

The emails were just one of Clinton's issues of ethics and entitlement.

Bill and Hillary Clinton's speaking fees were another. In 15 years after leaving the White House, CNN reported during the campaign, the Clintons between them billed over $150 million in speaking fees. He usually charged $500,000 per speech, while her standard fee after leaving the State Department in 2012 was $250,000 (which is what she billed for an October 2014 appearance at Canada 2020 in Ottawa, not including the cost of a private jet to fly her and her entourage in).

Then there was the question of pay-for-play at the Clinton Foundation, with seven-figure donors receiving face time with the Secretary of State. In most places, this would be called influence peddling.

Many voters decided that after seeing the Clintons on stage for a quarter century, they had seen enough. In a sense, they concluded that they knew her all too well. It wasn't the usual "throw the bums out" vote directed at a government; it was directed at a brand people had long ago had their fill of.

In the end, she is still expected to win the popular vote by as many as 2 million votes or about 1.5 per cent (several million votes are still uncounted in California, where she is leading by a 2–1 margin). But given the campaign Trump ran, it should never have been anywhere near that close and it doesn't do her any good in the Electoral College, where Trump has won by 306–232, far more than the 270 needed to win. It's quite different from Al Gore losing Florida and the White House to George W. Bush by 537 votes in 2000. The final score in the College that year was 271–267, and it was 97,000 Florida votes for Ralph Nader as the Green candidate that tipped the balance to Bush.

Clinton lost the battleground states of Florida, North Carolina and Ohio to Trump. But she also lost the Blue Firewall states of Pennsylvania, Michigan and Wisconsin (a state so reliably blue she didn't even bother to campaign there). Had she held those last three states, with their 46 electoral votes, she would have won the election.

She lost those states and the swing states because she lost the white vote, among both men and women – and not just among blue collar whites – while failing to get out enough Hispanic and black voters to offset them.

Exit polling showed white men voted for Trump by a 63–31 margin, while white women supported him by 53–43 per cent. Trump also won 54 per cent of white male university graduates, and 45 per cent of white female college grads.

How did Trump win? Well, as nasty as his rhetoric was, he was the candidate of change, running against the "rigged system" of Washington and Wall Street. Not to mention "Crooked Hillary" as the candidate of that system.

But his message wasn't hope and change, Barack Obama's signature slogan of 2008. It was grievance and change.

Even with the Republicans now controlling both the executive and legislative branches of government, the normal checks and balances of the system should curtail most abuses of power by the White House. And since the election, Trump has been saying that it is a time for healing, and spoken graciously of both Clinton and Obama. Winning the White House can be quite humbling.

But after staying off Twitter in the closing days of the campaign, he's been up to his old tricks @realDonaldTrump. On Sunday morning after the election, he was attacking the New York Times. "Wow, the @nytimes is losing thousands of subscribers because of their very poor and highly inaccurate coverage of 'the Trump phenomena.'"

He meant phenomenon. But never mind. He's going to be president of the United States. He needs to get off Twitter.

November 2016

FOR CANADA, TRADE TRUMPS ALL

In two months, on January 20, Donald Trump will stand on the West Front of the U.S. Capitol and be sworn in as the 45th president of the United States.

In delivering his inaugural address, he will be looking out directly to the Canadian Embassy, just a couple of blocks away on Pennsylvania Avenue.

Canadians gathered at the chancery for the occasion, as well as officials back in Ottawa, will be parsing his words for policy positions arising from the politics of the Trump era.

Canadians will be weighing Trump's words in three policy envelopes – economics and trade, energy and the environment as well as foreign and defence policy.

It would be a mistake to make it about us as Canadians, with our famous penchant for self-absorption. Former Vermont governor Howard Dean, speaking to the Canadian-American Business Council in Ottawa the other night, remarked that he'd been coming to Canada for 40 years, and always hearing complaints from Canadians about being ignored by the Americans. He then suggested, to appreciative laughter, that might be the best thing that could happen to Canada over the next four years.

On trade, for example, Trump hasn't been thinking about Canada when he has repeatedly called NAFTA "the worst deal in history." He was thinking about Mexico, and U.S. manufacturing jobs re-locating there over the last 20 years.

He wasn't thinking about Canada when he called the TransPacific Partnership trade deal "a disaster" negotiated by the outgoing Obama administration with 11 Pacific Rim nations including Canada.

But Canada can certainly be sideswiped by his promise to either re-negotiate or "tear up" NAFTA. As for the TPP, with U.S. and Japan alone having a veto, the White House acknowledged in not sending to Capitol Hill for debate during the lame-duck session of Congress that it was dead in the water. Trump needn't say another word about it.

But on NAFTA, if he really means to do something about it on Day One, he can go to the Oval Office after reviewing the inaugural parade and sign an executive order giving the required six months notice to invoke the cancellation clause of the continental trade agreement. It would be his first act as president, one that shows he means business. Then he could call the Canadian prime minister and Mexican president and politely say he'd like to renegotiate the deal.

Justin Trudeau would not have a problem with that. On the day after the U.S. election, his ambassador to Washington, David MacNaughton, told the Canadian media in a conference call that if the Americans wanted to renegotiate, Canada would be "at the table."

Trudeau himself the next day told a media availability: "If the Americans want to talk about NAFTA, I'm happy to talk about it."

This pre-emptive Canadian gambit may have got the Trudeau government out in front of Trump's NAFTA fixation, but the PM has also been criticized for opening up the deal before being asked. "Not a good move for Canada," former Pennsylvania Senator Rick Santorum and Trump supporter, in Ottawa for the CABC event, told CTV's Question Period in its Sunday morning broadcast.

Trudeau himself followed up during his visit to Cuba at the start of his South American swing last week with a perfectly sensible comment. "The fact is," he said, "that we are all committed to continuing to have strong relations with the new American administration."

Trudeau may have had a "bromance" with Barack Obama, but he will almost certainly find a way to strike up a cordial relationship with Trump. Trudeau has demonstrated a knack of building inter-personal relationships at the top. In his first year in office, he has hardly put a foot wrong on the international stage.

Besides, the bilateral trading relationship is a matter of overriding importance to both Canada and the U.S.

Canada is the most important customer for 35 U.S. states. You can be sure that 35 state governors and 70 members of the U.S. Senate are very aware of that.

No fewer than nine million jobs in the U.S. depend on trade with Canada. In Canada, some 2.7 million jobs, about one-seventh of the work force, depend on trade with the U.S. In 2015, Canada purchased US$338 billion in goods and services from the U.S., while exporting US$332 billion. On merchandise trade alone, Canada bought C$363 billion from the U.S. last year, while exporting C$397 billion.

The incoming U.S. vice president, Mike Pence, has a very close up understanding of this as the outgoing governor of Indiana. In 2014, Indiana sold US$12.2 billion of goods to Canada, or 35 per cent of the state's global exports. No fewer than 190,000 jobs in his home state depend on Canadian customers.

More than US$3.5 billion of these exports were in auto parts, automobile and trucking industries, where the supply chains constantly go back and forth across the border. Now the chair of Trump's transition team, Pence is looking very much like the chief operating officer of the incoming administration.

As a governor, he knows the Canadian trade file cold, and in the White House, could emerge as a solid and sensible friend of Canada.

The energy-environment and foreign affairs-defence files are also major policy concerns for Canada during the transition and beyond.

But trade is a major job creator and driver of prosperity for both countries.

For Canada, trade Trumps all.

November 2016

AN INAUGURAL ADDRESS UNLIKE ANY OTHER

It was not a speech, as they say in Rome, *urbi et orbi*, to the city and the world.

Donald Trump's inaugural address was a campaign speech, reiterating the isolationist, protectionist and nativist themes of the unlikely election result that made him the 45th president of the United States.

I meant what I said then, he said now. Power to the people, he declared. The people who put him there. Never mind the people sitting behind him, including four of his predecessors and the leaders of both parties in both Houses of the United States Congress.

As former Ronald Reagan speechwriter Peggy Noonan noted in her weekend *Wall Street Journal* column, the speech was "utterly and uncompromisingly Trumpian. The man who ran is the man who'll reign."

Get used to it.

"For too long," Trump said, "a small group in our nation's capital have reaped the rewards of government, while the people have borne the cost.

"Washington flourished – but the people did not share in its wealth. Politicians prospered – but the jobs left and the factories closed. The establishment protected itself but not the citizens of our country."

Fact check on job creation under the former presidents on the dais: 9 million new jobs under Jimmy Carter; 20 million under Bill Clinton; 11 million under Barack Obama, with slightly negative job growth under George W. Bush because of the Great Recession. Obama inherited unemployment of 10 per cent in 2009, and leaves unemployment at 4.7 per cent in 2017. The American economy is forecast to grow by a robust 2.8 per cent this year.

"This American carnage stops right here and right now," Trump declared, apparently oblivious to the strong economy bequeathed to him by his predecessors who paid him the courtesy of showing up for his swearing-in, only to hear him belittle their achievements in office.

But at least Trump stayed on his populist message, and stuck to his text, without improvising any of the mocking outbursts that marked his campaign. In preparing for the occasion, Trump had said he took the inaugural addresses of John F. Kennedy and Ronald Reagan in 1961 and 1981 as standards of excellence. Trump did emulate JFK's inaugural in one respect – at 16 minutes, his speech was a model of brevity.

But in Trump's inaugural there was no clarion call of patriotism, no echo of "Ask not what your country can do for you, ask what you can do for your country." No reminder to the world of American leadership, that America "would pay any price, bear any burden, meet any hardship, support any friend, oppose any foe, to assure the survival and the success of liberty."

Trump instead proposed a narcissistic and inward-looking America, engaging with the world strictly on its own terms. "From this moment on," he declared, "It's going to be America First."

On the economy and trade: "We will follow two simple rules: Buy American and Hire American."

This wasn't even speechifying, just sloganeering.

Within an hour of the inaugural address, the policy specifics were posted to the White House website, Trump's new internet address.

Referring to "failed trade deals," the link was unambiguously aggressive: "President Trump is committed to renegotiating NAFTA. If our partners refuse a renegotiation that gives American workers a fair deal, then the president will give notice of the United States' intention to withdraw from NAFTA."

Hello Canada, and hockey fans in the United States! Hola, Mexico!

Well, any of the three signatory countries can withdraw from NAFTA on six months notice. In Canada's case, we would then revert to the Canada-U.S. Free Trade Agreement.

In a congratulatory call on Saturday, Prime Minister Justin Trudeau reminded the president that Canada was the largest international customer of 35 American states. The other relevant bullet points would be that 9 million American jobs depend directly on trade with Canada, that $2 billion of goods cross the border each day, and that when trade in services is included, the U.S. enjoys a modest surplus with Canada in our $800 billion relationship. (It was a $100 billion bilateral relationship before the FTA was implemented in 1989.)

You can be sure that the governors of those 35 states and their 70 members of the U.S. Senate are aware of these numbers, or have been reminded of them by Canadian federal and provincial officials. These have also been the main talking points of Team Trudeau in their private talks with Team Trump.

For his part, Trump said Sunday: "Anybody hear of NAFTA? I ran a campaign somewhat based on NAFTA." His incoming Secretary of Commerce Wilbur Ross has indicated both publicly and privately that the U.S. has two major re-openers on NAFTA – rules of origin and the dispute settlement mechanism (DSM), both first adopted in the original Canada-U.S. FTA. This would be a major demand on Canada, which has benefited from generous rules of origin which, for example, classify foreign fabric as domestic content in the clothing industry. As for the DSM, the deal maker in the Canada-U.S. round, it was extended to the NAFTA and was the model for the World Trade Organization. The Americans have long thought Canada does too well on dispute settlement, and re-opening it could be a way for them to do better. They'll have to deal with Canadian trade officials, who are among the best in the world because they have to be – sitting across the table from the Americans.

It's not clear whether Trudeau and Trump spoke of the Keystone XL pipeline project, which is not mentioned in the energy policy on the White House site (whitehouse.gov). But Trump has been unequivocally supportive of the $10 billion pipeline from Alberta to Nebraska and from there to Gulf Coast refineries on an existing route. Trudeau had also endorsed Keystone, and expressed disappointment when his friend Obama killed the TransCanada project.

With all the approvals in Canada still in place, as well as approvals from states on the route, all that's needed for Keystone to proceed is for Trump to sign an executive order issuing a presidential permit.

Moving ahead on Keystone would get Trudeau's relationship with Trump off to a positive start, and in Canada-U.S. relations progress starts at the top.

In the meantime, the Canada-U.S. file is in the capable hands of Foreign Minister Chrystia Freeland, the smartest person in the room.

Canada-U.S. relations and the NAFTA renovation have been the dominant topic at the two-day cabinet retreat in Calgary, where Blackstone CEO Steve Schwarzman, chair of the President's Strategic and Policy Forum, made the opening presentation Monday morning. Schwarzman's appearance was arranged by former prime minister Brian Mulroney, lead director of Blackstone, who has been advising the Trudeau government at their request. Schwarzman also figures in Freeland's 2012 book, The Plutocrats, and with a portfolio valued at $11 billion, he certainly qualifies for what Freeland, then a financial writer living in New York, called "the 0.1 per cent." Schwarzman was reassuring, saying Canada is "a model for how trade relations should be. It's a positive sum game. Canada is well positioned."

During their first phone conversation following the November election, Trudeau already invited Trump to make his first foreign visit to Ottawa, as many presidents have done.

But this may be one occasion where Canada might defer to Trump visiting another country first. A Trump visit to Ottawa would almost certainly see thousands of protesters converging on the capital. And as we were reminded by Trump's churlish response to the Women's March on Washington, and countless other cities, it's all about him.

January 2017

14

HERE AND THERE

OUT ON THE MIRA

Nobody flies to Cape Breton anymore. No one can afford it. (Well, almost no one – but more on that later.)

I found out for myself just how expensive it was last weekend, when I had to fly to Sydney for a family memorial service. Getting to Halifax with Air Canada would be easy; connecting to Sydney would cost about $1,500 return.

"I want to go to Sydney, Nova Scotia, not Sydney, Australia," I told my travel agent, Mike Pacifico. In fact, I could have flown to Australia for less.

This is a real sore point in the smaller regions of the country, where Air Canada still enjoys a virtual monopoly, and can charge uncompetitive fares.

"The only people who fly to Sydney," one relative later put it, "are coming home from Fort McMurray." These would be workers from the oil sands, coming home with cash stuffed in their jeans. Other folks, going south for a winter holiday, drive to Halifax and park their car at the airport for a week or two.

Suddenly, fly and drive became an option. Even with the price of gas, the saving would be about $1,300. My mother, who was famously parsimonious, would have approved of such savings in honour of her memorial – the burial of her ashes beside my father, next to his parents, in a Cape Breton country cemetery at Hillside, Mira.

"Do you have a map?" I asked the young man at the Budget car rental desk.

"No maps," he said. "They did away with them with the recession."

No problem. Turn right at Truro, straight through New Glasgow and Antigonish to the Canso Causeway, where Nova Scotia ends and Cape Breton begins. Up either side of the Bras d'Or Lakes to Hillside, on the Mira River, halfway between Sydney and Louisbourg (pronounced Lewisburg). If you know the song, Out on the Mira, that's where it is, a farm home that has been in the family for a century and a half.

This is a road, the Trans-Canada Highway, that I occasionally travelled as a boy with my grandfather, Angus J. MacDonald. Half a century later, they are still building it.

The four-lane portion of the TCH ends at Peter MacKay's front doorstep in New Glasgow. The rest is two and three lanes that pass right through the middle of several towns: Antigonish, for example, a busy university town with three traffic lights. A week ago Friday, with traffic at a standstill and backed up halfway to New Glasgow, it took an hour and a half just to get through it. Well, there was a nice view of St. F.X.

MacKay happened to return my call, as I was sitting in the middle of this traffic.

"Don't you have some influence in this province?" I asked. "Can't you do something about this?"

"We're on it," replied the defence minister, who is also the senior Atlantic minister in the federal government. "We're building a bypass at Antigonish, $58 million. It's the biggest construction project in the province."

And guess what? There's a labour shortage. All those guys working in Fort McMurray, and flying into Sydney. This is called labour mobility, and it's one of the issues underlying the EI debate. If the threshold to qualify for benefits is lowered to 360 hours of employment, as the opposition is demanding, recipients won't necessarily look for work in other regions of the country.

MacKay, briefly encountered on the return trip through New Glasgow, was in the middle of his summer rounds, from strawberry socials to tartan festivals.

Sitting in his backyard, sipping a Nova Scotia-brewed Keith's, he said he detected no appetite for an election anytime soon, least of all over EI, an issue that's very well understood in Atlantic Canada. Of course, it all depends on the Liberals, and whether Michael Ignatieff wants to jump off that ledge.

In an extended-family focus group in Cape Breton, there was equally a strong sense that politicians had more serious business to do, in the current economic context, than plunging the country into an unwanted election. And while there was no great affection for Stephen Harper in the room, he was the devil they knew, whereas Ignatieff was the one they didn't.

Cape Bretoners are exactly like Quebecers: they bring far too much food to family events, and the first thing they ask is: "How long since you've been home?"

Far too long, not since Gracie was a baby, and that was 18 years ago. The house is as it has always been, with my grandmother's rocking chair still in the front hall at the bottom of the stairs. Martha Anderson MacDonald knew everyone in Cape Breton. "Now she was a MacAskill from Marion Bridge," she would say, "who married a MacInnis from Gabarous."

Most of them, it seems, are buried in this lovely country cemetery, of which my grandfather was president, and where I spent summers helping the caretaker mow the grass before the annual memorial service in mid-August.

This time we had our own, well worth the drive, and the journey home.

August 2009

DIEF'S GIFT LONG FORGOTTEN

This week marks the 50th anniversary of the proclamation of the Canadian Bill of Rights.

Not the Charter of Rights, but the Bill of Rights proclaimed on August 10, 1960.

John Diefenbaker's Bill of Rights.

No celebration marked the event on Tuesday, nor was much notice taken of it.

Which kind of makes the point that Diefenbaker is very much underappreciated for his achievements as Canada's 13th prime minister.

His greatest political contribution to Canada was breaking the back of a 22-year Liberal dynasty with a Progressive Conservative minority in 1957, followed by the biggest landslide in Canadian history in 1958. Dief provided the alternative that is the lifeblood of a competitive democracy.

He was reduced to minority status in 1962 before losing the 1963 election to Lester B. Pearson, whom he taunted and tormented for four years as leader of the opposition.

Diefenbaker remains the only Conservative leader since Sir John A. Macdonald to win three consecutive elections.

His policy legacy looms much larger in retrospect than it may have in his lifetime, in that it is part of an impressive continuum. So much of what he accomplished paved the way for what happened later, the Bill of Rights being an obvious example.

While it did not have the entrenched constitutional force of the Charter of Rights, most of the key provisions of the Charter – including freedom of speech and religion, and the right to life, liberty and the security of person – were first articulated in the Bill of Rights.

The building of a civil society was the great passion of Diefenbaker's life.

The themes of tolerance and empowerment are found in Diefenbaker's appointment of the first woman, Ellen Fairclough, to Cabinet in 1957. He gave aboriginal Canadians the right to vote without losing their treaty status. He named James Gladstone as the first aboriginal senator in 1958. Diefenbaker took important first steps on the road to bilingualism when he cut government cheques in both languages and introduced simultaneous translation to the House of Commons.

His appointment of the Hall Commission, led by Judge Emmett Hall of Saskatchewan, was a landmark – it led directly to medicare. The Glassco Commission reshaped the organization and administration of government. The Bladen Commission made recommendations resulting in the 1965 Auto Pact, forerunner of the Free Trade Agreement.

A decade before Pierre Trudeau's diplomatic recognition of Red China, Diefenbaker opened the door with wheat sales to China. And then there was Diefenbaker's Northern Vision, with its Roads to Resources program. Half a century later, his Conservative successor, Stephen Harper, has made Arctic sovereignty and sustainable development of the North a centrepiece of his policy agenda.

Diefenbaker was ultimately defeated by reneging on his pledge to accept nuclear weapons in BOMARC missiles on Canadian soil. Half a century later, no Canadian leader advocates nuclear weapons stationed in Canada.

Perhaps on this anniversary of the Bill of Rights, it's a moment to reconsider his achievements.

It you look closely at his statue on Parliament Hill, he is holding the Bill of Rights.

August 2010

MEECH, 25 YEARS ON

Coming out of the Langevin Block on the morning of April 30, 1987, I ran into former Alberta premier Peter Lougheed, who was in Ottawa on business.

"This is a very doable deal," Lougheed said of the meeting the prime minister had called for that day with the premiers on the Constitution at Meech Lake. Lougheed had been consulted by both Brian Mulroney and his own successor, Don Getty. He knew the contents of the federal proposal, and he saw it as a low-cost deal for obtaining the signature of Quebec, which was missing on the 1982 Constitution Act (patriated with the Charter of Rights, over the objections of Quebec).

Mulroney also consulted another important former Conservative, Bill Davis of Ontario, who like Lougheed had been at the table in the 1981 round. "Lougheed and Davis both took the view that a final round was needed to bring in Quebec," he later said. "That was their sense of it."

"I don't think we'll get a deal," Mulroney told me at the time. As he later said: "It was only there, at Meech Lake, that the dynamic enabled us to do what we did."

There was something about the sylvan setting, a very Canadian place in the Gatineau Hills of Quebec, that somehow created a good feeling in the upstairs room at Willson House. There was also the fact that the first ministers were meeting alone, without officials and without advisers, except for two note-takers.

Finally, there was a lot of goodwill around the table toward Quebec Premier Robert Bourassa. They recognized the risks he was taking in re-opening the constitutional file and the price of failure in Quebec.

Getty and Ontario's David Peterson were especially in Bourassa's corner. As chairman of the Premiers' Conference, Getty was the author of the 1986 Edmonton declaration saying a Quebec round was needed to address a five-point agenda put forward by Bourassa's government. As for Peterson, he liked to say: "You can't run the country without Ontario and Quebec, it's that simple."

And he saw it as three-way partnership, or as he called it, "Brian, Robert and me."

At one point, Bourassa had to get up and leave the room to take a call from his finance minister, Gérard D. Lévesque. "I have a budget leak," he said.

His colleagues knew immediately what that meant, that he might have to leave the meeting and fly back to Quebec. They wouldn't have been surprised if he'd set it up himself as a pretext for leaving without walking out.

I was standing a few feet away from Bourassa as he spoke to Lévesque. Since the leak was broadcast on the supper-hour news, he noted, the markets were closed, and budget secrecy intact. He told Lévesque to simply table the budget that evening and returned to the meeting.

That was the moment the other premiers realized he was serious about making a deal. There were five items on the Quebec agenda: entrenching its three seats on the Supreme Court, constitutionalizing an existing immigration accord, limits to the federal spending power, Quebec as a distinct society within Canada and a veto in the amending formula (which all provinces already had, in that it required unanimity to change it).

To which Mulroney added a sixth point: pending Senate reform, appointments to the upper body of Parliament would be made from lists provided by the provinces.

This was an incentive to the western provinces, where there was strong support for an elected Senate.

At mid-evening, Mulroney called a break. Officials huddled at the bottom of the staircase wanted to know what their bosses were up to.

"This is the dangerous moment," quipped New Brunswick's Richard Hatfield, a veteran of all the constitutional wars since the early 1970s. "Get these people out of here."

But the mood and momentum for a deal held, and there was a sense of history being made in the room.

"You're holding a bit of history in your hands," Bourassa told the Quebec press corps when the media were admitted around 10 o'clock that night. Several of them asked him to autograph the communique announcing the details of the deal.

One of the reasons they got Meech was that they ran it under the radar. Once the interest groups and opponents were jolted awake, the dynamic changed. As the all night meeting at the Langevin proved only a month later, it was one thing to get a deal in principle, quite another to agree on a legal text.

And the three-year ratification period for Meech proved that time can be a big enemy in politics. Ratified by eight legislatures, Meech died in June 1990, when Newfoundland Premier Clyde Wells cancelled a scheduled vote in his province on the pretext that it had been blocked on procedural grounds in Manitoba. It was a suicide pact between Wells and Manitoba's Gary Filmon.

On Monday, 25 years to the day, the *Globe and Mail* ran a picture of Mulroney and a smiling group of premiers at Meech Lake

"I'd completely forgotten about that," Mulroney recalled. "Twenty-five years ago today."

Many of us who were there, as privileged witnesses to history, have often wondered how things might have turned out differently for Quebec and Canada if Meech hadn't died.

But that night, as I handed Mulroney his statement, there was a sense the first ministers had made a historic breakthrough.

"This has been a good day for Canada," he began. And so it was.

May 2012

∞

A PMs' CLUB

On holiday in Maine, I've been reading *The Presidents Club*, a bestselling narrative history by Nancy Gibbs and Michael Duffy on the relationship between sitting U.S. presidents and their living predecessors.

As the subtitle confirms, it is "the world's most exclusive fraternity," never having had more than six members, and then only once, when Bill Clinton took office in 1993, and the other members were the first George Bush, Ronald Reagan, Jimmy Carter, Gerald Ford and Richard Nixon.

Currently, there are five members of the club – Barack Obama, George W. Bush, Clinton, Bush Sr. and Carter.

It doesn't matter that they belong to different parties, or even that some of them ran against and defeated one another, they are members of the club, which can be convened any time by the sitting president, who usually calls upon them to attend state funerals or appraise natural disasters. Quite on their own, they attend fundraisers and openings for their presidential libraries.

Along the way, mortal political foes have become close personal friends. In 1981, on the way home from the funeral of slain Egyptian president Anwar Sadat, Ford and Carter talked for the duration of the flight, striking up an enduring friendship. "We found that we had a lot of things in common," said Ford, who was defeated by Carter in 1976. Later they agreed that whichever one died first, the other would give the eulogy at his funeral, as was the case at Ford's death in 2006.

When the disastrous tsunami struck south Asia in 2004, and Hurricane Katrina hit New Orleans and the Gulf Coast in 2005, George W. Bush sent his father and Clinton to the scenes. Together they raised millions in relief. By then, they had become close friends, despite the elder Bush's loss to Clinton in 1992. Clinton is a regular house guest at the Bush summer family estate in Kennebunkport, and they've been known to drop in at Barnacle Billy's, a renowned seafood restaurant at Perkins Cove in Ogunquit.

When a devastating earthquake struck Haiti in 2010, Obama asked George W. Bush and Clinton to be presidential envoys, and they raised more than

$50 million for relief and rebuilding. They, too, have become friends, even appearing together at paid speaking engagements such as the occasional TD-Canada Trust events moderated by Frank McKenna.

The four living presidents sat together at the funeral of Reagan in 2004, where a remarkable eulogy was delivered by Brian Mulroney, the only foreign leader ever to speak at the state funeral of a U.S. president.

But it isn't just funerals and fundraisers that former presidents attend together. Occasionally, the sitting president will convene them for political leverage. In September 1993, Clinton invited the elder Bush, Ford and Carter to the White House for their endorsement of the North American Free Trade Agreement. Seeing the four of them arrive together, and hearing their arguments for NAFTA, was an important moment. After that, from our vantage point at the Canadian Embassy, opposition to NAFTA collapsed in Congress.

They may be in the business of burnishing their legacies – Richard Nixon spent 20 years rebuilding his after Watergate, and Carter made human rights the template of his post-presidency. And they've all had to go out and raise money for their libraries. But they've all sat in the president's chair, and there is no adequate preparation for that.

For a Canadian reader, the question arises as to how we treat our former prime ministers, and whether they're called upon by the prime minister of the day.

The answer is, not very well, and not very often.

There are no prime ministerial libraries on campuses in their home provinces, and their papers simply disappear into the National Archives. Former PMs aren't sent on diplomatic errands, except to attend funerals.

There's nothing like a PMs club in Canada, though there are seven living prime ministers, including Stephen Harper.

David Mitchell had the idea of honouring the former PMs two months ago on the occasion of the 25th anniversary of the Public Policy Forum, the think tank of which he is president. Five out of six showed up at the gala in Toronto: Mulroney, John Turner, Joe Clark, Paul Martin and Kim Campbell. The sixth, Jean Chrétien, was a no-show, apparently because he didn't want to appear with Turner or Martin, his predecessor and successor as Liberal leader.

While his absence didn't spoil the evening in Toronto, neither did it go unremarked. The others spoke about public policy issues close to their hearts – Turner about Parliament, Martin about First Nations, Clark about foreign policy, Mulroney about the public service. Campbell spoke wistfully of being PM as the best job she ever had, one that opened other doors for her. It was one of those nights when everyone won, except the absent former prime minister.

We need more such occasions in Canada, where the service of our prime ministers is celebrated.

July 2012

FREE TRADE AT 25

On the evening of October 3, 1987, Brian Mulroney was in his office in Parliament's Langevin Block, on a conference call with his team in Washington that had just initialled the Canada-U.S. Free Trade Agreement.

It was almost literally five minutes to midnight and the expiration of U.S. President Ronald Reagan's "fast-track authority" to negotiate a deal without amendments by the U.S. Congress.

The Americans, led by Treasury Secretary Jim Baker, had finally agreed to an independent dispute settlement panel, which they had refused before on the ground that it would impede their sovereignty. For Mulroney, the dispute-settlement mechanism was his deal breaker, as he had told Baker that evening in a conversation that proved decisive.

Mulroney explained to Baker that he would be calling Reagan at Camp David and asking him to explain how the Americans could make a nuclear arms-reduction deal with their worst enemy, the Soviets, but couldn't make a trade deal with their best friends, the Canadians.

Baker asked for about 20 minutes, and later burst into his own boardroom at the U.S. Treasury, where the Canadians were gathered, threw a piece of paper on the table, and said, "There's your goddamn dispute settlement mechanism."

It was the making of an historic deal, 25 years ago today. On the open call to his delegation, Mulroney asked one question: "Is this better than what we've got?"

It was a moment when time stood still. The answer, from his chief of staff, Derek Burney, in Washington:

"Yes, Prime Minister."

"Then go ahead."

Later, in the wee hours of Sunday morning, Mulroney met the media at the bottom of the Langevin staircase and said: "A hundred years from now, all that will be remembered is that it was done, and the naysayers will be forgotten."

"We're a much more confident, outward-looking people," he says a quarter century later. "We're much more confident and competitive because we know we can compete and succeed with anyone in the world. Look, if you can do it with the United States of America, you can do it with anyone."

And in a 25-year impact study, BMO Capital Markets deputy chief economist Douglas Porter concludes that the Canada-U.S. Free Trade Agreement, and subsequently the North American Free Trade Agreement of 1992, "were critical ingredients in helping modernize the Canadian economy, and have ultimately played a big role in transforming Canada from a relative underachiever among industrial world economies to a relative overachiever."

There are two particular standouts: bilateral foreign direct investment, and energy trade, notably oil and gas. The BMO study notes that "U.S. direct investment in Canada has jumped from $76 billion in 1988 to $326 billion today," or nearly 19 per cent of Canada's gross domestic product. Canadian foreign direct investment in the U.S. has also jumped, from $81 billion then to $276 billion now, or 16 per cent of our GOP.

Energy has been a huge winner under free trade. The deal in the Free Trade Agreement was security of access to the U.S. in return for security of supply from Canada. Exports of oil and gas, including refined product, were $102 billion last year, or 22 per cent of all our merchandise exports to the world. That's up from $17 billion and 11 per cent of exports in 1992, according to BMO Economics. More than 99 per cent of all our oil and gas exports go to the U.S., where it sells at a discount, but a $100-billion export segment is a stunning number.

Other sectors of the economy that were supposed to be losers under the Free Trade Agreement have come up big winners. Examples: the wine and clothing industries. Instead of producing plonk, Ontario and British Columbia are now making world class wines. Peerless Clothing of Montreal is the world's largest maker of men's suits. And in transportation, Canadian National does nearly half its business in the U.S. After a decade of spectacular growth, exports to the U.S. levelled off in the first decade of the new century. The loonie is now a petro currency, at exchange-rate parity with the U.S. dollar. There was the thickening of the border after 9/11, and the financial crisis and recession of 2008–09, which hurt trade. But overall, it's clear that Canada is a more prosperous place because of the Free Trade Agreement.

Finally, there's the intangible benefit of a change of mindset.

"I think that's one of the big achievements of the Free Trade Agreement," Mulroney says: "The transformation of our attitudes from being somewhat timorous about the Americans, and somewhat fearful of the Americans, to a situation where Canadians are not only confident about dealing with our friends in the U.S., but also around the world."

October 2012

A CAMPAIGN FOR THE AGES

Three weeks before the free trade election on November 21, 1988, Brian Mulroney's campaign plane was about to take off from Ottawa for a critical weeklong swing across Canada. He was sitting alone in the front row, looking out the window, when I handed him his speaking notes for the first event in Vancouver.

"How are you feeling?" I asked.

"He's got the momentum," Mulroney said of John Turner. "Now we're going to find out what we're made of."

What he remembers most about that election, 25 years later, is getting a phone call the previous day at 24 Sussex from a senior Conservative campaign official, informing him that a new poll "shows us dropping significantly and the Liberals running ahead."

"My challenge that day," Mulroney recalls now, "was how could I make sure that there's no hesitation on my part to shore up the troops, that we're going to win nothing less than a majority government."

He hadn't really thought about what Turner had said in the English-language debate on October 25, "because I'd heard it all before, but Canadians were focused for the first time during the campaign, during the debates, the debates are important, and Turner, to his credit, performed well in the debates." What Turner said during the debate came down to a single sound bite: "I believe you have sold us out."

In that moment, Turner tapped into the deep-seated insecurity of Canadians regarding their relations with the United States. Even worse than ignoring us, they were going to take us over.

"People were told you're going to lose your medicare, your pensions, your water, your culture, your identity, and most of all you're going to lose your sovereignty," Mulroney says. "And I wanted to sell out my country and be the governor of the 51st state."

There were actually two campaigns in 1988, the one before the debates, and the one after them. The pre-debate campaign was boring and scripted. The post-debate campaign was the most exciting and momentous of the modern era.

Just before leaving 24 Sussex for that crucial campaign swing three weeks before the vote, Mila Mulroney's advice was simple: "Go out there and campaign like only you can."

And for the next 10 days, as Conservative campaign director Harry Near put it at the time: "Mulroney carried the entire campaign on his back."

For the duration of the campaign, Mulroney never said a word about anything except the Canada-U.S. Free Trade Agreement, and the benefits it would bring. And most of the time, he spoke without a text.

The crowds were huge, and not always friendly. In Kingston, there were so many protesters outside the event that the head of the RCMP detail asked Mulroney on the bus if they could go in by the back door. "No," Mulroney said, "we go in by the front door." And the Mulroneys waded through the shouting and shoving of the protesters.

In Victoria on November 2, the Conservatives staged the biggest event of the campaign, with 2,000 people at a morning rally. Mulroney's speech was continuously interrupted by three hecklers who kept shouting about free trade meaning the end of health care and social programs.

"I'll tell you what," Mulroney said at one point. "You let me finish my speech and I'll meet you afterwards."

And so he did, for an impromptu debate, covered by the media. It was a major turning point, and a very Canadian democratic moment. It turned out that Mulroney knew the details of the deal cold, and three hecklers got an open debate with a prime minister.

Mulroney also enjoyed an inherent advantage in the vote splitting between Liberal leader Turner and the NDP's Ed Broadbent. "For every two votes that came out," Mulroney says now, "I got one and they had to split the other."

And then Mulroney received a huge third-party endorsement from Emmett Hall, the father of health care in Canada. Judge Hall had been appointed head of the royal commission on health care by John Diefenbaker, and his recommendations were adopted by the Pearson government. In retirement, he was chancellor of the University of Saskatchewan. Ray Hnatyshyn, the top Tory in Saskatchewan, had known Hall since Dief named him to the bench and his father, John Hnatyshyn, to the Senate. He persuaded Hall to do a news conference. Hall put his hand on the FTA as if it were the Bible and said nothing in it effected health care in any way, and any suggestion that it did was a lie. Such was the impact of Hall's news conference that the Conservatives got Claude Castonguay, the father of health care in Quebec, to come out the next day and say the same thing.

"That was the end of the election, right there," Mulroney says. On November 10, as he returned to Ottawa for Remembrance Day, Mulroney took a call from his pollster, Allan Gregg. The Liberal numbers had collapsed, and the Conservatives were on course to a majority. The next day, as he greeted the governor general at the National War Memorial, Jeanne Sauvé said she was concerned and asked how "we" were doing. "There's nothing to worry about," he told her. "The election's over."

But the campaign wasn't. The next day, as his bus rolled from Quebec City to Baie-Comeau, he said he wanted to say something personal about his parents' generation, who had built a town out of a forest. "My father dreamed of a better life for his family," he said that night, "I dream of a better life for my country."

A quarter century later, sitting in his corner office at his law firm in Place Ville Marie, Mulroney reflects on the campaign and its outcome. He works at a desk that once belonged to Sir A. Macdonald, and is the only Conservative leader since to win consecutive majority governments. While he thought free trade would be good for Canada, he acknowledges he couldn't be sure what would happen.

The numbers speak for themselves – hundreds of billions of dollars of increased exports, and millions of jobs. But what strikes him most "is the psychological transformation of Canada from a little Canada to a nation of winners." All the trade deals since, including the Canada-EU deal, are the FTA's children.

None of them would have happened without a campaign for the ages.

November 2013

McGUINTY'S MESSY LEGACY

One of the most important things in politics is how a leader leaves the public stage, the moment partisanship ends and the legacy begins.

In Dalton McGuinty's case, we are watching a very messy exit.

In announcing his resignation as Ontario Liberal leader on Monday night, he also prorogued the legislature for the indefinite period of the party's leadership race.

The *Ottawa Citizen*'s big banner headline on Wednesday got it just right: "Queen's Park closed for business."

Under the headline was a huge colour photo of an empty legislative chamber on Tuesday.

Then the *Globe and Mail* weighed in Thursday with a rare front-page editorial, top of the page: "Prorogation an abuse of power."

Well, as the *Citizen*'s subhead pointed out, 132 bills died on the order paper.

McGuinty's pretext for dismissing the provincial parliament was, as the *Globe* editorial put it, "so that he could focus on the government's negotiations with public sector workers and the implementation of a wage freeze."

How's the legacy management team doing so far?

Actually, a public service wage freeze is precisely the sort of thing that should be debated on the floor of the legislature. The NDP and Andrea Horwath would certainly have a view about a wage freeze among public service unions. The Conservatives and Tim Hudak would have to decide whether it was in their interest to side with the NDP and possibly trigger an election, or side with the government and contain costs in the public service.

There's another reason McGuinty doesn't want the legislature in session – the cancellation costs of two gas power plants, already approaching $250 million, with a damaging paper trail of emails in the thousands of pages. Project Vapour? It's got cover-up written all over it.

There's no doubt in our Westminster tradition that a prime minister or premier has the authority to establish the calendar of parliament.

At the federal level, no governor general has ever refused a PM's request to prorogue the House. As we saw in the 2008 parliamentary crisis, Stephen Harper drew on this precedent to avert the defeat of his government by the Three Stooges coalition of the Liberals and NDP, propped up by the Bloc Québécois.

Conveniently, since Harper's throne speech had just passed, as Brian Mulroney's had been in the short free trade implementation session after the 1988 election, there was never any doubt that the GG would accede to his request.

So, while McGuinty is on solid constitutional grounds, his dismissal of the House, for who knows how long, raises questions of legitimacy. Why is the Leg not sitting when it's supposed to be in session? Because the government party is in a leadership race. There are dynastic presumptions about this, and the word arrogant comes to mind.

As for the inconvenience of imposing a public sector wage freeze in a minority legislature, that is the hand McGuinty was dealt in last October's election, when he was fortunate to do as well as he did. Actually, he was fortunate to have Hudak talking about "foreign workers." I digress.

McGuinty came tantalizingly close – at 53 seats, only one short of a majority at Queen's Park. Still, he came up short.

In a bid to graduate to majority territory, McGuinty opened the Conservative seat of Kitchener Waterloo by appointing Elizabeth Witmer chair of the Workplace Safety and Insurance Board, a job that pays $188,000 a year.

Presumably the Liberals had poll numbers telling them they could win the seat. Instead, the NDP pulled off an upset over the Conservatives, while the Liberals finished third.

This may have been a psychological tipping point for McGuinty, the numbing realization that he was stuck with a minority House.

Evidently, his heart was no longer in it.

As for the legacy, any assessment of an Ontario premier begins with the management of fiscal frameworks. This is not a happy story for McGuinty.

When he took office in 2003, he inherited a surplus of $117 million, and a net provincial debt of $132.6 billion, or 28 per cent of provincial GDP.

As he leaves, Ontario has a current deficit of $14.4 billion, and a debt of $257.6 billion, or 39 per cent of GDP, according to BMO Economics.

In other words, Ontario's debt has nearly doubled during his premiership. There are mitigating circumstances – the thickening of the border after 9/11 hurt exports to the U.S., exchange rate parity of our petro currency and the 2008–09 financial crisis and global recession.

But the fact remains that, during the McGuinty years, Ontario became a have-not province, a recipient of equalization payments from Ottawa, amounting to $3.2 billion this year.

Ontarians don't see themselves as a have-not province.

Welcome to legacy management.

October 2012

IF THE WALLS OF THE CHÂTEAU LAURIER COULD TALK

That was Paul Martin walking through the lobby of the Château Laurier Monday afternoon, just a few minutes before Alison Redford left the hotel following a speech. They both walked by Salman Rushdie, who was sitting at the front of the lobby, checking text messages on his phone.

For the storied Château, marking its 100th anniversary this year, it was just another day at the office. Winston Churchill slept there. Pierre Trudeau swam there. Yousuf Karsh had his photo studio there. And everyone who is anyone in Canadian public life has spoken there.

Brian Mulroney remembers attending his first leadership convention there in 1956, and riding in an elevator with John Diefenbaker. After becoming Conservative leader in 1983, he lived for months in Room 496, the best room in the Gold section, the same room where John Turner lived when he was organizing his transition to government in 1984. Mulroney stays in that room to this day. If the walls could talk.

Redford, the Alberta premier, was there to receive the EVE award from Equal Voice, a women's advocacy group, at a sold-out meeting of the Canadian Club. Instead of speaking about energy issues, she spoke about women's issues.

Her message was simple – if women have come a long way, they still have a way to go. She spoke about the importance for young girls of role models, of which she has become one, in a province where both the premier and the opposition leader are women in their 40s. She said her own role model was her mother, a community volunteer.

Paul Martin was there to attend a cocktail in honour of Herb Gray, an iconic Liberal figure. Five of the party's leaders were there – Martin, Stéphane Dion, Bob Rae, Turner and Gray, who was leader of the opposition in the interim between Turner and Jean Chrétien.

Which is not where Rae and the Liberals find themselves now, sitting in the far corner of the House, in third place with only 35 MPs.

But this did not look like a third-place party whose popular vote plunged to an all-time low of 19 per cent only 18 months ago. On the eve of Sir Wilfrid Laurier's birthday, the joint was jumping with about 500 people.

You need to be very careful about writing off the Liberals. They may have fallen to third place, but they still have huge equity in their brand. And they still have a rank and file, and proved it at their convention last January, when 3,400 people paid their own way to Ottawa.

Many of Rae's would-be successors were in the room, including a few you've never heard of, and two with definite name recognition: Justin Trudeau and Marc Garneau. Trudeau and Martin had a moment in the middle of the room, and Liberal activists crowded around for photos. Trudeau works a room very well – he's gracious, he's personable, he's patient and he lets the room come to him.

The leadership campaign is already exacting a certain toll on him, in that he's got two young children at home in Montreal. But he said he manages to get home "two or three nights a week," and is also able to work on the Quebec side of the campaign from there.

Ian McKay, the Liberal party's national director, should have been very happy with the buzz in what amounted to a campaign kickoff, leading to a party convocation in Toronto next April 6, before a week of voting.

The date is an interesting one – it was on April 6, 1968 that Pierre Trudeau became leader of the Liberal party.

November 2012

"ICH BIN EIN BERLINER"

Fifty years ago, on June 26, 1963, John F. Kennedy made a speech in which he famously said: "Ich bin ein Berliner." The Berlin speech was just seven paragraphs on the page, and only nine minutes in a delivery continuously interrupted by cheering and applause from a throng of hundreds of thousands of people.

But in those nine minutes, Kennedy tautly defined the terms of the Cold War, and correctly predicted the outcome. The heart of the speech was the refrain: "Let them come to Berlin."

Standing in front of the Berlin Wall, he declared: "There are many people in the world who really don't understand, or say they don't, what is the great issue between the free world and the communist world. Let them come to Berlin. There are some who say communism is the wave of the future. Let them come to Berlin. And there are some who say, in Europe and elsewhere, we can work with the communists. Let them come to Berlin. And there are even a few who say that communism is an evil system, but it permits us to make economic progress. Lass' sie nach Berlin kommen. Let them come to Berlin."

And of the Berlin Wall, erected in 1961, he then said: "Freedom has many difficulties, and democracy is not perfect, but we have never had to put a wall up to keep our people in, to prevent them from leaving us."

From West Berlin and East Berlin to Berlin. From West Germany and East Germany to Germany. Who could have foreseen that then? Kennedy did, in a single sentence: "When all are free, we can look forward to that day, when this city will be joined as one, and this country and this great continent of Europe in a peaceful and hopeful globe."

He was predicting the fall of the Berlin Wall, the reunification of Berlin and Germany, the emergence of the European Community and the end of the Cold War.

And finally: "All free men, wherever they live, are citizens of Berlin, and therefore, as a free man, I take pride in the words, Ich bin ein Berliner."

And as they used to say, the crowd went wild (it's on YouTube, and many other websites).

But even as Kennedy was poking a rhetorical stick at the Russian bear, he had launched a summer peace campaign with Soviet Chairman Nikita Khrushchev. Earlier in June 1963, Kennedy gave a commencement address at the American University in Washington in which he proposed to end nuclear weapons testing. The resulting treaty, negotiated over the summer of 1963, was approved by the U.S. Congress and presented to the United Nations, all before Kennedy's death in Dallas in November of the same year.

And as the American economist Jeffrey Sachs notes in a timely and powerful new book, *To Move the World: JFK's Quest for Peace*, Kennedy and Khrushchev were united by having peered at the nuclear abyss during the October Missile Crisis of 1962, in which the world as we know it could easily have ended. Subsequently, they were partners invested in taking steps away from war, and toward peace.

One of the tests of politics is the policy continuum from one government to the next. Kennedy's Berlin speech met that test, as well setting a rhetorical standard.

Nearly a quarter-century later, on June 12, 1986, Ronald Reagan made the second famous Berlin speech, also renowned for four words: "Tear down this wall."

Standing in front of the wall at the Brandenburg Gate, Reagan directly challenged Mikhail Gorbachev: "Mr. Gorbachev, open this gate.

"Mr. Gorbachev, tear down this wall."

But even as he was challenging Gorbachev, Reagan offered the outstretched hand: "We welcome change and openness," referring to Gorbachev's signature policies of perestroika and glasnost.

And they were already at work on the same agenda as Kennedy and Khrushchev – arms control. At their Reykjavik summit in October 1986, they came very close to a major agreement, only to fail at the last minute. But Reykjavik set the table for the December 1987 agreement to eliminate short and medium range missiles.

In November 1989, the Berlin Wall was breached and neither the East Germans nor the Soviets made any attempt to close it again. It was the end of the Warsaw Pact. And at the end of 1991, the Soviet Union itself ceased to exist. In 1990, Berlin and Germany were reunified, the great project of Chancellor Helmut Kohl. Gorbachev did not oppose reunification.

Later, in private life, Kohl's office was in the former East Berlin.

All of which began exactly half a century ago with Kennedy's clarion call, in seven paragraphs and nine minutes that proved what Sachs calls "the power of oratory."

It was by no means the most elegant or eloquent of Kennedy's speeches – for that, you need look no further than his splendid address to the Irish Parliament only two days later. But no speech in modern times has proven more prescient or consequential. Let them come to Berlin.

June 2013

REMEMBRANCE DAY

It's an anomaly of Remembrance Day that even as the ranks of veterans are thinning, the crowds keep growing by the year. Where they once numbered in the hundreds, they are now counted in the thousands, in Ottawa and across Canada. Where poppies were once worn for a week or so before Remembrance Day, they now appear after Thanksgiving.

The Royal Canadian Legion has a lot to do with that, with their student essay contests and veterans speaking at schools. The mainstream media, led by the CBC, have provided huge coverage.

Don Newman anchored CBC-TV's Remembrance Day coverage for more than 20 years until 2008, and as he writes in his new memoir, crowds and television audiences "began to grow after 1994 and the celebration of the 50th anniversary of the successful D-Day landing in Normandy on June 6, 1944 that marked the beginning of the end of the Second World War."

"We seemed to go through a period there in the 60s, 70s and 80s where the crowds really thinned," Peter Mansbridge was saying Monday night following a special on the CBC's main channel from the National War Museum on the coming centennial of the First World War. "But the change began in the 90s after the D-Day specials and the VE (Victory in Europe) anniversary in 1995. But most of the credit goes to the veterans for going into the schools."

The veterans of the Second World War are now three generations removed from today's school children, but they have made a magical connection. And the students' essays speak of the bravery of ordinary Canadians, from the trenches of one war to the beaches of the next.

And now social media are driving interest in Remembrance Day. Ninety per cent of the posts to my Twitter account on Monday morning were tributes in 140 characters or less to the writers' parents or grandparents.

In our family, my father, Art MacDonald, was in the army for the duration of the Second World War. He joined as a second lieutenant and became the youngest major in the forces, in charge of electrical installations on the east coast of Canada.

As for my mother, Marian Agnes Roach, she served on the home front as a nurse and later became the matron of the Queen Mary Veterans' Hospital.

My parents belonged to what Tom Brokaw later called "the greatest generation," who fought the war, won the peace and created the prosperity we enjoy today. They had many friends from the war, but never talked about it.

Because of his service, our first home was an apartment at Benny Farm in Montreal, a post-war federal housing project for veterans and their families.

From the First and Second World Wars, down to the present day service in Afghanistan, Canadians have always punched above their weight. In a country of only nine million people, Sir Robert Borden raised one of the largest armies in Europe. Which, at his insistence, got Canada its own seat at the Versailles peace conference of 1919. In the Second World War, Mackenzie King hosted the Quebec conferences of 1943 and 1944 with Franklin Roosevelt and Winston Churchill. The first conference settled the plan for the liberation of Europe, and the second the shape of the post-war world.

As for Afghanistan, it is too soon to say whether our mission there has been worth it, in terms of helping the Afghans put down the roots of democracy, and making their schools safe for girls. It is not too soon to say that our men and women in uniform took on the most dangerous assignment in that broken country – the Kandahar region, home of the Taliban. There have been far too many come home in coffins to CFB Trenton, where the 401 to Toronto becomes the Highway of Heroes.

At least those soldiers have been buried with full honours. The Harper government has come under fire for what a *Globe and Mail* editorial called "failing to properly fund the Last Post Fund," a non-profit to ensure "all former soldiers, some of whom are impoverished to the point of homelessness are given a proper burial."

Ottawa has also been criticized for cuts to veterans funding and closing of Veterans' Affairs offices. The Veterans' Ombudsman says new compensation rules would, according to the *Globe*, "leave more than 400 severely disabled veterans in poverty after the age of 65." If there's a problem with veterans' funding, Ottawa should simply fix it in the next budget. The government can't honour veterans one day, and stiff them the next.

A dignified end of their days is the least that's owed those who marched in the cold past the National War Memorial on Monday. They are among two million who have served, while more than 115,000 Canadians never came home. As for Remembrance Day, it has been become as big an event as Canada Day, not as a celebration but as an occasion.

November 2013

FOUNDERS' INTENT: AN APPOINTED SENATE

The Supreme Court has replied to the Harper government: Since you asked, the answer is no, you can't.

No, you can't change the method of selecting Senators, or introduce term limits, without a constitutional amendment through the "7/50" general amending formula requiring the consent of Parliament and seven provinces representing at least 50 per cent of the population.

And, no you also can't simply abolish the Senate without the unanimous consent of the provinces. Don't even think about it, said the Supremes, who were themselves unanimous in knocking down the questions put by the government in the Senate reference case.

In doing so, the High Court interpreted as never before the intent of the Fathers of Confederation in the British North America Act, now styled the Constitution Act, 1867. In the U.S., they would call this "framers' intent."

"The Senate is one of Canada's foundational political institutions," the Supremes wrote. "It lies at the heart of the agreements that gave birth to the Canadian federation."

In other words, the framers' intent for Canada's bi-cameral legislature was that the House of Commons would be an elected body, while the Senate would be an appointed one, free of short-term political pressures.

The judgment noted that introducing "consultative elections for the nomination of senators would change our Constitution's architecture, by endowing senators with a popular mandate which is inconsistent with the Senate's fundamental nature and role as a complementary chamber of sober second thought."

Then they said it again, referring to the Senate as "a complementary legislative body rather than a perennial rival to the House of Commons."

That the Senate has taken a reputational hit in the expenses affair is hardly relevant to the Court. They're telling us how the Fathers of Confederation envisioned the Senate's role. That it was an appointed rather than an elected chamber "was not an accident of history."

And in that regard, the Supremes are strict interpreters of the Constitution.

For example, the government thought it had leeway to impose term limits of eight or nine years, based on the 1965 precedent of senators taking mandatory retirement at age 75, where previously they had been appointed for life. Parliament acted alone on that.

Nope, said the Supremes. It's a 7/50.

Consultative elections for Senate nominees? Sorry. Also a 7/50.

This is interesting in that Alberta has had consultative elections since the late 1980s, asking voters their preferential choice for the Senate in the event of vacancies. Alberta's first "elected" senator was Stan Waters, though he was appointed by Brian Mulroney in 1990. Subsequently, the Chrétien and Martin governments declined to appoint Alberta "senators-in-waiting" and it wasn't until Stephen Harper came to office in 2006 that Alberta got its next "elected" senator in 2007. Last year, Harper appointed two more "elected" senators from Alberta, Doug Black and Scott Tannas.

Alberta is, of course, the heartland of the Triple-E Senate movement.

Since the time of Preston Manning and the Reform Party, Alberta has called for a Triple E Senate – equal, effective and elected. None of which is in the offing, certainly not after the Supreme Court ruling.

So what now for advocates of an elected Senate?

"Significant reform and abolition are off the table," Harper said. "I think it's a decision that I'm disappointed with. But I think it's a decision that the vast majority of Canadians will be very disappointed with, but obviously we will respect that decision."

Canadians, he said, were "stuck with the status quo."

In a way, the Court has taken Harper off the hook on the issue of Senate reform. He can simply shrug and say, "What can you do?"

Nothing.

It's not Harper's style to call a First Ministers' Conference, let alone one to discuss the Constitution.

And in the event he ever did, it wouldn't be limited to Senate reform. Quebec would show up with its agenda, with the ghosts of Meech Lake. First Nations would have to be there, too. And even if there were an agreement on the Senate and other issues, there's a three-year period for constitutional amendments to be ratified by provincial legislatures. Which is how Meech Lake died in 1990, when the Manitoba and Newfoundland legislatures ran out the clock.

None of which is the Supreme Court's problem. The role of the Supremes is to interpret the Constitution, not to re-write it.

Nor is it the Court's problem if the Senate is seen as a dysfunctional body, or one in danger of falling into disrepute.

And if you don't want them to settle a constitutional question, don't ask.

April 2014

SCOTLAND: YES OR NO

Could Scotland be an independent country? Of course it could.

Truth be told, Scotland has all the attributes to be a sovereign country – the Scots are a people with their own geography, history and institutions.

"Should Scotland be an independent country?" That's a very different question. It also happens to be the exact question in Thursday's referendum. Six words, please answer Yes or No.

There's quite a bit riding on it, starting with the future of Scotland and the United Kingdom. There's a lot more than six words to that. But at least it's an honest question. There's no deliberate ambiguity, quite different from the tormented question posed by the Yes forces in Quebec in 1980.

The 1980 referendum question on so-called sovereignty-association was 114 words in French, 107 words in English, on the Quebec government's "proposal to negotiate a new agreement with the rest of Canada, based on the equality of nations; this agreement would enable Quebec to acquire the exclusive power to make its laws, levy its taxes and establish relations abroad-in other words, sovereignty-and at the same time to maintain with Canada an economic association, including a common currency; any change in political status resulting from these negotiations will only be implemented with popular approval through another referendum."

The 1995 referendum question was a comparative model of brevity, at 41 words in English, the heart of which asked: "Do you agree that Quebec should become sovereign after having made a formal offer to Canada for a new economic and political partnership?" The Yes side was going nowhere until three weeks before the vote, when Bloc Québécois leader Lucien Bouchard was named chief negotiator, which transformed the referendum campaign into a cliffhanger that nearly resulted in the breakup of Canada.

Similarly, in Scotland, a late surge by the Yes side has upended the assumption of a walk in the park for the No side. Only 10 days before the vote, The *Sunday Times* of London published a poll which put the Yes ahead for the first time, 51–49.

What followed was a week of panic in political circles and financial markets.

Campaigning in Scotland, Prime Minister David Cameron said this was not an election question about thumping "the effing Tories," but a question of country, "and I care more about my country than I do about my party."

But it was Cameron who insisted on the up-or-down question, with no third option such as devolution on the ballot, though he's certainly been talking a lot about that in the last week. The three British Westminster parties all agree on it.

Meanwhile, the financial markets served reminders that they don't like uncertainty, and Scotland-based banks and insurance companies served notice that they would vote with their feet and leave Scotland for London in the event of a Yes.

By the weekend, a fresh batch of polls showed that while the referendum was still too close to call, it was trending back to the No, mostly as a matter of head over heart. The *Sunday Times* poll this week had the No side ahead

50.6 to 49.4 (the result, to the decimal percentage point, of the 1995 Quebec referendum). A *Guardian* poll on Friday had the No side leading 54–46, while the last word on the weekend belonged to *The Observer* which on Sunday had the No ahead 53–47.

There are too many questions about the consequences of a Yes to which its leadership has no good answers.

For Quebecers and Canadians who've seen this movie twice, it's pretty much Groundhog Day.

It starts with the question of a common currency. Or not. All three Westminster parties – the Tories, Labour and Liberal Democrats – have rejected a monetary union and would not share the pound with Scotland.

Mark Carney, the Canadian governor of the Bank of England, was quite explicit last week when he said "a currency union is incompatible with sovereignty."

For his part, Scottish First Minister and Yes leader Alex Salmond dismissed this as fear mongering and said Scotland could simply adopt the pound as its own. He's right – nothing would prevent Scotland from using the pound, but it would have no seats on the central bank board, and no voice in monetary policy, a fundamental attribute of sovereignty to almost any country.

Then, there's the question of Scotland assuming its share of the British national debt. Forget about it, says Salmond, unless Scotland is allowed to share the pound. But a country can't walk away from its financial obligations, not without paying huge borrowing costs. Scotsman Gordon Brown, the former PM and chancellor of the exchequer, has called this "the road to ruin."

As it happens, based on its population of 5.3 million out of 63.7 million people in the UK, Scotland's share is 92 billion pounds out of Britain's national debt of 1.3 trillion pounds.

On the business side, the Royal Bank of Scotland, Lloyds Banking Group and Standard Life have all said they'd move their head offices from Scotland to London in the event of a Yes victory. We've been through that in Quebec in the 1970s, when Sun Life noisily moved its head office from Montreal to Toronto after the PQ's election in 1976, while Royal Bank and Bank of Montreal quietly moved their operations to Toronto, while maintaining legal head offices in Montreal. These guys aren't kidding, either.

Then, who would be citizens of Scotland, and could they be dual British citizens? The Yes side says all Scottish-born British citizens, and Scottish residents, would automatically become citizens of Scotland. The Union side is silent on this question.

What about the border with England? The pro-independence forces want Scotland to become part of the Common Travel Area within the UK, though it wouldn't be in the United Kingdom any more.

Then, there's the European Union, and whether Scotland would qualify for automatic membership since it's currently part of the UK, or whether it would have to apply on its own. And if it did, would it then join the 17 members of the euro area? Which goes back to the common currency question.

There's one further similarity between the No side in Quebec in 1980, and Scotland in 2014. They've had the same campaign slogan, "No Thanks." Which, now as then, says it all in a polite but firm manner.

There are those in Canada who worry that a victory by the Yes side in Scotland will help revive the slumbering separatist forces in Quebec. But 2014 isn't 1980, when the Yes forces were energized by the youth cohort. In last spring's provincial election, the 18–24 age demographic voted Liberal, as did every other demo by double digit margins, excepting only the 55–64 age group, who were nostalgic for another era.

And the close call of 1995, which saw divided families and broken friendships, is an experience very few Quebecers want to live through again.

But the Quebec independence movement does have one thing in common with its Scottish cousins – the absence of a rationale for breaking up a great country.

September 2014

THROW THE BUMS OUT

Turning around a losing campaign is tough enough for a governing party in an election where the ballot frame is "time for a change." It becomes impossible when the voters move beyond change to "throw the bums out" – which is what happened in Alberta.

After nearly 44 years, they threw the bums out. The longest reigning party dynasty in Canadian political history was kicked out of office. "Time for a change" was a sidebar.

Four short weeks ago, no one predicted an NDP majority government in Alberta – or even that Rachel Notley might end up as leader of the opposition.

No one foresaw the end of Conservative party rule, supposedly renewed under Jim Prentice, much less the Tories being relegated to third place in the Alberta legislature. And no one saw the Wildrose Party – dumped by their own leader when Danielle Smith and eight colleagues crossed the floor to join the Tories – enjoying the delicious revenge of regaining their role as official opposition under Brian Jean.

What happened? Well, campaigns matter. And Notley clearly won the campaign, as the vivacious agent of hope and change. There was nothing not to like about her, especially after the leaders' debate, which she clearly won.

Prentice not only lost the campaign, he lost a lot going into it – by dropping the writ a year ahead of Alberta's fixed-election date of May 2016, for starters.

Prentice was the consensus choice to lead the Conservatives after Alison Redford was forced out by her own caucus in the wake of her tone-deaf entitlement crises. Prentice did well at first, selling off the Alberta government's plane fleet and making other useful gestures, such as pay cuts for cabinet ministers.

But Prentice made what proved to be a fatal mistake when, a week before Christmas, he accepted Smith and eight other Wildrose floor-crossers into the Conservative fold. In a dynasty already 43 years old, the government had overthrown the opposition; it's supposed to work the other way around. As they talked about it around the dinner table over the holidays, Albertans decided it was undemocratic.

Then, with the collapse of oil prices, Prentice was looking at a very tough spring budget – one with a cyclical $5 billion deficit, to say nothing of structural issues such as the highest-paid public service in Canada and the lowest tax rates. "Look in the mirror," he told Albertans in March. It wasn't the message they wanted to hear.

Then Prentice's budget offered 59 personal tax and user fee hikes – but no corporate tax increases. The voters didn't like that, even in free-enterprise Alberta.

And a week later, with budget blowback already building, he dropped a pre-emptive election writ when he could have taken the summer to see how it had all played out, and when he could he have spent 10 days in July at the Calgary Stampede.

Then came the leaders' debate, in which he deliberately pivoted to Notley and, while discussing the cost of her platform, spoke those famous words "I know, the math is hard."

So now Prentice is out; he wisely chose to resign and move on with the rest of his life. It won't be in public life, which is Canada's loss. Had he won the Alberta election, he would have been an obvious candidate for the federal Conservative leadership after Stephen Harper. Whenever that happens, Prentice won't be part of the federal leadership conversation.

Whoever assumes the leadership of the Alberta Progressive Conservatives will be looking at a long re-build. Though the PCs won 28 per cent of the popular vote (four points more than Wildrose) the WRP won 11 more seats, 21 to 10. The Conservatives lost 59 seats on Tuesday.

And what does Rachel Notley do on the morning after her historic victory?

Well, she is forming a majority social-democratic government in the oilpatch. The first person she should meet is Richard Dicerni, the head of the Alberta public service, who will give her the transition books his staff has prepared.

She should know that Dicerni is one of the great Canadian public servants of the modern era, a senior deputy minister at Queen's Park and Ottawa, where he was Prentice's DM at the Industry ministry. The first thing she should do is ask him to stay on.

And for grace notes, it's impossible to beat Notley's speech thanking Prentice for his service to Alberta and Canada, congratulating Jean for his courageous campaign in the wake of losing his son, and thanking the people of Alberta "for putting their trust in our party." A brilliant acceptance speech.

Now for the hard part: Government, ready or not.

May 2015

GETTING IT WRONG

There was consternation in the public service and confusion in Ottawa's political class when Justin Trudeau ditched Janice Charette as clerk of the Privy Council and secretary to the cabinet, replacing her with her deputy clerk, Michael Wernick.

The public service was shocked at the timing of the clerk shuffle – days before a deputy ministers' retreat that Charette would have chaired, with the announcement itself being made in a news release by the prime minister from the Davos conference in Switzerland.

So Trudeau was out of town and out of the country. Bad form. Mind you, it's happened once before – in 2009, when the Prime Minister's Office announced the departure of Kevin Lynch as clerk while Stephen Harper was visiting Canadian troops in Afghanistan. In both instances, the PMO's approach was insensitive and inelegant.

The confusion among politicos arose from the second paragraph of Trudeau's announcement – which said that "the prime minister has asked Mr. Wernick for advice on a process to fill the position on a permanent basis."

Consulting and lobbying firms were immediately inundated with calls and texts from clients asking whether filling "the position on a permanent basis" referred to Charette's new assignment, or – more likely – "a process" for filling the clerk's role on a permanent basis. In other words, part of Wernick's mandate is to help find his own replacement.

So, was Wernick clerk, interim clerk or a placeholder for someone else? Those questions would have been very much on the minds of his colleagues as they gathered at the DMs' retreat.

The clerk is not only secretary to the cabinet, but also head of the public service.

Wernick has been in the public service since he joined Finance 35 years ago, and notably survived eight years as DM at Aboriginal Affairs from 2006–14, a tumultuous period even by the standards of a department which historically has been a graveyard for many careers. Wernick's time covered Stephen Harper's apology to First Nations, the appointment of the Truth and Reconciliation Commission, the Idle No More movement and the sabotaging of the First Nations Control of Education Act by dissident chiefs. As clerk, he's uniquely qualified to lead the implementation of the TRC's sweeping recommendations, Trudeau having accepted all 94 of them.

But as a placeholder. The question is – who's next?

The obvious candidate is Matthew Mendelsohn.

Who? He's an academic from McGill and Université de Montréal, a poli-sci prof at Queen's turned public servant at Queen's Park, founder of the Mowat Centre think tank at University of Toronto, and adviser to the Liberals in the fall election and transition.

Most of Ottawa missed Mendelsohn's appointment as deputy secretary in PCO, probably because it was made two days before Christmas. He's heading a new secretariat called "results and delivery," the re-branded Priorities and Planning secretariat reporting to the cabinet committee on "agenda and results," the former P&P inner cabinet committee chaired by the PM.

As a younger prof in the mid-1990s, Mendelsohn took a leave of several years to work in PCO in the intergovernmental affairs secretariat during a period that included the 1995 Quebec referendum. In the mid-2000s, he took another leave from Queen's to become a deputy minister in several portfolios at Queen's Park during the Dalton McGuinty era. That makes him a close colleague of Trudeau's principal secretary, Gerry Butts, who held down the same role in McGuinty's office during the time Mendelsohn was there.

Mendelsohn has impressive credentials as an academic, deputy minister and public intellectual. The Mowat Centre, in the six short years since he founded it, has done some important work and has become one of the country's leading think tanks. He took a leave to work on the 2015 Liberal campaign and was one of the authors of the Liberal platform. And as the *Ottawa Citizen's* outstanding public service beat writer Kathryn May noted in a mid-January profile, "he also worked with Trudeau's transition team to help craft Trudeau's mandate letters for ministers – fittingly penning the passages about how ministers will be expected to track and report on government priorities."

Which makes him, as the *Citizen* headline put it, "Trudeau's go-to guy."

It also helps explain the changing of the guard in PCO but it does not explain why Charette has been treated so shabbily by PMO. One explanation may be the Liberals' annoyance at the fact that PCO issued orders-in-council during the lame duck period, approving 33 Conservative appointments to government boards that took effect only after the election. As if a clerk of PCO could say no to a prime minister.

In his statement from Davos, Trudeau had the good sense to thank Charette "for her exemplary service to Canada," as well as for guiding "the public service through an election year and my government through a seamless transition."

But it's not a seamless transition in PCO, far from it. In the normal course of events, Trudeau would have waited until the summer, allowing her more than just 15 months on the job.

There's a protocol for how former clerks are treated. Usually they are named privy councillors, meaning they are known as "the Honourable." As for what they do next, that normally depends on what they want to do. An appointment to a Canadian embassy in a G7 country is one option, as was the case with Mel Cappe, named high commissioner to London by Jean Chrétien in 2002, and Alex Himelfarb, named ambassador to Rome by Harper in 2006. Other clerks, such as Paul Tellier and Lynch, decided on business careers.

When Brian Mulroney asked Tellier what he wanted to do after seven years as clerk in 1992, he replied that he wanted to lead the privatization of CN, which he did brilliantly as CEO over the next decade. Lynch opted for a career on Bay Street as vice-chair of BMO and a corporate director, while developing his work for universities and think tanks. Charette, highly popular with her staff and well regarded by the PS, has been left "pending." The town has taken note.

Trudeau and his entourage got this wrong. They got something else wrong this week in his keynote speech at Davos. "My predecessor wanted you to know Canada for its resources," he declared. "I want you to know

Canadians for our resourcefulness." A lovely turn of phrase, but completely the wrong note.

It is very inappropriate to take domestic political differences abroad, and to personalize them like that. It's considered very bad form to trash a former opponent in an international setting. It's time for Team Trudeau to stop campaigning and start governing. In other words, it's time for "results and delivery."

January 2016

BAILING OUT BOMBARDIER

At first glance, you'd think Bombardier winning a huge breakthrough order for 75 CSeries jets from Delta Airlines, with an option for another 50, would relieve the pressure on Ottawa to match Quebec's $1.3 billion investment in the aircraft program.

The Delta order comes only two months after Air Canada signed a letter of intent to buy 45 CS300s at a list price of US$3.8 billion, with an option for another 30.

So, Bombardier doesn't need Ottawa buying into the CSeries, right? Not exactly.

The Delta order is two years away from deliveries beginning in 2018, and has been negotiated at a steep discount, believed to be as much as two-thirds off the list price of US$5.6 billion. Similarly, Air Canada will be negotiating an aggressive discount. Cash flow from these deals is years away.

In the meantime, Bombardier still has liquidity issues around the CSeries, which is two years behind schedule and $2 billion over budget.

So an injection of cash would obviously be welcomed by Bombardier, with Quebec Premier Philippe Couillard aggressively urging Ottawa to support the Montreal-based company just as it rescued Ontario-based General Motors and Chrysler in the global financial meltdown of 2009. Couillard is not wrong about that – without Ottawa's $10 billion equity investment in GM and Chrysler seven years ago, they would have left Canada.

Nor is Bombardier a Quebec-only company. It also employs some 3,700 aerospace workers in Ontario, where its Downsview plant makes the Q400 turbo prop that is the backbone of the Porter and Air Canada Express fleets. If you're flying out of Toronto Island, you're flying the Q400. Bombardier also employs nearly 2,500 more Ontarians in its rail division, whose Thunder Bay plant makes subway vehicles, street cars and GO trains for the Greater Toronto Area. Not to mention Ontario-based suppliers in both aerospace and rail. Which is reason enough for Ontario Premier Kathleen Wynne to have endorsed Couillard's call for a federal investment in Bombardier.

So there's important political cover for Justin Trudeau as his Liberal government considers Bombardier's ask. The prime minister is personally on the record praising the CSeries as an "extraordinary airplane," adding: "Our question is very much how do we make sure that the airplane is a success and how are we making sure it is a Canadian success story?"

The point is that aerospace is a high tech industry, with highly paid jobs all along the supply chain in both Quebec and Ontario. And rail is going to be a key component of government infrastructure spending worldwide, which is why the Quebec pension plan, the Caisse de dépôt, has invested $1.5 billion for a 30 per cent stake in Bombardier Transportation.

Still, it's not just a question of Ottawa writing a cheque for $1.3 billion. There's due diligence to be done by the office of Economic Development Minister Navdeep Bains. For arm's length advice, the government has also hired New York investment banker Morgan Stanley, and a major commercial law firm, Osler Hoskin, as advisers on the Bombardier file.

There's one area of disagreement between Ottawa and Bombardier over how an investment would be structured, as well as a potential deal-breaker over the company's dual class shares which keep control of the company in the hands of the Bombardier-Beaudoin family.

Evidently, Ottawa's preferred route is credit financing, while Bombardier is asking Ottawa to match Quebec's equity investment in the CSeries.

As for the family's multiple-voting dual class shares, they are not about to relinquish control of the company, something the market is demanding. Among other things, Bombardier maintains the share structure protects the company from a foreign takeover.

At the end of the day, this is Trudeau's call. As a Montreal MP, he knows very well the importance of the aerospace industry to Quebec, not just in economic terms but as a matter of pride. So does Transport Minister Marc Garneau, who as a former astronaut and head of the Canadian Space Agency, knows all about the economic benefits of R&D in the industry.

Among other advantages for Bombardier, a federal investment would be a signal to the world that the government of the company's home country stands behind it on the global aviation stage.

Canada doesn't have many industrial world champions. Barrick Gold in mining is one that comes to mind. Peerless Clothing in men's suits is another. Bombardier in aerospace and rail transportation.

There's no doubt that the Delta announcement takes Bombardier and the CSeries to a higher-level in an extremely competitive and cutthroat industry.

As Delta President Ed Bastian noted at the announcement at Bombardier's Mirabel plant: "The decision by Delta, in our opinion, brings Bombardier as a third competitor into the mainline aircraft marketplace with Boeing and Airbus."

As the second-largest airline in the world, Delta is a global trend-setter in terms of modernizing and replacing its fleet. The Bombardier deal means other major airlines will take a serious look at the CSeries.

Among the plane's comparative advantages is that's it's environmentally friendly – 20 per cent more fuel efficient than its competitors.

Which would be one reason for airlines to buy it, as well as for passengers to fly it, and for Trudeau to get involved.

April 2016

THE 24 SUSSEX FIXER-UPPER

The last time any renovations were done on 24 Sussex, the work began during the summer election campaign of 1984, and it wasn't until months later that Brian Mulroney moved into the prime minister's official residence.

The makeover cost over $1 million then, and Mulroney, concerned about the optics, wrote a personal cheque to cover more than $200,000 of the home reno.

The governor general of the day, Jeanne Sauvé, strongly advised him against it.

"Brian, don't do it," she told him, "you'll never get any credit for it in this town."

She was right. All he got for his trouble was a story in the *Globe and Mail* about a shoe closet with room for dozens of pairs of Guccis and his wardrobe of tailor-made suits.

Ever since, no prime minister has gone anywhere near the need to upgrade Sussex. Not Jean Chrétien, not Paul Martin, and not Stephen Harper.

The place is a dump, literally falling apart. There's no central air conditioning in the 34-room house, although there is asbestos in the walls, and the ceilings need to be fixed up. The limestone exterior is in serious need of sandblasting.

It's a Confederation era house, built by lumber baron and MP Joseph Merrill Currier between 1866 and 1868. The government acquired the property in 1950 and it has been the PM's residence since 1951. John Turner never lived there, but at the country residence at Harrington Lake, during his brief summer as prime minister in 1984. Neither did Kim Campbell when being PM was her summer job in 1993. But Louis St.-Laurent, John Diefenbaker, Lester B. Pearson, Pierre Trudeau, Joe Clark, Mulroney, Chrétien, Martin and Harper have all called it home.

And a lot of history has been made there. The queen has been there many times on the watch of her 11 Canadian prime ministers during her remarkable 63-year reign. On the morning of Canada Day in 1992, the country's 125th birthday, she was sitting with Mulroney in the alcove of the dining room, reviewing her remarks. "Prime Minister," she said, "we really should mention your peacekeepers in the former Yugoslavia." She wrote it in her marginal notes, and was lustily cheered when she said it on Parliament Hill.

Ronald Reagan had lunch there in April 1987, and changed his Joint Address to the House to include references to Canada's claims on the Northwest Passage and positive comments on the talks that led to the Acid Rain Accord. Speaking of which, the first George Bush told the media at Sussex that he "got an earful" on acid rain at a lunch with Mulroney in 1989.

But Sussex has fallen into such a state of disrepair that a prime minister wouldn't want to invite anyone there. Barack Obama has never set foot in the place. His one visit to Ottawa in 2009 was entirely on Parliament Hill, with a stop in the Byward Market at a cookie shop he made famous.

In 2008, the then auditor general, Sheila Fraser, recommended $10 million in renovations. Harper's chief of staff at the time, Ian Brodie, said he saw an estimate of at least twice that amount. Even Fraser's lower number would come in around $15 million today.

It was no surprise the other day when it was announced that Justin Trudeau and his family would not be moving in. Instead, they are moving to Rideau Cottage, the gracious 22-room residence of the secretary to the governor general on the grounds of Rideau Hall.

That makes a great deal of sense. For one thing, it's behind the stone gates of the GG's residence, and the RCMP insists the PM live in a secure residence. The other two official residences in the neighbourhood, Stornoway and 7 Rideau Gate, are not fenced in.

Now the question is what is to be done with Sussex?

Whatever decision is made, Trudeau shouldn't be any part of it. He should never have to wear the cost of any decision, to renovate or re-build Sussex, or to acquire another property for the PM's residence.

The National Capital Commission runs the official residences, but these decisions are made on the advice of the Privy Council Office. Some thought might be given to each recognized party in the House naming one MP to an advisory oversight committee that could recommend what to do. A bi-partisan process, one in which all parties had ownership, would shield Trudeau from any political flak.

There are several other possibilities. One would be to buy Earnscliffe, Sir John A. Macdonald's historic home on Sussex, long the residence of the British high commissioner. It comes with a requisite stone gate, and the same river view as at 24. However, it's not on the market. The Brits have recently completed their own renovation of Earnscliffe, and they are quite attached to the place. Among other advantages is its location, across the street from the Pearson Foreign Affairs Building.

When Jim Flaherty was finance minister, and the cost of renovating 24 Sussex came up in 2008, he had another idea. "Tear it down," he once said, "have a competition among Canadian architects, and build a modern new residence for the PM."

The final option is to renovate 24 Sussex, whatever the cost, media bush league behaviour be damned.

Canada is a G7 country. It's time we acted like one.

October 2015

SOPHIE'S CHOICE

Sophie Grégoire-Trudeau says she needs help around the office, as well as at home. And she's right.

She's been trying to manage the many demands on her time with only one assistant, and with no space of her own at the Prime Minister's Office in the Langevin Building.

"I'd like to be everywhere but I can't" she told *Le Soleil* on the margins of an appearance in Quebec City before FillActive, a group promoting fitness and healthy activity for teenaged girls. "I have three children at home and a husband who is prime minister. I need a team to help me serve the public."

Her comments have caused predictable push back by the opposition Conservatives and NDP, as well as a viral response on social media such as Twitter, where most people apparently have no institutional memory.

As it happens, there's a precedent for solving Sophie's problem. You can look it up under Mila Mulroney, who had a staff of three assistants, and an office on the first floor of Langevin.

Her office was one of the busiest and best in the building. And her executive assistant, Bonnie Brownlee, was a valued adviser not only to her but to her husband.

Every prime ministerial spouse has her own style and way of doing things. Aline Chrétien and Sheila Martin often appeared with their husbands, but had very few events of their own. Laureen Harper was a volunteer or spokesperson for many causes such as the Red Cross and the National Arts Centre, but had only one staffer and no space in Langevin.

The Trudeaus are more like the Mulroneys in the sense that they came to government not just as a couple, but as a political team. They are also similar in that when they took office, they had young kids at home. When the Mulroneys went to 24 Sussex in 1984, they had three children aged 10 and under, and a fourth who would come along a year later. The Trudeaus also arrived with three children Xavier (8), Ella Grace (7) and Hadrien (2).

Like the Mulroneys, the Trudeaus have faced scrutiny about nannies on the public payroll. When asked about the Mulroneys' child care provider, a senior aide named Fred Doucet denied that she was one, famously saying she was a maid who "interfaces with the children in a habitual way." But an assistant press secretary, given the person's name and asked her role by Canadian Press, replied: "Oh, that's the nanny."

Or, in the case of the Trudeaus, two nannies, both of them carried on the public payroll as exempt staff within the existing budget of the official residence. *iPolitics* investigative reporter Elizabeth Thompson broke a story last week that the annualized cost of the nannies will come close to $100,000 a year. She also noted that when the Trudeaus take the kids on official foreign travel, as they have to Europe and Washington, the cost of the nannies accompanying them is billed to Foreign Affairs. When the family travels on vacation, as they did to the Caribbean over Christmas, Trudeau himself evidently pays for their equivalent commercial air fare and accommodation. Which seems like a sensible division of costs.

Since the nannies are taxpayer-funded, this story is legitimately in the public domain. That it's also become a bit of a political football is not surprising. Conservative Finance critic Lisa Raitt, herself a mother of two, jumped all over the story. "I believe the child care of the prime minister is something that should be paid for by the prime minister, not by the Canadian taxpayer," she said. "He's the only one getting daycare provided by the state in this country."

For her part, the NDP's employment critic Niki Ashton said Trudeau was "failing to show leadership in a national child care plan," and of "relying on nannies paid for by the taxpayer when child care is an increasing burden" for most families.

In other family news, the Conservatives have criticized Trudeau for having his mother and Sophie's parents invited to the state dinner at the White

House. Trudeau has quite properly pointed out that these particular invitations came personally from Barack Obama, who in his toast mentioned Margaret Trudeau's work on mental health. Besides, who wouldn't want his mother at such a special event?

Undeterred, the Conservatives wondered in the House this week why Natural Resources Minister Jim Carr didn't make the dinner guest list, but Liberal Party president Anna Gainey and Trudeau's chief fundraiser, Stephen Bronfman, were invited. This just in: party prez and bagman invited to dinner. In Bronfman's case, he's also a leading member of Montreal's Jewish community, and represents the third generation of a family that has made great contributions to Canada.

At the White House, Sophie probably got a glance at the machine that works for the First Lady. Michelle Obama has a staff of nearly 25 people working for her in the East Wing. And in the White House, the First Lady has played a significant representational role since the time of Eleanor Roosevelt.

Not so in Canada. The prime minister's spouse is usually referred to as the Chateleine of Sussex, though not currently since the Trudeaus aren't living there. But there is no official role, it is whatever she makes of it.

Sophie Grégoire-Trudeau would evidently like to make a lot of it. She's clearly interested in helping young girls break out; with her background in television, she's obviously interested in arts and culture. And she's already become an ambassador for the Canadian fashion industry. Her wardrobe choices for the White House visit were written up in the *New York Times*.

All of which looks good on her. She deserves the help she needs to play her role to the max.

May 2016

MISREADING THE HOUSE ON DEMOCRATIC REFORM

The toxic behavioural syndrome that infected Parliament in the last month has been a direct result of the Liberals trying to stack the deck in their own favour in striking the special committee on parliamentary reform.

It was a serious political miscalculation and misreading of the mood of the House on an issue fundamental to our democratic way of life – how people vote, and how their votes are counted.

The negative consequences began immediately after the Liberals served notice of a motion on May 10 to give themselves a majority of six seats including the chair on a 10-member special committee, with the Conservatives having three members and the NDP only one, while the Greens and Bloc would each be allowed to sit in on proceedings, but not to vote. That's exactly what standing committees look like. There was nothing special about it at all, except for the Liberals' presumptuous sense of the prerogatives of power.

While terming the simple plurality system unfair, a party with less than 40 per cent of the vote under first-past-the-the-post, was awarding itself 60 per cent of the votes on a committee to reform it. Yeah, right.

The push back from the opposition parties was immediate and unrelenting. This issue of parliamentary process dominated question period on every single sitting day over the last four weeks. The entire atmosphere of the House was poisoned by the government's totally tone deaf rollout of the special committee.

The following Monday morning, the opposition forced a vote on a non-money bill when the government was short of members. With a 139–139 vote, the Liberals needed the speaker's vote to break a tie on Bill C-10, regarding maintenance outsourcing by Air Canada, a cause dear to the heart of the NDP and trade unions. It was a near miss, and the bill would have been defeated had two Conservative MPs not been locked out in the lobby when the vote was called.

Stunned and infuriated, the Liberals then introduced Motion No. 6, which would have allowed ministers to dictate time allocation and hours of sitting on their bills, such as C-14, the legislation on assisted dying, a delicate moral and medical issue and a question of conscience for MPs. This only redoubled the anger of opposition members. When a vote was called on C-14, and some NDP members lingered chatting on the floor of the House, Justin Trudeau crossed the aisle in a fury, manhandled opposition whip Gord Brown, accidentally elbowing NDP member Ruth Ellen Brosseau in the process. As he steered Brown toward his seat, Trudeau yelled some very unparliamentary language and in a second crossing of the aisle moments later, got into an unseemly shouting match with NDP Leader Tom Mulcair, who called him "pathetic."

The incident was a shocking breach of parliamentary protocol – there's a reason the government and opposition parties sit a symbolic two swordlengths apart. While it was a low moment in the life of his government, it also provided Trudeau and the Liberals with the opportunity, actually the imperative, of making amends in the House. Over the next day, the Liberals withdrew the offensive Motion No. 6., while Trudeau apologized frequently, profusely and abjectly, saying it was "all on me." *Mea culpa, mea culpa, mea maxima culpa.*

Fortunately for the Liberals, a break week for the Victoria Day holiday intervened, allowing for a cooling of emotions on all sides, and enabling the government to consider a second rollout of the reform committee process. The Liberals also concluded correctly that there was no great enthusiasm among their own MPs and ministerial staff for expending so much political capital on a unilateral project. Not to mention that some 150 freshman Liberal members of the House did very well under FPTP, thanks very much, and many of them have little enthusiasm to throw out the system that got them elected.

So the Liberals needed to climb down from their self-serving opening play on the committee's composition, and their Winnipeg convention last weekend provided the occasion for Democratic Institutions Minister Maryam Mosef to give an interview to the *Toronto Star*. "The Liberals will abandon their plans to overhaul Canada's electoral system if they don't have widespread public support," the *Star* reported, and quoted Monsef saying: "We will not proceed with any changes without the broad buy-in of the people of this country ... so Canadians can rest assured that unless we have their broad buy-in we're not moving forward with any changes."

Well, that served the purpose of getting everyone's attention when the House re-convened on Monday. Then the NDP gave notice it would use its opposition day on Thursday to put forward amendments to the government motion, suggesting five Liberal members on the special committee, three Conservatives and two NDPers, with the Bloc and Green leader Elizabeth May not only sitting but also each having a vote.

By mid-week, the NDP motion had become an offer the Liberals couldn't refuse, a way out of a dead lock and dead end over process, and a way to go forward on substance.

In the debate on the motion Thursday morning, Monsef rose to accept the amendments of NDP critic Nathan Cullen, and offered a couple of her own. "The government will not proceed without the broad support of Canadians," she declared. "In this respect, the mandate of the committee needs to include recommending to the government the best method of ensuring that any proposal has the full or broad support of Canadians."

She was opening the door to a referendum, the key demand of the Conservatives as the main defenders and proponents of the status quo. But the Tories, seething with anger, denounced the "back room deal" between the Liberals and the NDP.

As if there's any other kind of deal in politics. The Charter of Rights was a back room deal. The Meech Lake Accord was a back room deal. The Canada-US Free Trade Agreement was a back room deal. Deals aren't made on the floor of the House, they're announced there.

The Conservatives have a strong hand in that three Canadians in four in polls think there should be a referendum on what the committee recommends and the government decides. But the Tories also sound like a One-Note Johnny, with nothing else to say except, "referendum." So, shouting and spitting, the Conservatives will vote against the enabling motion next week, though they will sit on the committee. They look obstinate, obstructionist and, frankly, politically stupid.

Yes, the Liberals and NDP together will constitute a majority of seven on the 12-member committee. But the New Democrats would never support a Liberal call for a preferential ballot, of which they would be the main beneficiaries as the second choice party, to the detriment of the NDP. The NDP propose some form of proportional representation, possibly partial or PPR. In order to be seen as constructive participants, the Conservatives need a product of their own, possibly a mixed member proportional (MMP) system that would retain first past the post at the riding level but add a certain number of seats proportionately by the vote in each province.

An initiative that was bogged down in process, going nowhere and doomed to failure, now has legs and life, thanks to the NDP proposing it and the Liberals getting it.

As Trudeau said on Thursday: "We heard the opposition's concerns that we were perhaps behaving in a way that came to resemble the previous government rather than the kind of approach we promised throughout the campaign."

In other words, the Liberals got their head out of their ass. And not a moment too soon.

June 2016

O CANADA

Going up the escalator at the Bell Centre before a Canadiens game last season, a woman said to her friend: "I don't know the words to O *Canada*. I only know the bilingual version we sing at the hockey game."

Or the version we sang in school.

In my generation, it went like this:

O Canada,
Our home and native land!

True patriot love, in all thy sons command.
With glowing hearts, we see thee rise,
The true north strong and free!
And stand on guard,
O Canada, we stand on guard for thee.
O Canada, glorious and free!
O Canada we stand on guard for thee,
O Canada we stand on guard for thee.

There were so many standing on guards that one of them could be replaced years later, when O *Canada* officially became the national anthem in law on July 1, 1980.

One stand on guard became: *From far and wide, O Canada.*

"From far and wide," was meant to please multicultural Canadians for whom Canada was their home, but not their "native land."

And then they dropped an O Canada and brought God into it: *"God keep our land, glorious and free."*

They wouldn't do that today, given the number of Canadians who worship another deity, or none at all.

But because the national anthem is now enacted as law, any change to the lyrics requires another act of Parliament, as we've seen with Bill C-210, Mauril Bélanger's private member's bill to make the second line of the English version gender neutral.

True patriot love in all thy sons command, in Bélanger's bill, becomes *True patriot love in all of us command.*

The bill will receive third reading Wednesday, and will pass easily, with the support of the Liberals and NDP. From there it will go to the Senate where it could also be adopted before the end of the sitting and from there to the governor general for his signature. With any luck, the gender neutral second line could be sung on Parliament Hill on Canada Day, the 36th anniversary of O *Canada* officially becoming Canada's national anthem.

For Bélanger this is more than a change he has advocated for at least two years, it is also about his personal and political legacy. Since the election last October the MP for Ottawa-Vanier has been diagnosed with ALS, Lew Gehrig's disease, a debilitating terminal illness that is usually life-ending within two to five years.

In Bélanger's case his physical deterioration has been alarmingly fast and poignantly visible. After dropping out of the speaker's race last December, he was named honourary speaker for a day, where he was able to use a walker to enter the House and sit in the speaker's chair. When he appeared in the House last week, he was confined to a wheelchair, and was visibly shrunken and frail.

Had Bélanger not been able to attend the House, his bill would not have been called for debate at third reading, and would have gone to the back of the PMB queue. When Liberal whip Andrew Leslie offered to stand-in as sponsor of C-210, the Conservatives churlishly refused. An earlier version of Bélanger's bill avoided going to the back of the line only when one of his Liberal colleagues, Linda Lapointe, graciously offered him her turn.

The Conservatives have strenuously, even ferociously opposed Bélanger's bill with procedural delaying tactics. In one sense, they were just playing their role, and reflecting the opposition of their base. Conservative Heritage critic Peter Van Loan told the House: "When it comes to national symbols, when it comes to the things that make us what we are, we have taken them from the people, not given them to the people."

Actually, we've taken them from Robert Stanley Weir, a Montreal lawyer who wrote the English lyrics for *O Canada* in 1908.

And guess what? The original second line was not *True Patriot Love, in all thy sons command*. It was *True patriot love, thou dost in us command*.

It was only in 1914 that Weir changed the lyric to "all thy sons command."

Bélanger's change to "in all of us command," quite apart from being gender neutral, clearly respects the author's intent in writing the original first verse of the anthem.

And here's an ironic note for Conservatives to consider. In their own 2010 speech from the throne, read by then Governor General Michaelle Jean, the Conservatives said Parliament would revert "to the original gender neutral wording of the national anthem."

However, 75 per cent of Canadians polled after the throne speech opposed the change and within two days the Conservative government capitulated and cabinet announced there would be no change to the lyrics.

By the way, there have never been any changes to the original French lyrics written by Adolphe-Basile Routhier to music composed by Calixa Lavallée. The song was commissioned by the St. Jean Baptiste Society and performed in Quebec City on St. Jean Baptiste Day, June 24, in 1880.

It's occasionally been suggested that one line in particular should be changed: *Il sait porter la croix!* Canada is not only ready "to wield the sword" but also "to carry the cross." Not only is the overtone religious, it equally connotes a crusade, but then consider who it was written for. One of the historic ironies is that for the last half century, the St. Jean Baptiste Society has been a strident advocate of Quebec nationalism and separatism, while *O Canada* has become the very symbol of Canadian unity.

Bélanger's bill is certain to pass, perhaps by an even larger margin on a free vote than the 219–79 margin in favour at second reading on June 1. Having made their point, the Conservatives would be wise to stand aside. They risk looking mean-spirited and cheap. While it is not Parliament's role to grant a dying man his wish, a certain generosity of spirit is appropriate in the circumstances.

On Wednesday, the House will stand on guard for Mauril as well as for Canada.

June 2016

∞

A MORAL DILEMMA

By the time she was in her 80s, a good part of my mother's mind had left us, and she decided the rest of her wanted to leave, too.

"Do you believe in euthanasia?" she once asked me over tea at her apartment.

"No, I don't."

"You're no help," she shot back.

The thought had never occurred to me. She was, after all, a devout Catholic, and the church had views on that, and still does.

She was a health care professional, a head nurse who had been the matron of Queen Mary Veterans' Hospital in Montreal. She had seen enough of men's minds drifting away to know when she was doing so herself. She was always, as she said, "getting ready," updating her will, filing away her monthly investment statements and making boxes. One of the boxes had my father's service medals, and his watch. "These are for you," she said that day.

In her mid-80s, she closed her apartment and moved into a seniors' residence in Westmount, and later an assisted living home, where she never left her bed except when helped into a wheelchair. In those years, she no longer recognized my daughter, and once introduced me to someone as "my husband." She lived to be 93, with no memory of her life, and completely oblivious to her surroundings. It wasn't Alzheimer's, just old age. When she finally slipped away seven years ago in the quiet of a late afternoon, it was the deliverance she had asked for a decade earlier.

I wonder what she would have made of the debate we're having now. In a euphemistic world, it is no longer called euthanasia, or even "doctor assisted suicide" but, as in Bill C-14, "medical assistance in dying."

Euphemisms don't change the profound moral dilemma around the issue of assisted dying. While many terminally ill patients understandably wish to be relieved of their suffering, usually with the support of their loved ones, it is health providers – doctors and nurses such as my mother – who will expedite their departure from this life, either by administering a fatal dose or writing a prescription for one.

They are the ones who bear the medical and moral burdens on assisted dying. A doctor's mission, as set out in the physician's oath, is "to do good or to do no harm."

There isn't a medical association, legal society, religious denomination, or stakeholders' lobby in this country that doesn't have unambiguous views on either side of the assisted dying debate. Practically from the moment C-14 was tabled, mainstream and social media were flooded with predictably outraged missives that it went too far, or not far enough.

And the bill is, indeed, as striking for what was left out as for what was written into it. It does not go as far as the Supreme Court decided in February of last year, when it ordered the government to come up with assisted dying legislation within a year. Nor does it go as far as a Joint House-Senate Committee recommended to the government this winter. The Court also put the government on notice of its impatience when it extended the deadline for passing legislation by only four months, to June 6.

In its judgment in the now landmark case of *Carter v. Canada*, the court unanimously determined that assisted dying fell under the Charter of Rights and Freedoms, specifically Section 7 which states that "everyone has the right to life, liberty and the security of the person and the right not to be deprived thereof."

In other words, the high court has deemed assisted dying a Charter right, a constitutional right. In an era of judge-made law, this crossed a new threshold of jurisprudence.

If you asked about framers' intent, it's worth noting that during the debate on the Charter in 1981, Pierre Trudeau wrote a private letter to Cardinal Emmett Carter of Toronto assuring him that he would invoke the Charter's notwithstanding override clause, as Brian Mulroney wrote in his *Memoirs*, "to countermand any law permitting abortion on demand." Years later, the same Section 7 on security of the person was successfully cited in the 1988 Morgentaler case for affirming a woman's unequivocal right to choose, now both settled law and conventional political wisdom on which most Canadians agree. There has been no abortion legislation on the books in Canada ever since, and there never will be again.

Assisted dying is likely the most difficult and divisive moral and medical issue since then, one on which there is equally only one outcome.

In overturning the ban on doctor-assisted dying, the court wrote of people who were "grievously and irredeemably ill" facing "a cruel choice" between either suicide or "intolerable suffering" until death by natural causes.

C-14 is notably less sweeping, and medically-assisted dying would apply to mentally competent adults over 18 with "incurable illness or disability" who are "in an advanced state of irreversible decline in capability." And they must be Canadian residents eligible for health care – no assisted death tourism will be permitted.

"Their natural death," C-14 says, must have "become reasonably foreseeable, taking into account all of their medical circumstances, without a prognosis necessarily having been made as to the specific length of time that they have remaining."

There's no shortage of legal qualifiers in that, and you can imagine the debate around the drafting table at the Department of Justice. You can also imagine the debate at DOJ, in light of the high court ruling, as to whether the bill is "Charter proof," a question they usually ask over there.

There are also 11 "safeguards" written into the bill, including "immediately before providing the medical assistance in dying," giving "the person the opportunity to withdraw their request and ensure that the person gives express consent to receive medical assistance in dying." Failure by health professionals to comply with any of the safeguards would be a criminal offence punishable by "a term of imprisonment" of up to five years. Wow.

Furthermore doctor or nurse practitioners or pharmacists receiving written requests for information on medically assisted dying must do so, unless exempted by Health Canada.

The health minister can make regulations, not requiring a bill, "exempting, on terms that may be specified, a class of persons from the requirement."

To state the obvious, no doctor or nurse or hospital should be coerced into assisting in a life-ending procedure or prescription to which they object or moral or ethical grounds. For example, any Catholic hospital, or order of nuns who are nurses, or individual doctors or nurses.

I can't helping thinking what my mother would have done as a nurse, or wished for herself in the closing years of her life.

April 2016

SOBER SECOND THOUGHT

The Senate was, exceptionally, sitting on Friday to consider its response to the House reiterating the government's original language in Bill C-14 on medically assisted dying.

The House version says death must be "reasonably foreseeable" before medical assistance and life-ending medication may be provided. The Senate amendment adopts the broader language of the Supreme Court's 2015 ruling that medical assistance in dying is permissible when a patient's condition is "grievous and irremediable."

This was one of seven amendments adopted by the Senate Wednesday night in passing C-14 by a vote of 64–12. On Thursday, the House re-adopted the government's "reasonably foreseeable" line by a vote of 190–108, and sent the bill back to the Senate again.

But this is not necessarily a standoff or a game of ping-pong, back and forth between the House and the Senate. Or at least, it needn't become one.

The government did accept the other amendments, four minor ones and two technical changes, adopted by the Senate along bi-partisan lines. One amendment is on consultations on palliative care before medical assistance in dying. Another concerns information to be provided on death certificates. A third one excludes anyone signing on behalf of a patient from being a beneficiary of a will or estate. And the final amendment calls for a status report back to Parliament on medically assisted dying within two years.

So the Senate has already served its constitutional role as the chamber of "sober second thought." The government and the House, for their part, have accepted six amendments which clarify C-14 in some respects and improve it in others.

Far from being a stalemate, this is the essence of the Canadian compromise. It's also very much what the founding fathers had in mind in drafting the Constitution Act 1867, with an elected House and an appointed Senate. As the Supreme Court put it in its 2014 reference on the Senate: "The Senate is one of Canada's foundational political institutions. It lies at the heart of the agreements that gave birth to the Canadian federation." In other words, the Senate is central to the Canadian constitutional experience.

The question here is what is the sense and mood of the Senate? Has it played out its role, and is it now time to bow to the will of the elected House, or does it want to keep on?

Interestingly, it the former Senate Liberals booted from caucus by Justin Trudeau in 2014, now sitting as independent Liberals, who seemed determined to persevere with the Supreme Court's more permissive language on "grievous and irremediable" illness.

For Serge Joyal, author of the major amendment rejected by the government, it is a question of "solemn conscience." For Jim Cowan, the onetime Liberal leader in the Senate, "my position would be that we should stick to our guns."

He went on: "I think we should broaden it. Otherwise, I don't think the bill will pass constitutional muster. I think it will be struck down."

In that regard, Joyal suggested the government refer C-14 to the Supreme Court. That's been rejected by the government, with Justice Minister Jody Wilson-Raybould saying she was confident C-14 would pass constitutional muster. The bill may end up at the High Court anyway, but Wilson-Raybould is correct in the sense that it's the government's role to write laws and the court's job to interpret them.

What this was coming down to Friday was the mood of the Red Chamber. And having made their point in six amendments accepted by the government, they deferred to the elected House on the narrower language for assisted dying, defeating Joyal's re-offered amendment, with its added reference to the court, 44–28.

"Senators on the whole feel they have improved the bill and brought it to public attention where there has been debate and discussion," said Manitoba Conservative Senator Janis Johnson, who has been in the Upper House for the last 25 years, and reads the place very well. "I think senators have to keep in mind the temper of the times and how the public views the Senate. It is a good opportunity to say we have done our job, made positive amendments, engaged public discourse and the House has the final say."

Johnson added: "This will, I hope, give the Senate a boost in the public's mind. It is a start and reflects the new independent Senate."

For example, when the Senate sat as a committee of the whole on June 1, cameras were permitted to televise the proceedings as senators grilled Raybould-Wilson and then Health Minister Jane Philpott for four hours on C-14. Conservatives, independent Liberals and independent senators alike put them through their paces, but both ministers made a solid account of themselves, giving as good as they got.

The senators were inquisitive, the ministers were insightful, and the entire four hours was informative and even illuminating.

There's no more sensitive medical or moral issue than assisted dying. In both houses of Parliament, a difficult and divisive conversation has been conducted with dignity and respect for the deeply held beliefs of others.

That's greatly to the credit of MPs and senators on all sides.

June 2016

∞

BEER, WINE AND FREE TRADE

While the Trans-Pacific Partnership, the Canada-Europe free trade agreement and protectionist U.S. election rhetoric have taken up most of the oxygen on trade recently, Canada's interprovincial trade liberalization process is heating up, and both the political and economic stakes are high.

The Canadian Constitution is very clear about interprovincial trade. Section 121 of the 1867 Constitution Act stipulates that "all articles of the growth, produce and manufacture of any of the provinces shall, from and after the Union, be admitted free into each of the other provinces."

But it hasn't worked out that way, particularly in two economic segments where provincial governments are key participants – liquor and procurement. In beer and wine, provincial liquor boards historically have excluded products from other provinces. In government procurement, the provinces always have looked after local industries first in terms of both content and jobs.

As a result, we have BITs – barriers to interprovincial trade – which the premiers' club in the Council of the Federation addressed two weeks ago at the biannual meeting of provincial and territorial premiers in Yukon. They've agreed to update the 1994 Agreement on Internal Trade (AIT) so that, as the Canada Free Trade Agreement (CFTA), it aligns with the Comprehensive Economic and Trade Agreement (CETA) between Canada and Europe, which, if implemented next year, would give European business access to some provincial market segments denied to other provinces.

The premiers haven't said what's in the deal, or what's being left out. But they're calling it, in the words of Ontario Premier Kathleen Wynne, "an agreement-in-principle," details to follow after they've been worked out by ministers and officials.

That could take months. But Prime Minister Trudeau is calling a First Ministers' Meeting for the fall, probably in October, to discuss province-by-province carbon emissions reduction targets for meeting Canada's commitments to the Paris Agreement on climate change. The provinces also would like to discuss the terms of a new federal-provincial health care agreement to follow the expiration next year of the 2004 health accord.

While they're at it, the prime minister and premiers can talk about BITs, particularly in booze and government procurement. It wouldn't be the first time a PM has had such talks with the premiers.

Politically, for Trudeau, it's an issue of managing the federation, one of several he has put on the fed-prov agenda. After two decades of suspended animation for federal-provincial First Ministers' Meetings during the Chrétien and Harper years, Trudeau has gone out of his way to engage the premiers – one of his key indicators that there's a new CEO in Ottawa. The Trudeau government has identified fed-prov collaboration as a leadership issue, and in this regard Justin Trudeau is much more like Brian Mulroney than like his father.

On the economic side, business and investors in the broad sense stand to win from lowered BITs, not just in trade but in services. The interprovincial trade narrative is one littered with nonsensical, worst-practices barrier fables – some apocryphal, some not. The Ottawa-Gatineau cab story is a good example that MPs, bureaucrats, and national reporters deal with every day. You can take a Blue Line cab from the Fairmont Château Laurier in Ottawa to a federal office building or conference across the Ottawa River in Gatineau, but the driver can't get in line to bring passengers back, much less be hailed on the street. Works the other way against Gatineau cabs. And this in the age of Uber.

In 1986, Mulroney's Progressive Conservative government launched the negotiations with the Reagan administration that led to the 1987 Canada-U.S. Free Trade Agreement. Wine and beer, as well as procurement, were at the centre of backstage conversations between Ottawa and the provinces.

Then Ronald Reagan played his hand on liquor in a toast at Rideau Hall during a visit to Ottawa in April, 1987. Raising a glass to Governor General Jeanne Sauvé, he said Americans looked forward to the day when they could toast such an occasion with "fine California wines."

As a Californian, he wanted to deliver for an important industry in his home state. It was clear to Mulroney that this was one of Reagan's personal bottom lines. As Mulroney later told his negotiating team: "Wine is in, beer is out."

The Canadian wine industry strenuously opposed the inclusion of wine in the FTA. But Ottawa provided generous funding for Canadian winemakers to transition out of plonk – and today, Canadian vintages are world-competitive.

As for beer, it was never going to make it into the Canada-U.S. FTA, since the provinces then required that it be home-brewed. As Mulroney used to say at the time: "You can buy a bottle of Moosehead in New York, but not in Montreal," because it was brewed in New Brunswick but not in Quebec.

On government procurement, while the Canada-U.S. talks were ongoing in 1986–87, Ontario Premier David Peterson created an issue when he insisted that the steel used in the construction of Toronto's SkyDome – now the Rogers Centre – had to be made in Ontario, at Hamilton and other local plants. In any trade talks with the U.S., it's pretty difficult to exclude the interests of the American steel industry.

Thirty years on, Alberta Premier Rachel Notley is insisting that "local benefits" account for 20 per cent of the contracts for the re-build of Fort McMurray over an initial four-year period. Other provinces have objected, but Quebec and Ontario have gone along with it – not just to keep the peace but because their industries will be major beneficiaries in a re-build that may see as much as $5 billion in federal funding.

On liquor, you can always count on the provinces to defend the interests of their provincially-owned distribution boards, as dividends are a big part of their fiscal frameworks. For example, the Liquor Control Board of Ontario (LCBO) returned a dividend of about $1.9 billion to Queen's Park last year. The Societé des alcools du Québec (SAQ) returned a $1 billion dividend to Quebec in 2015.

In New Brunswick, NB Liquor returns $160 million to the province – which is why Fredericton is appealing an April ruling by a provincial court justice that a $300 fine against retiree Gérald Comeau for bringing more liquor than permitted (a 12-pack of beer and a bottle of wine) across the line from Quebec was unconstitutional.

Judge Ronald LeBlanc ruled the NB Liquor Control Act violated that key section, 121, of the Constitution Act. This one is headed to the Supreme Court, which – 150 years after they made their deal – may rule on what the Fathers of Confederation actually meant when they spoke of interprovincial trade.

Imagine – free trade among provinces. What a concept.

August 2016

LOSING POLITICAL CAPITAL FOR NOTHING

The Liberals are on a bad roll, one entirely of their own doing, on things that were completely preventable such as tears for Fidel Castro and pay for play fundraising events.

As a result, they are losing political capital for nothing at precisely the time they need the party's brand equity, and Justin Trudeau's, in support of important decisions on pipelines, carbon pricing, defence procurement, peacekeeping and electoral reform.

The prime minister has only himself to blame for the mawkish and fawning tone of his weekend tribute to Castro, which inspired merriment and scorn worldwide on the web.

There was trouble from the first to last line of the statement, which began with a reference to Castro as "Cuba's longest-serving president," as if he had been elected to the office time and again rather than creating a brutal communist dictatorship. This is the sort of thing that occasionally happens when a leader is eight time zones away, as Trudeau was in Madagascar, and a statement is put out in the middle of the night back at home without being vetted by anyone.

When Trudeau praised "one of the world's worst dictators," Opposition Leader Rona Ambrose asked in question period Tuesday, "what was he thinking?"

At least Trudeau's office got ahead of the story on Monday, by asking the governor general to attend a memorial service for Castro in Havana, while putting it out that the prime minister's schedule did not permit him to attend the funeral of his father's friend.

If the PM's office hadn't acted as quickly as it did to kill the story, it would have followed Trudeau and the Liberals around in QP all week, rather than just his first day back in the House.

As it happens, there's another story with a life of its own, the cash for access fundraising saga, a gift that keeps on giving thanks to the *Globe and Mail*'s Robert Fife and Steven Chase, who've been producing serial scoops.

The latest instalment in Tuesday's edition of the *Globe* revealed that Bill Blair, parliamentary secretary to the justice minister, attended a Toronto-area riding association fundraiser last April hosted by a downtown Toronto law firm whose guest list included representatives the Cannabis Friendly Business Association.

While the $150 per person cocktail was well within the legal limit of $1,525 per year, it again violates Trudeau's Open and Accountable Government guidelines to ministers and PS's that "there should be no preferential access or appearance of preferential access." A Liberal spokesperson said the CFBA member donations "are now in the process of being returned to avoid any appearance of conflict of interest" between a registered lobby and the government.

As it happens, the task force on the legalization of marijuana, chaired by former Justice Minister Anne McClellan, is scheduled to deliver its recommendations to cabinet by Wednesday and she predicts the report will "engender a lot of interest."

But that wasn't the story line in question period Tuesday, where the opposition had one more freebie on fundraising. The Conservatives haven't had so much fun in QP in ages. Tony Clement accused the Liberals of "taking money from the marijuana lobby, from Big Weed" and that "all their claims about following the rules have gone up in smoke." Blaine Calkins quipped that "we're just trying to weed out the truth here."

The pay for play story line began last April when Justice Minister Jody Wilson-Raybould attended a $500 per person fundraiser at the Bay Street law firm of Torys. Lawyers representing clients to her department got to socialize with the justice minister, who also names members of the legal profession to the bench.

While in the midst of pre-budget consultations in October, Finance Minister Bill Morneau was the guest at a $1,000 per person fundraiser attended by 15 people at the home of a wealthy Halifax businessman. All the right people were there. Naturally. In November, he was the guest at a $500 per person fundraiser for a Liberal riding association in the Greater Toronto Area.

And then there's Trudeau's own attendance at a $1,500 per person fundraiser with wealthy Chinese and Chinese Canadian business leaders in Toronto last May. One of the prominent figures from the Chinese Canadian community, Shenglin Xian, was waiting for federal approval to start a new bank, which he received a couple of months later. Which isn't to say he discussed his bank application with the PM. A billionaire attendee from China, Zhang Bin, could not donate to the party as he was not a Canadian citizen. But he soon turned out to be one of two major donors of $750,000 to the Université de Montréal law faculty and $200,000 to the Pierre Elliott Trudeau Foundation. Another $50,000 will pay for a statue of the first prime minister Trudeau at the university. All in, $1 million.

Justin Trudeau stepped aside from the Trudeau Foundation board after becoming Liberal leader, and is clearly arms-length from its affairs, though hardly disinterested. He was instrumental in persuading then-PM Jean Chrétien to endow the Trudeau Foundation with $125 million in federal funding in 2002. No other former prime minister has a federally funded institute, library or think tank.

There's no doubt that Trudeau is trying to set a higher standard of transparency in political fundraising, but in doing so he risks falling into a double standard when the Liberals fall short.

But a sense of perspective is also helpful. No one should think a cabinet minister can be bought for $1,500. Fundraising has also changed for the better. In the months before the 1997 election, the Chrétien Liberals wanted to raise another $1.5 million for their campaign in Quebec.

Chrétien hosted seven sit-down dinners for 10 people in the dining room of 24 Sussex, and the Liberals easily raised the $1.5 million, mostly in corporate donations. That would never happen today. It wouldn't be legal.

November 2016

AN HISTORIC DAY IN THE HOUSE

Write down the date – March 8, 2017. It will be remembered in the annals of the House of Commons as one of the most progressive and productive days in the modern era of Canadian politics and public policy.

First came the Daughters of the Vote, 338 young women aged 18–23 occupying the seats of MPs from their own ridings. And then, perhaps partly influenced by the presence and eloquence of the Daughters, MPs then voted three times across party lines in favour of private members' bills, with Liberal backbenchers joining opposition MPs on two of them against the advice of their own government.

In more than four decades of going to the House, I've never seen anything quite like it. I was there the day in September 1983 when Pierre Trudeau and Brian Mulroney spoke brilliantly in favour of a resolution on French-language minority rights in Manitoba. Trudeau's speech was an intellectual *tour de force*, while Mulroney spoke in deeply moving emotional terms. You could have heard a pin drop through both speeches, which were quite enthralling.

In September 1988, Mulroney famously delivered an apology to Japanese Canadians for their having been interned and their property seized by Ottawa during the Second World War. There was hardly a dry eye in the galleries as the survivors and their children watched the unprecedented apology.

In June 1990, Nelson Mandela chose Ottawa as the first foreign parliament in which he spoke because Canada and Mulroney opposed apartheid and championed his release from imprisonment in South Africa. That was a celebration not only of his freedom, but of Canada's unique role in securing it.

Last Wednesday in the House will be remembered not for one or two speeches, but for the inspirational presence of those young women, and then MPs deciding that they were more than just numbers in votes, but parliamentarians who were there to make a difference.

Watching the Daughters from the visitors' gallery, Lisa MacLeod called it "one of the proudest days of my life." A prominent Progressive Conservative member of the Ontario legislature from the Ottawa riding of Nepean-Carleton, MacLeod recalls a two-hour cell phone brainstorming session with Nancy Peckford of Equal Voice in 2015. "I was at Canadian Tire in Barhaven and she was at McDonald's in Kemptville," MacLeod says. "And the idea was to bring 338 young women to Parliament Hill." MacLeod says Peckford took the idea to the Harper government before the election and got over half a million dollars of federal funding under the Canada 150 umbrella from the new Trudeau government a year ago.

Equal Voice interviewed and selected a remarkable number of culturally diverse and indigenous representatives. Air Canada and VIA Rail made generous value-in-kind donations to get them to Ottawa, where they remained for a week of working breakfasts and lunches, plenaries and breakouts and evening social events at venues such as the Museum of History and the National Arts Centre. The 70 indigenous girls formed their own caucus.

By the time the Daughters occupied their members' seats in the House, says MacLeod, "they were sisters, they had built relationships, they were there for each other." This was evident in the standing ovations they gave fellow Daughters during their statements and their highly pertinent interventions in a question period with Prime Minister Justin Trudeau. In five or 10 years time, many of the Daughters are going to be back as MPs, senior staff on the Hill or rising stars in the public service.

For MacLeod, who as a school girl in the Nova Scotia riding of Central Nova, couldn't afford to make her class's trip to Ottawa, it was indeed a proud moment marking International Women's Day, the 100th anniversary of women first getting the federal vote in 1917, as well as Canada 150. "The rest," she wrote "is HERstory."

Part of the "herstory" that day was Opposition Leader Rona Ambrose and her bill, C-337, that prospective appointees to the bench must first complete a course on sexual assault law. When she made this case to the Daughters, they responded with cheers and standing ovations. She made it again later in QP, in the lights of the shocking "knees together" comment by an Alberta judge who would resign last Friday, as well as the "clearly a drunk can consent" remarks by a Halifax judge in dismissing a case against a cab driver.

"Countless legal experts have pointed out the mistakes in this judgment," Ambrose told the House. "I have introduced a very common-sense bill to make sure that judges are not making basic errors or, even worse, painful comments that make victims think twice of ever pursuing justice."

Some honourable members: "Hear, hear!"

Then the House unanimously agreed to fast track Ambrose's motion to committee before third reading, bypassing debate on second reading. Exceptionally, the motion was moved by NDP Leader Tom Mulcair. "When it comes to how our system handles cases of sexual assault," Mulcair said, "we must all come together and say: we believe survivors."

Then during an hour of private members' business, Liberal MPs joined the opposition to pass two bills from the Senate, one on bail reform for making bail, and the other to enable patients from disclosing results of genetic tests to insurance companies.

Wynn's Law, bill S-217, is named for Alberta RCMP Const. David Wynn, who was gunned down in 2015 by a habitual criminal who made bail despite dozens of outstanding charges against him. The government opposed S-217, but enough Liberal backbenchers joined the opposition parties to adopt it on second reading, 154–128. Const. Wynn's widow, Shelley MacInnis-Wynn had been in Ottawa advocating for the Conservative bill, and sitting in the gallery as she heard the result, reportedly burst into tears.

On S-201, fully 105 Liberal backbenchers joined the opposition in supporting the bill to prevent genetic discrimination. Trudeau had said publicly the government opposed the bill because it was "unconstitutional." Justice Minister Jody Wilson-Raybould went so far as to write provincial premiers urging them to come out publicly against the bill, which had been proposed by now retired Liberal Jim Cowan in the Senate, and piloted through the House by Liberal backbencher Rob Oliphant. In the House, in the space of about 20 minutes, the anti-genetic discrimination bill was adopted 222–60, with essentially only the cabinet and parliamentary secretaries toeing the government line, while the Liberal back bench voted overwhelmingly in favour of it.

"A great day for Parliament," Oliphant declared on Twitter. For its part, the government quickly announced it would refer S-201 to the Supreme Court. Which means that Governor General David Johnston won't be asked to sign it anytime soon.

Meanwhile, Liberal MPs have asserted an unprecedented degree of independence, one of the most remarkable aspects of a truly historic day in the House.

March 2017

IT'S HARD TO SAY WHO'S HAVING THE WORSE WEEK – BOMBARDIER OR THE NHL

The Bombardier file is one they'll be teaching in communications courses years from now – an object lesson in how *not* to run public and government relations. The NHL's decision not to participate in the 2018 Olympics is typical of its corporate greed and disregard for its fan base. With its usual arrogance, the NHL said Monday: "We now consider the matter closed."

Last Wednesday, Bombardier disclosed that its top six executives received compensation of US$32.6 million in 2016, an increase of almost 50 per cent over 2015 – and this in a year which saw the company lay off 14,500 workers worldwide in its aerospace and rail divisions. In 2016, Bombardier lost nearly US$1 billion, an improvement over its US$5.3 billion in net losses in 2015.

The Quebec and federal governments are heavily invested in the success of the Montreal-based company in both planes and trains. Quebec has paid US$1 billion for a 49.5 per cent equity stake in the CSeries passenger jet project. The Quebec Pension Fund, the Caisse de dépôt et placement du Québec, paid US$1.5 billion for a 30-per-cent share of the rail division. And Ottawa recently loaned Bombardier $372 million for the CSeries commercial jetliner and the Global 7000 business jet.

The public furor over Bombardier's executive compensation was so intense that company brass had to do something corporations seldom do. They announced over the weekend that they would defer more than half of the US$32.6 million the executives received in compensation in 2016 until 2020.

This was, of course, after workers had staged a noisy protest outside Bombardier's corporate office on Boulevard René Lévesque, and Quebec government officials, starting with Premier Philippe Couillard publicly expressed their displeasure with the company.

In the Commons on Monday, Opposition Leader Rona Ambrose had a field day in question period.

"Mr. Speaker," she began. "Millionaire Bombardier executives are giving themselves a 50 per cent raise and bigger bonuses with tax dollars. This is a company and a CEO who said that he did not even need the money the prime minister gave him. Also, it is a company that is firing 14,000 workers in a year.

"This is not helping the middle class. This is lining the pockets of the 1 per cent of the 1 per cent with tax dollars. Is the prime minister not embarrassed? How is this helping the middle class?"

Justin Trudeau pointed out that what the federal government gave Bombardier was a repayable loan "that will ensure good jobs in the CSeries and Global 7000 and ensure the long-term viability of the aerospace industry in Canada." As for the pay packages, Trudeau allowed that "we are obviously not pleased with the decision that Bombardier made around its remuneration for its executives, but we are happy to see it make decisions that are fixing that for the confidence of Quebecers and Canadians."

Ambrose was having none of it.

"Mr. Speaker, Canadians work hard for their money," she resumed. "They feel nickel-and-dimed while the prime minister is taking away tax credits for their kids' sports, arts and music lessons. He is even taking away their tax break for bus passes. Meanwhile he is handing out millions of dollars that are being used for bonuses for Bombardier executives, all while they fire 14,000 middle class workers. Is this the prime minister's way of standing up for the middle class? If so, he should sit back down."

Ouch. Ambrose was at it again on Tuesday – her first four questions were on the Bombardier deal "leaving taxpayers with the bill." There was a similar opposition rout of the government in Quebec's National Assembly on Tuesday.

Part of the problem with Bombardier is an embedded sense of entitlement that comes with the Beaudoin family's control of the company through its dual class share structure. Preferred shares, majority-controlled by the family, account for 90 per cent of the shareholder votes, while the subordinate shares make up only 10 per cent. The family's refusal to relinquish its control is one of the reasons Ottawa made a loan to Bombardier, rather than investing in it.

The dual class share structure has led to a certain tone-deafness in Bombardier's engagement with public opinion, which views public investments in the company as corporate welfare rather than as efforts to build a world champion in aerospace, a sector that is heavily subsidized worldwide.

As for the NHL, it's been engaged in a dialogue of the deaf with the International Olympic Committee and the National Hockey League Players' Association (NHLPA).

"The IOC has now expressed their position that the NHL's participation in Beijing in 2022 is conditioned on our participation in South Korea in 2018," said the NHL in its statement. "And the NHLPA has now confirmed that it has no interest or intention of engaging in any discussion that might make Olympic participation more attractive to the clubs."

The NHL owners' position, summarized: *What's in it for us?* What do the owners get for taking the trouble to shut down the schedule for three weeks in mid-season and making it up after the Games? What would be their share of the live gate and TV money from the Olympic tournament, in which the NHL has participated every four years since 1998? It is the most important, most watched event of the Winter Games.

Who doesn't remember that golden goal in Vancouver in 2010? As sports-video.org noted at the time, "about 22 million people, or two-thirds of the Canadian population, were watching when Sidney Crosby scored in overtime (against the U.S.) that sealed the gold for Canada." It was the largest TV audience in Canadian history.

The NHLPA did not conceal its displeasure with the league. "The players are extraordinarily disappointed and adamantly disagree with the NHL's short-sighted decision not to continue our participation in the Olympics," the NHLPA said in its reply on Monday.

So they should be. The game – *our* game – doesn't belong to the owners. It belongs to the players and the fans. They want to see Crosby, Connor McDavid and Carey Price wearing Canada's colours at the Olympics. They want to see the best of Team Canada against the best of Team USA. They want to see Alex Ovechkin leading the Russians.

There's no better place to put pressure on the seven Canadian NHL owners than question period in the House. Like shooting a puck on a empty net.

April 2017

O'LEARY OUT

A funny thing happened during lunch on Wednesday: Kevin O'Leary dropped out of the Conservative leadership race and endorsed Maxime Bernier.

This stunning development happened only hours before O'Leary and 13 other candidates were to meet in Toronto for the last debate before the leadership vote exactly a month away, on May 27.

No frontrunner has ever dropped out of a leadership race before the first ballot in living memory in this country. Some have been overtaken in subsequent ballots in delegated conventions, as was the case with Joe Clark (overtaken by Brian Mulroney) in 1983, and Michael Ignatieff (passed on the inside by Stéphane Dion) in 2006 at the Liberal convention.

And make no mistake: O'Leary was the frontrunner. Only hours earlier, the *iPolitics* weekly Mainstreet poll of some 2,100 Conservatives had O'Leary growing three points from the previous week to 26 per cent, Andrew Scheer moving into second place at 17 per cent, and Bernier slipping to third at 14 per cent. The other candidates are all also-rans, in the single digits.

The O'Leary campaign claims its internal numbers were even better than that. "They show us in the low 30s," O'Leary said privately a few weeks ago in Ottawa. His campaign wasn't just polling donors registered with Elections Canada, but other party rank-and-file. His campaign also signed up about 35,000 new paid members of the party, most of whom probably knew him as a TV star rather than a politician.

O'Leary's problem wasn't leading on the first ballot, but growing to a majority in subsequent readouts of the preferential ballot. He was not the second, third or even fourth choice of enough Conservatives to put him over the top.

Among other things, O'Leary was hobbled by the 'MacKay clause' in the Conservative rulebook – the one which says all 338 ridings are created equal, with 100 votes, no matter how many members they have.

This rule dates from the 2003 merger of the Progressive Conservatives with the Canadian Alliance. For then-PC leader Peter MacKay, the equality of ridings was a deal-breaker.

What this means in 2017 is that the ten ridings in the Calgary area have more Conservative members than all of Quebec combined – but only 1,000 votes in the leadership race, compared to 7,800 for Quebec. (With 33,800 votes nationwide, the winner needs 16,901.)

And O'Leary was nowhere in Quebec. Though born and raised in Montreal, he doesn't speak French (highly unusual for someone of Irish and Lebanese descent, as those are two of the more linguistically integrated communities in the city). He said at the outset of the campaign that by the time the next election rolled around, he'd be bilingual. Apparently he hired a French tutor, but he wasn't making the sort of progress that anyone could notice. And he wasn't gaining any ground in Quebec, where Bernier is obviously a favourite son.

O'Leary admitted as much in a letter e-mailed to Conservatives Wednesday afternoon: "I am extremely strong in the West but have not generated material support in Quebec."

He also acknowledged his second ballot vulnerability: "Because I am an outsider, I have very weak second ballot support … The Quebec data is a different kind of issue and a big problem for me." Without significant support in Quebec, O'Leary admitted, he couldn't win a general election against Justin Trudeau in 2019. "Without growing the Conservative base in Quebec, beating Trudeau in 2019 would be a huge challenge."

And so … "I'm withdrawing my candidacy and throwing my full support behind (Bernier). I'm going to do everything I can to ensure he gets elected, and I'm going to ask my supporters to do the same."

How many of his supporters will follow him to Bernier? And how many of O'Leary's organizers will move with him? Fresh polling from Mainstreet suggests most Conservative party members are unwilling to let their preferred candidate tell them how to vote. O'Leary's campaign director, Mike Coates, is one of the best operatives in the business. Bernier already has a strong ground game, and Team O'Leary can only help.

With Bernier suddenly emerging as the front-runner, and Scheer growing to a clear second place, the party appears to have a choice between a libertarian and a social conservative – a prospect that should have the Liberals rubbing their hands with glee.

No one else has emerged from the back of the pack as the candidate representing the moderate, centrist wing of the party – the Red Tories, socially progressive but economically conservative.

One thing's for sure: The also-rans who had been taking shots at O'Leary will now have Bernier, and to a lesser degree Scheer, firmly in their sights.

Bernier will start taking heat for advocating the abolition of supply management, and Scheer will be scrutinized more closely for his conservative views on family issues.

To that extent, O'Leary's candidacy will be missed. He brought some interest and ideas to a listless leadership campaign. And always – as he has proved again – he was his own man.

April 2017

THE HYBRID CONVENTION

In the end, the Conservative leadership race was a hybrid between ranked mailed-in ballots and an old-style delegated convention decided by the delegates on the floor.

Maxime Bernier had the polling numbers, but not the votes when it mattered. Andrew Scheer, the consensus second choice, overcame the libertarian's lead on the 13th and final vote count, after all the other contenders had been eliminated.

While 132,000 Conservative party members returned their preferential ballots by mail, another 9,000 voted Saturday at polling stations across the country. The "live" vote, just in the hall at the Toronto Congress Centre, may have been enough to tip the balance in Scheer's favour as the safer choice.

Consider the final score, with 100 votes per 338 ridings and 16,901 points needed to win. Scheer won 17,221 points or 50.95 per cent, while Bernier won 16,579 points or 49.05 per cent. Leading on the first 12 ballots, Bernier fell just 322 votes short on the last one.

And events at the convention could have accounted for his shortfall. At Friday night's keynote session, he used most of his 10-minutes of speaking time with a video rather than a speech, and his brief remarks were quite weak. Rather than making a convincing closing argument, he failed to clinch the deal.

Then, Bernier's staff took a premature victory lap. His deputy campaign director Emrys Graefe gave an interview to Janice Dickson of *iPolitics* that turned into a Saturday morning mishap for Bernier. In terms of positions at party headquarters, he said Bernier's team should have "dibs on the good positions first." Then he made an entirely gratuitous remark. "There are some silly old fuddy-duddies who believe they have a clue about things out in the real world and they don't," he said. "And I include Andrew Scheer in that because he's the oldest 38-year-old I've ever known." Rule one: the staff should never become the story. Rule two: they should never pose for a photo.

Nor was Bernier's campaign helped in the closing week by a *Maclean's* piece that dissected his health care platform and concluded he would dismantle the Canada Health Act and make medicare an exclusive provincial jurisdiction with tax points transferred from Ottawa. A Bernier spokesperson confirmed the act would be "unenforceable."

But what may have sealed Bernier's fate was his promise to end supply management in agriculture, notably dairy, poultry and eggs. Farmers across the country took out Conservative party memberships, and supported anyone but Bernier. In Quebec alone, four Conservative MPs endorsed Scheer for his strong support of supply management. On the final round, Bernier lost his own riding of Beauce to Scheer by 51 to 49 per cent. While the Beauce is known as a hub of small business, it's also known for its dairy farms. Those farmers signed up to vote against their own MP.

As for Scheer, the Liberals are already making the argument that he owes his victory to the social conservative faction of the Conservative party and that he'll revive the debate on abortion, same sex marriage and LGBTQ rights.

It's true that the two avowedly "so-con" candidates in the race, Brad Trost and Pierre Lemieux, took 15 per cent of the points on the first round. Trost ran a surprisingly strong fourth place and was on the ballot until the 11th round, after which about two-thirds of the so-con vote broke to Scheer.

But that doesn't mean Scheer, himself a social conservative, is in thrall to the so-cons. While he's obviously pro-life rather than pro-choice on abortion, he's promised not to raise the issue again in the House. And while he voted in favour of a failed Commons motion to re-open the definition of marriage in 2006, he also supported the party's 2016 resolution to drop the definition of a marriage as between a man and a woman.

The so-cons going to Scheer brought him to within two points of Bernier in the penultimate round, but it was the moderate and progressive wing of the party who delivered his victory. Supporters of Michael Chong, Lisa Raitt and Chris Alexander, among the also-rans, coalesced around Erin O'Toole, giving him 21 per cent in the 12th count.

They then broke to Scheer by a 60–40 margin, choosing his genial manner over Bernier's libertarian platform.

And then there was the caucus, where Scheer had the endorsement of 32 MPs and senators, while Bernier had only a handful. Advantage Scheer, as most MPs are able to deliver their electoral district associations.

The caucus was noisily united behind Scheer Monday morning, when reporters and cameras were invited into the meeting. Scheer was magnanimous in his remarks about Bernier.

"Your bold campaign reignited the passions of Canadians everywhere I've travelled," Scheer told Bernier. "We all thank you for what you've contributed and I'm excited to work with you in building that excitement."

In the House, Bernier was given a front row place, three seats to the left of the new leader, quite visible in the longer TV shots for question period. In his first QP as leader, Scheer focused on fiscal frameworks and the defence deployment against ISIS, both reliable Conservative themes. His first encounter with Justin Trudeau, in Rome to meet the pope, will come another day.

Suffice it to say that, at 38, Scheer has time to grow into his new role. And while it's hard to imagine the voters turfing the Liberals in 2019 after only one term in office, it's easy at Scheer's age to suggest that he has more than one election in him.

May 2017

INCUMBENCY VS. CHANGE

It would be highly unusual for Canadians to kick out a majority government after only one term in office. The one exception in the 20th century was the Conservative government of R.B. Bennett in 1935, and he had the terrible misfortune of governing through the Great Depression.

More frequently, voters have put first-term majorities on notice by reducing them to minorities, as was the case with Conservative John Diefenbaker in 1962, and Liberal Pierre Trudeau in 1972. In Trudeau's case, it was a near thing, with the Liberals winning a plurality of only two seats, 109 to 107 for the Conservatives, leaving the NDP holding the balance of power at 31 seats in the-then 264 seat House.

Realistically speaking, and rhetorical posturing aside, reducing the Liberals to a minority in 2019 would be a significant achievement for the Conservatives and their new leader, Andrew Scheer. From a minority House, the Conservatives would be better positioned in the subsequent election, probably in 2021, to make the case for change.

In the meantime, Scheer needs to move the Conservative brand closer to the centre on social issues while holding to the narrative of responsible fiscal frameworks on the right. It is not by pandering to the social conservatives who helped elect him Tory leader that he'll reach out to a broader mainstream of moderate voters. Though a so-con himself, Scheer will not be reviving debates on abortion, same sex marriage or LGBTQ rights. There is no path to power in any of that, and Scheer's personal brand is one of a smiling face and a genial disposition. He's likeable.

He may be on to something in caricaturing the Liberals as the party of entitled elites. "The Liberals can take their cues from the cocktail circuit," Scheer said Monday. "We will take ours from the soccer fields, from the legion halls and the grocery stores." In other words, the middle class that Justin Trudeau is always talking about.

But Trudeau has two significant advantages, incumbency and his own considerable gifts as a retail politician. Incumbency gives him a seat on the world stage, as it has for the last week at the NATO and G7 summits, his audience with the pope at the Vatican, and his bilateral visit to Rome with his speech to Italian parliamentarians. He didn't look out of place in any of those international settings.

At home, the economy is in good shape. Unemployment of 6.5 per cent in April was the lowest since October 2008, the lowest since the start of the Great Recession. The Bank of Canada is forecasting economic growth of 2.6 per cent this year, with a core inflation rate below the 2 per cent target, and no need to increase interest rates in the near term.

Trudeau and the Liberals remain highly popular in the polls. In a May Nanos survey, the Liberals polled at 42 per cent, the Conservatives at 29 per cent and the NDP at 18. That's way into majority territory, even above the 2015 election when the Liberals won 184 seats in the new 338-seat House with 39.5 per cent of the vote, while the Conservatives elected 99 MPs with 31.9 per cent. The Conservative must cross the 30 per cent threshold to be become competitive again, and they also need the NDP to take votes from the Liberals on the left, rising to somewhere over 20 per cent.

But the Liberals do need to keep a close eye on political events, such as those unfolding in British Columbia this week, and the upcoming NAFTA renegotiation with the U.S. and Mexico.

BC Green Leader Andrew Weaver throwing his three seats behind NDP Leader John Horgan with 41 seats in the legislature will give the two opposition parties a bare majority in the 87-seat house. Liberal Leader Christy Clark won a plurality of 43 seats and has every constitutional right to form a government, but the NDP-Green alliance means she'll be defeated on her throne speech.

And that may well mean the end of Kinder Morgan's $7.4 billion plan to twin its Trans Mountain pipeline from Alberta to Vancouver. It may also mean the end of Clark's $11.4 billion liquid natural gas project and the $6.6 billion Site C hydroelectric dam project. Both the Greens and NDP oppose all three projects.

Scheer was very much onto this off the top of QP on Tuesday. In Rome, Trudeau held to the line that his government's approval of Trans Mountain was evidence-based. "The decision we took on Kinder Morgan was based on facts and evidence on what is in the best interests of Canadians and, indeed, all of Canada," he told a news conference. "Regardless of the change of government in British Columbia or anywhere, the facts and evidence don't change."

Trudeau's proposition is responsible economic growth in moving resources to tidewater, balanced by a carbon tax to help meet the emissions reductions targets of the Paris Agreement on climate change. If Trans Mountain is killed, the carbon tax could be another casualty, at least in Alberta where it was a trade off between Trudeau and Premier Rachel Notley.

On the NAFTA talks, the least that can be said is that negotiating with the Trump administration, Canada will be in uncharted waters.

As Harold Macmillan famously said: "Events, dear boy, events."

May 2017

THE NDP LEADERSHIP RACE

The people behind the NDP leadership debates seem to be giving Canadians what the Conservative leadership race conspicuously lacked over a span of more than 18 months: good TV, interesting content.

With as many as 14 contenders elbowing each other on stage, the Conservative race was doomed from the outset to be a dreary, predictable enterprise of candidates pitching platitudinous soundbites to the party's right-wing base.

The NDP has only five candidates on the set, which allows them to mix it up in longer exchanges. All of them are experienced parliamentarians, extremely well versed on the issues from a progressive perspective. And all of them are bilingual – again, an improvement over the overcrowded Conservative field.

You could tell by the way the other candidates went after Jagmeet Singh in Sunday afternoon's debate in St. John's that they regard him as the front-runner.

British Columbia MP Peter Julian, 55, was particularly critical of Singh for not opposing Kinder Morgan's Trans Mountain pipeline – a project he said 60 per cent of British Columbians voted against in last month's provincial election, soon to bring a minority NDP government to office. Julian also pointed out the federal NDP opposes Kinder Morgan.

Singh replied – politely but pointedly – that he would be meeting both BC NDP Leader John Horgan and Alberta NDP Premier Rachel Notley, who has endorsed the twinning of the existing Trans Mountain pipeline from Edmonton to Vancouver. In other words, Singh wants to avoid a fight in the NDP family.

Singh has been deputy leader of the Ontario NDP at Queen's Park, a political arena renowned for high-sticking and elbowing in the corners. In the exchange with Julian he demonstrated what everyone in the provincial legislature already knew – that he can take a punch, and not just in the mixed martial arts bouts in which he has competed.

At 38, Singh has an interesting personal narrative: born in suburban Toronto of Punjabi immigrant parents, raised in St. John's and Windsor, attended high school in Detroit. Somewhere along the way, he also learned French. A criminal defence lawyer, he's been in the legislature since 2011 and is the only Sikh member there. He's known a stylish dresser – certainly the only NDP member who's ever been featured in GQ.

Charlie Angus, who could emerge as a consensus second choice on the ranked ballot, also has a fascinating personal story. As a young man in Toronto in the 1980s, he co-founded two bands that recorded seven albums. He still sings and plays bass guitar, and launched his leadership campaign at the Toronto club where he used to hang out as a teenager.

As a Catholic social justice advocate, he founded a shelter for homeless men in Toronto. Returning to his birthplace of Timmins in the 1990s, he became a community activist. He's been in the House since 2004. At 54, he's the author of seven books, including *Children of the Broken Treaty*, a searing indictment of the treatment of First Nations children. Nobody in the House knows more about northern or aboriginal issues. His campaign slogan – "I've got your back" – is no idle boast. On Monday, he won the endorsement of the Public Service Alliance of Canada.

Niki Ashton, 34, from Churchill in northern Manitoba, is probably the most left-leaning of the leadership candidates. When they were asked to comment on the Trudeau government's foreign and defence policy reviews, Ashton jumped at the opportunity to lambaste the Liberals for promising $15 billion in new defence spending just to please Donald Trump. That's a message that resonates in the NDP.

Guy Caron, 49, has been in the House from Rimouski since 2011 and, as the party's former finance critic, is closer to the progressive centre of the NDP.

Several obvious candidates chose to sit out the race; Nathan Cullen, Alexandre Boulerice and Megan Leslie all had compelling family or career reasons not to jump in. But the five in the field all belong in it, and the NDP has done a good job of organizing the leadership campaign. Sunday's debate was the fourth. All of have them have been interesting, especially when the candidates are asking each other questions in addition to the ones chosen from party members' submissions. There are five more debates to come.

And at the end of the day, the NDP will prolong the suspense by having members vote each week in October until someone obtains a majority of preferential ballots (unlike the Conservatives, who rolled out 13 rounds in one day).

As always, the NDP faces an existential quandary – whether it's enough to be the conscience of the country on the left, or whether it should broaden its base and play to win. From J.S. Woodsworth to Tommy Douglas, CCF and NDP leaders have endured Liberals hijacking their ideas, from pension plans to universal health care.

As the party's former national director Robin Sears writes in a forthcoming *Policy* magazine article on the NDP, "this hits the most painful internal struggle faced by any party of principle of left or right. Is power and its necessary compromises more important than principle? Does being right always take precedence, even if the price is certain defeat?"

Ed Broadbent and Jack Layton both played to win. The NDP would do well to remember that.

June 2017

MID-TERM MUDDLE

As the House lurches towards the end of the spring sitting, there's a sense that while there's a lot going on in Ottawa, not much is getting done.

It's the mid-term muddle which hits most majority governments halfway through their first mandates, where the Trudeau Liberals are now.

From parliamentary reform to climate change, from the fiscal framework to defence procurement spending to Canada's place in the world, the government's record is somewhere between a work in progress and a disappointment to many Canadians who voted for change in 2015.

Much has happened since then that wasn't on the radar, much less in the Liberal platform – notably Donald Trump winning the American presidency, calling NAFTA a "disaster" for America and subsequently dismissing NATO as "obsolete." You can't blame Justin Trudeau for any of that. It is his job to cope with it, though, since they touch on the two most important files in Canada's most important diplomatic relationship: trade and security.

The prime minister's challenge is to get along with Trump without going along with him. How he strikes that delicate balance will have an immediate impact on how voters perceive him. He has to manage the bilateral relationship while keeping his distance from Trump on his protectionist and isolationist agenda, which amounts to nothing less than an abdication of American leadership in the post-war world of the last 70 years. How Trudeau strikes that tone of differentiation may determine his standing with progressive voters and, as a result, his prospects in the 2019 election.

NAFTA renegotiation talks are booked to begin mid-August. You shouldn't expect Trudeau to reveal Canada's position anywhere but at the bargaining table. This is not, as he told the Commons on Monday, a matter for QP.

As for the relationship between the two leaders, Trudeau is stepping very, very carefully. "Of course," he replied when asked during an interview on Global's West Block on Sunday whether he "respects" the president. On the question of whether he trusts Trump, Trudeau waffled. (Sensible. As Ronald Reagan famously told Mikhail Gorbachev, "Trust, but verify.")

In the meantime, there's lots going on, but not much going down. The government announced a long-awaited defence review two weeks ago, in which it pledged to increase military spending by 70 per cent to $33 billion a year over the next 10 years. But none of it is in current spending envelopes, and all of it is back-end loaded. The finance department says the spending increases won't add to the deficit. No one really believes that.

The Liberals say they will add 15 new ships to the naval fleet and 88 fighter jets to the air force. What kind of jets? That's to be determined by a competition, which could well bring the F-35 stealth fighter back into the picture. Meantime, there's a general consensus that the purchase of 18 Boeing Super Hornets as an interim replacement for the aging CF-18s is a bad idea, as it would add another platform to maintenance costs.

Conveniently, Ottawa is in the middle of a trade dispute with Boeing, which has filed a complaint with the U.S. Commerce Department over Canada's loan to Bombardier for the CSeries commercial jet. Which is as good a pretext as any to cancel the $7 billion Super Hornet option.

In terms of the larger parliamentary agenda, it's much the same story: lots of back-and-forth, not much closure. The inertia in Parliament is reflected in the high vacancy rate among its officers. The ethics, lobbying, chief electoral officer and official languages commissioner posts are all unfilled. The selection of Madeleine Meilleur for the official languages post blew up because she was a former Liberal cabinet minister at Queen's Park and a donor to Trudeau's campaign. Notwithstanding her good work as a champion of Ottawa's Montfort Hospital and francophone rights in Ontario, she was a partisan nomination to a non-partisan role; the Trudeau team should have known better.

The current parliamentary argument is on the government's budget implementation bill, an omnibus bill with enabling legislation tacked on to create the Canada Infrastructure Bank. In opposition, the Liberals quite rightly condemned the Conservative government of the day for forcing omnibus budget bills through Parliament. In government, the Grits are doing the same thing.

The Liberals claim that because the infrastructure bank was announced in the budget, it's part of the budget, even though there's no money in it yet.

Many senators didn't buy that, and the government narrowly averted a defeat on it Monday night, when the Senate voted a 38–38 tie to reject a motion to sever the bank from the budget bill. This is not the old Senate of party hacks, but the new chamber of independent senators created by Trudeau.

Well, not entirely. CBC pollster Éric Grenier ran the numbers on how the new Senate has been voting and found that in all but a few cases, the 27 senators named by Trudeau and 13 previously appointed independents have been voting overwhelmingly with the government. Oddly enough, it's the 18 Senate Liberals – kicked out of caucus by Trudeau three years ago – and the 38 Conservative members who've been joining forces to hold up government bills. This is the revenge of the Senate Liberals, who now hold the balance of power in the Red Chamber.

In the midst of all this, the Liberals introduced two new bills Monday and Tuesday, an unusual occurrence in the last week of a sitting. One is an updated

Access to Information bill, the first since ATI was introduced 34 years ago, and the other is on national security. Both are important bills, and neither has any hope of being adopted before the recess, though they may allow the Liberals to say they're keeping two campaign promises. Several bills have passed in the last week, including a new Citizenship Act, but the Liberals have still passed only half as many bills as the Conservatives did in the first session of their 2011 majority mandate.

This is a sitting, and a session, that needs to end now. Approaching mid-mandate, the prime minister normally would be looking at a summer cabinet shuffle and a new throne speech in the fall. But there's no sign the government plans to prorogue, and there's ample precedent for that. At mid-mandate in 1986, the Mulroney government prorogued only at the end of August, even as it was writing a throne speech for early October.

The mid-term muddle. To be continued.

June 2017

QUEBEC'S FUN FÊTE NATIONALE

The St. Jean Baptiste holiday used to be a rallying event for the sovereignty movement, with separatist leaders marching at the head of the parade and Québécois artists bringing up the rear, singing the movement's anthems.

No longer. The parade is hardly even covered as a news event; it's become a peaceful walk down St.-Denis Street rather than a militant march down Sherbrooke Street. And the concerts on Montreal's Mount Royal, which once drew hundreds of thousands, are a thing of the past.

As for politicians showing up – the most prominent one on the weekend was Justin Trudeau, who had events scheduled in five Quebec cities and towns over two full days, culminating with a family event in his Montreal riding. No Canadian prime minister has ever had such an intensive schedule of St. Jean Baptiste events. "Bonne fête nationale du Québec!" Trudeau tweeted.

Throughout those events, Trudeau looked like he was on the campaign trail, playing his outstanding retail game, having the time of his life. And in a way he was, reminding everyone he was Quebec's favourite son in Ottawa.

It's now nearly half a century since his father was loudly booed for having the temerity to sit on the reviewing stand at the June 24 parade the night before his election in 1968. On Saturday, his son posed for selfies with young admirers in his riding of Papineau in East End Montreal, once the heartland of the separatist movement. No longer.

The Parti Québécois has been floundering since the 2014 campaign, ever since star candidate Pierre-Karl Péladeau famously pumped his fist, called for renewed efforts to "make Quebec a country" and transformed the election into a referendum on another referendum – the last thing most Quebecers wanted, having lived through the near-miss of the 1995 referendum, which resulted in divided families and broken friendships. Later as PQ leader, Péladeau quit in 2016 after less than a year on the job. Under Jean-François Lisée, the PQ has put off any question of a referendum off until 2023, after the next two provincial elections in 2018 and 2022.

But the voters aren't buying anything the PQ is selling. A Léger Marketing poll for Le Devoir published on Quebec's national day showed the PQ in third place at 22 per cent, behind the Liberals at 31 per cent and the Coalition Avenir Québec at 28 per cent, with the leftist-separatist Québec solidaire growing to 15 per cent.

Only five months ago, in January, the PQ was at 29 per cent with the QS in single digits at 9 per cent. The Liberals were then at 32 per cent, with the CAQ in third at 23 per cent. Every single point the QS has gained came at the expense of the PQ.

Bryan Breguet of the polling site Too Close To Call has extrapolated the Léger numbers in the 125-seat National Assembly and projects 51 Liberals, 45 CAQs, 22 Péquistes and seven QS members of the legislature. That would be a razor-thin Liberal minority, with the CAQ as the official opposition and the PQ relegated to third party status.

This happened once before in the 2007 election, which produced the first minority legislature since 1874, with the Liberals under Jean Charest winning 48 seats with 33 per cent of the vote and Action démocratique du Québec under Mario Dumont taking 41 seats and 31 per cent of the vote, while the PQ won 36 seats and 28 per cent of the vote.

But that was a three-party house, not a four-party legislature. The PQ wasn't outflanked on the left and on the sovereigntist vote, as it now is by QS. Dumont's ADQ has been supplanted by François Legault's CAQ on the centre right. A former PQ cabinet minister from 1998–2003, Legault previously was co-founder and CEO of the charter airline Air Transat. If he can grow a few points among non-francophone Liberal voters in the Greater Montreal Region, he might even be able to form a minority government next year.

The current political puzzle in Quebec is the unpopularity of the first-term majority Liberal government of Philippe Couillard. The Liberals have balanced three budgets in a row, and in March delivered $1 billion in tax cuts and $4 billion in new program spending, mostly in health and education. The province's unemployment rate is tracking below the national average.

But the Couillard Liberals have been taking hits on charges against former ministers on fundraising abuses and governance issues dating back to the Charest years that have been killing them in the legislature and the media.

Couillard may have thought he could change the conversation this month by suggesting a re-opening of the Constitution to recognize Quebec as a distinct society. For Quebecers, being distinct, he said on releasing a 200-page position paper on June 1, "is our way of being Canadians." Shades of Meech Lake – except that constitutional re-openers would now include three northern territories as well as First Nations and Inuit at the table. Good luck with that.

Trudeau was having none of it. "You know my views on the Constitution," he replied the same day. "We are not opening the Constitution."

There was a time when Trudeau's abrupt dismissal of Quebec's constitutional initiative would have been widely denounced by the Quebec political class and media.

Not this time. The story disappeared without a trace. Quebecers are evidently no more interested in another constitutional round than they are in another referendum.

On to Canada Day.

June 2017

TRUMP'S NAFTA WISH LIST

We've finally got Donald Trump's NAFTA renegotiation wish list – and once again it turns out the president's bark is worse than his administration's bite.

Trump was barking away at a Made-in-America products rollout at the White House Monday afternoon, an event that featured everything from a fire truck on the South Lawn to baseball bats and guitars in the Blue Room.

But by his standards, his rhetoric was relatively restrained, and he appeared to stick to the text on his Teleprompter. "No longer will other countries drain our wealth," he declared. He said he wanted a level playing field with Canada and Mexico, "but if it's slanted our way a little bit, I'd accept that, also."

To his base in the rust-belt industrial states of Pennsylvania, Ohio and Michigan – which delivered him the White House – he promised: "We are going to stand up for our companies, and most of all for our workers … wait till you see what's up for you."

An hour later, the United States Trade Representative issued a 17-page shopping list of objectives for the NAFTA renegotiation, meeting a congressional deadline of 30 days before the talks begin in mid-August. While it obviously seeks advantageous outcomes for the Americans, none of it is written in stone, and it's a very professional piece of work.

Topping the wish list for the USTR: "Improve the U.S. trade balance and reduce the trade deficit with the NAFTA countries."

Canada is not the problem here. According to USTR's own numbers, the U.S. exported US$266 billion of goods to Canada in 2106, while importing $278 billion, for a deficit in goods of $12 billion. But on trade in services, the U.S. had a $24.6 billion surplus with Canada, for an overall surplus in trade in goods and services of $12.5 billion.

Clearly, the Canada-U.S. trade relationship is balanced and beneficial to both countries. As Prime Minister Justin Trudeau reminded the National Governors Association last Friday, Canada is the largest customer of two-thirds of American states and "buys more from the U.S. than China, Japan and the U.K. combined."

Mexico is a different story. The U.S. exported US$231 billion in goods to Mexico last year, while importing $294 billion, for a deficit of $63 billion. When trade in services was included, the deficit was still $55 billion. And yet – again, according to USTR – U.S. exports of goods to Mexico have increased 455 per cent since NAFTA took effect in 1994, with exports in services up 200 per cent.

Trump's trade deficit issue is with China. The U.S. exported $116 billion of goods to China last year, while importing $463 billion, for a deficit of $347 billion.

Reducing trade deficits may be an objective, but it's hardly negotiable at the trilateral NAFTA table. As previously signalled by Commerce Secretary Wilbur Ross, the Americans have two major re-openers – rules of origin and the dispute settlement mechanism – that will be issues for Canada.

As the USTR paper puts it, the U.S. objective is to "update and strengthen the rules of origin, as necessary, to ensure that the benefits of NAFTA go to products genuinely made in the United States and North America."

This might be an issue for integrated industries. While vehicles are assembled in all three countries, for example, not all of the parts come from North America. USTR wants to "ensure the rules of origin incentivize the sourcing of goods and materials from the United States and North America." So what would that mean to, for example, the apparel industry, which relies on international wool markets?

As for dispute settlement, the Americans want to "eliminate the Chapter 19 dispute settlement mechanism" of NAFTA. The dispute settlement clause was a deal-breaker for Brian Mulroney in the 1987 Canada-U.S. free trade talks, and it was only minutes before the expiry deadline for the negotiations passed when the Americans agreed to it. Canadian firms have won their share of cases under Chapter 19; without it, their only recourse might be American courts. Good luck with that.

On trade in services, the Americans are focused on telecommunications and financial services. The U.S. wants market access for American telecom providers and "market opportunities for United States financial services suppliers to obtain fairer and more open conditions of financial services trade."

It's not clear that the big three Canadian telecom providers – Rogers, Shaw and Bell – would welcome competition from American firms, but the public might. The Canadian telecoms are also off-limits for prospective U.S. buyers. As for Canadian banks – notably RBC, BMO and TD – they have flourished in the U.S. and should have little to fear from an American presence in Canada.

In agriculture, the Americans are taking aim at supply management in dairy – without naming it – as they "seek to eliminate non-tariff barriers to U.S. agricultural exports."

On government procurement, the U.S. wants more opportunities for American firms to bid on public projects, without offering reciprocity. In fact, the U.S. wants to "exclude sub-federal coverage (state and local governments) from the commitments being negotiated." Well, then, the Canadians could do the same, couldn't they?

In terms of modernizing NAFTA (which Trudeau says "we welcome"), the Americans would like to start with some online cross-border shopping, raising the duty-free purchase amount from $20 in Canada to US$800. That's certainly customer-friendly. The Americans also are looking for "secure commitments not to impose customs duties on digital products."

In all, the Americans are setting an ambitious agenda for a negotiation they hope to complete in the months before the mid-term congressional and governors' races primary season begins early in 2018. The Mexicans want it done and off the table before their national election next July.

Trudeau is under no obligation, as Trump was, to publish his agenda for the NAFTA talks. Nor should he. He should play Canada's hand very close to the vest. Up to now, he's done a first-rate job of managing his relationship with the mercurial Trump, as have his ministers and staff in managing the issue in Washington and reaching out to the states and major stakeholders in industry.

Canada's bottom line on NAFTA is as obvious as the Hippocratic oath: First, do no harm. Also: if it ain't broke, don't fix it.

July 2017

INFRASTRUCTURE: A DOABLE CROSS-BORDER DEAL

Amid the chaos of the Trump presidency, there are two important files from his campaign platform that Canada can work on with his administration.

The first, obviously, is trade and the coming NAFTA renegotiation. The second is infrastructure – where the Trudeau government has a strikingly similar agenda of partnering with private sector investors.

Trump is talking about "a great national infrastructure program" worth $1 trillion; he hopes that $200 billion in federal funding will attract another $800 billion in private and local government investment. So far, it's just talk. Trump hasn't shown anyone the money, hasn't gotten around yet to asking Congress for it. He's expected to do so in the fall.

Indeed, Justin Trudeau's team is way ahead of the Trump administration in producing a plan on infrastructure. Enabling legislation to establish the Canada Infrastructure Bank was approved by Parliament as the House rose for the summer. The government this month appointed a chair, Janice Fukakusa, former CFO of Royal Bank, and is searching for a CEO. Even before the CIB was approved, the government brought in Jim Leech, former head of the Ontario Teachers' Pension Plan, as a special adviser.

The CIB will spend $35 billion on infrastructure projects, $20 billion of it in equity partnerships with pension funds and private investors. The hope is to generate $4 to $5 of private investment for every government dollar spent. Overall, Ottawa plans $180 billion of infrastructure spending over the next 11 years.

The prime minister personally hosted an infrastructure summit in Toronto last November organized by BlackRock Inc., with $21 trillion in assets represented around the table. The Canada Pension Plan Investment Board and Quebec's Caisse de dépôt were among the Canadian players at the meeting.

Caisse President and CEO Michael Sabia, a member of Trudeau's advisory council on economic growth, knows something about infrastructure investing. In 2015, the Caisse bought the British government's 30 per cent stake in Eurostar International, owner of the Chunnel train service between London and Paris. The Caisse is also putting up $3 billion to build a new light rail commuter train network in the Greater Montreal Region, with Ottawa and Quebec slated to pick up the remaining $2.5 billion.

Trudeau also said last month that once the CIB was up and running, Quebec and the Caisse could "identify the project as an opportunity for independent opportunity and analysis by the bank."

There's no shortage of projects the bank can consider, "in Canada or partly in Canada," as mandated by the enabling legislation. That means cross-border infrastructure, like the Gordie Howe Bridge from Windsor to Detroit, will be eligible for CIB funding. As it stands now, Canada will pay the $4.8 billion cost of the bridge and border stations at the busiest crossing between Canada and the U.S., with the costs to be recouped from tolls. It fits right in with the bank's mandate on trade and transportation corridors, the other main aspects being green infrastructure and public transit.

There may be a significant trans-border infrastructure project in the works on the West Coast. The Canadian Press reported that the state of Washington is looking at the CIB to be a "financing option" for a multi-billion-dollar high speed train service linking Vancouver, Seattle and Portland. As CP reports, a high-speed train would facilitate trade and transportation in the 'Cascadia Innovation Corridor' between Seattle and Vancouver, the home region of Microsoft and other high-tech leaders. Trudeau apparently discussed this in a May meeting with Washington State Governor Jay Inslee, and one of his advisers told CP's Andy Blatchford: "They talked about this as an idea whose time has come."

So, with the Canadians moving forward through the CIB on trans-border infrastructure files, the question becomes: When will the Trump administration get moving on infrastructure?

Washington is a town that is gridlocked in normal times. These are not normal times.

There's the matter of the Russians, and whether the Trump campaign was on a "collusion course" with them in meddling in last year's election. Former FBI director Robert Mueller is a special counsel to the justice department on that; there are rumblings that Trump might end up firing him if his investigation gets too close to the president himself or members of his family such as son Don Jr. or son-in-law Jared Kushner, who met with Russian sources last June at Trump Tower.

Now, of course, Trump is saying that if he had known Attorney-General Jeff Sessions would recuse himself from the Russia probe, he wouldn't have appointed him in the first place. Trump has been tweeting his disappointment in Sessions lately, accusing him of taking a "very weak position" on "Hillary Clinton crimes" and information leaks from his own administration. The president also tweeted over the weekend that the president has "the complete power to pardon anyone," including family members and himself (probably not true).

No wonder the cable new channels ratings are through the roof. *House of Cards* can't come up with story lines this crazy.

Speaking of Russia, the Senate voted nearly unanimously to curtail Trump's ability to lift economic sanctions against Russia; Trump accepted the measure with amendments on the weekend. Had he vetoed it, the Senate would have overridden his veto. The Senate GOP voted today to open debate on repealing Obamacare, bringing the president an inch closer to realizing the Republicans' long-stated goal of replacing the health care legislation. But they've still got an awful long way to go; the Obamacare repeal project is polling very badly and senators still don't have a clue what shape the replacement bill ultimately will take.

In short, Trump desperately needs a couple of wins. Trudeau can help him on trade and infrastructure. With his skill at interpersonal relations, the prime minister has managed to form a good working relationship with Trump. "Justin is doing a spectacular job in Canada," Trump said at the G20 this month. "Everybody loves him and they love him for a reason, so congratulations on the job you are doing."

Such an effusive third-party endorsement, especially considering the source, may have left Trudeau blushing … with embarrassment. But it also opens doors at the White House and throughout the administration.

On infrastructure and trade, there are two key cross-border issues: investment and procurement. In its paper on NAFTA objectives last week, the office of the U.S. Trade Representative called for "rules that reduce or eliminate barriers to U.S. investment in the NAFTA countries."

That's a reciprocal issue. Similarly, the USTR is seeking to "increase opportunities for U.S. firms to sell U.S. products and services into the NAFTA countries." That's also a two-way street, not a "Buy American" or "America First" preference when it comes to building infrastructure, in which Canada has considerable experience in Public-Private Partnerships. Canadian construction and consulting engineering firms also have world-class expertise in building roads, bridges and energy grids.

In short: Get over it, Donald. And get on with it.

July 2017

DISPUTE SETTLEMENT A NAFTA RED LINE FOR CANADA

On the night of October 3, 1987, the clock was ticking towards the midnight expiration of U.S. President Ronald Reagan's fast-track authority to negotiate a free trade agreement with Canada, to be voted "up or down" by Congress without amendments.

There was only one issue remaining – a deal-breaker for Canada: a dispute settlement mechanism. Canada wanted bi-national panels to settle disputes on issues such as anti-dumping and countervailing duties. The Americans maintained it would be an infringement of their sovereignty, as U.S. Treasury Secretary James Baker told Prime Minister Brian Mulroney on the phone.

"I'm going to be calling President Reagan at Camp David," Mulroney told Baker, "and I'm going to ask him one question."

"What's that?" Baker asked.

"How come the United States can make a nuclear arms deal with its worst enemy, the Soviet Union, but can't make a trade deal with its best friend, Canada?"

"PM," Baker replied, "Can you give me 20 minutes?"

Half an hour later, Baker burst into his own board room in Washington, where the Canadian negotiating team was camped out, and threw a piece of paper on the table.

"There's your goddam dispute settlement mechanism," he said. "Now can we send a messenger to Congress?"

It was literally five minutes to midnight. Both sides stopped the clock. Later, as he met the press at the bottom of the staircase in the Prime Minister's Office, Mulroney said, "A hundred years from now, the naysayers will be forgotten."

But first, the 1988 election would be transformed into a referendum on the Canada-U.S. Free Trade Agreement. And in the 1993 election, Liberal leader Jean Chrétien campaigned against the North American Free Trade Agreement signed a year earlier by Mulroney, the first President George Bush and Mexican President Carlos Salinas.

The bi-national dispute settlement panels established in Chapter 19 of the FTA were also incorporated as Chapter 19 of the NAFTA.

A quarter century on, NAFTA has been re-opened by Donald Trump for re-negotiation; talks begin in two weeks in Washington. Now, as it was 30 years ago in the FTA round, the dispute settlement mechanism is looming large.

The Office of the U.S. Trade Representative is required by Congress to publish its negotiating objectives one month before trade talks begin. This time the USTR put out a 17-page position paper which included a call to "eliminate the Chapter 19 dispute settlement mechanism."

In its place, the Americans want to "establish a dispute settlement mechanism that is effective, timely, and in which panel determinations are based on the provisions of the Agreement and the submissions of the parties and are provided in a reasoned manner."

Team Trump has put a lot of other issues on the table, from rules of origin to procurement, investment, intellectual property, trade in services and digital online trade, which did not exist 25 years ago. There's no doubt that NAFTA needs to be updated.

But when it comes to dispute settlement, Prime Minister Justin Trudeau made it clear last week that Chapter 19 is as much a deal-breaker for him as it was for Mulroney 30 years ago.

"A fair dispute settlement system is absolutely essential for Canada to sign on to," the prime minister declared last Tuesday at an Ottawa news conference.

The good news for Trudeau is that, after a series of self-inflicted policy defeats, Trump desperately needs a win – which means a win all around. Trump's recent shuffle of his White House, bringing over Homeland Security Secretary John Kelly to be his chief of staff, may finally introduce a measure of order to the chaotic West Wing. (A retired four-star Marine general, Kelly's first act was to oust Anthony Scaramucci as White House communications director after only 10 days on the job – during which 'The Mooch' constantly broke the rule that staff should never become the story.)

The NAFTA file is one that's already under adult supervision in Washington. Trump's USTR, Robert Lighthizer, is a Washington trade lawyer who previously served as deputy USTR in the first Reagan administration. The U.S. chief negotiator, John Melle, has been assistant USTR for the Western Hemisphere and has worked at the trade office since 1988.

The Canadian chief negotiator is Steve Verheul, who worked for years on the Canada-Europe trade talks and helped then-Trade Minister Chrystia Freeland close the deal last fall. Retaining responsibility for the NAFTA file as foreign minister, Freeland obviously picked a trusted trade hand to be at the table.

Mexico's lead negotiator, a man with the unlikely name of Kenneth Smith Ramos, worked on the original NAFTA negotiation and is currently head of trade and NAFTA at the Mexican embassy in Washington. These veteran trade officials are deeply seasoned professionals, and all three countries will be well served by them.

There remains the question of whether the latest Canada-U.S. softwood lumber dispute can be resolved before the NAFTA talks begin. The obvious trade-off would be for the U.S. to remove its up to 24 per cent countervailing duties and 7.7 per cent anti-dumping duty per cent duty on Canadian softwood in return for Canada accepting a phased-in deal limiting its share of the U.S. market a few points below its current 31 per cent share.

After a visit with Lighthizer and Commerce Secretary Wilbur Ross last week, new B.C Premier John Horgan sounded optimistic. "I'm pretty confident," he said, "based on Mr. Ross's view that he wants to get this done before the middle of August."

That's not to say the U.S. Lumber Coalition is of the same mind, of course. For them, it always comes down to the lower Canadian stumpage fees from Crown-owned forests, as compared to privately-owned land in the U.S.

It's another Canada-U.S trade story that's been around for the last 30 years – a constant reminder that, in international trade talks, the past is always prologue.

August 2017

THE NAFTA TALKS

The best thing you can say about the first round of NAFTA talks is also the least thing you can say about them:

Donald Trump hasn't tweeted about them. Yet.

He was too busy on other fronts – for instance, abdicating the moral authority of the American presidency in the aftermath of white supremacist rioting in Charlottesville. With the Trump presidency preoccupied with its implosion, the White House is doing damage control 24/7 and has left the NAFTA file in the hands of United States Trade Representative Robert E. Lighthizer and his team of professionals.

That's the good news: The grown ups are at the table. Led by Steve Verheul, the Canadian team had 75 negotiators in more than a dozen meeting rooms at a Washington hotel during the opening five days of talks; officials discussed more than two dozen issues. They'll reconvene in Mexico City September 1–5 and somewhere in Canada in late September.

The Americans were throwing their weight around, of course. It's what they do. In drafting a joint communique at the end of the opening round, the U.S. wanted to refer to the talks as a "renegotiation," while the Canadians and Mexicans preferred to call them a "modernization." They compromised, agreeing to describe the talks as "a renegotiation to modernize NAFTA."

The three countries also declared they were "committed to an accelerated and comprehensive negotiation process that will upgrade our agreement and establish 21st century standards." In other words, the Americans don't want the talks caught up in next year's mid-term elections, and the Mexicans don't want negotiations going on during their presidential and parliamentary elections next July 1.

The Americans made it very clear that dispute settlement and rules of origin are their major re-openers, and that their top priority remains reducing the U.S. merchandise trade deficit. Oh, and they want access to government procurement contracts in Canada and Mexico, while maintaining an America First position at home. Evidently, they define 'reciprocity' a little differently in D.C. these days.

Not surprisingly, USTR Lighthizer held to the demand in his July 17 Summary of Objectives for the NAFTA Renegotiation to "eliminate the Chapter 19 dispute settlement mechanism." Equally unsurprisingly, this is a deal-breaker for Prime Minister Justin Trudeau, just as it was for Brian Mulroney in the first round of free trade talks 30 years ago.

But the language of the American position paper on trade remedies is not objectionable. They want to "establish a dispute settlement mechanism that is effective, timely and in which panel determinations are based on the provisions of the agreement and the submissions of the parties."

What the Americans are talking about is similar to the existing dispute settlement mechanism at the World Trade Organization and the one they negotiated with 11 countries, including Canada and Mexico, for the 2015 Trans-Pacific Partnership – which, ironically, Trump walked away from in an executive order on his fourth day in office last January.

As long as the principle of bi-national panels is respected, the language establishing them should be a secondary concern. The point is to avoid litigation in American courts. Neither Canada nor Mexico would ever agree to that.

On to rules of origin: The Americans want to increase the North American content in the auto industry from the current level of 62.5 per cent. But the Big Three automakers, and parts makers such as Magna and Linamar, are all opposed. In the assembly process, autos go back and forth across the borders half a dozen times, and some of the parts come from Asia.

As for Trump's obsession with the American merchandise trade deficit, the president and his officials neglect to mention their surplus in trade in services. A modest Canadian surplus of US$12 billion in goods becomes a deficit of $12.5 billion when the American surplus in services is included. The Mexican merchandise trade surplus of $64 billion is mostly in auto and petroleum exports – but it's still smaller than the U.S. deficit with Germany and it's negligible when compared with America's $350 billion deficit with China.

None of which even touches on the question of whether trade deficits are even an accurate reflection of a nation's economic prosperity. In a Monday editorial, the *Wall Street Journal* tore through what it called Lighthizer's trade deficit "preoccupation" and the "bizarre economics" at the centre of

Trump's trade agenda, which the paper called "dangerous to American prosperity." As Foreign Affairs Minister Chrystia Freeland put it at the start of the talks last week, "Canada doesn't view trade surpluses or deficits as a primary measure of whether trade works."

Of course, Trump is merely playing to his blue-collar base in the rust-belt states of Pennsylvania, Ohio and Michigan, which delivered the presidency to him last November. "Great trade deals coming for American workers," he tweeted last week before the talks began.

The question is whether the continuous chaos his presidency generates weakens his hand in the trade negotiations, or whether he might even undermine the talks on his own to placate his base.

Most American presidents have understood the difference between the job and the role they play as America's moral leader. Trump doesn't, because he has no sense of history – and no class. His tumultuous news conference last week, during which he said there was "blame on all sides" for Charlottesville, may have been a tipping point for his presidency. (As if there could be any moral equivalence between armed Klan members and neo-Nazis and the protesters who confront their repulsive messages.)

Of all the issues on which an American president is supposed to lead, race relations is the most sensitive and most important. Which explains why the private sector is fleeing Trump's taint at a dead run: CEOs resigned en masse from the president's two business councils, as did every member of his arts council, and at least nine major charities have cancelled events scheduled for his Palm Beach estate, Mar-a-Lago. It's why the five Joint Chiefs of Staff put out statements denouncing racism and extremism, distancing themselves and their services from the Commander-in-Chief.

Watching a presidency in crisis while negotiating NAFTA 2.0, officials from all three countries must have been relieved Trump wasn't intervening in the talks. And if Trump does go on Twitter, they might be best advised to ignore him.

August 2017

∞

NOT VIRTUE SIGNALLING

On the NAFTA renegotiation, Rona Ambrose got it right in her initial response: aligning the Conservatives with the Liberals in a united front. Andrew Scheer, on the other hand, got it wrong – in differentiating the opposition from the government at this early stage of the game.

Conservative foreign affairs critic Erin O'Toole was dismissive of what he called Liberal "virtue signalling" last week – a reference to the Trudeau government's attempt to negotiate new NAFTA chapters on gender equality, Indigenous peoples and the environment. Instead, O'Toole said, Team Canada should be focusing on a softwood lumber deal and export access in the North American auto industry.

Actually, Foreign Minister Chrystia Freeland and U.S. Commerce Secretary Wilbur Ross are very close to a deal on softwood, one that would see the Americans withdraw duties in return for Canada accepting a cap on market share. The obstacle is the powerful U.S. Lumber Coalition, but in the wake of the devastating hurricanes in Texas and Florida, the needs of the U.S. housing industry likely will take priority.

As for the 62.5 per cent North American rules-of-origin in automobiles, the industry likes things the way they are right now, with vehicles crossing the borders half a dozen times in assembly. Donald Trump can complain all he wants about U.S. plants relocating to Mexico, but he's complaining about the wrong thing; most American auto job losses are due to the spread of automation and artificial intelligence.

In short, there's nothing wrong with Canada proposing chapters on gender, Indigenous and environmental issues. Even if they're more aspirational than achievable, they represent values and goals on which there's a Canadian political consensus. Maybe the Liberals are playing to the gallery – but they can hardly be faulted for that.

Prime Minister Justin Trudeau took the ammo O'Toole offered and used it during a Monday appearance at the Women in the World Summit, organized by former *New Yorker* and *Vanity Fair* editor Tina Brown.

"The pushback we're getting is actually not from south of the border," he told Brown. "The pushback we're getting is from Canadian Conservatives who said, 'Oh no, this is about economics, it's about jobs … it's not about rhetorical flourishes or being good on the environment or good on gender.'

"To see that there is a supposedly responsible political party out there that still doesn't get it about gender equality, as well as many other things, that environmental responsibility is fundamentally an economic issue, highlights that we still have a lot of work to do in Canada."

Trudeau pointed out that there was a chapter on women's rights in the recently negotiated Canada-Chile free trade agreement, and said he hoped to persuade the U.S. and Mexico to accept a similar chapter in NAFTA.

If Trudeau wants a starting point on this with Donald Trump, he need look no further than his daughter Ivanka and son-in-law Jared Kushner, who worked with the PM's office in establishing the Canada-U.S. Council for

Advancement of Women Entrepreneurs and Business Leaders, which had its first meeting with the PM and the president at the White House last February.

On Indigenous peoples, it's probably stretching credulity to suggest they might get their own NAFTA chapter this time. Putting them on the Canadian ask list was, however, clearly a precondition for Assembly of First Nations National Chief Perry Bellegarde accepting Trudeau's invitation to join the government's new NAFTA Advisory Council, a blue-ribbon panel that includes Linamar auto parts CEO Linda Hasenfratz, outgoing Bank of Montreal CEO Bill Downe and former Conservative leader Ambrose.

While a chapter on Indigenous peoples is probably out of reach, they could easily be accommodated in a preamble. Indigenous issues vary by country. Canada has 1.8 million Indigenous people comprising 5.6 per cent of the population. Mexico has 25.7 million Indigenous people, or 21.5 per cent of the population, while the U.S. has 5.2 million North American Native Indians, according to the Census Bureau – less than 2 per cent of the population.

As for the environment, the Americans themselves in their July statement of objectives from the United States Trade Representative asked that environmental and labour standards be included as full chapters in the NAFTA rather than as side deals. That's what Bill Clinton demanded as a condition of signing after becoming president in 1993.

As Freeland put it in her Canadian agenda-setting speech at University of Ottawa last month, "we can make NAFTA more progressive first by bringing strong labour safeguards into the core of the agreement, second by integrating enhanced environmental provisions to ensure no NAFTA country weakens environmental protection to attract investment, and that fully supports efforts to address climate change."

Trump remains in denial about climate change and global warming, even in the wake of hurricanes Harvey and Irma. But even though Trump announced his intention to withdraw the United States from the Paris Accord, the parties to the accord can't leave until three years after it came into effect last November 3, and only then upon giving a year's notice. That would put the date of withdrawal on the day after the next U.S. presidential election.

And there's nothing to prevent negotiations on the environment from continuing separately from trade talks. The landmark Montreal Protocol on ozone depletion was signed 30 years ago this week, less than three weeks before the Canada-U.S. trade deal was announced. The Canada-U.S. acid rain accord was signed in March 1991, ahead of the first NAFTA round.

Trade was a signature issue for the prime minister of the day. But so was the environment – which is why Brian Mulroney was named Canada's greenest prime minister in 2006.

Neither trade agreements nor environmental accords are achieved without leadership – something Trudeau clearly understands.

Scheer obviously has a role to oppose, and a duty to do so if the Liberals mess up the NAFTA file. But he should be careful to avoid finding himself on the wrong side of history.

September 2017

JOHN TURNER

There is a saying in politics that honour is due. In John Turner's case, it is long overdue.

Finally, Turner's life and career in politics receive appropriate recognition in *Elusive Destiny: The Political Vocation of John Napier Turner*, a biography by Carleton University historian Paul Litt that is one of the best Canadian political books of the year.

It captures all the qualities, as well as the faults, of Turner. His brief season as prime minister, his wilderness years as opposition leader, and what he called the fight of his life against free trade don't end very well. But what comes across in all the chapters of his life is his sense that politics is an honourable calling. At the end of the story, as he leaves public life in 1989, there is a sense that his honour is not only undiminished, but very much enhanced.

Two guys who don't come out of this book looking particularly good are his predecessor as Liberal leader, Pierre Trudeau, and his successor, Jean Chrétien. They constantly undermined his leadership and in the end helped destroy it. Litt has the goods on them both, and the portraits of self-absorption (in Trudeau's case) and disloyalty (in Chrétien's) are quite damaging. Then again, the two were successful and long-serving prime ministers, while Turner was not.

Far from providing a smooth transition, Trudeau forced Turner to make a raft of patronage appointments

15

PEOPLE

that proved to be his undoing during the ensuing 1984 campaign. "There isn't a Grit left in town," said Conservative leader Brian Mulroney, smelling blood on the day the writ dropped. "They've all gone to Grit heaven."

Which led to the defining moment of the campaign, the exchange in the leaders' debate in which Turner lamely said of the appointments: "I had no option."

"You had an option, sir," Mulroney retorted. "You could have said; 'I'm not going to do it. This is wrong for Canada and I'm not asking Canadians to pay the price.' You had an option, sir, to say no."

"I had no option," Turner repeated.

"That is an avowal of failure," Mulroney shot back. "That is a confession of nonleadership, and this country needs leadership. You had an option, sir. You could have done better."

After that the bottom fell out of the Liberal campaign. Mulroney won the biggest landslide in Canadian history, while Turner led the Liberals to their worst showing ever up to then, with 28 per cent of the vote and only 40 seats.

Which left Turner in opposition, the last place he expected to find himself, constantly watching his back from the Chrétien crowd scheming for his job.

Litt captures all the drama and intrigue of the 1988 election, which Turner transformed into a referendum on free trade. But not before he had to survive a putsch mounted by the Liberal Party's senior advisers, who tried to persuade him that he should resign in the middle of the campaign, with Chrétien coming in as his replacement. Even worse than the would-be coup, Peter Mansbridge got wind of it and broke the story on CBC News.

Somehow, Turner pulled himself together for the debates the following week, and in the English debate he scored heavily when he told Mulroney: "I believe you have sold us out."

Turner tapped into a deepseated emotional insecurity in Canadians about the United States. He had found his voice, and his cause. This time it was the Tory numbers that tanked overnight.

At a lunch and book-signing in Toronto last week, I said to Turner: "I was on the other team. You scared the hell out of us."

He forced Mulroney to raise his game by abandoning a safe and scripted campaign and going for broke in the last four weeks.

As Mulroney himself put it: "He's got the momentum; now we're going to find out what we're made of."

It was the most exciting campaign of the modern era, and the most consequential.

That Turner lost, partly because of what Litt terms the Liberals' failure to close ranks behind him, does him no discredit. The first part of Turner's biography, on his early years and his terms as justice and finance minister, has a much happier ending.

Once an Olympic sprinter and the fastest man in Canada, Turner, now 82, has been much slowed by physical ailments. But his mind and wit are still sharp.

And he's clearly enjoying his season in the literary spotlight. If I had to recommend one political book for Christmas, this would be it, the highly readable biography of John Napier Turner, truly a right honourable gentleman.

December 2011

NIGEL WRIGHT

Back in the day when Nigel Wright was a young staffer in the policy shop of the Prime Minister's Office, I commented on his youthful appearance, wondering if he was old enough to vote.

"Be nice to Nigel," commented Bill Fox, then communications director to Brian Mulroney. "We'll all be working for him some day."

Then a law student at the University of Toronto, Wright was executive assistant to Charley McMillan, who was senior policy adviser to the prime minister. After two years, he returned to Toronto to finish his degree, picked up a Harvard master's in law, and joined the mergers and acquisitions practice of Davies Ward in Toronto.

Since 1997, he has been a top dealmaker for Gerry Schwartz at Onex Corp., of which he's now managing director. Along the way, he has made a ton of money, and a legion of friends, which can't be said of everyone on Bay Street.

Now he has accepted Stephen Harper's offer to be the next PMO chief of staff and at 46, is returning to the Langevin Block. It is only a few steps down the second floor corridor from the office he occupied a quarter century ago to the PM's corner suite, but it's also a very long journey.

Wright is an interesting choice in several respects. Although he knows the system inside-out, he's coming in from the outside, without an agenda or any baggage. His background in business and finance suggests Harper will be moving away from wedge-issue politics driven by ideology, to big-picture economic issues that will be the main policy frame until the election. Finally, Wright is decidedly from the Progressive Conservative wing of the party, not the former Reform crowd on the hard right.

"There will be more common sense and less blind ideology," says McMillan, Wright's onetime boss. That would be refreshing all the way through the system, from the public service, which has put down tools with this government, to the permanent political class of lawyers, consultants and lobbyists with whom any government must co-exist in Ottawa.

The outgoing chief of staff, Guy Giorno, has two young children, which is a very legitimate reason to leave a burnout job after two and a half years. He will leave behind a decidedly mixed record. His PMO has done an excellent job of managing big files such as the auto bailout and Haitian relief.

But this PMO's fatal flaws have been an obsession with tactics, and an absence of strategic communications to flesh out decisions with narratives. For example, the PM's maternal health initiative was announced in a single paragraph in a speech to the Davos economic forum, without any communications support to answer questions about a funding envelope, to say nothing of the availability of birth control and therapeutic abortions in the developing world. This is why Harper was completely blindsided by the predictable blowback.

Proroguing the House at Christmas was a major decision that needed more of a narrative than "recalibrating" to back it up. Ending the long form census in midsummer, when the government was off the air, was a stunning example of abdicating the "air game" to the opposition parties and every interest group in town.

It's not as it they don't have folks working on communications in Langevin. There are 30 people working on "comms" in the PMO, and another 100 upstairs in the Privy Council Office devoted to the PM's and the government's message. So, where's the product, other than juvenile attack lines and talking points that Tory talkers are too embarrassed to repeat on the air?

In Ottawa, the story over the summer was that Giorno was staying until the end of the year. A few weeks ago, the story became that he was leaving by the end of the year. It's exactly the same story, the only difference being that Giorno is now a lame duck.

Normally, a departing PMO chief of staff hands over the files and leaves in short order. A four-month transition period is unheard of and, now that his successor is known, probably untenable.

The Ottawa game just changed.

September 2010

LEE RICHARDSON

The House of Commons will be a poorer place without my friend Lee Richardson, the Calgary MP who has resigned his seat to become principal secretary to Alberta Premier Alison Redford.

First elected as a Progressive Conservative in the class of 1988, returning with the reunified Conservatives in 2004, the five-term member is known for his civility, collegiality and conviviality.

During his farewell remarks to the House last week, Richardson was interrupted by three standing ovations from all sides of the House, an extraordinary response to a backbencher announcing his resignation.

Then, even while leaders of all parties joined in personal tributes to Richardson, about 200 MPs lined up to shake his hand as he stood at his front-row seat by the door at the far end of the House. It was a good half-hour before he could leave the House. In four decades of attending the House, I've never seen anything quite like it.

"Well, that was quite something," he told friends after doing a scrum with reporters in the foyer of the House.

The cheers and applause were for both the messenger and the message: an honourable and decent man, calling for more honour and decency in the conduct of our public affairs.

"If I could share one thought with colleagues, it would be this," he said. "While we advocate for different ideas of Canada, we're all Canadians and we all love our country."

Which provoked a thunderous standing ovation from all parties.

"We would all, I think, do well to remember that," he continued, "and leave the partisan furies at the water's edge."

Few parliamentarians are better at extending a hand across the floor than Richardson, 64, renowned for hosting MPs of all parties at the Calgary Stampede. On caucus Wednesdays at the parliamentary restaurant, a bipartisan parade would inevitably stop by his table for a friendly word.

This is precisely what is missing in our public discourse today, and most MPs know it.

They generally run for office with the highest motives, but once they arrive in Ottawa are stunned by the dysfunctional environment in the House.

The obscurity of a backbencher's role is frustrating enough, the toxic atmosphere even more exasperating.

The media are not blameless in this. In the 24/7 news cycle, journalists are under constant pressure to get out the story, any story, preferably a drive-by shooting. First the 30-second clip was replaced by the 10-second sound bite.

Now the news agenda is increasingly driven by Twitter and other social media. Reporters aren't developing sources, let alone breaking stories, when they're talking to each other all day on Twitter. And 140-character postings provide little insight to politics and public policy.

Richardson has been around long enough to remember the two-minute clip, documentary length in today's terms, of which Peter Lougheed was the acknowledged master when Lee worked for him in the Alberta premier's office in the 1970s.

Richardson stayed on for nine years with Lougheed, becoming chief of staff in 1979, before leaving to become deputy chief of staff to Brian Mulroney in the opposition leader's office in 1983, playing the same role in the PMO after the 1984 Tory landslide.

Which is where our friendship of all the years since began when I worked there as Mulroney's principal speechwriter from 1985–88.

"He's our house commie," Lee once told a colleague in the PM's office in the Langevin Block. In fact, he protected me from the right wingers in the office. He had my back.

Among politicians of all stripes, no attribute is more highly valued than loyalty. When Mulroney was summoned to the star chamber hearings on Karlheinz Schreiber's accusations in 2007, and Conservative MPs were urged to stay away from the circus, Lee would have none of it. "My prime minister is coming into the building tomorrow," Richardson told the Conservative caucus. "I'm going to be there to meet him. Does anyone have a problem with that?"

No one did.

His two prime ministers, actually. He's been very supportive of Stephen Harper, who as he pointed out in the House, reunified the right and brought it back to power, and whose caucus management skills are comparable to Mulroney's in terms of leading a united caucus.

Wednesday in Calgary, Richardson will introduce Lougheed at a tribute dinner to his former premier where the keynote speaker will be his new premier, Redford, whose seat in the Alberta legislature overlaps with his Calgary seat in the House. When her election campaign nearly went south in April, he had her back, too, and she knew it.

As a moment in time, a passage, it's only perfect.

June 2012

RICHARD DICERNI

In a public service career spanning more than 40 years, Richard Dicerni has seen it all. He has served five of the past seven prime ministers, from a minister's staff under Pierre Trudeau to deputy minister of industry under Stephen Harper, a role he has played for the last six years.

He also spent more than a decade in Ontario, first as deputy minister of environment and energy under Bob Rae's NDP government, then as deputy of education, post-secondary education and intergovernmental affairs in the Mike Harris Conservative government and later as CEO of Ontario Power Generation, the provincial electrical utility.

In all of these roles, Dicerni has expressed great pride in the loyalty of the public service to the government of the day. As he put it in an appearance before the Industry, Science and Technology Parliamentary Committee last week: "There is one characteristic that is common to all deputy ministers: we are serially monogamous in our loyalty to the government of the day." It was his 27th and final appearance before the committee ahead of his retirement, Which, at 63, he has announced for the end of July. One of the truly outstanding public servants of his generation is leaving an exceptional legacy of service.

As the 31-year-old head of the Canadian Unity Information Office during the 1980 Quebec referendum, Dicerni ran a federal propaganda machine outside the auspices of the official No committee.

He was the invisible hand, the unsung hero of the federalist forces and their 60–40 victory. The leader of the No forces, Claude Ryan, had decreed his side would do no polling. Dicerni simply gave all the federal polls to the No campaign without Ryan's knowledge.

By the time of the second Quebec referendum in October 1995, Dicerni was working with new Ontario premier Harris. In 1995 the siren song of the sovereignty messenger, Lucien Bouchard, was "*le partenariat*," a partnership with the rest of Canada, starting with Ontario.

Dicerni brought me in to work with him on Harris's important speech to the Canadian Club of Toronto. He needed to make the point that, while the two provinces were already joined by geography and economics, Ontario had no interest in a partnership with a separate Quebec. And he needed to say so in clear, but courteous terms. Harris had perfect pitch that day: "Ontario's answer is a friendly, but firm, '*Non, merci!*'" The speech had an echo effect where it was needed most: Quebec.

In a referendum where the margin of victory was slim, 50.6 to 49.4 per cent, the contribution by Harris and his deputy minister was important.

"He worked very hard on that speech," Dicerni recalls today. "He had me over to his home and went over the speech line by line." But Harris also thought it was important to patch things up with Quebec, and so they flew to Quebec City for a meeting with Bouchard, by then premier. "They talked about their kids," Dicerni remembers, "and they had a lot in common, being from small towns." Harris noted that Bouchard had greeted Dicerni by his first name, as had Jean Chrétien in a meeting with the prime minister. Dicerni had worked for Bouchard when he was secretary of state and for Chrétien when he had oversight of the 1980 referendum.

When Dicerni first went to work on Parliament Hill as a 20-year old staffer in 1969, they were still using rotary phones. The first cell phones wouldn't be in use until the late 1980s, and smart phones would be an invention of the new century. Twenty years ago, the Internet was in its infancy, long before the explosion of web platforms such as Twitter.

All this technology and innovation stuff is what makes the Industry department important. The files are complex, and the stakes incredibily high. The wireless telecom space is just one example. If there's a ministry that's about the economy and the future, it's Industry. Canada's $12-billion share of the $60-billion 2009 North American auto bailout was a file managed by Dicerni and industry officials.

Without the bailout, he says: "The auto sector would have suffered the same catastrophic fate as the financial services sector in the U.S." Three years later, the loans have been paid back, and the industry is thriving.

Industry is actually three portfolios in one, with two junior ministries, Science and Technology and Tourism and Small Business, to go along with the senior ministry. In six years since his return to Ottawa, Dicerni has had four senior ministers and several more junior ones. He's much too discreet to rate them, but does not disagree that Jim Prentice was the best.

Prentice, now vice chair of CIBC, equally feels he worked with the best. "It was one of the finest partnerships I ever had," Prentice says. "He has had a remarkable career and quite simply in six years has built Industry into a strong department. He has an incredible record of service."

But Prentice remembers Dicerni most fondly for a personal intervention. He was in New Orleans with Harper for a trilateral summit of the three amigos – Canada, the U.S. and Mexico – when he learned his daughter had been rushed to hospital in Chicago. "I've got you booked on the next flight to Chicago," Dicerni told him. "The PM has many ministers, but your daughter has only one father."

June 2012

MARK CARNEY

It's difficult to imagine a central banker as a rock star, but that's what Mark Carney has become in his four and a half years as governor of the Bank of Canada.

At international conferences, from the G20 to Davos, Carney and Finance Minister Jim Flaherty were major players, not because of the offices they held but because of the story they had to tell, of steering Canada safely through the financial crisis of 2008–09.

In spite of stimulus spending to get through the Great Recession, Canada has by far the lowest deficit-and debt-to-GDP ratios of any G7 country. Inflation has fallen from just under two per cent when Carney took office, to just over one per cent today.

Canada has the best job-creation rate since 2008 of any G7 country with the exception of Germany. All the jobs lost in the recession have been replaced, and then some.

And then there's the Canadian banking system, ranked strongest in the world for the last five years by the World Economic Forum.

The Big Five Canadian banks all rank in the top 10 in North America in terms of assets and market cap. At the bottom of the recession in 2009, Flaherty put $350 billion of standby credit aside for the banks, and they never took a nickel of it. Nor did they ever miss a dividend payment.

That may be because they weren't carrying toxic assets on their books, derivatives, sub-prime mortgages and the like. Carney knows this complex world from his years as an investment banker at Goldman Sachs in London and New York.

As associate deputy minister of finance under the Martin government, he was a logical candidate to become deputy minister under the Conservatives. When that didn't happen, Flaherty pushed hard for his appointment to the Bank instead. Which proved to be providential, in view of the crash of October 2008, only six months after he was named governor.

Carney and his colleagues, notably Ben Bernanke at the Federal Reserve in the U.S., aggressively intervened to pump liquidity into their economies by lowering interest rates to near zero, and using every instrument of monetary policy at their disposal.

In the close circle of G7 and G20 finance ministers and central bankers, Carney's flair caught the attention of his colleagues, notably for his creativity and persuasiveness. A year ago, Carney was named head of the Financial Stability Board, the G20's oversight committee on banking and finance. This part-time role was another line in Carney's international résumé. He would have been a natural candidate to head one of the international financial institutions, except that since their founding, the World Bank has always been led by an American, while the International Monetary Fund has always been headed by a European, with neither the Americans nor the Europeans likely to relinquish their control of either.

Which meant that in terms of what he might do next at age 47, Carney would have to look elsewhere. About six months ago, he was rumoured to be shortlisted to succeed Mervyn King as governor of the Bank of England. Asked about this at the time, Carney said he looked forward to talking to the next head of the Bank of England.

Which turns out to be him. Announcing his appointment in the mother of all parliaments, Chancellor of the Exchequer George Osborne called Carney the outstanding central banker of his generation and said: "He is quite simply the best, most experienced and most qualified person in the world to do this job."

From London, as Carney and Flaherty both noted, he'll be able to keep a closer eye on the euro crisis, to say nothing of the challenges in British banking and markets, in an economy just coming out of a double-dip recession.

And while he's technically a foreigner, a first for the Bank of England, it's not as if he doesn't know the place.

He did his master's and doctorate in economics at Oxford, where he met his British wife, Diana, mother of their four daughters. He worked in the City, London's financial district, for seven years. The Brits are lucky to be getting him, and they know it.

Carney apparently represents a trend to reverse colonialism in high places in London. First, Moya Greene, head of Canada Post, was named head of the Royal Mail in 2010. And now Carney to the Bank of England.

A girl from Newfoundland, and a boy from Fort Smith in the Northwest Territories. It's a remarkable journey for both of them, and it says something about the quality of the Canadian public service that the British are stealing our best people.

November 2012

JEAN CHAREST

To those asking about Jean Charest's political legacy, the answer is quite simple: He saved the country.

And he did so on several different occasions, beginning with the 1995 Quebec referendum, a one-point game that could have well gone the other way without Charest's unrivalled performance.

As the leader then of a Progressive Conservative remnant of only two members of Parliament, he was at first relegated to the "B" circuit in what became a momentous October campaign. By the end, Charest waved his Canadian passport as a prop. But fundamentally, he restored pride and passion to the Canadian option when it was needed most. It was Charest, not Jean Chrétien or Daniel Johnson, who energized the crowds in the final week, when the federalist forces finally reversed a dangerous slide.

The ensuing result – 50.58 per cent for the No side, to 49.42 per cent for the Yes – was as close as it gets. If less than six-tenths of one per cent of the vote had gone the other way the country would have been lost. And it was Charest who gave the No side the rhetorical lift when it mattered most.

The 1995 referendum also paved the way to Charest's assuming the Quebec Liberal leadership, when Johnson stood down early in 1998.

The referendum changed Charest's career path, and it also damaged Chrétien's legacy in that he responded by creating the sponsorship program, leading to the scandal that taints the federal Liberal brand in Quebec to this day.

While he would have preferred to remain in Ottawa rebuilding the Tory party, Charest knew he had no choice but to come to Quebec.

Quebec elections are unique among provincial campaigns in that they are the only ones in which the future of the country is at stake.

And the 1998 election was no exception. Bouchard, by then premier and leader of the Parti Québécois, proposed his famous "winning conditions" as a prerequisite for another referendum. Charest stormed down the home stretch of the campaign, and though Bouchard won a majority of seats, Charest won a plurality of votes, 43.6 per cent to 42.9 per cent.

What that meant was no winning conditions, and Bouchard knew it. By early 2001, only halfway through his mandate, he abruptly resigned to spend more time with his family. Never again would he campaign for sovereignty.

In 2003 and again in 2008, Charest won majority governments, which automatically precluded the possibility of another referendum. Only in the 2007 election, when Mario Dumont emerged as the alternative to Charest and reduced the Liberals to minority status, was the future of Canada not in play.

And even in the 2012 election, amid all the turmoil in the streets and accusations of official corruption, Charest still saved the furniture, not only for the Liberals, but for Canada itself. He somehow delivered 50 seats, by winning 31.2 per cent of the vote, to 54 seats and 31.9 per cent for the PQ. With such a weak minority government, Pauline Marois could not call another referendum.

"A minority government would have been very difficult for us," he says now, especially with the Charbonneau Commission hearings ongoing, not to mention rioting students in the streets. Having lost his own seat of Sherbrooke, Charest got to walk away and start a new life, with a national and international law practice at McCarthy Tétrault.

Historians will have good material on his mistakes in office. But there are also impressive achievements. On inter-provincial relations, he founded the Council of the Federation. In the 2004 Health Accord with Ottawa, he won recognition of asymmetrical federalism in that Quebec alone would decide how to spend its share of $41 billion in new federal funding.

Within his own cabinet, he achieved gender parity, and appointed women to such major portfolios as finance and education. On his watch, Quebec created 400,000 new jobs, and today has an unemployment rate lower than that in Ontario and the United States. And he had a big idea, *Plan Nord*.

Through the worst of times, his caucus always remained loyal. This was something Charest learned in Ottawa from Brian Mulroney, who often said that "you can't lead without the caucus." Even in the turmoil of 2012, Charest's caucus was rock solid behind him.

But above all, it is his contribution to keeping the country whole that constitutes the major piece of his legacy. It doesn't get any bigger, or better, than that.

March 2013

MIKE LAZARIDIS

Two years ago, Research in Motion co-founder Mike Lazaridis was hosting a conference called Innovation Nation at the Perimeter Institute, which he created in Waterloo, Ontario.

The think tank where I was then working was one of the organizers of the event, and at the plenary session I happened to be sitting next to the man whose company invented the BlackBerry and, later, the smart phone.

I told him that when I first went on the road as a reporter in the 1970s, we filed with portable typewriters and telecopiers that moved hard copy at six minutes per page. The first generation fax machines weighed about 40 pounds, and typewriters were nearly as heavy.

"Today," I said, "I can hold this in the palm of my hand, write my column on it, and push the send button. That's how much things have changed in one working lifetime."

"That's a great story," he said, "you should write it."

It turned out to be a bad day at the office for Lazaridis. As we were speaking on September 15, 2011, RIM's stock was tanking, nearly $6 in one session, on an earnings miss.

But you would never have known it from his demeanour. There were no assistants whispering urgent messages in his ear. He stayed for the entire symposium, and then hosted a dinner for the presenters, including Finance Minister Jim Flaherty.

Lazaridis never gave the slightest indication that anything had gone wrong that day. It was an amazing display of grace under pressure.

In retrospect, RIM was already in trouble, bleeding market share to the iPhone, Android and other smart phones. Its PlayBook tablet was launched without email or text messaging. And its new line of smart phones, the BlackBerry 10, seemed to be years in development. And this in an industry where a week is an eternity.

Months later, Lazaridis and his co-chair, Jim Balsillie, stepped aside and made way for Thorsten Heins. The company re-branded itself as BlackBerry and rolled out the BlackBerry 10 in January of this year.

The reviews were good but sales apparently were not. Last month, BlackBerry put itself up for sale. Last Friday it announced it had nearly $1 billion of unsold phones and was laying off 4,500 people, one-third of its already slashed work force.

On Monday it announced a conditional sale to Fairfax Financial, a Canadian insurance group headed by investor Prem Watsa. Fairfax would take it private. The preliminary offer bid is really establishing a floor figure, of US$4.7 billion, or $9 a share.

The offer is 6 per cent of RIM's 2008 peak price of nearly $150 per share. It probably represents the hard value of the company's assets, with no debt, $2.6 billion in cash, a security network worth $1 billion, $1 billion in patents and its real estate. At this point, Fairfax has no partners from the technology space, and no other investors signed up. The Canada Pension Plan Investment Board might take a look at it, as might the Ontario Teachers' Pension Plan. Then again, they might not. Lazaridis himself is reported to be talking to a private equity group in New York, and might join the bid or make one of his own.

What's clear is that the Fairfax offer is the only one on the table, unless and until a better one comes along. The offer was apparently cobbled together over the weekend, said one Fairfax senior executive, to "get in quickly," and keep BlackBerry "whole and stabilizing it."

There is no shortage of expert opinion on the reasons for BlackBerry's fall from grace – from dominating the smart phone space to a global market share of only 3 per cent. At some point, BlackBerry stopped making what teenagers wanted on their cellphones. And it never had the kind of retail presence Apple did at its stores, where people lined up to get in.

The most important question is about BlackBerry's future. The *Wall Street Journal* reported Tuesday that "the company said Friday it would stop selling its phones after weak demand, and few analysts ascribed any value to BlackBerry's namesake smartphone business."

Watsa said in an interview, "we think over time," BlackBerry "can be successful again. We think in a private setting, this company can do well, without all the noise from the marketplace."

But if BlackBerry is planning to leave the smartphone segment, that becomes something of a self-fulfilling prophecy.

There is still a hard core of BlackBerry loyalists, who love their phones for features like the key board. A real key board, not a virtual one. One you can punch.

As for Lazaridis, people shouldn't forget how much he's changed the world, the way we communicate and the way we work.

September 2013

JOHN BAIRD

The death of Jim Flaherty was "a turning point" for John Baird, he told a friend after his statement to the House on his resignation as Foreign Affairs minister.

Flaherty and Baird had been friends and colleagues for many years – nearly two decades at Queen's Park and Ottawa. "Jim is the first close friend I've lost in politics," Baird said at the time of Flaherty's death.

And after a lifetime in politics, Flaherty's death got him thinking, at age 45, about a life after politics.

"I did not," he said, "want to leave Parliament in a coffin."

Instead, he leaves for new opportunities, as yet unspecified, in the private sector. Lots of international companies would be interested in talking to a former foreign minister of a G7 and G20 country with a network on five continents. Along the way, he's also been at Treasury Board, Environment and Transport, not to mention a stint as government House leader.

There were many things Baird and Flaherty had in common. Both came up through Queen's Park, a very tough provincial league where players need to keep their heads up in the corners. But when they graduated to Parliament, they were ready to play in the majors, and both turned out to be happy warriors in the House.

Both were senior Ontario ministers, Flaherty for the Greater Toronto Area and Baird for the National Capital Region. Both – exceptionally in a government run by control freaks – were allowed to shape their own messages, and both were strong messengers.

They were also known for having the two best office staffs on Parliament Hill, Flaherty at Finance and Baird wherever he went. They also encouraged their staffers to regard their time on the Hill as a formative experience and move on to the private sector – as nearly all of them have, still united, almost as family, by their service to their former ministers.

"Behind any successful minister are great staff," Baird told the House, "and that is truly the case for me."

Every now and then, Baird would turn up after work at the bar at Hy's, take over a corner booth and buy drinks for his staff. They were definitely not the Harper PMO, the team that fun forgot.

But in all his portfolios, Baird not only did Stephen Harper's bidding – he was often his go-to guy on important files.

The Harper government's first piece of legislation, even before the 2006 budget, was the Federal Accountability Act. It was the first of Harper's Five Priorities and it was Baird's baby at Treasury Board, for better or worse. The FAA imposed campaign contribution limits of $1,100 per person, down from $5,000 under the Liberals. "You're the guy who killed the MPs' golf tournaments," Baird was once told. "Yeah," he replied, "I hate golf."

The FAA also imposed strict post-employment guidelines on cabinet ministers and staff, forbidding them to lobby government for five years after leaving it. The upshot was that it was very difficult to recruit good people to work in ministers' offices, for all the career constraints on leaving them. Everyone in Ottawa knows the five-year post-employment ban was a mistake.

As minister of Transport and Infrastructure during the economic crisis of 2008–09, Baird moved $12 billion of infrastructure spending out the door in the 2009 budget. All of it was shovel-ready, and none of it was a bridge to nowhere.

At Foreign Affairs since 2011, Baird has always understood that a foreign minister has only one client – the prime minister. Out with the "honest broker," in with what Baird termed a "principled foreign policy" – including unequivocal support for Israel and condemnation of Russia and Vladimir

Putin for annexing Crimea and invading Ukraine. Or, as he put it Tuesday: "Side by side with the only liberal democracy in the Middle East, strong relationships in the Arab world, firm in our objection to militaristic expansionism in Eastern Europe ..."

Baird also took on causes, such as gay rights in Russia and the forced marriages of girls and young women. As NDP Foreign Affairs critic Paul Dewar noted in the House: "He stood on the world stage and spoke out against discrimination against people, wherever in the world, who are being discriminated against because of their sexual orientation. As minister he led like no other minister on the world stage when it came to the persecution of gays, lesbians and transsexuals."

Coming from the opposition bench, it doesn't get any better than that. Like Dewar, Liberal foreign affairs critic Marc Garneau thanked Baird for inviting them to Iraq last September and said that "to have allowed us to join him demonstrated what is often lacking in this place, and that is the dropping of the gloves in the national interest and putting away partisanship."

Not that Baird wasn't partisan – he just learned how to rise above it. He was both combative and collegial. Which is why a Tuesday morning sitting of the House, when even getting a quorum can be a challenge, was nearly as crowded as question period in the afternoon.

As with Flaherty's resignation, six weeks before his death, Baird's departure leaves a gaping hole for Harper in the run-up to an election.

Baird is the 27th Conservative member who won't be running again, an attrition rate of 16 per cent. Harper's time in office is beginning to show.

Until Tuesday, Baird had been there for all of it, nine years less three days.

He may have made an escape.

February 2015

PETER MACKAY

Peter MacKay says he has "neither sought nor secured other employment." He needn't worry – once he leaves office after the election in October, the Bay Street law firms will come calling.

- He's been foreign minister of a G7 and G20 country. *Check.*
- He's been defence minister of a NATO country. *Check.*
- He's currently justice minister, which entitles him to practise law in any province in the country. *Check.*

There isn't a national or international law firm in Canada that wouldn't want to talk to him. Some major corporations would also offer him board directorships.

MacKay and his wife, Nazanin Afshin-Jam can settle down in Rosedale or Forest Hill with their young family. Their son Kian recently turned two. A baby girl is expected in the fall.

"I love what I do," MacKay said on Friday, "but, simply put, I love my family more." He's often said that he felt the absence of his father, Elmer, a long-time Conservative MP and cabinet minister, when he was growing up in Nova Scotia.

"For entirely personal reasons," he continued, "the time has come for me to step back from public life and concentrate on my young and growing family."

There is no doubt that marriage and fatherhood have changed MacKay. Attending a Parliament Hill event on Autism Awareness Day in early April, his eyes lit up when talking about his son's second birthday. As for his brilliant and beautiful wife, the Iranian Canadian human rights activist, MacKay knows he won the lottery. "You married up," I once told him. "I know," he replied. "Believe me, I know."

And now, at 49, he has just made the great escape, staged with elegance and class, to his own voters.

Unlike John Baird's departure in February, Stephen Harper didn't hear about it on the evening news. He went out of his way to be in Stellarton in MacKay's riding of Central Nova for a joint news conference.

"Peter MacKay is an outstanding public servant, a great person and an historic figure," Harper said. "He is a team guy in every sense of the word."

Historic figure? Well, as Harper noted, MacKay was co-architect of the merger on the right that "changed the course of Canadian politics."

Harper was altogether generous and gracious, a side of him that isn't seen often enough. He was also right. Without MacKay, as leader of the Progressive Conservative party, agreeing to the merger with Harper's Canadian Alliance in October 2003, the last decade in Canadian politics would have been very different. But together they seized the moment, and changed the course of history.

"I've said many times that it takes two to tango," says former Conservative Prime Minister Brian Mulroney. "You don't merge with yourself. Peter created the conditions for a merger of equals. What Peter did to bring this about was huge."

His tenure at Foreign Affairs, from 2006–07, was not very memorable, though it was a good learning experience for him. Some of the people MacKay met along the way, such as U.S. Secretary of State Condoleezza Rice, became good friends.

His six years at Defence were marked by the Afghan war and the loss of Canadian lives, as well as the procurement cost overruns of the F-35 fighter jet. But MacKay was on the front line of the department, well-liked by both the brass hats and the troops. He also founded the Halifax International Security Forum, an annual conference that's become a magnet for NATO political leaders and international media.

His two years at Justice have proven that he's indeed a team player, especially in difficult times. The Harper government's conservative agenda, from legal appointments to Senate reform to law-and-order, has been battered by one defeat after another in the Supreme Court. The government's national security legislation, Bill C-51, has been widely denounced for invading privacy rights and diminishing civil liberties, and may not survive constitutional tests in the courts. Through it all, MacKay has loyally carried on.

There's no doubt that the announcement of his departure comes at an inconvenient time for Harper – just five months before the election. MacKay is the fourth minister to stand down, after Baird, Shelley Glover and Christian Paradis. In all, 30 Conservative caucus members won't be running again. That's a very high attrition rate.

It also plays to the narrative that this government has been around for nearly a decade and that, in the normal course of events, its time would be up. MacKay is obviously a serious loss for Harper from the Progressive Conservative side of the house. While Red Tories are not an endangered species, they don't exactly recognize themselves in this government.

And then MacKay represents a huge loss for the Conservatives in Atlantic Canada, where he's been senior minister for the region. Nothing got done in the Atlantic, from highways to fishing ports, without his sign-off.

The Conservatives are already in deep trouble in Atlantic Canada. In this week's EKOS-*iPolitics* poll, the Liberals lead the NDP in the region by 41–24 per cent, with the Conservatives trailing badly at 21 per cent. A 20-point deficit translates to a Liberal romp and a Conservative rout in the race for the region's 32 seats. With MacKay's departure, even his own seat of Central Nova may be in play.

There is no corner or community of the riding he doesn't know, having travelled it constantly since his father's time. When Elmer MacKay stepped aside to give Brian Mulroney a seat, Peter was the new PC leader's driver during the 1983 by-election campaign. In time, Mulroney would become MacKay's political mentor, though MacKay didn't ask the former PM's advice on this move.

On a personal note, on a drive from Cape Breton to Halifax Airport in the summer of 2009, I stopped at MacKay's place in New Glasgow for lunch.

He talked about the Festival of the Tartans, a big summer event in New Glasgow, which had recently been held. I said I'd probably missed my chance to buy a tartan skirt for my newly-born daughter, Zara.

A few days later, a package arrived from MacKay's office. It was a skirt for a little girl, in the Clanranald MacDonald tartan. That's Peter MacKay.

May 2015

ED BROADBENT

At 80, Ed Broadbent has found a second calling as chair of the progressive policy think tank that bears his name. Like the Manning Centre on the right, the Broadbent Institute does important work on the left that the Conservative and New Democratic parties don't, and can't, do. Canada 2020 has equally served as an important convener of policy conferences that have informed Liberal platforms.

Parties and their leaders have only one job – winning. Think tanks like Broadbent, Manning and 2020 discuss ideas and shape agendas that find their way into party platforms and messages.

For 2020, the payoff for their events is that they can now deliver cabinet ministers, as at their Canadian Open Forum Dialogue on the public service at the Shaw Centre. As CTV's Glen McGregor has reported, it also turns out 2020 can now deliver government funding for its events. Across town, the Broadbent Institute convened its third annual Progress Summit (without government funding).

You'd never know the NDP had been pummeled in last October's election, judging by the 900 fun-seeking delegates who jammed the Delta hotel's lobby and convention floor for an opening night cocktail featuring a very loud mariachi band.

The conference itself was rich in content, and not just Canadian navel gazing. Gloria Steinem delivered an opening keynote that demonstrated why, more than four decades after founding *Ms* magazine, she remains an American thought leader. From the European left there were interesting keynotes from *Guardian* columnist Owen Jones and former French socialist justice minister Christiane Taubira, who resigned in January over the Hollande government's policy to strip terrorists of their citizenship. (Sound familiar?) A Friday night beer bash on the Democratic presidential race featured Hillary Clinton strategist Mitch Stewart, Bernie Sanders supporter Rafael Navar and CNN political commentator Sally Kohn, who rocked the house. For Canadian content, a plenary on climate change saw Environment Minister Catherine McKenna share the stage with her Alberta colleague Shannon Phillips and Vancouver city councillor Andrea Reimer. A Saturday afternoon debate on democratic reform saw columnist Andrew Coyne and former clerk of the Privy Council Alex Himelfarb hold for proportional representation, while Conservative MP Michelle Rempel and conservative pundit Tasha Kheiriddin were against it.

Broadbent himself opened the conference, and he was in high form.

"I want you to know that I've decided to seek the leadership of the NDP leadership at next week's convention," he began, to sustained applause. "April Fool!"

Which was a good-humoured way of speaking to the elephant in the room, the mandatory leadership review for Tom Mulcair at the Edmonton policy convention. Mulcair, sitting in the first row, had pulled his own April Fool's stunt, with a tweet of his face lathered up with shaving cream as he held a barber's razor to his cheek. #losethebeard would have been a very popular hash tag last fall.

As leader of the NDP for 14 years and four elections from 1975–89, Broadbent couldn't address the leadership review, but nor could he avoid saying something about a campaign in which the NDP started in the first place in the polls, only to finish a distant third on election day.

"There can be no doubt," he allowed, "that for the NDP it was disappointing."

That's an understatement, even though the NDP's 44 seats were its second-best performance ever, exceeded only by Jack Layton's Orange Wave and the 103 seats they won in 2011, driven by *le bon Jack*'s 59 seats in Quebec. From 37 per cent in an Angus Reid Institute poll three weeks into the campaign in the last week in August, the NDP plummeted to 19.7 per cent on October 19.

They're still in free fall. An EKOS poll for *iPolitics* this past week had the NDP at 11.7 per cent, the Conservatives at 32 per cent (where they were on election day), and the Liberals still in honeymoon territory at 42 per cent.

The NDP haven't been in such dire straits since 1993, when Audrey McLaughlin led them to 7 per cent of the vote and nine seats.

It's no mystery what happened to the NDP in the campaign – they got outflanked by the Liberals on the left, with Justin Trudeau promising a stimulative deficit while Mulair ran on budgetary balance. It's still going on, as reflected inadvertently in Broadbent's remarks. He noted that the Liberals had rescinded anti-union legislation and delivered $8.4 billion for Indigenous peoples in the Liberal budget.

This is the eternal quandary for the NDP. Is it enough for them to be a party of conscience prodding the Liberals to the left, or do they play to win, as they often do in the provinces?

This, as Broadbent put it, is a debate between "bold ideas" and a party that can deliver the vote. His role is now on the ideas side of the conversation, which isn't to say he doesn't know the other side of it.

He should be thanked for his continuous service to our country.

April 2016

∞

JASON KENNEY

Jason Kenney's departure from the federal scene leaves two lingering questions about the Conservative leadership race. First – would he have it won it? And second – did he regard it as a prize worth winning, given the prospect of a second Liberal majority term starting in 2019?

It's not at all clear that Kenney would have won the Tory leadership. For one thing, he didn't appear to have a whole lot of support in the Conservative caucus. You can't lead without caucus – there's no point in even trying.

In private conversations with Conservative MPs, two theories prevail. One is that, following Stephen Harper, it's simply not the time for another middle-aged white guy from Calgary. It's time for someone from Eastern Canada.

The other is that the party needs to move closer to the progressive centre of the political spectrum if it's to regain traction in urban areas such as the 905/416 belt of the Greater Toronto Area, where the Conservatives won only five out of 54 seats last October.

That's what snitch lines and niqabs got the Tories – just two of the low points in a disgraceful and stupid campaign based on identity politics, with the Ford brothers thrown in for good measure. For all of Kenney's efforts in reaching out to multicultural communities over the previous decade, those urban voters (along with Red Tories) deserted the blue banner in droves. In such a race, Kenney might well have been kingmaker – but not king.

And it seems highly unlikely at this point that the Conservatives will be returned to office after only one Liberal term in government. After a decade of Conservative rule, it was time for a change. It's also clear that Canadians like what they've seen of Justin Trudeau.

Lately, he's used the trappings of office entirely to his own political benefit. After hosting the North American Leaders' Summit and Barack Obama at the House of Commons at the end of June, Trudeau presided over Canada

Day on the Hill. He then flew off to Eastern Europe for a NATO summit in Warsaw – where he confirmed Canadian troops would be posted to Latvia – had a moving visit to Auschwitz, then moved on to Ukraine, where he laid wreaths and signed a bilateral free trade agreement.

At no point did he look as if he didn't belong. At all times, he appeared quite at ease in the role of prime minister. And on Friday, he was at the Stampede in Calgary,

Trudeau's approval rating won't be going south anytime soon. For the next year and a half, he's going to be presiding over Canada 150 celebrations – a time for the country to feel very good about itself (unless the economy tanks, and that's not in any of the forecasts).

The latest Forum Research poll puts the Liberals at 52 per cent, the Conservatives at 28 per cent and the NDP at only 11 per cent. While the Conservatives and NDP are between leaders, all of those numbers should concern the Tories. The Liberals are 13 points *above* their vote on election day, the Conservatives four points below theirs, and the NDP nine points lower than their share of the vote last October.

In fact, the NDP's slide should be particularly worrying to the Conservatives. They need the NDP to be at least at 20 per cent – splitting progressive left-leaning votes with the Liberals – to have any hope of being competitive, much less winning an election.

Even if he'd fought for and won the Conservative leadership, Kenney would have been looking at the likelihood of at least another term in opposition. Not just four more years – closer to seven. Considering the alternative, it's no surprise he fancied a shot at winning the Progressive Conservative leadership in Alberta, uniting the right in a merger with Wildrose, and becoming premier in 2019.

Of course, *that's* not a done deal either. Wildrose is the official opposition in Edmonton and its leader, Brian Jean, is no pushover. He has borne the death of his son, and then the loss of his house to the Fort McMurray wildfire, with great courage and grace. At Harper's annual Stampede barbecue last week, Jean received an ovation as loud as Kenney's – the man Harper and interim Conservative Leader Rona Ambrose were there to endorse for the PC leadership.

Kenney also got it wrong two days earlier at his leadership announcement when he said the election of Rachel Notley and the NDP last year was "an accident."

It was no accident; it happened because Albertans decided to throw the PC bums out after 43 years in power. That process started, more or less, when Wildrose Leader Danielle Smith and eight members of her caucus crossed the floor to join the Conservative government of Jim Prentice. Voters were unimpressed; they instinctively understood that it's the *opposition's* role to overthrow the government, not the other way round.

Then Prentice told Albertans to "look in the mirror" on unsustainable program spending costs in his first budget, and called an early election on it rather than summering at the Stampede. Finally, in a defining election debate soundbite, Prentice sailed this ill-considered quip at Notley: "I know math is hard." So, *not* an accident.

It's also unclear how Kenney, as a candidate from the right, can unite the more centrist urban elements of the Alberta PCs. This was once the party of Peter Lougheed, the guy who built modern Alberta. Kenney is more of an heir to Ralph Klein.

But Kenney does begin the race for a delegated convention with one clear advantage: he is a great organizer and will have a strong ground game in all 87 provincial ridings. He also begins with very high name recognition in his home province.

Kenney has enjoyed a lot of "unearned" earned media in the last few weeks. Part of that is due to summer being a slow season for political news. Part of it is due to skill. But from here on out, he may have to earn it.

July 2016

ELIZABETH MAY

Reflecting on her future over the last two weeks, the one thing that never occurred to Green Leader Elizabeth May was to cross the floor and join the Liberals.

That wouldn't have been her, she said at a news conference. "I'm Green." And to be clear, she had no conversations with the Liberals.

Standing in front of the Green logo at the National Press Theatre, it was clear she wasn't going anywhere. "It's not a good idea for me to join another party," she said. "The reasons for staying are far more compelling."

Among other reasons why joining the Liberals was a complete non-starter for her was a very compelling one – it would have cost May her seat and her vote on the special committee of the House on electoral reform.

When the 12-member committee was established in the spring, May was named to it as the member from Saanich-Gulf Islands, not as leader of the Green party.

For the rest, the Liberals have five members, including the non-voting chair, the Conservatives three members, the NDP two MPs and the Bloc one. (In a normal standing committee the Grits would have had six members, the

Conservatives three, and the New Democrats one seat, with the Bloc and May sitting as participants without votes.) Had she joined the Liberals, she would no longer have sat as the member from her riding, and would have gone to the back of the Liberal line.

Furthermore, she's a proponent of some form of proportional representation as the means of leveraging the Green vote into more than the one seat she currently occupies in the House (the very last seat in the very last row of opposition MPs). The Liberals have a previously stated preference by Justin Trudeau for a preferential or ranked voting system, though they haven't been pushing that button in committee.

This is not where May is coming from and not where she is going on the committee, which is hearing more expert testimony in Ottawa before heading across the country in the next two months on a 17-city road show, before submitting its report by early December. She called the electoral reform committee "a wonderful, exciting and challenging opportunity to change the way we vote."

For May the committee has become a full-time job, and the only role she's interested in filling in the fall session. As she said at her newser: "What's our goal for this year? Electoral reform, electoral reform, electoral reform."

As for the process debate within the party, between consensus and majoritarian voting at Green conventions, May made it clear that "this is now off my plate," adding that "I'm not participating in that debate. I'm out of it."

Majority voting and Roberts Rules of Order enabled proponents of BDS – boycott, divestment, sanctions – to pass a motion against Israel for the 2014 Gaza conflict, which left the Greens bitterly divided at their convention early this month, and led to May's period of reflection about her future.

Travelling to and from a family vacation in Cape Breton last week, May found herself being stopped by strangers telling her she had to stay on as Green leader. Alluding to this Monday, she looked to be having a Sally Field moment on Oscar night: "You like me, right now, you like me."

"Yes," May said, "it was my Tom Sawyer moment, attending my own funeral."

It's no mystery – while the Greens currently poll only around 5 per cent in voting intention, May's approval rating in a recent EKOS poll is 54 per cent, compared to 52 per cent for Conservative leader Rona Ambrose and 45 per cent for Tom Mulcair. Only Trudeau scores higher approval numbers than May, at a stratospheric 65 per cent. May's brand is strong.

What the party does about process, and how it reviews the BDS vote, may be considered at a special meeting, which will not be convened until after the electoral reform committee releases its report in early December. The Green federal council, which has asked May to remain as leader, will be in charge of the process and review of the BDS resolution and several other contentious motions adopted at the convention.

The federal council will be acting on recommendations of the Green shadow cabinet on BDS and other resolutions.

"I'm against it," May says flatly of the BDS motion, but she struck a somewhat conciliatory note with its advocates Monday, saying that "people who are part of the BDS movement are people of good will."

May could be seeking a tenable middle ground with BDS advocates led by Dimitri Lascaris, who happens to be justice critic in the Green shadow cabinet.

But here is something to consider – in the Westminster tradition, just as ministers are chosen by the prime minister, so are shadow critics named by the opposition leaders.

Even in the Green party, it is no different.

"That is, in fact, the party policy," May said during our conversation. "I'm very much aware that that is my call."

She's got the hammer.

August 2016

RALPH GOODALE

Every government has a steady hand on the wheel, and in the present Liberal government, it's Ralph Goodale, the minister of Public Safety.

In a speech to the Canadian Association of Chiefs of Police the other day, Goodale took them through the hot files on his desk since the Liberals took office. First, re-settling 25,000 Syrian refugees in Canada. Then, the Black Friday terror attack in Paris last November and the response of western governments to terrorists targeting civilians as they did again in Nice on Bastille Day.

Last May, there was the northern Alberta wildfire, and the evacuation of 90,000 people from Fort McMurray in the biggest Canadian natural disaster of modern times.

And just last week there was the coordinated police takedown of Aaron Driver, a 24-year old ISIS sympathizer with an improvised explosive on his person. The device went off in a cab near London, Ontario, where Driver was evidently on his way to a mall, having made a video promising to shed Canadian blood for the terrorist ISIS cause.

To every one of these situations, Goodale has brought his characteristic demeanour, which is to keep calm and carry on.

In the takeout of Driver by the RCMP, the OPP and local police, the cops were acting on information posted to social media by the ISIS acolyte, and picked up by the FBI. Asked about cooperation between the RCMP and FBI, Goodale replied that it happens all the time – the Americans share information with us, and we share it with them. Next question.

Driver had frequently broken a "peace bond" with a judge, in which he promised to avoid weapons and proselytizing for ISIS on social media, and Goodale mused that the government may look at a peace bond law requiring "an individual to engage with counter radicalization professionals."

In any event, Goodale said, the Driver incident demonstrated the need to "up our game" in deprogramming potential homegrown terrorists and that Ottawa will hire a deradicalization adviser with an annual budget of $10 million and a mandate to work with cities on their own deradicalizing efforts. As for cyber security, Goodale stated the obvious need to balance security requirements with the imperative of protecting personal privacy. Asked by CBC's *Power and Politics* whether police could compel divulgence of telephone encryption codes, Goodale pointed to Apple refusing to do so with the FBI, and said it was a debate in progress.

Amending the previous Conservative government's anti-terror legislation, Bill C-51, is another delicate dossier on Goodale's desk. The Liberals promised in the election campaign to "repeal the problematic elements of Bill C-51," and Goodale has spoken of "a series of very specific amendments to what we believe is wrong in C-51" he said, "but we want to hear from Canadians about what else they think needs to be added to the list." In other words, consultations before any bill in the House, which may preclude amendments to C-51 during the fall sitting.

At 66, Goodale doesn't get excited about stuff like that. It's not that he's inscrutable so much as imperturbable. One former senior staffer describes Goodale as "prudent – you can't be anything but prudent when you're a Liberal from Saskatchewan." He is the lone Liberal MP from Saskatchewan, and has been for the last three elections. He has served 28 years in Parliament, from 1974–79, and again since 1993 as a member from Regina.

This means Goodale is always up to date on the Saskatchewan Roughriders. "How are the Riders going to be this year?" he was asked at an Ottawa reception in June. "This is going to be a re-building year," he put it mildly and, indeed, the Roughriders are firmly entrenched in last place in the CFL West. He also would have been following Saskatchewan's Graham DeLaet in the Olympic men's golf tournament, where he finished out of medal contention but with a very good score of four under par. Nothing about his home province is off Goodale's radar.

There are two elements to Goodale's style. First, he's a problem solver, and then he's a team player.

This was evident in the government's management of the refugee file. Some 25,000 Syrian applicants were processed and cleared at refugee camps in Turkey, Jordan and Lebanon, then flown to Canada and re-settled in their new country in the dead of winter. Since they were all families, there wasn't a terror suspect among them. No fuss, no bother. Take that, Donald Trump. Several cabinet ministers and many officials, including Immigration Minister John McCallum, deserve credit for the successful resettlement effort, but Goodale was a leading member of the team, although he would be the first to say that Canadians themselves deserve the credit for opening their communities and homes to the Syrians.

During the terrible wildfires that swept northern Alberta in May, Goodale was in charge of the government's response. At one point, he assured Fort Mac residents: "We're standing with you and we have your back." Encountered walking from Parliament Hill to the Château Laurier one day in the midst of the wildfire crisis, Goodale was congratulated for his management of the file. He replied that he was just doing his job. He was certainly doing what he does – problem solving.

And it wasn't a job he wanted or expected when the Liberals took office. It's no secret that Goodale would have liked to be Finance minister again, as he was when the Martin government produced two surplus budgets in 2004 and 2005. When you consider the other portfolios Goodale has held, from Agriculture to Public Works to Natural Resources, he's uniquely experienced in this government. But he's also crossed the desert with the Liberals, as House leader during their wilderness years from 2006–15.

Every government has one cabinet minister who enjoys the complete confidence of the prime minister. In Pierre Trudeau's time, his go-to guy was Marc Lalonde. In Brian Mulroney's government, Don Mazankowski was chief operating officer. In Jean Chrétien's decade in office, Paul Martin was indispensable, until he wasn't. During the Harper years, Jim Flaherty was a powerhouse at Finance but also a political actor with superb instincts. Nothing ever flustered Flaherty, who was interested in working through issues and getting things done.

Goodale is rather like that. And on any list of strong ministers in Justin Trudeau's government, his name would be right at the top.

Just don't ask him how the Roughriders are doing this season.

August 2016

BRIAN MULRONEY

Brian Mulroney becomes the first Canadian prime minister to receive France's highest civilian honour Tuesday evening when he is inducted as a Commander of the Legion of Honour.

The ceremony, at the French Embassy residence on Sussex Drive, is largely in recognition of Mulroney's role as co-founder of la Francophonie 30 years ago along with French president François Mitterrand.

Previous attempts to create a global organization of French-speaking nations had foundered over Quebec's place at the table. In the fall of 1985, Mulroney negotiated an agreement with then-premier Pierre Marc Johnson that enabled Quebec to speak on its own behalf from within the Canadian delegation on matters of provincial jurisdiction. Officially bilingual New Brunswick was accorded the same status. The first summit of la Francophonie was then held at Versailles in 1986.

"There were 31 members at the first meeting," Mulroney recalled at his Montreal law office in Place Ville Marie. "Today it has expanded to 57 member states and governments, and the secretary-general, Michaëlle Jean, is a Canadian."

Among its achievements in the Mitterrand-Mulroney start-up period was the creation of TV5, the global French-language television network, and the forgiveness of billions of dollars of debt owed by francophone countries in sub-Saharan Africa.

"It's not very well known," Mulroney said, "that Canada is the second most powerful francophone country in the world, just as in the Commonwealth it's the second most important country after the UK in the English-speaking world."

When Mitterrand and Mulroney first proposed African debt forgiveness, they were the only proponents around the G7 summit table. "When we wrote it off," Mulroney said "we were the first industrialized country to do so. All the other G7 countries were against it."

At the time, he reasoned, since the sub-Saharan francophone states weren't going to pay the money back anyway, writing it off was inevitable as well as the right thing to do.

"I tried," Mulroney said, "to direct Canada's affairs in a way that helped the country do the right thing in foreign affairs."

He leveraged his relationships with Mitterrand and other G7 actors to give Canada a wider role on the world stage. Today, his political legacy is defined to a surprising degree by his positions on foreign policy.

As it happens, France is the fifth country to confer such an honour on this former foreign leader. The others were Haiti (the Order of National Honour and Merit in 1994), Ukraine (the Order of King Yaroslav the Wise in 2007), Japan (the Order of the Rising Sun in 2011) and South Africa (Supreme Companion of the Order of Oliver Tambo in 2015).

In Haiti, Mulroney and then-U.S. president Bill Clinton were honoured for their role in the 1994 restoration of the democratically elected government of Jean-Bertrand Aristide, who had been ousted in a 1991 coup.

In Ukraine, Mulroney was honoured as the leader of the first country to recognize Ukraine's independence from the Soviet Union in 1991, over the objections of the first George Bush and Soviet leader Mikhail Gorbachev. Bush was worried it would undermine Gorbachev's leadership at home. The failed coup against Gorbachev on August 24, 1991, occurred on the same day the Ukrainian parliament declared independence. Canada announced its recognition on December 2, three weeks before Gorbachev's resignation on Christmas Day, with the Soviet Union itself dissolved the following day.

Mulroney recalled: "I told Gorbachev, 'this is something Canada has to do. We have one of the largest Ukrainian diasporas in the world. The Ukrainians have been waiting for independence since the end of the Second World War.'" In Canada, where he had named Ukrainian Canadians Ray Hnatyshyn as governor general and John Sopinka to the Supreme Court, no one in the Ukrainian community of 1.2 million has forgotten Canada's trailblazing recognition of Ukraine's independence.

In Japan, they honoured Mulroney for advocating the Japanese receive a permanent seat on the UN Security Council as well as for his role in the redress for Japanese Canadians who had lost everything and been wrongly interned in prison camps during the Second World War. Survivors filled the galleries in September 1988 when he formally apologized in the House for their ordeal, and there was hardly a dry eye in the chamber.

Mulroney said Margaret Thatcher called him to complain about his proposal to expand the P5 at the UN, and that he told her: "Margaret, what the founders did at San Francisco was right for the times. This would be right for these times. You wouldn't lose your veto. Japan has earned it." A major financial supporter of the UN, Japan was then the world's second largest economy and Canada's second largest trading partner. Mulroney was also very close in the G7 to Yasuhiro Nakasone, perhaps the most influential Japanese prime minister of the day.

In South Africa, the Tambo award is given uniquely to foreigners, and in Mulroney's case it was obviously for his fight against what he called "the scourge of apartheid" and the imprisonment of Nelson Mandela. From his first speech to the UN General Assembly in 1985, Mulroney notably parted company with Ronald Reagan and Thatcher, otherwise his conservative soulmates. As he told Thatcher at the 1987 Commonwealth Summit in Vancouver: "Margaret, you're on the wrong side of history." Mitterrand was also with Mulroney on the right side of that history, as was German Chancellor Helmut Kohl.

The awarding of the Legion of Honour comes at the end of a season of honours for Mulroney and his wife, Mila. In late October, they attended the announcement of the creation of the Brian Mulroney Institute of Government at his alma mater, St. Francis Xavier University in Nova Scotia. He's raised $60 million for a new building and scholars' program, while the Mulroneys have donated $1 million themselves as well all the administration costs.

Last week, Mila Mulroney was honoured at a dinner in Montreal for her three decades of volunteer service in the fight against cystic fibrosis, for which she has raised millions of dollars. She used to say about volunteerism, "pick one cause and stick with it." At the $1,000 per couple black tie dinner for 600 people, the CF hosts announced an important benchmark of progress. Thirty years ago, CF victims lived to an average age of only 13. Today, they live an average of 53 years, thanks to breakthroughs from funded research in Canada and the U.S.

"That number just blew everyone away," Mulroney said. Their four children and spouses were all in the room, and their son Ben was the emcee.

It is obviously a happy time for the Mulroneys.

"We're at the top of the mountain," said Mulroney, now 77. "But I mean that in a nice way. There's a good feeling about life, my family, the people around me and so on. I just feel great."

The French are giving him one more reason to feel even better.

December 2016

RONA AMBROSE

As Rona Ambrose takes her leave, the question gets asked: What she has accomplished during her short time as opposition leader and interim leader of the Conservative party?

Well, consider what she inherited in November 2015 – a party that was defeated, divided, dispirited and discredited among mainstream Canadians. A party whose brand had become toxic with multicultural Canadians (whose support is critical to winning in the cities) because of its proposed ban on niqabs at citizenship ceremonies and its pitch for a barbaric practices 'snitch line'.

In the House, she made the Conservatives credible and competitive again in question period – no small feat given the poisoned well she inherited, not to mention the internal divisions inherent in a ludicrously overcrowded leadership race. In the country, she had "sunny ways" of her own – of civility and decency.

"She changed the perception of the party for the better," says former Conservative prime minister Brian Mulroney. "She understood her role well. She changed the water. A significant achievement."

Mulroney was one of the former leaders Ambrose consulted on assuming the interim leadership, and he advised her to avoid allowing the caucus to fall into "recriminations."

Her own instinct, she said in her final speech as leader Tuesday morning, was simple: "No blaming, no grudges. Learn from it. Focus on the positive and get busy.

"Canadians asked us to change over time, and we changed over time."

Such was the positive perception of her leadership that many Conservatives came around to the view that the leader they needed was the one they already had – which led to a 'draft Rona' movement to change the rules of the game so that the interim leader could step down and enter the race. Ambrose was having none of it; in the process she maintained her reputation for being as good as her word. At the Conservative convention in Vancouver last May, her spouse J.P. Veitch appeared wearing a T-shirt that said: "She's not running."

And so she leaves at a time of her choosing, *la tête haute*.

And as far as the timing of her departure goes, she couldn't have picked a better forum than her final speech as leader to a Canadian Club breakfast in Ottawa Tuesday, and her final statement in the House later in the day, with tributes from all sides following QP.

Her speech came just 10 days before the Conservative leadership vote in Toronto next weekend. And her retirement announcement came during the last week of the House sitting before the Victoria Day holiday break week – the only day of the week Prime Minister Justin Trudeau would be in the House to join in the tributes.

It also came the day after the House passed her private member's bill to educate judges on sexual assault law – destined to become a significant part of her legacy.

She also took a bow Tuesday for the Conservatives raising their party and leadership fundraising and membership numbers during the first quarter of

2017. "In the first quarter, we raised $9 million while the Liberals managed only one-third of that," she said. Approaching the convention, the Conservatives have 259,000 members – "150,000 new paid members since January," Ambrose added. She also noted Conservative favourability numbers among those "who would consider voting Conservative up 10 points in the last year."

Those are all positive measures of her leadership. "She's done a fantastic job bringing people together," says Conservative finance critic Gérard Deltell. "I'm not sure if anyone else could have done it."

Mulroney suggests another leadership benchmark – "when she wrote to Justin Trudeau to take a bi-partisan position about NAFTA" in the coming talks with the Trump administration. She also made her position very clear during her own visit to Washington.

Not that she hasn't regularly raked the Liberals over the coals on issues such as fiscal frameworks, cash-for-access fundraisers, a culture of entitlement and a string of broken promises. In that, she was just doing her job. She was doing it again yesterday, asking Trudeau again about whether he had met with the ethics commissioner to talk about his Christmas holiday at the Aga Khan's island in the Caribbean.

All in all, this is a good time for Ambrose to leave.

"I am going to be resigning after the House rises for the summer," she told the Canadian Club audience at the Fairmont Château Laurier. "It is time for a new chapter in my life."

And so, at 48, she is moving on. And why not? Why would she stay on in a shadow cabinet when she's already led a shadow cabinet? Why would she return to Alberta to work under Jason Kenney in provincial politics when she has served a decade in national cabinet portfolios?

Not that she didn't have her bad moments. As a rookie environment minister in 2006, she got badly mauled at the annual UN Conference of the Parties Conference in Nairobi on climate change. The Canadian environmental movement took her apart on the world stage, and Prime Minister Stephen Harper's response was to throw her under the bus in his first cabinet shuffle two months later, demoting her to Intergovernmental Affairs and president of Privy Council.

Rather than being scarred by the experience, Ambrose grew from it. And in her subsequent portfolios – Public Works, Labour, Western Diversification, Status of Women and Health – she kept stakeholders close and managed expectations. In all, she served in eight ministries in nearly 10 years in office.

In retirement, she'll be eligible for most of her MP's pension, plus her cabinet top-up, at age 55. The remainder, after changes made in January 2016, kicks in at 65. After five terms and 13 years in the House, and a decade less three months in cabinet, her pension will kick in at around six figures.

Just the sort of thing that riles up the Canadian Taxpayers Federation – but no one elected them. The voters in Ambrose's Edmonton riding have chosen her in the last five elections.

She has the sort of diversified political resume that will serve her well in her post-Ottawa life. Post-employment guidelines prevent her from speaking to government for five years, but national and international companies and consulting firms will come calling, as will corporate boards. One leading Washington think-tank, the Wilson Center, has signed her up already as a senior fellow at its Canada Institute.

After QP yesterday, the House devoted 45 minutes to thanking her for her service and cheering her final remarks in the House as opposition and Conservative leader.

Trudeau, with his strong sense of occasion, struck the perfect note in his farewell tribute. "I hope," he said, "that she knows that, thanks to her leadership, she is leaving this House a much better place." And he crossed the floor to exchange a warm *bisou*.

For her part, she said that if new members were wondering "how long it takes for people to say something nice about you, actually you don't have to wait. You just have to quit."

And finally, in a gesture that showed her obvious respect and affection for Trudeau, she told the House: "It must be said that never again will two competitors be so matched out for best hair."

She left them laughing.

May 2017

16

TRIBUTES

TOM VAN DUSEN

Tom Van Dusen, who has died at 90, was a senior adviser to two Conservative prime ministers, John Diefenbaker and Brian Mulroney.

"There aren't many people alive who can say that," Mulroney was saying upon Van Dusen's death last weekend in Ottawa.

He was also the patriarch of a remarkable and prominent family, married for 64 years to Shirley Hogan, an Ottawa landscape and portrait artist whose paintings of Parliament Hill adorn many offices and boardrooms in the capital. At 85, she is still painting.

He was the father of seven accomplished children, many of them in the news media. And he had 14 grandchildren, including my daughter, Grace MacDonald, whose mother, Lisa Van Dusen, is the youngest of that talented brood.

If you went to their house in Russell, Ontario, east of Ottawa, on a Sunday afternoon, they would all be there, shouting to be heard in the kitchen, while assorted grandchildren added to the din.

Tom enjoyed every moment of it. He loved nothing better than goading his own children into a family argument. He was also a gifted and very funny raconteur, with great stories to tell of his half-century in journalism and politics on Parliament Hill.

More than an adviser to Dief, he was also one of his biographers, and his book, *The Chief*, is on display in a glass case at the Diefenbaker Centre at the University of Saskatchewan.

Tom was one of the honourary pallbearers at the Chief's funeral in 1979, and rode the famous Diefentrain all the way to his final resting place in Saskatoon. And oh, the stories he told about that.

When Mulroney became Conservative leader in 1983, he brought Tom back to the leader's office, first in opposition and then at the Prime Minister's Office, as head of caucus relations.

It may not sound like a very important position, but in Mulroney's world, nothing was more important than the caucus.

"Anyone who didn't think it was an important role wouldn't have known me or the party very well," Mulroney says. "Nothing is more important than the caucus. You can't lead without the caucus."

Adds the former prime minister: "This is the Conservative Party we're talking about here. The Conservative caucus destroyed Dief's leadership, it destroyed Bob Stanfield's leadership, and it destroyed Joe Clark's leadership."

Van Dusen had a hideaway office down the hall from the PM's office and the cabinet room on the third floor of the Centre Block. Many Tory MPs who needed something done in their ridings, or wanted to convey a message to the boss, would find their way to Tom's office. Many things got done that way, occasionally over a glass of something.

"Tommy didn't just advise me on the caucus," Mulroney says. "He would send me notes; he would write speeches." And he represented institutional memory, something nowadays in short supply in Ottawa.

"He had wisdom," says Charley McMillan, who as Mulroney's senior policy adviser worked across the hall from Tom in the Langevin Block. "And he had class."

On May 1, 1987, the morning after the surprise negotiation of the Meech Lake Accord, Van Dusen was one of five advisers in the PM's Centre Block office, the others being press secretary Marc Lortie, chief of staff Derek Burney, secretary to the cabinet for federal-provincial relations Norman Spector, and me, the speechwriter.

"Congratulations, Prime Minister," Tom told him. "It's a remarkable achievement." From all his years in politics and government, he knew that getting such a deal was an odds-against proposition.

At times Tom could be unsparing in his advice. "A prime minister doesn't have friends," he told Mulroney. "He can't afford friends. He has to be able to fire anyone."

Van Dusen would be among the very last advisers Mulroney would have fired. But as he turned 70, he took his leave and retired. Mulroney took him to a farewell lunch at the National Press Club, then the most public place in town.

For the next decade, until he grew increasingly frail, he went on being the much-beloved patriarch of his remarkable clan. His grandchildren adored him. He told them stories of pet monkeys and assorted animals that once had the run of the family's earlier home in Wychwood, near Aylmer.

In such a large family it was always somebody's birthday. At our cottage at Lac-St.-Pierre-de Wakefield in the Gatineau Hills, he essentially presided over Gracie's annual July birthday barbecue, featuring her many cousins. His relationship with her, and all his grandchildren, was magical to behold.

I couldn't have loved my father-in-law more if he'd been my own father.

As his second prime minister says: "He was a wonderful man."

September 2011

PETER LOUGHEED

Arriving at a tribute dinner in his honour in Calgary last June, Peter Lougheed had that old steely look in his eyes. Though he had been in failing health, he could still get up for the big event, and he was clearly ready.

He had been named Best Premier of the Last 40 Years by a *Policy Options* panel of prominent Canadians, on the occasion of the 40th anniversary of the Institute for Research on Public Policy.

All 30 members of the jury had picked him in their Top Five list, and 21 of them, including 10 out of 13 from Ontario, chose him as best premier. It wasn't even close. As the results came in, his lead kept lengthening. As I later told him, it was like watching Secretariat win the Belmont by 31 lengths.

Lougheed said he was deeply honoured, and he was delighted to attend the sold-out fundraising dinner in his honour at the ballroom of the Fairmont Palliser, scene of his many victory nights. Former federal cabinet minister Jim Prentice, a fellow Calgarian, later said he'd never felt such warmth and affection in a room as that night.

Scheduled to speak for only 10 minutes before dinner because of concerns over his health, Lougheed instead spoke for half an hour, from handwritten notes. He had two main messages: "We were Canadians first." And that his caucus, not his cabinet, set the agenda for his government in his 14 remarkable years in office.

Yes, Lougheed was a champion of Alberta's cause, in all the energy and constitutional debates with Pierre Trudeau. But Canada was always first in his heart. And yes, his caucus ruled the roost, as cabinet members and staff discovered. He liked to say that caucus made policy and the premier's advisers implemented it.

As for his legacy, it is simply unmatched in modern times.

He created a political dynasty that endures to this day. From no seats in the Alberta legislature before 1967, his Progressive Conservatives won four consecutive elections beginning in 1971. Alison Redford recently won the party's 12th consecutive election. And he played a role in that, too, making a strong televised endorsement for her 10 days before the election, at a time when she was trailing Danielle Smith and Wildrose badly in the polls. Lougheed's intervention came at a decisive moment, when undecideds were deciding.

In terms of substance, Lougheed was the builder of modern Alberta, of its new universities and technical colleges, of its modern hospitals and network of roads. He established the Alberta Heritage Fund, and built it into a $12-billion nest egg for a rainy day. And he made the oil sands feasible by allowing developers to get their costs out.

The price of oil tripled twice during his premiership, in 1973 and in 1979, and Alberta was transformed as result. The per capita income of Alberta, $17,000 when he took office in 1971, was $50,000 when he left in 1985.

When Trudeau brought in the confiscatory National Energy Program in 1980, Lougheed reminded him that the resource belonged to the province, and was delighted when Brian Mulroney dismantled it soon after taking office in 1984. Lougheed famously said that where Trudeau had previously been on his front porch, he now found him in his living room.

Lougheed himself would say his most significant achievement was on the Constitution, patriated with the Charter of Rights in 1981.

Quite simply, without Lougheed there would have been no deal. He insisted on the general amending formula, requiring the approval of Ottawa and seven provinces representing 50 per cent of the population, the 7/50 clause. His deal breaker was the notwithstanding clause. He insisted on the ability of the legislature to overrule the courts. While Ottawa has never invoked it, he didn't hesitate to use it in Alberta.

He was famous for his relationships with his fellow premiers, particularly Bill Davis, Allan Blakeney, Robert Bourassa and René Lévesque. He liked to tell of the time he and Davis left a first ministers' meeting in Ottawa, not walking out, but simply going back to the hotel to watch NFL *Monday Night Football*. Even when he and Davis disagreed on energy issues, they still got along. As for Bourassa, Lougheed took Quebec as his model for having a strong presence on the federal-provincial scene. Looking back at these premiers, we are standing on the shoulders of giants.

None stood taller for Alberta and Canada than Peter Lougheed. As it was said of Sir Christopher Wren, if you would seek his legacy, look around you. All around you.

September 2012

JIM FLAHERTY

This was written through tears, on a train passing through Oshawa–Whitby, Jim Flaherty's home. He was my friend of all the years.

On our high school hockey team at Loyola – undefeated senior city champions in 1965 – Jim was a star forward. He proudly wore number 16, like Henri Richard, another little guy with a big heart. We used to say, "Don't get between Jim and the net."

Many years later, in 2007, when I was on the board of our school, we were looking for a commencement speaker and I suggested Jim.

"Do you think he'd do it?" someone asked.

"He'd change his schedule to do it," I replied.

"Of course, I'll do it," he said, when I asked him the next day outside the House. "I'd be honoured."

Jim never forgot where he came from – Lachine and then Belmore Avenue in west end Montreal, right next to the school.

On commencement day, he arrived with his mother, Mary, then 91, a sprightly old lady in red. She had been president of the Loyola Mother's Guild, and when he proudly introduced her from her seat in the third row, she received a huge ovation.

It fell to me to introduce Canada's finance minister. "Jim personifies the difference between graduates of LCC and graduates of Loyola," I said. "*They* may own the country, but *we* run it."

"We were Irish Catholics," he said. "And so I was supposed to be a Liberal." By then, he had the crowd in the palm of his hand. And what did he learn at school? "Hard work, self-reliance and service to others," he said.

Loyola, he said, formed him, "intellectually, spiritually and physically." As one of eight children from a family of modest means, he wouldn't have gotten to Princeton without a scholarship, or from there to Osgoode Hall law school in Toronto.

He wouldn't have met Christine Elliott, the love of his life and the mother of their triplet sons, Galen, Quinn and John. Jim and Christine wouldn't have opened a law practice together in Whitby, where they bought an old stone farmhouse, scene of the best Christmas parties ever. He wouldn't have gone to Queen's Park as the MLA from Whitby-Oshawa in the 1990s, serving as finance minister before the Conservatives' defeat in 2003.

And when he went to Ottawa from the same riding in 2006, his experience at Queen's Park made him the logical choice to become Stephen Harper's finance minister. Until last month, he was this government's only finance minister – for eight years, one month and 12 days. He resigned on the morrow of St. Patrick's Day, wearing a trademark green tie.

In time, he became the ranking finance minister in the G7 and G20. And he guided Canada safely through the shoals of the Great Recession of 2008–2009 to the shore of recovery.

Canada came out of the economic crisis in sounder shape than any G7 country, with the strongest job creation – one million new jobs – and lowest debt-to-GDP ratio of any of the leading industrialized nations. Canada recovered because of the stimulus spending, beginning with the 2009 budget and a $56 billion deficit.

Over the next five years, he ran up nearly $160 billion of new debt – but in what turned out to be his last budget in February, he came within a hair of balancing the books with a $2.9 billion deficit, 0.1 per cent of GDP and a $3 billion contingency reserve. He forecast a $6.4 billion surplus for next year.

He had a good message, and he was a great messenger. He was fond of saying that Canada's banking system was the strongest in the world, six years in a row; that Canada was ranked the second-best place to do business in the world by Bloomberg, thanks to the lowest business taxes in the G7. He himself was named the world's best finance minister by *Euromoney* magazine in 2009.

This became a ritual shout-out on the golf trips he led to Ireland in August of 2011 and 2012. Twelve guys on a bus, and a week of rollicking laughter. "THE BEST FINANCE MINISTER IN THE WORLD!" they would shout at dinners in Irish pubs. At one 19th hole, the hostess came over and asked where we were from. "Canada," someone said. "This is our country's finance minister, Jim Flaherty."

"Oh!" she responded. "Can you come over here and help us out of all this trouble?"

Jim did not stand on ceremony. When he was hosting the G7 finance ministers and central bankers in February 2010, he merrily told off officials who wanted to hold the meeting in Ottawa. He decided to have it in Iqaluit. They all went on snowmobile rides in their parkas. Flaherty loved that.

He loved stories and he loved telling them, like the time in Washington in October 2008, at the height of the financial crisis, when the G7 finance ministers personally wrote the communique about pumping stimulus into their economies.

One night, a couple of springs ago, Jim invited me to dinner at the parliamentary restaurant. He wanted to write a book, and asked me to work with him on it. We weren't sure whether it would be a biography or an autobiography. But he wanted it to be honest and authentic, and he wanted it to be in his own voice. He kept talking about it, never quite getting around to it.

We talked about it again in February, over dinner in the bar of the Rideau Club. "I still want to do the book," he said. "Let's talk about it again after the budget." We never did.

He was the best-read man I knew, surrounded by books in the study of his beautiful family home, the oldest house in Whitby. When my last book came out in the fall of 2009, Jim spoke at the Ottawa launch. "I'll buy 100 copies," he said, "if you'll sign them at the house at the Christmas party."

The last time I saw him, we were doing a Q&A on the budget for *Policy*, my magazine. Two mornings after the budget, we talked for half an hour in the board room of his Centre Block office. It was a wide-ranging conversation, one that had a certain valedictory tone to it.

He looked tired that morning, but he also said he was feeling much better after a difficult year of health challenges, and had recently been given a clean bill of health by his doctor.

When he resigned, I remembered that Christine and their boys had been in the balcony for the budget speech. They already knew it was his last one.

I thought he might never speak in the House again, but simply move on, having served our country so well. That was the thing about Jim – he was a happy warrior, a man without malice. That is why he was loved on all sides of the House.

And Jim had empathy. He never failed to ask about Zara, my four-year old daughter who has Asperger's Syndrome, and lives with her mother near the Flaherty home in Whitby.

As it happened, Flaherty's last budget had an initiative for vocational training for people with Autism Spectrum Disorder.

"There are hundreds of thousands of Canadians who can't work who are labeled with some sort of disability," he said at the end of our interview. "We need them."

It turned out to be his last interview – the last time I ever saw him. I had tickets for the last Canadiens home game of the season, and when I offered them to him and his family, his eyes lit up. But last week, he had the tickets returned, saying he would be travelling instead.

And so he is, as it turns out, on his way to heaven.

April 2014

JEAN BÉLIVEAU

Montreal Canadiens owner Geoff Molson got it exactly right when he said Jean Béliveau was the most respected hockey figure in the world. He was also the most revered.

For all the years he played, and in all the years since, no one else represented our game with such elegance, grace and class.

His record speaks for itself. Ten Stanley Cups – five as captain of the Canadiens – and another seven as a team executive. No other player in the history of the game even comes close. As Molson told the *Montreal Gazette*'s Dave Stubbs: "His name is on the Stanley Cup 17 times, but he's even more than that."

So much more than that. Like Maurice Richard before him, Béliveau understood that his role as a public figure did not end with his retirement and his last Stanley Cup in 1971. The Rocket knew that he was expected to go on being a hero, and so he did, playing and refereeing in old-timers games in countless small towns throughout Quebec. Even in retirement, Richard was still fire on ice. When Dickie Moore once told him, "You know, Rock, you could pass it to me if you like," Richard replied, "Dickie, they come to see me score."

Béliveau, the majestic prince of the game, went on to become its greatest ambassador and its most beloved figure. And he did so with the same special grace that had always distinguished his play. It was a representational role he was born to play, and it began with his kindness to strangers, often those at lower stations in life.

In 1969, on a day the Forum ice was unavailable to them, the Canadiens came by bus to practice at the Loyola College arena. Béliveau helped the rink manager, a Latino immigrant named José, install the net after re-making the ice. Then he patiently signed autographs for every college kid hanging over the boards.

A quarter century later, when we were members of the same golf club in Montreal, Béliveau would occasionally invite me to join his regular Saturday morning game. He was unfailingly considerate of his playing partners, and while he was always happy to discuss hockey, he loved talking about politics. But he also talked to the caddies. "Are you having a good season?" he would ask, and he would always buy them lunch after nine holes.

Whether he was talking to a rink manager, a golf caddy or a prime minister, Béliveau's demeanour was always the same.

"Innately, he was a great gentleman," recalls former Prime Minister Brian Mulroney, a friend of nearly 40 years. "He had all the instincts of a great gentleman. He was the genuine article."

Six weeks ago, in late October, Mulroney received a call from Élise Béliveau saying that her husband would like to see him.

"I went and spent about an hour and a quarter with him in his bedroom," Mulroney said. "He was obviously not well, but he was very much still with it." They talked about hockey and politics.

"For the first time in my life," Mulroney told him, "I'm looking at a guy who turned down the Senate."

"I thought I turned it down twice," Béliveau replied. And so he did. He did not want a partisan line on his resume.

Jean Chrétien had the idea of making him governor general in 1994. He invited him to 24 Sussex and offered to appoint him to Rideau Hall. Béliveau thought about it, then declined for family reasons – his daughter Hélène had lost her husband, and he thought his two granddaughters needed a father.

Why would a hockey player be offered the country's most important constitutional role, as head of state representing the Crown? Even in a hockey country?

Well, because he was so much *more* than a hockey player. There was his humanity, his humility. There was his integrity, his character and, yes, his incredible class. He was a regal figure.

Most of all, Jean Béliveau was a unifying figure, a *rassembleur,* who brought people together. Never was this more apparent than in the raucous years from 1976 to 1980, when Quebecers and Canadians lived through two divisive debates – one on the language issue, and another on the future of Canada itself.

Le Gros Bill didn't need to make speeches. In all his public appearances he simply led by example, giving Montrealers and Quebecers a lesson in staying together and not being torn apart. But long before that, Big Jean had become, among hockey players, a uniquely pan-Canadian figure. In other hockey towns they might have hated the Canadiens – but everyone admired Béliveau.

Only one distinction is missing from his career: He never got to play for his country. Had he not retired at age 39 in 1971 – had he played just one more season – there is no doubt who would have been captain of the first Team Canada when they played the Soviets in September 1972, just after he turned 41. (Does anyone think a team led by Jean Béliveau would have been forced to the last minute of the last period of an eight-game series before finally beating the Russians?)

In his last playoff season, the Canadiens played the Big Bad Bruins of Bobby Orr and Phil Esposito in the first round of the playoffs. Down one game in Boston, and down 5–1 after two periods in the second game, Béliveau famously led the Canadiens to a 7–5 comeback in the third period. After that, the Canadiens seemed to have destiny behind them, defeating Boston in seven games and winning the Stanley Cup in Chicago in game seven against the Blackhawks of Bobby Hull and Stan Mikita.

It was the first time a captain carried the Stanley Cup around the ice. "I wanted," Béliveau told me years later, "to bring the Cup closer to the fans."

Later that night, when the Canadiens returned to Montreal, a customs agent asked if he had anything to declare. "Just the Stanley Cup," he replied. The officer said he would just mark it as "Canadian goods returned."

It was the last of his five Stanley Cups as captain of the Canadiens, and his 10th as a player. His first five Stanleys had been won from 1956–60, when he was the biggest star on the greatest team of all time – the only team ever to win five Cups in a row.

How great? Consider the power play – Big Jean at centre, the Rocket at right wing, Dickie Moore on left wing, Doug Harvey and Bernie "Boom Boom" Geoffrion on defence. Every one of them in the Hall of Fame. A power play so fearsome that the NHL changed its rules to align with the international hockey rule that allows a player out of the penalty box when his team had been scored upon.

"I was responsible for having that changed," Béliveau told me one day over lunch in 1998.

"How was that?"

"One night against Boston, I scored three goals in 44 seconds on a power play."

"Who was in goal for them?"

He paused and then said: "Terry Sawchuk." Not just any goalie, but perhaps the greatest of all time.

So there is the career of Jean Béliveau to be celebrated, and his life to be honoured. No organization does this better than the Canadiens, especially since the team has returned to the ownership of the Molson family. Geoff and Andrew Molson have inherited an impressive sense of occasion.

This was apparent as Jean lay in state at the Bell Centre Sunday and Monday. His closed casket lay at the south end of the arena, in what would have been the slot, his office during his brilliant career. Two huge photo banners – one of him hoisting the Cup and another of him passing the torch – were hung on either side of his retired number. Every important trophy he won, from the Stanley Cup to the first Conn Smythe Trophy as most valuable player in the 1965 playoffs, was displayed on either side of a sculpture of Big Jean. His sweater was draped over his seat near the Habs' bench, beneath a shaft of light.

For two days, Élise, Hélène and his two granddaughters shook the hands of thousands and thousands of well-wishers, who came not to mourn his passing so much as to express gratitude for his remarkable life.

In line behind me on Monday afternoon was a young boy, no more than 7 or 8, with his dad. He was incredibly patient, waiting for over an hour to pay tribute to a man he never saw play. He was wearing a Habs home jersey, with number 4 and the name Béliveau on the back.

For Jean Béliveau, the short two-block skate from the Bell Centre to his funeral service at Mary Queen of the World Cathedral would have been, like his incomparable career, an effortless turn on the ice.

December 2014

ANTONIN SCALIA

The sudden passing of Antonin Scalia has thrown all three branches of the U.S. government into unexpected turmoil in the midst of a presidential primary season.

In the judicial branch, the nine-member United States Supreme Court finds itself one justice short just weeks before a session in which it will hear cases on immigration, Obamacare and abortion, among the more than 20 cases on its docket. In any 4–4 ruling, a case is thrown out and the decision of the lower court is upheld.

In the executive branch, the White House will be nominating a successor to Scalia, the high court's ranking conservative intellectual of the past 30 years.

If confirmed by a majority in the Senate, a moderate appointee would swing a reliable 5–4 conservative majority to a liberal one.

Which is why, in the legislative branch, the Republican majority in the Senate is having none of it. Its leadership vows to block any nomination by President Barack Obama in his lame-duck year, saying the vacancy should be filled by the next president.

On the presidential campaign trail, both Democrats and Republicans went ballistic. For the Democrats, both Hillary Clinton and Bernie Sanders pointed out that Obama is president until January 20. Among the six Republicans, most sided with Republican Senate Majority Leader Mitch McConnell in opposing the idea of Obama sending up a nominee. As Donald Trump put it in a debate in South Carolina: "Delay, delay, delay."

What would Scalia have made of the polarizing effect of his death on the entire U.S. government? Well, he was a famous proponent of "originalism," or founders' intent, in his readings of the U.S. Constitution.

The American Constitution clearly vests executive power with the president, including the appointment of all federal and Supreme Court judges. As the Constitution clearly states: "The President shall nominate, and by and with the Advice and Consent of the Senate, shall appoint judges of the Supreme Court."

There's no mention of the role of the Senate Judiciary Committee, which by convention holds hearings before a Supreme Court nomination is sent to the floor of the Senate for an up-or-down vote.

According to Scalia's own doctrine of originalism, the committee might have no standing in a strict constructionist reading of the Constitution; there's nothing in it, or in American political convention, about the president not putting forward a nominee in an election year.

What a debate that would be – and what a debater Scalia was. Even when he was on the losing end of an argument, he had a gift for winning over his opponents – including the high court's most liberal member, Ruth Bader Ginsburg, who described them last weekend as "best buddies," an unlikely friendship that thrived on a shared love of food and opera.

I had the privilege of seeing Scalia up close and personal at a McGill Institute for the Study of Canada conference I was co-hosting with MISC director Antonia Maioni on the 25th anniversary of the Canadian Charter of Rights and Freedoms. We were looking for an act to close the conference on February 16, 2007.

Chris Manfredi, then dean of arts and now provost at McGill, was on the organizing committee and had the idea of inviting Scalia to debate a liberal member of the Supreme Court of Canada.

Yeah, right, I thought, good luck with that.

At the next meeting of the conference steering committee, Manfredi reported back. "Scalia," he said, "is a "yes.'" You could have knocked us over with a feather.

"I had written to Scalia in September," Manfredi recalled the other day, "invoking the name of my dissertation supervisor whom Scalia knew, and also reminding Scalia that we had met at a conference organized by the University of Western Ontario law school."

Manfredi didn't hear back at first. "There was silence for quite a while," he said, "probably due to the court's not being in session until the first Monday in October."

But then came Scalia's yes. Manfredi invited as Scalia's opponent Ian Binnie, one of the brightest lights of the Supreme Court of Canada and, as it happened, a McGill Law graduate who was unlikely to turn down his alma mater and who already had met Scalia at international events.

Binnie immediately accepted and the ensuing debate with Scalia was one of the most exciting, entertaining and educational events that could be imagined.

They blew the doors off the place. Binnie argued for the Constitution as a living tree, while Scalia made the case for originalism and the intent of the framers.

Bob Rae, acting as the good-humoured moderator, had the good sense to drop the puck and get out of the way.

Hardly anyone among the 300 students, academics and conference participants agreed with anything Scalia had to say. But they loved him anyway, because as Binnie was the first to acknowledge, he was "a rock star."

Binnie, it turned out, got the better of Scalia in the argument. "The issue is whether the framers intended a 'frozen rights' approach to our political institutions and rights and freedom," Binnie began. "Is the Constitution a living tree or a dead tree?"

As for "original meaning," Binnie said the question was whether "a theory of frozen rights, with no realistic prospect of a thaw, is correct for Canada."

In Canada, he said, "the ability of the courts to move with the times has served this country well." Indeed, in the 1982 Canadian Charter of Rights and Freedoms, the political framers enumerated rights but left interpretation to the courts.

Scalia retorted that interpreting the Constitution as a living tree "simply encourages judges to make anti-democratic decisions that extend rights to questionable groups." Typical Scalia – a man famous for his dissenting opinions and for not mincing his words.

But Binnie also made the better case on the American side of the constitutional framework. "Judge Scalia asks what gives a judge the special wisdom to evolve the Constitution over time," Binnie said. "Of course, the same question can be asked about how judges can divine the original meaning of a document written 230 years ago."

And he quoted two eminent American authorities who opposed originalism or 'frozen rights.' Thomas Jefferson, one of the greatest American founding fathers and presidents, said: "We might as well require a man to wear still the coat which fitted him when he was a boy…" And he concluded by quoting the great Justice Oliver Wendell Holmes writing on the Supreme Court in 1920: "The case before us must be considered in the light of our whole experience and not merely in that of what was said a hundred years go."

Game, set and match to Binnie. When the debate ended, the jam-packed hotel ballroom in Montreal exploded in applause for both Binnie and Scalia.

It was in the hours following the conference that we saw Scalia's innate grace and instinctive generosity. First, he mingled with the students while he sipped a glass of red wine. Then he dropped in on the Association of Italian-Canadian Jurists of Quebec, who had heard he was going to be in town. He had a good visit with them before a private dinner with Binnie and the McGill organizers.

The dinner was at Verses at the Nelligan Hotel in Old Montreal. Manfredi remembers that "by the time I arrived, Scalia was already there, enjoying a dry martini." He was clearly a *bon vivant*.

Scalia sat at the centre of a table for 12, looking out at Rue St. Paul. Binnie sat across from him, and they spoke in very warm and collegial terms. Scalia spoke at length of his friendship and affection for Ruth Bader Ginsburg.

By the time the evening ended, everyone at the table had been won over by Scalia. He was easy to disagree with, impossible to dislike. He was absolutely authentic, and kind to all.

Binnie won the debate. Scalia won the dinner.

February 2016

NELSON MANDELA

The best story in a long time is that of the 300 South African firefighters flying into northern Alberta to help extinguish the wildfire that has razed Fort McMurray and caused the evacuation of more than 80,000 Canadians from their homes.

Part of a national brigade of 5,000 young bush and forest firefighters, the South Africans took a crash course in Canadian forest fires, boarded an Air Canada charter, and flew 16,000 kilometres over 24-hours to Edmonton, where they landed Sunday night on their way to Fort Mac. Leaving Johannesburg and arriving in Edmonton, the young men and women sang and danced.

As the *Globe and Mail*'s Geoffrey York reported, the South African government "sees it as re-paying a debt to the Canadian people for their support for the anti-apartheid struggle." Speaking at the departure ceremony, a senior official said: "As South Africans we feel indebted to the Canadian people. Remember that these are the people who stood on our side in our times of trouble, so today we are paying back."

The South African firefighters, an all-black team in yellow shirts, will be in Alberta for about a month as part of an international contingent relieving exhausted Canadian firefighters after four weeks on the front where 5,200 kilometres of forest and thousands of Fort Mac homes and businesses have been consumed.

Reading this story in his Montreal office, Brian Mulroney said: "I'm looking at a picture of Mandela, and saying, 'thank you, Nelson. We were there for your people, now you're there for us.'"

From the time he took office as prime minister in 1984, Mulroney championed the anti-apartheid cause and called for Mandela's release from prison where he had languished since 1963.

He called the arrival of the South African firefighters "one of the unforeseen consequences of a foreign policy that you never think of."

Mulroney was honoured by the South African president last December when he was invested a Supreme Companion of the Order of Oliver Tambo, South Africa's highest award to a foreigner.

While Mandela languished in prison for decades, Tambo served as head of the African National Congress, and was received by Mulroney along with Bishop Desmond Tutu and other anti-apartheid leaders.

As Mulroney wrote in a *Globe* op-ed at the time he received the Tambo Award: "I told the cabinet that it would be a priority policy of my government to press the case for Nelson Mandela's liberation, the destruction of the apartheid system, the unbanning of the ANC and the building of a non-racial democratic society in South Africa."

Nor was Mulroney the first Canadian prime minister to take up the anti-apartheid cause. As a law student and young Progressive Conservative, he was deeply impressed by John Diefenbaker leading the movement to expel South Africa from the Commonwealth in 1961. To this day, Mulroney remembers the hero's welcome Dief received at the Château Laurier on his return from the Commonwealth Heads of Government Meeting in London.

As prime minister, Mulroney put Canada's money behind his anti-apartheid rhetoric, imposing economic sanctions against South Africa's segregationist regime. In this entire campaign, he was stridently opposed by Ronald Reagan and Margaret Thatcher, normally staunch conservative allies on the international stage.

"People forget but at the time we got Canada involved, Mandela was essentially forgotten," Mulroney says. "The first time I met Oliver Tambo I asked him what role if any he saw for a middle power like Canada in this. He said something like: 'Are you kidding? Canada is a G7 country and a leading country in the Commonwealth.'" When Mulroney first raised the apartheid issue at the G7 summit in Germany in 1985, he had virtually no support around the table, least of all from Reagan and Thatcher, and not even from the summit chair, Helmut Kohl. "Only François Mitterrand expressed support," Mulroney recalls, "and he was somewhat lukewarm."

At one point, even Mulroney's own officials were "somewhat lukewarm" to his policy. I had worked on a draft of his September 1985 speech to the United Nations General Assembly in which he threatened economic sanctions in the event of the minority white Afrikaner regime's continued refusal to act. External Affairs and the Privy Council Office insisted we take it out. Sitting in the holding room before speaking to the UN General Assembly, Mulroney asked Stephen Lewis, whom he had appointed Canada's ambassador to the UN, what he thought. His advice was to put the sanctions reference back in, and Mulroney did so.

Matters really came to a head with Thatcher at a CHOGM meeting in Vancouver in October 1987. Thatcher and the British delegation put out some numbers on Canadian firms' investments and operations in South Africa that gave the appearance of showing Canada's economic sanctions to be completely ineffective and even counterproductive.

Then Thatcher's press secretary, the ineffable Bernie Ingham, gave a stormy news conference at which a Canadian reporter asked if he thought the Canadians were hypocrites.

"If the shoe fits," Ingham replied, "wear it."

Watching this upstairs in his suite at the Pan Pacific Hotel, Mulroney had had enough of the Brits undermining him as conference host.

"I'm going downstairs in 20 minutes to meet Margaret Thatcher," he said, "and she's not going to like what I'm going to tell her."

Lewis, who was the only other person in the room, later remembered it as "a tongue lashing."

"Now that you've hoisted your colours, Margaret, you better look out for me," Mulroney told her. "You're on the wrong side of history."

When Mandela was released from prison in February 1990, he called Mulroney to thank him. He said he and his fellow prisoners had heard that Mulroney "had taken up my cause and South Africa's." He said they sometimes "listened to you" on BBC radio denouncing what Mulroney always called "the scourge of apartheid."

"Prime Minister, I want to thank you and Canada for everything you've done," Mandela continued. "And if you like, I'll make my first speech to a democratic parliament in Ottawa."

"Would you like me to send a plane for you this afternoon or tomorrow morning?" Mulroney asked, and they shared a laugh over that. "I'll come as soon as I can," Mandela replied.

It was the first time they had ever spoken, but it was the beginning of an enduring friendship.

When Mandela arrived in Ottawa in June 1990, you'd think the Beatles had landed at the airport. And when he walked into the Commons to speak to a joint session of Parliament, you never heard such cheers and applause.

Mandela said he was grateful for the opportunity to speak to the Canadian Parliament, when he could not speak before his own. Which was precisely the point. He didn't even have the right to vote, and his people lived "apart." Eight years later, when he returned to the House, he spoke as the democratically elected president of the Republic of South Africa. His "long walk to freedom" was complete.

And in 2001, at Jean Chrétien's invitation, he became an honourary Canadian citizen. The continuity of Canadian prime ministers, championing the cause of freedom in South Africa, stretches more than half a century from Diefenbaker to Justin Trudeau's elegant comments on Mulroney receiving the Tambo Award.

Now a young generation of South Africans has flown to the aid of Fort Mac, re-paying a debt of democracy by coming to fight the wildfire.

Mulroney was sitting in his den Monday night, watching Peter Mansbridge present a piece on *The National* showing the firefighters in uniform, dancing and singing at Edmonton airport.

"What a wonderful story," Mulroney said the next morning. "It's delightful to see them here. There is a kind of tissue of connectivity in life, a tie-in between policy and people."

June 2016

JACK LAYTON

Five years after the passing of Jack Layton, it's a good moment to re~~~~ what Canada gained from his life, and lost at his death.

As a politician, Jack played the long game, and he played to win. He didn't just solidify the NDP's base, he worked constantly to grow it.

"We had the fifth anniversary of his passing on Monday," says Brad Lavigne, NDP campaign director in 2011. "And the celebrations reminded us that he's still a tremendous force within the party."

When he became leader of the New Democrats in 2003, they had only 13 MPs, barely beyond the minimum of 12 members needed for recognized party standing in the House. At his passing eight years later, the NDP had just been elected official opposition, with 103 members, and most remarkably 59 MPs from Quebec.

Tragically, Layton died of cancer at 61 less than four months after his historic breakthrough in the 2011 election, when he ran a campaign for the ages. He was the man with the cane, whose physical courage was inspirational.

In Quebec, he became known as *le bon jack*, a good guy and a favourite son. At a campaign event in a Montreal sports bar during the hockey playoffs, Jack showed up wearing a Canadiens jersey. He might have moved from Montreal to Toronto decades earlier, but he was still a Habs fan. Voters in Quebec got that – you can change cities without changing teams.

Layton's campaign team first sensed something extraordinary was going on in Quebec during his taped appearance on Radio-Canada's hit show, *Tout le monde en parle*, when he got a standing ovation from the studio audience – in the rehearsal.

Most remarkably, he blocked the Bloc, which was reduced from 49 seats in the 2008 election to just four MPs in 2011. This is a significant aspect of Layton's legacy, and of his service to Canada – he put the separatists out of business in Ottawa.

By the end of the 2011 election, Layton had the NDP polling in the mid-40s in Quebec. At lunch in Montreal during the final days of the campaign, former Ontario NDP leader Stephen Lewis asked former prime minister Brian Mulroney what that translated to in terms of seats.

"Fifty-nine," Mulroney replied. "About 59 seats."

Lewis excused himself, saying he had to share Mulroney's prediction with Layton.

Flash forward to the 2015 election, in which the NDP was reduced to 44 seats, 16 from Quebec. From 31 per cent of the popular vote in 2011, the New Dems finished with less than 20 per cent in 2015. And this, after leading

ection, and during the first half of the campaign, ...ast month of the 78-day marathon campaign. ...s during the campaign, and through all the recrimi- ... Democrats have asked themselves one question: ...done? ...our national game, he knew that the worst thing you ...ad. And he would never have allowed himself and the ...ced on the left, as they were by Justin Trudeau and the ...r promise to run stimulative deficits, in contrast to Tom ..., balanced budgets.

Layton...lso a born campaigner, who was energized by crowds. He practised the politics of joy. Or as he himself put it in his final message to Canadians, written just two days before his death: "Love is better than anger. Hope is better than fear. Optimism is better than despair. So let us be loving, hopeful and optimistic. And we'll change the world."

The Orange Wave of 2011 was not an overnight occurrence, but a political development nearly a decade in the making. The long game.

In the 2004 election, Layton increased the NDP deputation in the House, with 19 seats and 16 per cent of the popular vote. In 2006, the New Dems grew to 29 seats and 17.5 per cent of the vote. In 2008 the NDP won 37 seats and 18 per cent of the vote.

Those were three successive minority Parliaments in which Layton held the balance of power, and managed to cut deals, first with Paul Martin's Liberals and then with Stephen Harper's Conservatives.

Through it all, the NDP worked through four campaigns out of owned rather than rented space at the corner of Bank and Laurier in downtown Ottawa. The story of the building, and how the NDP came to own it in late 2003, is one of Layton playing the long game.

"He got the idea from the communications and energy workers, who owned their own space," recalls Lavigne. The Chrétien government had recently passed a campaign finance reform banning corporate and union donations to parties that was to take effect in January 2004.

"Jack decided to get one last round of donations from the unions and buy the building," Lavigne says. Layton raised $2.3 million from the unions and ever since, the NDP have occupied the top floor, while tenants on the two floors below pay for the mortgage. Not only that, as Lavigne notes, "the party has collateral at the bank."

Thanks to Layton, the socialists are the only party to own their own space, while the others are tenants in downtown Ottawa. And now the NDP building is called the Jack Layton Building, having been named for him after his death.

His name is also on the Jack Layton Ferry Terminal on the Toronto waterfront, so named by Toronto city council in 2013, in honour of his many years of service as a member of council before he went to Ottawa. At the entrance to the terminal, there's a bronze statue of Layton sitting alone on the back seat of a bicycle built for two.

He could be waiting for his wife, Olivia Chow, to join him for a bike ride, or perhaps his beloved granddaughter, Beatrice, now seven years old.

Sitting in his Centre Block office one afternoon in 2010, Layton talked about his father and granddaughter. His father, Bob Layton, a former Progressive Conservative minister in the Mulroney government, also had cancer, a battle he eventually lost. Layton referred to him as "Dad," and you could hear the love in his voice. Asked about his granddaughter, his face simply lit up with joy.

Among his many qualities, one stood out – he was authentic. Five years on, Canada is a better place for his service to our country.

August 2016

MIKE ROBINSON

The last time I had lunch with Mike Robinson, he was talking about how much he was looking forward to spending the summer at his place on the coast of Normandy, after the completion of extensive renovations to his family's second home of some 30 years.

I asked him what it was like, as an English-speaking foreigner, dealing with notoriously difficult French tradesmen and suppliers.

"We get along," he said.

That was Mike. He got along with everyone. It probably helped that his beloved wife ML, Mary Louise Walsh, was always there. It probably didn't hurt that the Canadians were liberators of Normandy in the Second World War. With his strong sense of history, Mike would have known he never had to mention that.

And it was there that he died, suddenly, on Canada Day, at 65, at the beginning of what was to have been a summer doting on his four children and four grandchildren, to say nothing of constant visits of friends from home.

He wasn't going to be around all summer at his customary seat in the Earnscliffe booth at the Métropolitain restaurant on Sussex Drive. At the consulting firm he co-founded, the Met was known as the cafeteria. On Tuesday evening, the cafeteria was open for a reception for hundreds of Mike's friends, following a moving memorial service at Beechwood Cemetery.

With his flair for event management, Mike would have approved of both venues. Beechwood is Canada's national military cemetery, on the edge of Rockcliffe in the heart of a town he loved. It's the final resting place of a prime minister, Sir Robert Borden, and a governor general, Ray Hnatyshyn. Conservatives, to be sure, and Mike was nothing if not a Liberal, but he was a Canadian first. And the Met, well, that's where you could find him nearly every day at lunch, with bartender Mike Hannas always close at hand to refresh his glass of red wine and discuss the menu.

At Tuesday's reception, Hannas wasn't working, he was a guest, and a friend. So many friends, and so many stories.

Conservative strategist Harry Near told some great ones in his eulogy for his partner of more than a quarter century since they had co-founded the Earnscliffe Strategy Group, the government relations consulting firm named for the home of Sir John A. Macdonald.

Harry was telling the story of Mike doing a television panel during the 1993 federal election, where his Conservative counterpart John Tory, now mayor of Toronto, said the Liberals didn't have a plan for a particular campaign issue. Mike brandished the Liberal platform, the Red Book, and said, "it says so right here on page 55."

Harry had a punch line: "It turned out that the Red Book only had 46 pages."

And then he told a story from the Royal Ottawa Golf Club, where he and Mike were regulars in a group of eight members in a Sunday morning game that included Jean Chrétien, when he was prime minister. Mike had been chair of Paul Martin's leadership campaign in 1990, but every second Sunday he would be in Chrétien's foursome.

As Harry told it, Chrétien didn't wait for others to hit and with his RCMP detail would walk ahead of the foursome. On one hole, he said Mike hit two balls that came so close to the PM that the Mounties were concerned.

Later, Chrétien told Mike: "I know you guys want Martin to be prime minister, but you don't have to kill me to do it." Harry didn't have to impersonate Chrétien's famous accent. You could hear him saying it.

It would also be like Mike to get along with the Chrétien crowd, though there was never any doubt he belonged to the Martin camp. His prime minister was among the eulogists, and told several delightful stories at his own expense.

As Near also put it, Mike was "respected deeply as a stalwart ally or worthy opponent." He was a gentleman and a player, a man of influence admired on all sides.

His political opponents and business competitors were also his friends, such as Mike Coates, now president of Hill and Knowlton Strategies for the Americas in New York. "Mike gave me my first job back in the day of Public Affairs International," Coates recalled. They ended up on opposite sides of the table as representatives of the Liberal and Conservative parties in leaders' debate negotiations with the network television consortium during the 2006 election campaign. "He thought we were barbarians," Coates said with a chuckle.

As a competitor in the GR business, Coates and his H&K colleagues also had a deep respect for the brand that Robinson, Near and their colleagues had built over 27 years. From start-up space on Sparks Street in 1989, Earnscliffe now occupies a splendid heritage building with the firm's name on it overlooking the National War Memorial on Elgin Street. Mike understood succession issues, and he was in the process of moving on, but he still went to the office every day, and the staff adored him.

He was also a mentor, in business and politics. James Baxter, the founder and editor of *iPolitics*, recalls Mike encouraging him to start his news site. John Duffy, author of the award-winning *Fights of Our Lives* on great Canadian campaigns, said that "Mike made me" when he brought him in as a 20-something speechwriter for Martin in the 1990 Liberal leadership campaign.

There were many such stories told at the Met Tuesday night. Mike would have enjoyed them all. But perhaps he would have most enjoyed the one told by his son Drew, in his eulogy, about the love story between Mike and ML.

"He always said the secret of a happy marriage could be summarized by two words: 'Yes, dear.'"

Only perfect.

July 2016

JIM PRENTICE

Sitting in the memorial service for former premier Jim Prentice in Calgary, it was hard not to think that, had he remained at CIBC two years ago, he might have been on a different plane than the last one he fatefully boarded in Kelowna.

He might have been out on the campaign trail as a candidate for the federal Conservative leadership. He would have been very hard to beat.

But Prentice chose another path when he returned to Alberta to lead the Progressive Conservatives' flailing and failing provincial government in the fall of 2014.

In truth, he was answering a call, though some observers thought he had taken leave of his senses. But as he told his friend and former Tory caucus colleague Jay Hill at the time: "I don't want to look back on my children

...dren in a decade and know I could have done something to ...nd I chose not to."

...he essence of Jim Prentice – his life was about family and public ... told this story in his eulogy during the state memorial service ...ern Alberta Jubilee Auditorium, overlooking the city of Calgary ...loved.

...an 1,500 guests and members of the public filled the hall to near capacity for the 90-minute service. The VIPs included three former prime ministers, Stephen Harper, Joe Clark and Kim Campbell. There were five sitting premiers in attendance – Alberta's Rachel Notley, BC's Christy Clark, Saskatchewan's Brad Wall, NWT's Bob McLeod and PEI's Wade MacLauchlan. Three former Alberta premiers were there – Ed Stelmach, Dave Hancock and Alison Redford, whose political flameout in the spring of 2014 was the reason Prentice stepped in.

Led by Opposition Leader Rona Ambrose, there were dozens of current and former Conservative MPs, many of whom, in other circumstances, would have supported a Prentice bid for the party's national leadership. Jim would have enjoyed seeing them all. He knew how to work a room. He had the gift of talking to you and not looking past you.

Jim would have enjoyed the laughter that lightened the state occasion, and would have been touched by the tears.

He would have been incredibly proud of his daughter Cassia, speaking on behalf of her sisters Christina and Kate and their mother, Karen. He might have wondered, as many in the hall did, how she got through it in the doubly tragic circumstances of having also lost her father-in-law, Dr. Kenneth Gellatly, in the crash. When she said she still could not believe her father was gone, she had the room in the palm of her hand.

"My father was so much to so many, and he was absolutely everything to our family," she said. "His life was lived as a pledge to his parents – one of integrity, kindness, hard work and community. Those principles and the man who embodied them were bedrock to our family."

Stephen Harper's role was to speak of the cabinet minister to whom he gave several challenging roles, because of his ability to get things done while getting along with friend and foe alike.

"Let me tell you, there's a price to be paid for that," Harper said. "You get the tough jobs."

Did he ever. As chair of the cabinet operations committee from the beginning of the Conservative government in 2006, Prentice was, as Harper said, "chief operating officer" of the government. Which meant he was Dr. No to many Conservative ministers with big ideas for their departments, as well as to MPs with pet projects in their ridings.

At Indian and Northern Affairs, a department where conventional wisdom had long held that political careers went to die, Prentice fashioned the residential schools settlement and did the heavy lifting that led to the appointment of the landmark Truth and Reconciliation Commission. His interest in indigenous peoples began back in his Calgary law practice, where he represented First Nations in land claims cases.

At Industry, Prentice presided over a place of ideas that became a central agency in all but name. At Environment, he worked to reconcile climate change with the energy issues of the oil patch he represented in the House. It doesn't get any more politically challenging than that.

"We gave the hardest assignments to the people who could best handle them and Jim was always one of those people," Harper said.

When it came time to talk climate change with the new Obama administration in 2009, Harper said he told the new president, "Barack, I'm sending ... probably the most capable guy that I've got."

Obama replied that Harper's secret appraisal of Prentice was safe with him.

This was the Harper who, when he occasionally turned up as prime minister, you wondered where he was the rest of the time. The Harper who generously offered state funerals to Jack Layton and Jim Flaherty, and spoke so humorously and poignantly at Flaherty's service; the prime minister who invited Brian Mulroney and other former PMs to accompany him to the state funeral of Nelson Mandela in South Africa. Why didn't that guy show up more often? Canadians like a touch of class in a prime minister, which is one of the things they like about Justin Trudeau, whose tribute to Prentice at his death was both generous and gracious.

One of the final eulogies was delivered by Prentice's neighbour and mentor Dick Haskayne, a former CEO of Enbridge and TransCanada Pipelines. Jim had the gift, he said, that "he could tell you where to go in such a way that you'd look forward to the trip."

There was a table of Jim's mementos – his buckskin jacket, cowboy hat and boots, a hockey stick and Alberta hockey sweater with a captain's C, and the train set he loved to run with his grandson Jack.

The service ended with a photo montage over two country music songs, The Rodeo's Over and Alberta Bound. Entirely fitting, as Prentice in his rich life as a policy maker, politician, father and husband, had quite a rodeo.

Anyone considering the possibility of a career in politics need look no further for a role model.

October 2016

17

COTTAGE COUNTRY

ALL IS WELL WITH THE NEW DOCK

Greetings from cottage country, where it has been quite an eventful summer at the lake. First we built a new dock, the old one having collapsed into several pieces after two decades of service.

Then there was the earthquake, which knocked down the chimney. Finally, we closed off the cedar sun deck, which had been designed as an open concept, but that was before Zara's arrival in June of last year.

How to enclose the deck, all 40 by 15 feet of it? Someone suggested chicken wire, which might have served a functional purpose, but wouldn't have won any awards for esthetics. Zara's mom, Tasha, had a better idea.

"Why not," she suggested, "close it off with lattice panels?"

"We can do that," said my neighbour. Wolf Schwarz, designer of both the deck and the new dock, and off we went to McClelland's in nearby Poltimore, the largest hardware store and lumberyard in the Gatineau.

"How much do you need?" asked Darryl McClelland, who has been looking after cottagers and contractors alike for nearly half a century.

"Six panels of three by six feet," replied Schwarz, who found just what he was looking for in the back of the lumberyard –lattice siding that blended perfectly with the British Columbia cedar on the deck. Problem solved – the open deck was quickly transformed, with two security gates added for the stairs, to a secure play area for Zara.

It was our second stop at McClelland's yard this summer, the first one being to buy lumber and Styrofoam for the new dock, which was quite a production.

Let's put it this way: We spent nearly as much on foam as we did on lumber, which was treated pine wood from Goodfellow, the Montreal softwood producer.

And the foam was not an obvious choice, especially given the propensity of muskrats to take up residence in the space between the floaters and the wood. Molly the Muskrat raised a whole family while living under the old dock, but hasn't been seen yet under the new one.

A dock is a serious statement in cottage country, not just a swimming raft or a landing area for boats. It's a place for a flag, for family photos and for a Muskoka chair from which to watch the sunset. A glass of Chardonnay doesn't get any better than that. I should note that our Muskoka chair is authentic, not one of those awful hardware store plastic knock-offs in baby blue.

Schwarz had an idea of what he wanted to build – a 10-by-16-foot dock with a 3-by-16-foot apron. "Sounds good to me," I said. My job is policy, not operations. The finished product is stunning, so beautiful I've decided not to tie the fishing boat up to it. Why spoil perfection?

Schwarz was putting the dock in the water on the afternoon of June 23, when the earthquake struck.

"The whole place shook," he reported later. It took out half the chimney and cracked the foundations of the house. If we hadn't reinforced it with steel beams a couple of years ago, the living room might have ended up in the basement.

The epicentre of the earthquake, a 5.0 on the Richter scale, was at Echo Lake on the Quebec-Ontario border. It resulted in office buildings being evacuated in Ottawa, and caused damage throughout the Gatineau region.

"You're not covered for earthquakes, only for fire and theft," said the insurance company agent who seemingly took great pleasure in passing on the news. Thanks for that. A contractor came and looked at the cottage, and his suggestion was to tear it down and build a new one. Thanks for that, too.

But with the new dock, and the enclosed deck, we were ready for Zara's first visit to the lake with her mom.

It has been nearly 20 years since Grace was the last little girl on our beach at Lac-St.-Pierre-de-Wakefield.

Gracie's crib, in storage in Montreal all these years, turned out to be in remarkably good shape. And at the back of a closet in the guest room at the cottage, we just happened to find Gracie's stroller, also in great shape, and perfect for morning walks down to the babbling brook.

I was looking for something else in the shed when I came across a box full of Gracie's old beach toys, as well as her farm and Tonka truck. Zara was delighted with all of them.

Most of all, she was thrilled to meet the bullfrog, known as King, on the beach one day. Squealing with delight, and totally fearless, she ran right after him. Sensing danger, King quickly hopped under the new dock.

August 2010

A MUSKOKA CHAIR

It being the cottage, there's always something.

Last year it was the earthquake, a 5.0 on the Richter scale, which shifted the foundations and knocked down the chimney of our cottage on Lac Saint-Pierre-de-Wakefield.

Four years ago it was the tornado that roared down the lake with such force that it blew out windows and uprooted huge trees. Three nights ago it was the windstorm that appeared out of nowhere around 6.30 p.m. on Sunday evening. With winds later estimated at 140 kilometres per hour by Environment Canada, the storm uprooted three trees on our property, one of which fell on the power and phone lines.

"It was pretty scary," reported our neighbour, Sandy McDermott.

"Worse than the tornado?"

"Yes."

How bad was it? It lifted our Muskoka chair, designed to weather storms, off the dock and dumped it on the lawn 50 feet away. It lifted a neighbour's rubber raft, anchored by a 30 pound cement block, right out of the water. It flew 20 feet into the air before landing on their lawn. Forty-five minutes later, the same freak storm raced down the Ottawa River at 96 kilometres per hour and destroyed the stage at the Bluesfest on LeBreton Flats, sending the band, Cheap Trick, and nearly 10,000 spectators scurrying for cover, many of them at the nearby National War Museum. Miraculously, no one was seriously hurt at the concert site, although two people drowned on the river in storm-related boating incidents.

Normally I would have been at the lake on a Sunday evening in July, firing up the barbecue, or quite possibly out in our 16-foot canoe. Big Red is a very light boat, weighing only 48 pounds, and would not have done well in the storm.

Fortunately I was in Toronto visiting Zara, my 2-year-old daughter, helping her, her mother and grandmother celebrate the birthday of her grandfather, Fareez Kheiriddin, who turned 86 on Sunday.

By the time I got to the office in Ottawa on Monday, my neighbour, Wolf Schwarz, was on the phone with a damage report.

"No power since last night and my phone just came back on," he said. "You have trees on power lines at your place, and your phone is out. Hydro-Québec says you have to call an electrician to repair the connection to your metre."

At first Hydro-Québec said power would be back on by 6 p.m. Monday, then by 11 p.m., then by 7:30 a.m. yesterday, then by noon. As I was driving in to work yesterday on Highway 307, four Hydro-Québec repair trucks passed heading in the other direction. I hoped one of them was headed to our corner of the lake.

I'd been meaning to stop for ice for the freezer on the way to the lake Monday evening, but of course the stores in the village of Saint-Pierre were closed. "Fermé, panne électrique," advised a hastily drawn sign in the window of Tessier's, the local grocery. Never mind our fridge – what about theirs?

Well, I was planning on barbecuing anyway, and a steak was conveniently thawed in the freezer. For the rest, a gas barbecue does not depend upon electricity. And while we have a satellite dish at the lake, we don't really go there to watch television.

As for light, we have three antique gas lamps from the basement of my grandparents' house on the Mira River in Cape Breton. The house has been in the family for at least 125 years.

But we had no gas for the lamps.

"No problem," said Schwarz. "Just take a few of the solar lamps from the dock." The solar lamps are meant to warn boats at night, when the dock lights up like a runway. "They'll light the cottage right up," he said.

He was right. They did. My grandfather, Angus J. MacDonald, used to say you could read a newspaper by the light of a summer moon in Mira. I never thought of reading one with a solar lamp. Maybe that's the future.

Meantime, our Muskoka chair is back in its proper place under the flag at the end of the dock. The perfect place, with a glass of Chardonnay, to contemplate the remains of the day.

July 2011

TWENTY-FIVE YEARS AT THE LAKE

In 1988, Brian Mulroney forced a rare summer sitting of Parliament, partly because the Liberal controlled Senate was intent on staging a filibuster against the implementing legislation for the Canada-U.S. Free Trade Agreement.

In the Prime Minister's Office, it meant no one could leave town.

"If I'm going to be stuck here for the summer," I mentioned to PMO communications director Bruce Phillips, "maybe I should rent a cottage at some place like Wakefield and commute."

Just then, his secretary, who had been seconded from Foreign Affairs, looked up from an ad in the department's staff newsletter.

"Here's a place at St.-Pierre-de-Wakefield," she said.

"What does it say about it?"

"It says it's a three-bedroom cottage with a beach, a dock and a boat."

And a fieldstone fireplace. And sunsets off the end of the dock on Lac-St.-Pierre, 45 minutes north of the Peace Tower. I went to see it, but it wasn't for rent, only for sale. The owner was asking $85,000. I offered him $76,000, never thinking he would accept, but he did.

Little did I know then that he had picked up the place a few years earlier for $40,000 in a proceeds of crime sale against the previous owner, an Ottawa drug dealer.

That's how I got the cottage, by a complete fluke – a Senate filibuster, an overheard office conversation, and an ad in a departmental newsletter. It was the smartest thing I ever did, totally by accident.

In the 25 years since, going to the lake has been a constant pleasure, the highlight of every summer, and the greatest joy for my daughters.

Of course, it being the cottage, there's always upkeep. We are on our third dock, this one pushing 40 feet out into the lake.

We're also on our second cottage roof, and second sun deck, 36 by 12 feet.

Fortunately, my next door neighbour and friend of all the years, Wolf Schwarz, is also my contractor. Our deal is, my job is policy and his is operations.

This means I'm an excellent customer of J.B. McClelland & Sons, which is a grocery in the front, a hardware store in the middle, with a lumber yard and a boat repair shop in the back.

If you've ever been to Poltimore, you've been to McClelland's. The sons run it, their kids all work there, and the leader of the clan is Darryl McClelland. He's been there for more than 50 years, and has been in charge of the hardware store and lumber yard for all the 25 years I've been going there.

On any Saturday morning at McClelland's, you'll run into cottage people from Ottawa, seeking advice from Darryl and his brother Harold, who runs the grocery, and their brother, Kent, who is everywhere in the store.

Harold is the one behind the meat counter, or sometimes the post office, where you can also buy a fishing licence. He'll happily reserve all the weekend papers for you.

Darryl can be found in the back, sitting on a stool, talking to customers on one line, with two suppliers on hold, and cottage people lined up to ask him really stupid questions. He's famous for knowing where everything is in the store, and for his endless patience with city folks. This being the weekend of the Poltimore Fair, you might want to drop in to McClelland's on the way.

What's changed at the lake in 25 years? Well, the weather, for one thing. With global warming and climate change, summer storms are more frequent and much more severe than a quarter century ago. Any cottager, from the Rideau Lakes to the Outaouais, can attest to this. In 2007, a tornado tore down our lake, uprooted old growth pine trees, and smashed windows in cottages across the 53 kilometres and five bays of Lac-St.-Pierre.

In 2010, there was the 5.0 degree earthquake that split the foundation of our cottage, while closing downtown Ottawa office towers. In 2011, there was the windstorm that saw our windproof Muskoka chair fly 100 metres off the dock.

What hasn't changed? The pure joy of being at the lake with family and children.

Grace, now 23, has grown up at the lake. Zara, at 4, is just getting to know it.

Grace's July birthday party has long been an annual event in her Mum's large family, the prominent Ottawa media Van Dusens, presided over by her much beloved grandfather, Tom Van Dusen, and attended by her many cousins. Zara also loves the lake, swimming, fishing and canoeing, not to mention catching frogs and toads on the beach. So does her Dad, sitting on the dock at sunset, grateful for the accidents and the circles of life.

August 2013

ZARA AND "CAMOUFLAGING" TOADIE

A few months ago, Zara handed me an old children's story book, of which only the covers remained.

"Read me a story, Daddy," she said.

"What story, sweetie?"

"The one in my imagination," she replied. Which is not the only five-syllable word in her vocabulary. At the cottage two years ago, when she had just turned two, I was putting her in her stroller for our morning walk down to the bridge.

"We're going for our morning constitutional," she declared. Her mother explained that back home, she would take her out for their "afternoon constitutional." From afternoon to morning, Zara could tell one from the other, but she remembered her constitutional.

This summer, at age four, when she caught a toad on the beach at the lake, she and her Mummy made a home for it – turf, sand and water in a Frisbee, all in an inflatable wading pool. When Toadie disappeared from view, Zara said: "He's camouflaging in the habitat."

She also has a photographic memory.

Sitting out in her grandparents' backyard last summer, I pointed out a bird that flew by. "Look at that little yellow bird," I said.

"Daddy," she said, "that's a gold finch."

Her grandmother had been reading an illustrated book of birds with her, and she knew all the ones in the backyard.

It also turns out that she has perfect pitch, which is one of the reasons why she can't stand people singing off key. At her third birthday party last year, she covered her ears and began to scream when guests started to sing Happy Birthday.

From the age of two and a half, she began exhibiting many other sensory issues. She became extremely sensitive to sound and light, as well as touch. Once, when I was helping her into her car seat, my cheek brushed up against hers. "Oh, Daddy," she exclaimed, "you hurt me with your beard, but I love you anyway."

This is part of a diagnosis last fall that Zara has a moderate case of Asperger's syndrome, which is on the autism spectrum disorder (ASD) at the high performance end of the scale.

Zara has the vocabulary of a child perhaps twice her age.

"Did you go swimming today?" I asked her on the phone this summer.

Instead of a simple yes or no, I got the weather report.

"No, Daddy," she said, "it was rainy, and foggy and cold."

She has behavioural issues familiar to parents of Aspies. She has obsessive interests: for six months, she believed she was a bunny; currently, she will tell you she's a teenager. She is less interested in playing with her peers than older children and adults; until recently, she would tell kids her own age to simply "go away." At her preschool, she would not join circles, and preferred to do her own thing. She can be quite obstinate about getting her own way, and sometimes has meltdowns when she doesn't. She can say things that are very funny, but socially inappropriate.

One Canadian child in 68 has ASD, and Zara is one of the fortunate ones at the high end of the scale. All these children have special needs that are not covered by their health care cards.

Getting the kind of developmental therapy these kids need is expensive. Zara's mother recently enrolled her for daily half day sessions at a privately run exceptional learning centre near their home in the Greater Toronto Area. It's very expensive – like sending your kid to an Ivy League college, in pre-K. Yet at least, between us, we can afford it.

But what about the parents who can't afford therapy for children with special needs? And what about their kids, who could consequently fall between the cracks? The obvious answer is that we can help these families now, and help their children become productive, and potentially brilliant, members of society. Or we can pay for the costs of looking after them later.

Meanwhile, back at the lake, Zara was keeping a close eye on Toadie, "camouflaging in the habitat."

She sure didn't hear that from her Dad.

August 2013